DATE DUE

APR 0 8 2014			
OCT 0 8 2014			
JAN 0 5 2015			
			PRINTED IN U.S.A.

DISCARD

AUG 1 5 2013

dancing the new world

dancing the new world

AZTECS, SPANIARDS, AND THE CHOREOGRAPHY OF CONQUEST

Paul A. Scolieri

UNIVERSITY OF TEXAS PRESS ★ AUSTIN

This book is a part of the Latin American and Caribbean Arts and Culture publication initiative, funded by a grant from the Andrew W. Mellon Foundation.

Copyright © 2013 by the University of Texas Press
All rights reserved
Printed in the United States of America
First edition, 2013

Requests for permission to reproduce material from this work should be sent to:
Permissions
University of Texas Press
P.O. Box 7819
Austin, TX 78713-7819
http://utpress.utexas.edu/about/book-permissions

♾ The paper used in this book meets the minimum requirements of ANSI/NISO Z39.48-1992 (R1997) (Permanence of Paper).

LIBRARY OF CONGRESS CATALOGING-IN-PUBLICATION DATA
Scolieri, Paul A.
  Dancing the new world : Aztecs, Spaniards, and the choreography of conquest / by Paul A. Scolieri. — First edition.
      pages   cm
  Includes bibliographical references and index.
  ISBN 978-0-292-74492-9 (cloth : alk. paper)
  1. Aztec dance. 2. Indian dance—Mexico. 3. Dance—Anthropological aspects—Mexico. 4. Aztecs—First contact with Europeans. 5. Mexico—History—Spanish colony, 1540–1810.   I. Title.
  F1219.76.D35S36   2013
  972'.02—dc23
                                                    2012031508

doi:10.7560/744929

Contents

List of Appendices vii
List of Maps and Images ix
Acknowledgments xi

Introduction 1

1 On the *Areíto*
   Discovering Dance in the New World 24

2 Unfaithful Imitation
   Friar Toribio de Benavente "Motolinía" and the "Counterfeit" Histories of Dance 44

3 The Sacrifices of Representation
   Dance in the Writings of Friar Bernardino de Sahagún 56

4 Dances of Death
   The Massacre at the Festival of Toxcatl 90

5 The Mystery of Movement
   Dancing in Colonial New Spain 127

Conclusion 150

Appendices A–J 153
Notes 173
Bibliography 187
Index 197

APPENDICES

Appendix A. Two Accounts of the *Areíto* of Anacaona. Bartolomé de las Casas, *Historia de las Indias*, and Peter Martyr d'Anghera, *De orbe novo* 153

Appendix B. *Areítos* and *Bailes cantando* of the Indies. Gonzalo Fernández de Oviedo y Valdés, *Historia general y natural de las Indias* 155

Appendix C. *Areítos* of Nicaragua and Its Vicinity. Gonzalo Fernández de Oviedo y Valdés, *Historia general y natural de las Indias* 157

Appendix D. *Bailes* and Songs of the Indies. Bartolomé de las Casas, *Apologética historia sumaria* 162

Appendix E. *Bailes* of Mexico. Toribio de Benavente "Motolinía," *Memoriales* 164

Appendix F. *Macehualiztli* and *Netotiliztli*. Toribio de Benavente "Motolinía," *Memoriales* 167

Appendix G. Aztec Myth of the Origin of Music and Dance. Gerónimo de Mendieta, *Historia eclesiástica indiana* 168

Appendix H. Charges Drawn by the *Audencia* of Mexico against Pedro de Alvarado (1529). 169

Appendix I. Pedro de Alvarado's Response to Charges Brought by the *Audencia* of Mexico. 170

Appendix J. Founding of the First Dance School in New Spain. *Actas de Cabildo de la Ciudad de México* 172

MAPS AND IMAGES

Maps

Map 1: Aztec Empire and Surrounding Region (Molly O'Halloran) 15

Map 2: Tenochtitlan and the Ceremonial Precinct (Molly O'Halloran after Townsend) 16

Figures

0.1. Morisco dance. *Das Trachtenbuch des Christoph Weiditz* (1529) 8
0.2. Aztec acrobat in Spain. *Das Trachtenbuch des Christoph Weiditz* (1529) 10–11
0.3. *Ollin* (movement). *Codex Telleriano-Remensis* (ca. 1554) 19
0.4. *Cihuateteo*. *Codex Borgia* (ca. 1400) 21
1.1. Vespucci in Paria. Theodor de Bry, *America*, part 10 (1619) 26
1.2. *Voladores*. Gonzalo Fernández de Oviedo y Valdés, *Historia general y natural de las Indias* (ca. 1535) 37
2.1. *Netotiliztli*. Pieter van der Aa, *Naaukeurige versameling . . .* , vol. 9, part 1 (1707) 52
2.2. *Macehualiztli*. Pieter van der Aa, *Naaukeurige versameling . . .* , vol. 9, part 2 (1707) 53
3.1. Aztec dancers and musicians. *Florentine Codex* (ca. 1570) 65
3.2. Instruments and equipment for the dance. *Florentine Codex* (ca. 1570) 66
3.3. The *tlatoani*'s dance array. *Florentine Codex* (ca. 1570) 66
3.4. Atamalcualiztli. Bernardino de Sahagún, *Primeros memoriales* (ca. 1560) 69
3.5. Tlacaxipehualiztli. *Florentine Codex* (ca. 1570) 73
3.6. Tlacaxipehualiztli. Bernardino de Sahagún, *Primeros memoriales* (ca. 1560) 74
3.7. Discipline during Huey Tecuilhuitl. *Florentine Codex* (ca. 1570) 79
3.8. Thief dancing with forearm. *Florentine Codex* (ca. 1570) 82
3.9. Ochpaniztli. *Florentine Codex* (ca. 1570) 84
4.1. First encounter between Cortés and Montezuma. Bartolomé de las Casas, *A Brief Account of the Destruction of the Indies* (1598) 105

4.2. Montezuma watches as conquistadors attack his court dancers. Bartolomé de las Casas, *A Brief Account of the Destruction of the Indies* (1598) 106

4.3. The Massacre at the Festival of Toxcatl. Theodor de Bry, *America*, part 5 (1595) 107

4.4. The knight dances with Death. Hans Holbein, *Dance of Death* (1538) 108

4.5. The Massacre at the Festival of Toxcatl. Diego Durán, *History of the Indies of New Spain* (ca. 1581) 111

4.6. Drummer, conquistador, and Aztec warrior at Templo Mayor. *Códice Aubin* (ca. 1576) 116

4.7. Conquistadors dismembering Aztec drummer and decapitating Aztec dancer. *Florentine Codex* (ca. 1570) 117

4.8. Falling from the Templo Mayor. *Florentine Codex* (ca. 1570) 118

4.9. Encounter at the Templo Mayor. *Codex Azcatítlan* (ca. 1575) 120–121

4.10. Coyolxauhqui Stone. Museo del Templo Mayor, Mexico City (15th century) 122

4.11. "Dance of the Indians" at the Templo Mayor. Gerónimo de Mendieta, *Historia eclesiástica indiana* (1595) 124

4.12. "The Great Temple of Mexico." J. Fuller at the Dove in Creed-Lane, *The American Traveller* (1741) 125

4.13. "The Rejoicings of the Mexicans, at the Beginning of the Age." John Hamilton Moore, *A New and Complete Collection of Voyages and Travels, Vol. 2* (ca. 1785) 126

5.1. Eagle and jaguar warriors dancing before the Spaniards. *Códice de Tlatelolco* (ca. 1560) 129

5.2. Dance leader in Xocotl Huetzi. Diego Durán, *Book of the Gods and Rites* (ca. 1575) 135

5.3. Dancing at the *cuicacalli*. Diego Durán, *Book of the Gods and Rites* (ca. 1575) 137

5.4. Xochipilli, "The God of Dance." Museo Nacional de Antropología, Mexico City 139

5.5. Xochipilli and Xochiquetzal. *Codex Borgia* (ca. 1400) 140

5.6. Xochipilli drumming and Huehuecoyotl dancing and singing. *Codex Borbonicus* (ca. 1520) 141

5.7. "Of All the Manners of Strange Dances Among the Indians." Theodor de Bry, *America*, part 9 (1601) 142

5.8. Dance of the Emperor. *Crónica de Michoacán* (ca. 1788) 144

5.9. Dance of the Emperor Montezuma. Joaquín Antonio de Basarás y Garaygorta, *Origen, costumbres, y estado presente de mexicanos y philipinos* (1763) 145

5.10. Missionaries gazing at *voladores* and baptism. *Codex Azcatítlan* (ca. 1575) 147

ACKNOWLEDGMENTS

Dancing the New World began as a dissertation in the Department of Performance Studies at Tisch School of the Arts, New York University. I benefited immeasurably from the innovative scholarly environment created by its faculty and students, as well as from the outstanding mentorship of José E. Muñoz, Marcia B. Siegel, and Diana Taylor. For continually sharing her genius and encouragement, I owe a special debt of gratitude to Barbara Browning, my advisor.

As a faculty member at Barnard College, I received invaluable institutional support as well as endless inspiration from faculty, administrators, and students, especially from my distinguished colleagues in the Department of Dance, the Program in Africana Studies, the Consortium for Critical Interdisciplinary Studies, and the Center for the Critical Analysis of Social Difference at Columbia University. Special thanks to Mary Cochran, Lynn Garafola, Kim F. Hall, Janet Jakobsen, and Janet Soares.

In 2008–2009, the David Rockefeller Center for Latin American Studies at Harvard University invited me to spend the academic year in residence as the Peggy Rockefeller Visiting Scholar in order to conduct research for this book. I am deeply grateful to DRCLAS faculty and administration for the extraordinary experience, as well as to my cohort of visiting scholars, who generously offered advice that led me to important discoveries, directions, and depths.

Many archivists, librarians, and museum curators throughout Europe, Mexico, and the United States generously provided me with research assistance and permission to publish the astonishing dance-related images that appear in this book. I especially wish to acknowledge the Archive of Early American Images, John Carter Brown Library, Brown University (Providence, RI); Biblioteca Medicea Laurenziana (Florence, Italy); Museo Nacional de Antropología e Historia (Mexico City, Mexico); Houghton Library and Tozzer Library, Harvard University (Cambridge, MA); the Instituto Nacional de Antropología e Historia (Mexico City, Mexico); Museo del Templo Mayor (Mexico City, Mexico); and the New York Public Library, Manuscripts and Archives Division (New York, NY).

In the early stages of this project, I began to study Nahuatl (the Aztec language) at the Nahuatl Summer Language Institute at Yale University. I thank Jonathan Amith and Una Canger for their thoughtful instruction. R. Joe Campbell generously shared his remarkable research into the linguistic aspects of the *Florentine Codex*, which helped me to clarify several arguments I present in this book.

For sharing their expertise and insights regarding aspects of my research, I thank Lynn Matluck Brooks, Max Harris, and Frances Kartunnen.

Fiona Buckland, Pamela Cobrin, Alma Guillermoprieto, and Rhonda Rubinson read sections of the book in manuscript form and responded with characteristic grace and brilliance.

I thank Theresa J. May, editor-in-chief at the University of Texas Press, for her enthusiastic support of this book; Scott Metcalfe and Liam Moore for permission to publish their elegant translations; and Molly O'Halloran for her gorgeous maps.

Over the years I have had the pleasure of serving on the boards of directors of three scholarly organizations—the Congress on Research in Dance, the Society of Dance History Scholars, and the World Dance Alliance–Americas. I am grateful for the many opportunities to present my research at these organizations' conferences and for the incisive questions and suggestions I have received from dance scholars as a result.

I am eternally grateful for the affection and support of my family and friends, a few of whom I must mention by name: Catherine Murphy, for the conviction that dance is always meaningful; Marie Scolieri, for her ways with words; Bruce Glikas, for countless theatrical diversions; and my parents, Antonino and Genivieve Scolieri, for their endless encouragement.

And finally, for his indomitable belief in me and the distinct honor of his love, I dedicate this book to Lavinel Savu.

dancing the new world

Introduction

In their chronicles of the New World, explorers, conquistadors, missionaries, colonial administrators, royal historians, scientists, and travelers all surprisingly yet invariably wrote about "Indian" dances. Whether drawn to the topic by accident or by design, they wrote about dance in narratives of discovery, encounter, and conquest, in descriptions of indigenous sacred and martial ritual, and in accounts of missionary theater, the Church-sponsored dramas aimed at evangelizing the conquered native populations. The chroniclers could not avoid writing about dance, as it was a prominent aspect of the indigenous societies they sought to conquer. For some chroniclers, dance was an ideal topic for expressing the sense of wonder and terror they experienced in their encounters with natives. Others considered dance a serious threat to the enterprise of Spanish political and religious domination. This is especially true of Spanish missionaries who in the decades following the conquest of Mexico in 1520 extensively studied and documented indigenous dances in an attempt to identify and eradicate all forms of idolatry. An identifiable group of chroniclers evidently had never seen the dances about which they wrote, but instead plagiarized the writings of other authors, sometimes even claiming the experience of the spectator embedded in the text as their own. In so doing these very writers inadvertently left behind one of the most extensive archives of indigenous performance in the Americas, especially concerning the Aztec, the largest indigenous empire in Mesoamerica at the time of its European "discovery." That archive is the subject of this book.

The chapters ahead examine the transformation of the Aztec empire into a Spanish colony through the visual and written representations of Indian dances in colonial discourse—the vast constellation of chronicles, histories, letters, travel books, legal depositions, ecclesiastic writs, and council ordinances by Europeans in and about the New World. This book focuses on texts written in the late fifteenth and sixteenth centuries. It begins with Christopher Columbus's 1492 letter detailing his encounter with dancing Indians at his historic landfall in the New World, then concentrates on the "golden age" of missionary ethnography in mid-sixteenth-century New Spain, and concludes with the first chronicle of the conquest written by a full-blooded Aztec of the late sixteenth century.

The documentation, interpretations, and prohibitions of indigenous dance in colonial discourse provide a unique lens into the broader "encounter" between Europeans and Indians in the New World. In some instances these sources offer a direct view into the ways that bodily postures, gestures, and movements figured into Indian and European interactions with and perceptions of each other. In other instances, the sources reveal how representations of indigenous dances shaped and were shaped by conflicting perspectives on some of the central political, theological, and intellectual controversies of the era, such as the debates over the "noble" versus "savage" nature of the "Indian"; the methods and merits of the Christian conversion of "natives"; and the radically evolving principles and practices of historiography, particularly regarding the role of the "eyewitness" in the production of history.

As such, representations of dance in colonial discourse tell us as much about the political unconscious of the European writers and artists as they do about the realities of Aztec dance. Colonial discourse does not passively represent the New World and its "others" as much as it actively constructs them through what Michel de Certeau described as a "heterology," or a "discourse on the other," that is "built upon a division between the body of knowledge that utters a discourse and the mute body that nourishes it."[1] For writers in the New World, Indian dancers were among the many bodies that "nourished" the Spanish discourse of empire. Throughout the chronicles of the New World, we find innumerable references to dancing Indians—the presumed *mute bodies* of history—through whom the chroniclers dramatized their experiences of terror and wonder, repudiation and fascination, and estrangement and familiarity. Indeed, the chroniclers *choreographed history* in the sense that they memorialized, justified, lamented, and/or denied their role in the discovery, conquest, and colonization of the New World through the Aztec dancing body.

This idea is vividly illustrated by one of the earliest European descriptions of Indian dance. The account involves a performance by an Indian slave at the Spanish court of King Charles V—not some "barbaric" ritual held on a temple patio, wild shoreline, or any other exotic locale where the chroniclers were wont to find dancing Indians. In 1519, two years before the final fall of the Aztec empire, the infamous conquistador Hernán Cortés (1485–1547) sent his secretary Juan de Ribera from the New World to Spain with a shipment of riches accumulated for the king—a part of the "royal fifth," or the rightful share of spoils conquistadors were bound to relinquish to the Crown. Along with gold, jewelry, maps, garments, feathers, masks, and other objects Cortés sent six Indian "slaves."[2] Spain's first royal chronicler, Peter Martyr d'Anghera (ca. 1455–1526), commanded one of the slaves to demonstrate the function of the exotic objects contained in the shipment and described this outlandish experience in the first royal chronicle of the New World. The Indian gave an impromptu command performance on an open terrace of the king's palace for Martyr and a small audience of select courtiers and Ribera, who had learned to speak the Aztec language of Nahuatl and translated some of the explanations not readily apparent from the slave's demonstration. For his first performance, the slave reenacted a ritual of human sacrifice. Dressed in warrior array, he wielded a sword and a shield, and then stabbed at another slave who performed the role of his victim. He then grabbed his victim by the hair, dragged his body across the floor, and then proceeded to mime the action of cutting the victim's chest and removing his still-beating heart. The slave even pretended to wring his hands of excess blood. When the slave finished his demonstration, the courtiers moved into another room, where they waited for him to change costumes. For his second performance, the slave emerged carrying a "golden toy with a thousand different ornaments" and "a circle of bells." With these instruments, he began to sing and dance about the room as if joined by the massive number of celebrants that participated in the processions of his homeland. Martyr was particularly impressed by the salutatory gestures the slave made before his imaginary king—"never looking at the king and humbly prostrated." For his third and final performance, his most "faithfully sustained" role according to Martyr, the Indian performed the feints and falls of a naked drunkard at a sacred festival, going as far as to feign interactions with imaginary revelers and stumble along the crowded streets.

With this description Martyr established three major paradigms through which subsequent chroniclers described Indians: as barbaric performers of human sacrifices, as "obedient and faithful" noble subjects, and as inebriated tricksters. The scenario also brings into relief the inherent exercise of power exerted by the colonial gaze on the Indian dancing body. The slave performed a sacred rite that had hitherto been performed exclusively to appease Mesoamerican gods, yet was reenacted to satiate a

European desire to encounter an exotic other. This command performance was a deliberately staged encounter between Old and New Worlds, Christian and pagan, present and past, and self and other, wherein the Indian slave had to bear the burden of representing a bewildering alterity.

Moreover, Martyr's account is a salient example of the manner in which encounters between Spaniards and Indians were purposefully staged and memorialized as performances. Martyr makes no attempt to conceal the encounter as contrived. In fact, he openly explains how he controlled the *mise-en-scène* of the slave's performance to ensure its authenticity. (Although Martyr does stipulate that he had the obsidian blades removed from the slave's weaponry, just in case the reenactment became too real.) In other accounts, the chroniclers seemingly go to great lengths to persuade readers that theirs were encounters born of their expert skills in discovery and diplomacy or of divine will. The underlying logic of these performances of encounter (and encounters with performance) in the chronicles of the Americas is that performance granted unmediated access to the "other." Martyr, for example, asked the slave to perform, confident that he could circumvent the language barrier yet still penetrate the confusing rites of the Indian world. In turn, Martyr's account reads as its own type of performance—a spectacle of ventriloquism, wherein Martyr maneuvers the slave's "silent body" and in turn speaks for it.[3]

Above all, Martyr's account is relevant for the way it demonstrates the curious fact that with rare exception, references to dancing Indians in the early writings about the Americas almost always emerge in death scenarios—accounts of burial ceremonies, rituals of human sacrifice, narratives of conquest, and rites of ancestor worship. This connection makes sense, given that indigenous choreographies were intimately linked to rituals of sacred and political violence such as ceremonies of human sacrifice or reenactments of military conquests. Aztec ritual dance placed its celebrants in a "structured nearness" to death by creating conditions for performers to come into physical proximity to experiencing and witnessing death.[4] Aztec sacred choreographies dramatized the interplay between life and death, whether through priests dancing in skins flayed from the bodies of sacrificed slaves, warriors dancing with the bloodied limbs and heads of sacrificed victims, or staged and actual military contests between warriors. Aztec dances were neither representations nor allegories of violence, but state-sanctioned "killing performances" that expended the bodies of women, captive warriors, and children to discipline and coerce the Aztec subject into obeisance.[5] Dancing was a technique of terror. It was also a way to conspicuously display bodies in the riches begotten from terror by way of stylish processions of nobles drenched in exotic feathers, hides, and precious metals and stones that were extracted through an indigenous tribute system that was founded on and protected by violence.

More broadly, Aztec ritual was designed to coordinate the human cycle of life and death with the creative and destructive forces in the natural world, especially the spectacles of agricultural fertility on land and the movements of astral bodies in the heavens. Aztec dance not only reflected those patterns of transformation, but also aspired to harness their power. Dancing was a form of worldmaking—a technique for creating, representing, and maintaining the Aztec sacred and political order, for dancing was not only a form of social memory through which they recalled the past, but also a means through which the Aztec sought to body forth a world they envisioned. The New World chroniclers and missionaries exploited the association between dance and death, often inserting themselves into accounts of indigenous performance in order to symbolize their role in the annihilation of indigenous cultures and the birth of a new world order.

Martyr's account is no exception. Death figures prominently in his descriptions of the slave's performance—not only because of his reference to the slave's simulation of sacrificial violence, but also for his unwitting inscription of the phantoms summoned by the slave's pantomime. Martyr's account meticulously describes the scenarios and physical objects he observed with his "naked eye," yet it also registers his perception of the traces of absence summoned by the slave's gestures: the victim's still-beating heart and bloodied entrails, the illusory king, and the imaginary revelers—the world of the dead and absented that dance uniquely brings into awareness. Thus, even though Martyr attributes his authority to having experienced the performance in the same time and space as the slave (with his own "naked eye," no less), his account registers multiple indices of *other* times and spaces. The slave's performance was a reenactment of previously performed rituals that referred to multiple pasts and locales: to the ceremonies as they were performed in the Aztec empire, to the gestures and steps of ancestors who had performed them before him, and to the myths upon which they were based.

For the chroniclers, dance was a privileged figure for presence, liveness, and being, upon which they based their claims about Indian identity, reality, and history. The presence of the other assured their own existence in turn. However, as much as their writings cling to the seductive empiricism of the dancing body, their representations of dance are haunted by the traces of meaning that dance instantiates. Colonial discourse represents not only dancing bodies, but also the specters of gods, ancestors, and victims that were rendered through dance. It is equally fraught with bodies, gestures, and steps that are implied, conjured, or entirely falsely witnessed.[6] Thus, in the chronicles of the New World, dancing, so often the ultimate expression of vitality, presence, and strength, seems always haunted by the threat of death, absence, and annihilation.

The slave's pantomime and Martyr's account of it vividly reveal a tension between dance and death in colonial discourse. This tension animates almost every reference to dancing in the New World. For Martyr, the phantasms revealed by the slave's pantomime were easy to perceive and serve as a clear example of the far more obscure and haunting ways that dance "nourishes" the discourse of empire. In fact, Martyr likens the act of writing history to a form of martyrdom. His account of the slave's performance is preceded by the following statement that playfully yet provocatively suggests how the historian's own body is nourished by that of the other: "When the Hydra's heads are cut off they revive, and so it is with me; for I have hardly disposed of one narrative than a number of others spring up."[7] For Martyr, the mute dancing slave "nourishes" his discourse of empire. Yet he brings the slave into his self-sustaining narrative with little deference to the indigenous history, myth, and knowledge that the slave's pantomime ambiguously reveals through absence. In fact, de Certeau provides multiple images and metaphors for describing historiography as "a form of mourning, a burial rite that attempts to exorcise death through its insertion into discourse."[8] In that regard, Martyr's writing about the slave's pantomime unwittingly exorcises the ghosts that made the slave's movements meaningful and instead renders the slave's performance as a trace of the chronicler's own experience of seeing.

This book is about European encounters with indigenous dance in the New World and the written and visual representations of those encounters. Yet it is also about the ghosts that are embodied in and exorcised by those representations. The chroniclers' representations of indigenous dances set into motion a dizzying constellation of inversions, reversals, and transpositions of identities, bodies, and histories that disorient and disrupt the chroniclers' narratives of discovery, encounter, and conquest. Understanding the implications of this argument for the history of the New World means examining three of its underlying abstractions: colonial discourse, dance, and the "Aztec" empire.

Colonial Discourse

As royal chronicler, Martyr wrote the first "official" history of the discovery and conquest of the New World, yet he never set foot on American soil. Except for his attendance at the slave's performance, he had little direct experience with natives and thus in order to write his version of history he relied on eyewitness reports from abroad that were funneled through the Spanish court. For this reason, many of Martyr's contemporaries, especially those who had traveled to the New World, openly discredited his reliability and authority. By his own admission, Martyr relied on Ribera's translations of the slave's explanations of his performance in his native language of Nahuatl, yet in his account Martyr erases any indication of such mediation. Indeed, Martyr's seemingly straightforward description of the slave's performance attempts to occlude the complex issues of discourse (translation, interpretation, authority, and address) that condition his ability to speak for the other. These discursive operations mediate all the histories, ethnographies, and travel books that constitute colonial discourse.

Colonial discourse is "an ensemble of linguistically-based practices unified by their common deployment in the management of colonial relationships."[9] Thus, "colonial discourse" refers not only to material texts, but also to their shared "sets of questions and assumptions, methods of procedure and analysis, and kinds of writing and imagery" that conspire to produce colonial power. Indeed, colonial discourse does not provide a window through which we may objectively peer into the New World encounter—a perspective many colonial writers would have wanted to give their readers. Far from it: colonial discourse is animated by the chroniclers' patterns of logic, imagination, and belief. Put another way, Foucault described "discourse" as a set of "practices that systematically form the objects of which they speak."[10] The implication of this assertion is that the chroniclers formed the "objects" (and subjects) of their discourse, including a body of knowledge about Aztec dance, and that the objects and subjects of their discourse are necessarily limited by what the chroniclers could think and say. Thus, the formation of indigenous dance in colonial discourse more closely reflects the experiences, preoccupations, and languages of the chroniclers than any social reality about "Indians" and their dances.

Spanish humanist philosopher and grammarian Antonio de Nebrija expressed a similar reflection on the relationship between discourse and empire. In 1492 Nebrija famously presented Queen Isabella of Spain with his *Gramática de la lengua castellana*. The queen did not immediately realize what use she would have for a grammar book about vernacular Spanish, yet she was persuaded by Nebrija's remark in the book's prologue that "language has always been the companion of empire."[11] This statement was not merely a reflection on the power of discourse to unify subjects within the empire's Castilian and Aragonese regions, but also a mandate to deploy the power of discourse in the empire's efforts to expand overseas. His words could not have been more prescient, for at that time, within the span of a year, three critical events were occurring that helped to unify and expand the Spanish global empire: the enactment of the Alhambra Decree, which led to the military expulsion of Jews from the kingdom of Spain; the signing of the Treaty of Granada in 1491, which led to the end of the reconquest of territories controlled by the Moors in southern Spain, bringing to a close nearly five hundred years of military struggle; and the departure of Christopher Columbus, a Genoese sailor who at the behest of the Spanish Crown set out to discover a direct route between Europe and the Indies. Combined, these events set the stage for military and religious expeditions that within fifty years would claim territories that outsized the Iberian peninsula tenfold.[12]

Indeed, sixteenth-century Spain experienced an exceptional rate of expansion, acquiring territories in the Caribbean, North, Central, and South America, and Asia, which necessitated the development of a colonial administration that was in the service of the Crown. All forms of writing—letters, legal depositions, encyclopedias, royal histories, ethnographies, indigenous language grammars, and psalmodies—were undertaken in pursuit of developing and controlling that burgeoning empire. To control the expanding territories of the Spanish empire in the Americas, Spain established a number of administrative bodies. In 1503 the *Casa de Contratación* was formed to deal specifically with trade, commerce, duties, and immigration laws in the Indies.[13] In 1524 the Council of the Indies, a body consisting of Crown-appointed leaders from the church, military, and nobility, was formed to administrate the judicial and legal matters in Spain's new territories. Both of these bodies were located in Seville, Spain, and therefore required the creation and circulation of written reports, testimonies, and accounts concerning legal, theological, and economic matters in the young colony, especially regarding the *encomiendas*, the large estates that were designated to Spanish lords, often as compensation for their role in the conquest. *Encomenderos* famously exploited natives as sources of tribute and unpaid labor, and the *encomienda* system spurred major political, theological, and economic debates throughout the colonial era, some of which were resolved in 1542 with the New Laws, which prohibited enslavement of Indians. In 1527 the first *audencia*, or judicial court, was established. These administrative measures and bodies all led to the formation of the viceroyalty of New Spain in 1535, with the appointment of its first viceroy, Antonio de Mendoza. Centered in the former Aztec capital of Tenochtitlan—where now stands Mexico City—New Spain encompassed Mexico, Central America, and territories in the West Indies.

New Spain was formed as both a political and a religious colony. Through a series of papal grants known as *patronato real*, the Spanish Crown maintained authority over the Catholic Church in its new territories, where missionaries waged a "spiritual conquest" similar in scope and intensity to military operations. Missionaries built churches, established schools, taught Spanish, and above all, evangelized the natives. Some defended natives from the abuses of the *encomendero* system, whereas others were entirely complicit in its practice of subjugation. In 1523 three Flemish missionaries, including Pedro of Ghent (ca. 1491–1572), a blood relative of the king of Spain and Holy Roman emperor Charles V, arrived in New Spain and established a community in Texcoco, were he lived among and taught hundreds of thousands of natives.[14]

By order of Charles V, in 1524 a group of twelve Franciscan missionaries followed. These "First 12" included André de Olmos and Toribio de Benavente Motolinía, whose early research and writings in the 1530s established a foundation for a tradition of missionary ethnography that intensified throughout the mid-sixteenth century. This principally involved the collection of extant Aztec manuscripts known as *códices*—indigenous painted texts that native scribes known as *tlacuílos* created to preserve specialized information, including divinatory practices, calendars, maps, and dynastic histories. For the deep knowledge of Aztec beliefs and practices they contained, codices were systematically burned, confiscated, or otherwise destroyed in the years following the conquest. Some native nobles managed to successfully hide several codices, a few of which survive to this day in museums, libraries, and private collections throughout the world. Missionaries consulted the codices so as to better understand the ancient past and even ordered the recreation of some codices, a project that was later vehemently prohibited by the Spanish Crown.

One of the greatest works to emerge from that period of activity is the *Florentine Codex* (*Historia general de las cosas de Nueva España*), compiled by Franciscan missionary Bernardino de Sahagún, who arrived along with other missionaries in 1529. Based as it is on Sahagún's interviews with native informants, the *Florentine Codex* is widely considered the most authoritative source on Aztec culture. Book 2 of this twelve-volume encyclopedia is dedicated to descriptions and images of the eighteen major Aztec rituals. This remarkable text, with its unique descriptions of Aztec dance, is the pinnacle of the golden age of sixteenth-century missionary ethnography, as well as one of the earliest cross-cultural performance ethnographies of the early modern era.

Like most missionary ethnographies, the *Florentine Codex* was undertaken as an intellectual enterprise as well as a proselytizing tool. The missionaries were resolved to eradicate all aspects of indigenous belief systems and practices and recognized the importance of understanding indigenous ritual so as to identify vestiges of pagan religion in behaviors and practices, including dance. They also soon realized that the Aztec tradition of public spectacle could be put in service of Christian evangelization. As decreed in a papal bull of 1537, all colonial subjects were required to observe twelve annual Church festivals and attend services.[15] The services included the performance of religious dramas (*autos*) in the presence of the Holy Sacrament; these were aimed at teaching Christian morality and the merits of salvation through conversion. Some of the dramas included baptismal scenes, wherein native actors were baptized by a Spanish priest, sometimes as many as five thousand at a time. The policies and perspectives surrounding the role of the missionary theater, and methods of conversion more generally, varied from religious order to religious order.

There is no one unified European perspective about the "Indians" within the early writings about the New World. There were meaningful tensions concerning the treatment of Indians within the colonial administration and religious orders, as well as between them. These contradictory, shifting, and evolving perspectives of the "Indian" are dramatically revealed through the visual and written descriptions of indigenous cultural realities. Around the time of the quincentennial of Columbus's discovery in 1992, many scholars of the New World shifted their critical attention away from interpreting historical reality based on the chronicles and toward analyzing the chronicles themselves, often drawing upon the tools of literary analysis to interrogate their discursive dimensions. One of the major outcomes of this scholarship was the realization of the degree to which texts about the New World and its discovery were fictionalized so as to convey cultural realities.

This book directs the momentum of these critical gestures toward a neglected subject within colonial discourse: dance. Dance is an exceptional topic in the writings of the New World, for unlike the situation around other areas, such as military and dynastic history, warfare, trade, nature, and geography, there was no established European tradition for writing about dance. Before the discovery of the New World, dance was a peripheral topic of religious, cultural, and historical investigation. However, the chroniclers approached native dances with attention and intrigue, and included such descriptions within their "natural histories," legal tracts, and ethnographic analyses, for the native dances they encountered were as foreign and new a "discovery" as the peoples and lands of the New World. In some respect, the chroniclers introduced dance into historical discourse. As such, representations of dance in colonial discourse greatly contribute not only to our understanding of the New World encounters, but also to emerging early modern European notions of dance history.

Dance

By the time of the "discovery" of the New World, dancing had already become an established means for symbolizing ideals of imperial identity as well as threats of religious, racial, and class difference among Europeans.

Although Martyr mentions nothing about his previous exposure to dance before his encounter with the Indian slave, we can safely assume that he was familiar with dancing among European nobles, given his unique roles in the court of Ferdinand and Isabella, first as royal tutor and later as royal chronicler. An Italian-born chaplain, Martyr had developed a reputation for his humanist teaching. For this reason, Isabella invited him to establish a school for the children of the nobility at her court and entrusted him with the education of her daughters. Dancing did not have a role in Martyr's curriculum per se. As Barbara Sparti explains, "The humanist curriculum was directed at educating princes, upper- and upper-middle-class males—and some females. It was based on and aimed at producing moderate, ethical, self-sacrificing, and, above all, civic-minded statesmen, soldiers, and citizens."[16] Thus, dancing was "ignored—and at times even condemned" within the curricula at the courts of fifteenth-century Italy from which Martyr hailed.[17] However, while under Martyr's tutelage in the arts and sciences, the *infantas* simultaneously trained with a dancing master, who helped the young royal daughters cultivate the physical discipline, comportment, and grace required of their elite station, which meant learning French and Italian court dances.

Dancing was also a significant form of court entertainment. There is documented evidence of dancing at the Aragonese court as early as the fourteenth century. Pedro IV (ca. 1319–1387) patronized two French-inspired female dancing troubadours (Jacme Fluvia of Mallorca and Pere de Rius). Between 1465 and 1468, King Ferdinand (then Ferdinand II of Aragón) employed a dancing master named Guglielmo Ebreo da Pesaro (ca. 1425–1480) at his Neapolitan court.[18] Dance continued to flourish in the Spanish court in its Golden Age, especially during the reign of King Philip II (1527–1598), the great-grandson of Ferdinand and Isabella, who was an accomplished guitar player. He was also a notorious "devotee of dancing, court festivities, and rites of chivalry."[19]

One of the major influences on court entertainments was the exotic performances of the Moors, the North African Muslims who had invaded and settled the Iberian peninsula in the eighth century. For example, female Moorish dancers known as *alfuleys* performed in the court of Martín I of Aragón (1356–1410). Alfonso V (1396–1458) had several dancers associated with his court, including a famous *bailadora* from Valencia named Graciosa, and later a group of Moorish dancers (*moros balladors*).[20] Charles V also hosted Moorish dances when traveling with his court. According to David Coleman, the king enjoyed the exotic performances of *leylas* (Moorish

FIG. 0.1 Morisco dance. *Das Trachtenbuch des Christoph Weiditz* (1529), fols. 107–108. Courtesy of Germanisches Nationalmuseum, Nürnberg.

wedding dances) and *zambras* (secular dances performed by converted Moors known as Moriscos).

On the final night of a seven-month stay in Granada in 1526, a dance was held in Charles's honor.[21] A German artist named Christoph Weiditz (ca. 1500–1559) was traveling with the court and documented the Morisco performances in watercolor illustrations. These illustrations form part of his costume book *Das Trachtenbuch*, which catalogues the physical appearance, dress, and customs of local cultures he encountered during his travels throughout Europe. Several of his illustrations reference dancing. One depicts a group of Morisco dancers and musicians performing a *zambra* (fig. 0.1). Weiditz did not indicate whether the illustration documented a specific ceremony, such as the 1526 performance held for Charles V, or whether it was a generic portrait of the ubiquitous dance performed throughout Islamic Spain during the sixteenth century. The image gives no further clues as to the context of its performance, for it references neither the location of the event nor its audience. Instead, it emphasizes the musical instruments and the manner in which the dance was performed. The accompanying text tells us that a female dancer snaps her fingers, while a man manipulates his mantle by twisting a swath of its fabric with his right arm and draping another over his left.[22]

The influence of Moorish dancing extended beyond the world of the court to folk dances and rituals. The religious tension between Christians and Moors was a persistent theme in Iberian folk dances, such as the staged reenactments of military battles between Moors and Christians called *moros y cristianos*. Lynn Matluck Brooks notes that *moros y cristianos* commemorated and gave "choreographic form" to the centuries-long struggle between Christians and Muslims in Spain.[23] *Moros y cristianos* were performed against a backdrop of actual physi-

8 DANCING THE NEW WORLD

cal conflict precipitated by the Spanish Inquisition. Although the inquisition was established in the thirteenth century, it was revitalized by Ferdinand and Isabella in 1478 to combat heresy, particularly among converted Jews and Moors. One of the hallmarks of the reign of Isabella and Ferdinand was their attempt to eradicate influences of Moorish and Jewish culture on their Catholic empire. Following the Spanish conquest of the New World, *moros y cristianos* were performed throughout the colonies. Originally meant to dramatize Christian domination over the Moors, this dance was transplanted to the New World, where at Church-sponsored festivals and official colonial events missionaries enlisted recently conquered Indian natives to reenact their own military and spiritual domination under Spanish rule.

Anna Ivanova argues that during the reign of Ferdinand and Isabella, the Church utilized dance and theater to "proselytize the illiterate," especially among the recently converted Jews and Muslims of southern Spain.[24] Church-sponsored festivals staged religious dramas to teach and reinforce Catholic beliefs. Dance also evolved in religious ceremonies, especially those connected to the Corpus Christi festivals in Seville and Toledo, by way of *autos*, allegorical plays that often concerned the mystery of the Eucharist. Thus dancing figured both directly and indirectly into the dynamics between Moors and Christians, whether through the explicit dramatizations of military conquest or via the more circuitous implementation of dance as a method of spiritual conquest.

The above references to Moorish dancing at the Spanish court suggest that the Indian slave's command performance for Peter Martyr was by no means the first time the court staged a burlesque of religious and racial difference. Nor was it the last. In 1528, nearly a decade after Hernán Cortés had sent slaves and riches to the court of Charles V and two years after Peter Martyr's death, the conquistador himself returned to Seville for the first time. He brought with him acrobats, jugglers, tricksters, and humpbacks. These "exotic" and "noble" Aztec performers were part of the booty of riches presented to the court of Charles V in Toledo. Weiditz was also present when Cortés made his triumphant return. To commemorate this historic moment, Weiditz drew several scenes, including three sequential illustrations of a *juego de palo*, an indigenous log-rolling game that garnered the attention of many chroniclers (fig. 0.2). The images depict different phases of the game, which involved a man laying flat on a mat as he spins, tosses, and then catches a log with his feet. As with Weiditz's drawing of the Morisco dancers, these drawings are a rare visual record of the Indians' appearance and offer minute traces of the exceptional dances performed at the Spanish court.

Even before the Christian encounter with the Indians of the New World, and before that, the Christian encounter with the Moors, dance was an already established means for symbolizing relations of power within the Catholic Church. This idea undergirds one of the most popular themes within medieval European art, literature, and performance: the "dance of death." Variably known as *le danse macabre, der Totentanz,* or *la danza de la muerte,* the dance of death allegorizes the indiscriminate power of death through the figure of a dancing skeleton that seduces, manipulates, or otherwise coerces his victims into their untimely demise, and then leads the corpses in a choreographed procession to their graves. Dance of death imagery commonly appeared in church frescoes, paintings, ossuaries, and engravings. It also appeared as a theme in poems, musical compositions, and plays, most often as a dialogue between Death and his victims, who plead for their lives. There is even trace evidence that the dance of death began as a performance tradition that brought communities together to bear witness to the trauma of death.[25] One would imagine that the ritual involved the acting out of the dance of death scenario—a choreographed game of Russian roulette wherein a skeleton selects and then dances its victims to death.

The figure of the dancing skeleton was a reminder not only that death is constant—a type of *memento mori*—but also that it could strike any moment and take any victim. Gundersheimer suggests that "In an age of plagues, wars, and famines [the dance of death] represented a way of realizing graphically, and thereby perhaps somewhat domesticating, the dreadful fatality that hovered over even the most sheltered lives."[26] The dance of death inverted social order, indeed lampooned the conceit of a social hierarchy, by revealing that all were equal before

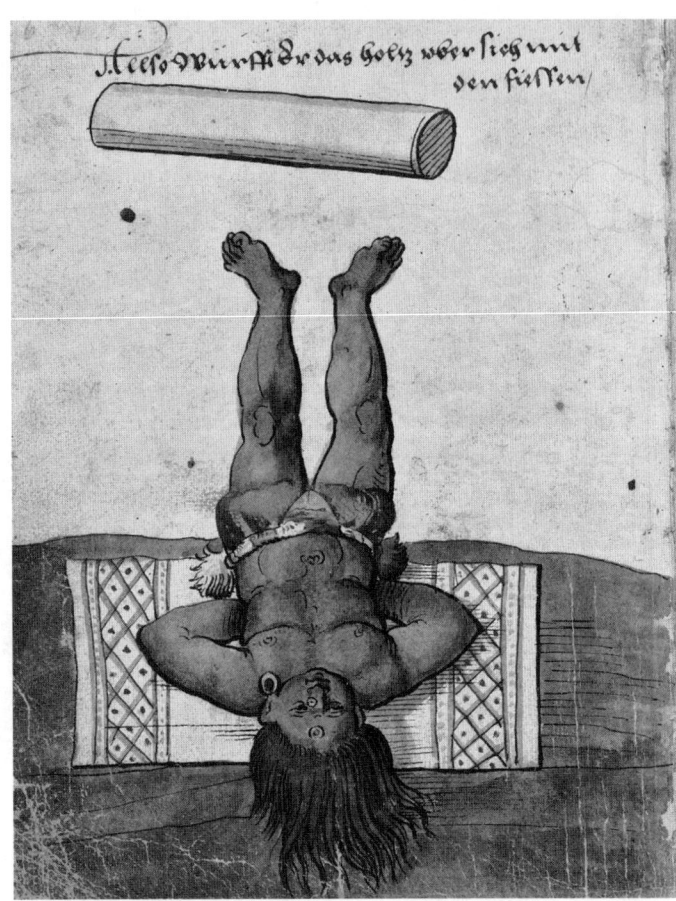

FIG. 0.2 Aztec acrobat in Spain. *Das Trachtenbuch des Christoph Weiditz* (1529), fols. 6, 8, 9. Courtesy of Germanisches Nationalmuseum, Nürnberg.

death. For example, the most distinguishing choreographic or iconographic feature of the dance of death was its "arrangement of characters by estate; carefully graduated in rank they are passed in review, each one with an appropriate vice."[27] In turn, Death's victims—from the king and the priest to the peasant and the child—perform their own "dance" in a futile attempt to escape Death's inevitable grip.

Clergy figure prominently among Death's victims in many examples of dance of death art and verse. For example, in Hans Holbein's famous series of dance of death woodcuts from 1538, more than a third of the victims are clergy: the pope, the cardinal, the bishops, the abbot, the preacher, the priest, the nun, and so forth. Yet beneath the dance of death symbolism lurks a deep anticlericism that sought to expose the Church's powerlessness or perhaps even neglect in protecting its flock from the ravages of earthly matters, the Black Plague most especially.

J. Mack Welford postulates that the dance of death developed as a result of the Roman Catholic Church's appropriation of pagan funerary rituals that involved frenzied dancing.[28] In its effort to convert pagan societies across Europe, the Church adopted and transformed their tradition of dancing in cemeteries into a didactic dramatic form that warned Christians to prepare for death. Although there are many examples of ecclesiastical denunciations of dance in the medieval Roman Catholic Church, vernacular and folk traditions such as the dance of death and the *moros y cristianos* suggest that the Church drew upon the symbolism of the dancing body to teach, convert, and subordinate its others—first pagan European societies, then the Moors, and ultimately the Indians. The dance of death tra-

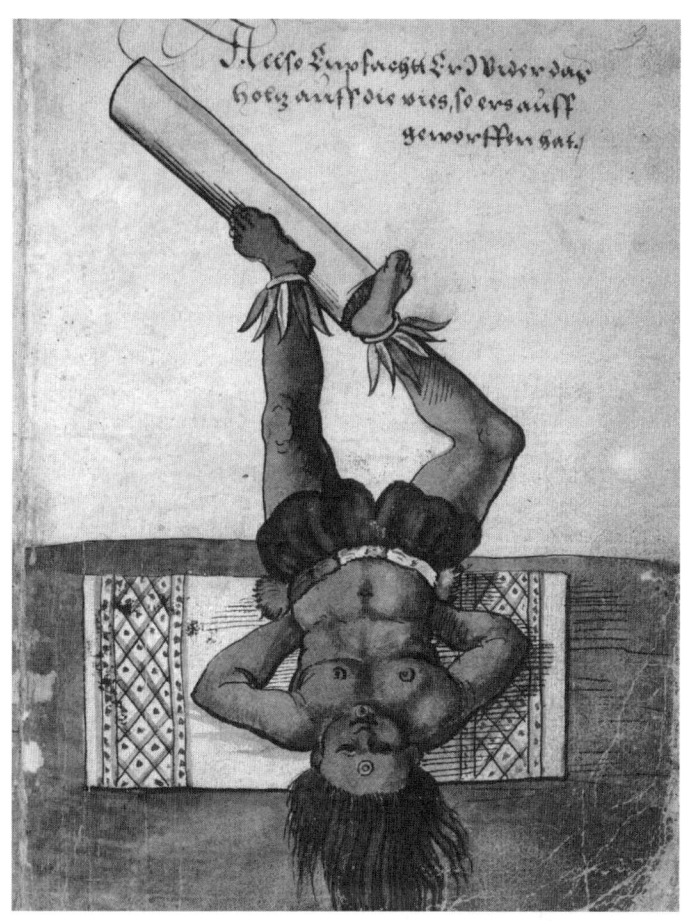

dition was just one of many lenses that framed European perspectives on Indian dance. Its configuration of dance, death, and religion exerted a direct and diffuse influence on sixteenth-century chroniclers of the New World, whose tendency was to allegorize violent and ultimately deadly encounters between Christians and Indians as a type of dance.

Although the chroniclers were familiar with dance's ability to allegorize power and exoticize difference, *writing* about dance was an entirely foreign enterprise. Although there are several extant European dance manuals from the fifteenth century, there was hardly an established tradition of documenting and interpreting dance. Thus, many chroniclers made allusions to classical sources, especially about the dances and bacchanals of ancient Greece and Rome. Others sought passages from the Bible to help reconcile their experiences with Indian dances.

However, neither the classical histories nor the Bible sufficiently explained the Indian dances they encountered. In their writings we can perceive how the chroniclers sought new methodologies, techniques, and discursive strategies to represent dance. They required not only new vocabularies, but also new conceptual models for understanding dance as a form of historiography, a sacred epistemology, and a form of political spectacle. In the absence of a tradition of dance ethnography, the chroniclers implicitly and explicitly articulated questions about the nature and function of dance as a sphere of meaningful human action: What is dancing? Is it a religious expression? A political weapon? A repository for history? And what is its relation to other rites, such as music, divination, sacrifice, and dress? What distinguishes "dancing" from other types of human movement? How can we know whether the ancient beliefs endure in the dances we see? Would prohibiting dance lead to the extinction of paganism?

The divergent and conflicting responses to these questions reveal themselves in the ways that writers "discovered," borrowed, and coined terms to refer to "dance." By the mid-sixteenth century, a growing lexicon of terms for "dance" had begun to emerge in colonial discourse. These words were drawn from multiple languages, including Spanish (*baile*, *danza*), the indigenous Caribbean language of Taíno (*areíto*, or "song-dance"), Nahuatl (*macehualiztli*, a form of sacred dance; *netotiliztli*, a form of social dance; *mitote*, or "dance"), and, to a lesser extent, Quechua (*taqui*) and Latin (*saltare*). These were used in addition to terms specific to dancers and dances (*sarabanda*, *tocotin*, *dançadores*) and choreographic elements (*coro*, *compás*) as well as broader performance and ritual events (*representaciones*, *bacchanal*, *sarao*). In some instances, chroniclers used pejorative terms such as *vicio* (vice), *idolatría* (idolatry), or *superstición* (superstition) when referencing a physical movement or action. Although the chroniclers do not critically reflect on the use of these terms, their circulation and application bring into relief the underlying ideas concerning history, politics, race, and religion that drive their use. What, for instance, does it mean that Bernardino de Sahagún, the most accomplished linguist and speaker of Nahuatl among the Spanish missionaries, refused to acknowledge the Nahuatl terms for

INTRODUCTION 11

"dance" and instead referred to Aztec dances by the Taíno term *areíto*? In contradistinction, why did the eminent indigenous historian (and descendant of Aztec nobility) Fernando de Alvarado Tezozómoc use the full range of polyglottal dance-related words in narrating the role of dance in the epic events of Aztec history—a history originally recounted to him in his family's tongue of Nahuatl?

By and large, the chroniclers used the Spanish terms *baile* and *danza* with the most frequency. Antonio de Nebrija's Spanish–Latin dictionary (the one given to Queen Isabella) includes entries for several Latin terms related to dance in the classical world, including *salto*, which Nebrija translates as *dançar o bailar*. He pairs these distinct terms as if they were interchangeable, which might explain why Spanish chroniclers almost always use the terms in similarly undifferentiated and interchangeable variations: *baile y danza*, *danza o baile*, *bailadores y danzantes*. However, there is a semantic distinction between them. In her study of processions and dances in Golden Age Spain, Brooks synthesizes several early modern comparisons between *baile* and *danza*. The first distinction relates to context: a *baile* is a popular dance whereas a *danza* is a noble dance. This relates to her second distinction, following Sebastián de Covarrubias's 1611 dictionary, which notes that the terms refer to different functions: "*baile* denotes action, while *danza* denotes the dance itself."[29] That is to say, *baile* refers to expressive and spontaneous movements that need not necessarily cohere to a prescribed choreography; *danza*, by contrast, refers to movements that conform to a predetermined sequence of specific steps, figures, actions, and gestures, such as dances held in court. This distinction is supported by Pedro M. de Olive's 1852 *Diccionario de sinónimos de la lengua castellana*: "'Danza' expresses more than 'baile.' It indicates more artifice, complexity, culture, delicacy, wealth, and luxury. It is a studied composition, prepared, arranged with an object, a plan of an action, expressive and representative movements, only with help of gestures, movements, and postures."[30] Olive argues that a *baile*, on the other hand, consists of jumping and leaping movements borne from happiness and praise.

Olive's definitions subtly suggest a hierarchy between the terms, which has less to do with the inherent qualities of the dances themselves than with the dancers who perform them. The New World chroniclers privileged *danzas*. They wrote with great esteem about "Indian" dances that exhibited the discipline of martial arts or dances performed as entertainments at court and repeatedly exalted the control and precision exhibited by dances that required synchronicity between dancers—dancing that revealed a predetermined logic, design, or narrative. By contrast, the chroniclers repudiated *bailes*. These included dances that were performed by the populace at social gatherings. The movements were seemingly more expressive, improvisatory, and uncontrolled. Their descriptions of these dances often pay as much attention to related rituals of drinking alcohol or ingesting mind-altering substances. *Baile* connotes expressivity—movement stirred by emotion, belief, or idea. *Danza*, by contrast, connotes a body disciplined by language, law, or choreography.

Of course, the term "choreography" is altogether absent from sixteenth-century dance writings of the Americas. This absence is easily explained by the fact that the term—or at least its neologistic predecessor "orchesography" ("the writing of dances")—was not coined until 1589, when French dance master and Jesuit priest Thoinot Arbeau (1520–1595) published his influential dance manual of the same name.[31] *Orchésographie* takes the form of a dialogue between Arbeau and his former student, Capriol, who returns to his dance master upon completing his legal training. Capriol comes to Arbeau in order to learn dancing so that he may "please the damsels" and excel in social spheres where dancing was an indication of good manners, health, and temperament. Capriol's return to his master soon gives way to a discussion that establishes the necessity for a system of dance writing that Arbeau calls *orchésographie*. Capriol urges his master "to set these things down in writing" so as to avoid losing "the knowledge of our ancestors."[32] Arbeau complies, and thus the manual includes an "inventory" of various sixteenth-century dances and instructions on how to perform them, as well as images that demonstrate some of the salient figures.[33]

Early in the course of their dialogue, the dance master and his student reflect on the history of dance and its role in producing a "well ordered society."[34] Capriol asks Arbeau why it should be that dancing reflects man's dignity, given the many famous condemnations against dance by figures such as Cicero, Moses, and King Alphonse. Arbeau responds to his student's query by listing the names of prophets, statesmen, and philosophers who held dance in high esteem. These include King David, Claudius, Socrates, and the god Vulcan. To this list he adds the Indians of the New World. He explains: "Indians worship the sun with dances, and those who have traveled in the New World report that the savages dance when the sun appears upon the horizon."[35]

Arbeau's reference to the New World chronicles is remarkable for two related reasons. First, Arbeau invokes these accounts to establish dancing's universality, emphasizing that "scores of others have praised and esteemed it."[36] He argues that if dance held such a sacrosanct role among the Indians of the New World, then surely the courts of Europe should recognize its great value. Second, Arbeau references the writings about Indian dances to bolster his case for a type of "dance writing." Arbeau did not specify which reports of New World travelers he had read, but it is safe to assume that these works would have memorialized indigenous dances in various states of extinction, disappearance, and prohibition. The impending loss of Indian dances inspires Arbeau to devise a means of memorializing European dance in writing, so as to avoid losing "the knowledge of [the] ancestors." When de Certeau argued that the discovery of the New World ushered in "a new function of writing in the West" that dealt principally with memorializing bodies, he most certainly did not have Arbeau's idea of orchesography in mind. However, the discovery of the New World—with the destruction of Indian dances and the European writings that memorialized them—indeed helped to usher in the development of "choreography" (the writing of dance) as a form of historiography (the writing of history). Arbeau's orchesography was fueled by the dancing master's desire to immortalize dances and to protect them from the ravages of time, memory, and, in the instance of the New World, death.

The various ideas about "dance" among early chroniclers raise a relevant question about my own use of the term "dance" and its critical capacity to interrogate the principles and practices of Aztec movement and their representation in colonial discourse.

Like the many terms employed to describe meaningful physical movement that surface in sixteenth-century colonial discourse, "dance" has its own history and history of practice that both overdetermines and underestimates the range of Aztec embodied practices and Spanish perceptions of them. Writing specifically about the relationship between performance and conquest, Diana Taylor argues that "taking a word developed in a different context to signal a profoundly different worldview to fit our analytical needs simply does violence to that term."[37] I heed her warning about the potential pitfalls in applying a historically and culturally specific term such as "dance" to describe either the Spanish chroniclers' ideas about dance or the principles and practices of indigenous movement they sought to describe. Instead, Taylor encourages the use of terms such as "theatricality" and "performance" to describe pre-Hispanic embodied practices, even though she admits that they, too, have their referential limits. I use the term "dance" as a critical lens for reading colonial discourse, while recognizing the fact that the Aztec maintained separate words for dance (*macehualiztli, netotiliztli, mitote*), practices, and institutions specific to dance that the broader term "performance" potentially erases. Although Aztec rituals synthesized expressive forms such as music, song, dress, masking, and dance in a manner that made them indistinguishable from each other, "dance" still maintained its own significance as a practice and a way of knowing. Thus, I use the term "dance" in a broad and flexible manner in order to encompass the conflicting and evolving set of indigenous and European ideas, practices, and perceptions of human movement approximated by the term "dance" in various languages.

This book is interested not in identifying or validating a single definition of "dance," but rather in examining the constellation of ideas about embodiment that emerged as a result of the New World encounter. The dances of the New World required that chroniclers, conquistadors, and missionaries see this art form anew. Looking across cultural divides, they began to recognize that dancing was intimately linked to the formation of religious, national, and class identity. As Jennifer Nevile succinctly puts it in her study of court dance in the age of European humanism, "Movements of the body were believed to be the outward manifestation of movements of the soul."³⁸ Indeed, the writings about dance in the sixteenth-century chronicles of the New World inspired an epistemic shift in thinking about dance, one that necessitated the development of a Western notion of "choreography."

Yet even as the dances of the New World animated new ideas about dancing, some practices remained the same. The Indians of the New World were cast in long-standing roles in spectacles of difference. The Indians, like the Moors before them, and the pagan Europeans before them, participated in choreographies of resistance and acquiescence to the power of the Church and its courts. In that respect, the Indian slave's command performance for Martyr at the court of King Ferdinand was exceptional in that it brought together the European historian and the dancing Indian for the very first time. However their meeting was just another instance within a much broader history wherein dancing served as a means of experiencing both the proximity and the distance between the self and the other. Whether through traditions such as the dance of death, staged military combats such as the *moros y cristianos*, or spectacles of exoticization such as the court entertainments, dancing was a viable way to negotiate perceptions of social, cultural, and religious differences in an ever-expanding world.

The "Aztec" Empire

For Martyr, the dancing slave symbolized the "Indian" writ large. Although Martyr mentions that the slave hailed from Tenochtitlan, he never gives the slave's name. Moreover, even though Martyr refers to the Indian performer as a "slave," in all likelihood he was an indigenous noble, for we know that Cortés selected Indians of noble blood to join him on his later expeditions back to Spain.³⁹ In some measure, the Indian was denied humanity altogether as he was transformed into a commodity as part of the Crown's "royal fifth." Like so many "Indian" dancers referenced throughout colonial discourse, Martyr's slave was anonymous, displaced, and misidentified, yet came to represent the authentic "Indian."

Many distinct indigenous cultures existed in the Americas on the eve of the European arrival. These cultures had different languages, histories, rituals, governance structures, and religious systems. Those differences were instrumental to the conquistadors, who leveraged existing interethnic tensions for their own gain. However, European chroniclers tended to erase those distinctions in pursuit of constructing a broader category of the "Indian." This book principally addresses the written and visual representations of dance among the Aztec, for there is more extant dance-related source material (both European and indigenous) about and from this civilization than from any other. This includes several surviving indigenous painted manuscripts (*códices*), physical evidence (such as sculpture and architecture), and collections of song-poems.

It was during the decades following the conquest that missionaries undertook some of the most sustained ethnographic studies of the Aztec world, and in turn created one of the most extensive archives on any native American society. This material includes information about Aztec dance, although of course not a complete portrait. Most of what exists is limited to ceremonies and rites pertaining to the Aztec ruling class. Through its size, wealth, and stratification, the Aztec empire created ever-expanding contexts for the Aztec to integrate dance into their sacred and social worlds. For nobles, elites, and warriors, ceremonial events provided endless occasions to publicly display their wealth and status. Other descriptions of Aztec dances focus on the major sacred ceremonies, the world of nobility and palace life, and the *cuicacallis* (houses of song), schools dedicated to the study of music and dance. The first indigenous chronicles from the sixteenth century also offer accounts of dances dating from the early fifteenth century. Thus, the archive is sufficiently ample, diverse, and deep to warrant an analysis of this almost completely overlooked topic.

It is worth describing a few aspects of Aztec culture and history here as a context for understanding its principles and practices of dance, beginning with the term "Aztec" itself. At best "Aztec" is a misnomer, and at worst a complete historical fiction. Scholars of Mesoamerican culture have debated the merits of the use of term "Aztec" to describe the indigenous people and culture that thrived in the island cities of Tenochtitlan-Tlatelolco and environs. The term was popularized by two influential nineteenth-century writers, Alexander von Humboldt, the German naturalist and explorer, and William H. Prescott, the American historian who wrote the monumental *History of the Conquest of Mexico* (1843). In 1945 R. H. Barlow made an impassioned argument against the utilization of the term "Aztec," noting that none of the first chroniclers, conquistadors, or missionaries used it, and neither did the "Aztec" identify themselves as such. The peoples of Tenochtitlan and Tlatelolco in fact referred to themselves as "Mexica," the name of the ancient tribe from which they descended. Alternatively, some "Aztec" or "Mexica" who lived in Tenochtitlan also went by "Tenochca," just as those "Mexica" who lived in Tlatelolca went by "Tlatelolca."[40] Adding to this list of referents, there is also the term "Nahua," which broadly refers to speakers of Nahuatl, the *lingua franca* of the Aztec empire.

Since this book is not exclusively about the Mexica, I use the term "Aztec" when referring to the broader range of Nahua-speaking cultures within the Aztec empire and use terms specific to ethnicity or geography (such as "Tenochca" and "Tlatelolca") when necessary and possible to make such distinctions. As we will see, the ability to distinguish the ethnicity, location, and class of the performers described in colonial writings on dance significantly illuminates the ways in which (and reasons why) the chroniclers were interested in documenting dances.

The term "Aztec empire" is equally fraught. Historian Inga Clendinnen memorably described the phrase "Aztec empire" as "a European hallucination" by which she meant that Tenochtitlan held on to its network of tribute cities more through domination than through the perceived shared cultural traits that "empire" might imply.[41] When speaking of the "Aztec empire" I specifically refer to the "Triple Alliance," a political entity formed in 1428 that united the cities of Tenochtitlan, Texcoco, and Tlacopan; this alliance was designed to allow the cities to more efficiently conquer and manage territories throughout the Mesoamerican valley and beyond.

At the time of its Spanish "discovery," the Aztec empire was the largest, wealthiest, and most powerful indigenous empire in Mesoamerica. With a population of approximately 250,000, the ruling Mexica

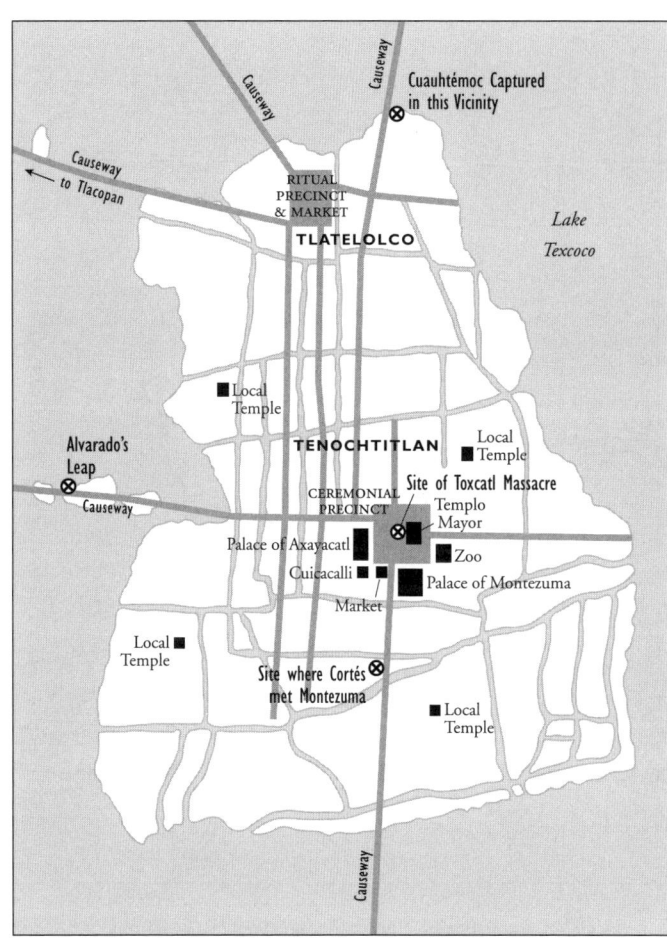

MAP 1 Aztec Empire and Surrounding Region (Molly O'Halloran).

made their home on the island city of Tenochtitlan-Tlatelolco, situated on Lake Texcoco in the Valley of Mexico[42] (map 1). Tenochtitlan was several hundred years in the making. It was originally founded in ca. 1325 by an indigenous tribe known as the Mexica, which since 193 CE had undertaken a great migration from their mythic homeland of Aztlán ("Place of Whiteness") to the Valley of Mexico. Their journey was guided by their patron deity, Huitzilopochtli ("Hummingbird of the South"), who instructed them to settle wherever they saw the vision of a snake-devouring eagle perched upon a *nopal* cactus. The Mexica came across this manifestation on the island of Tenochtitlan; over the course of several hundred years, they developed the site into a major administrative, trading, military, and ceremonial center. (The image of a snake-devouring eagle

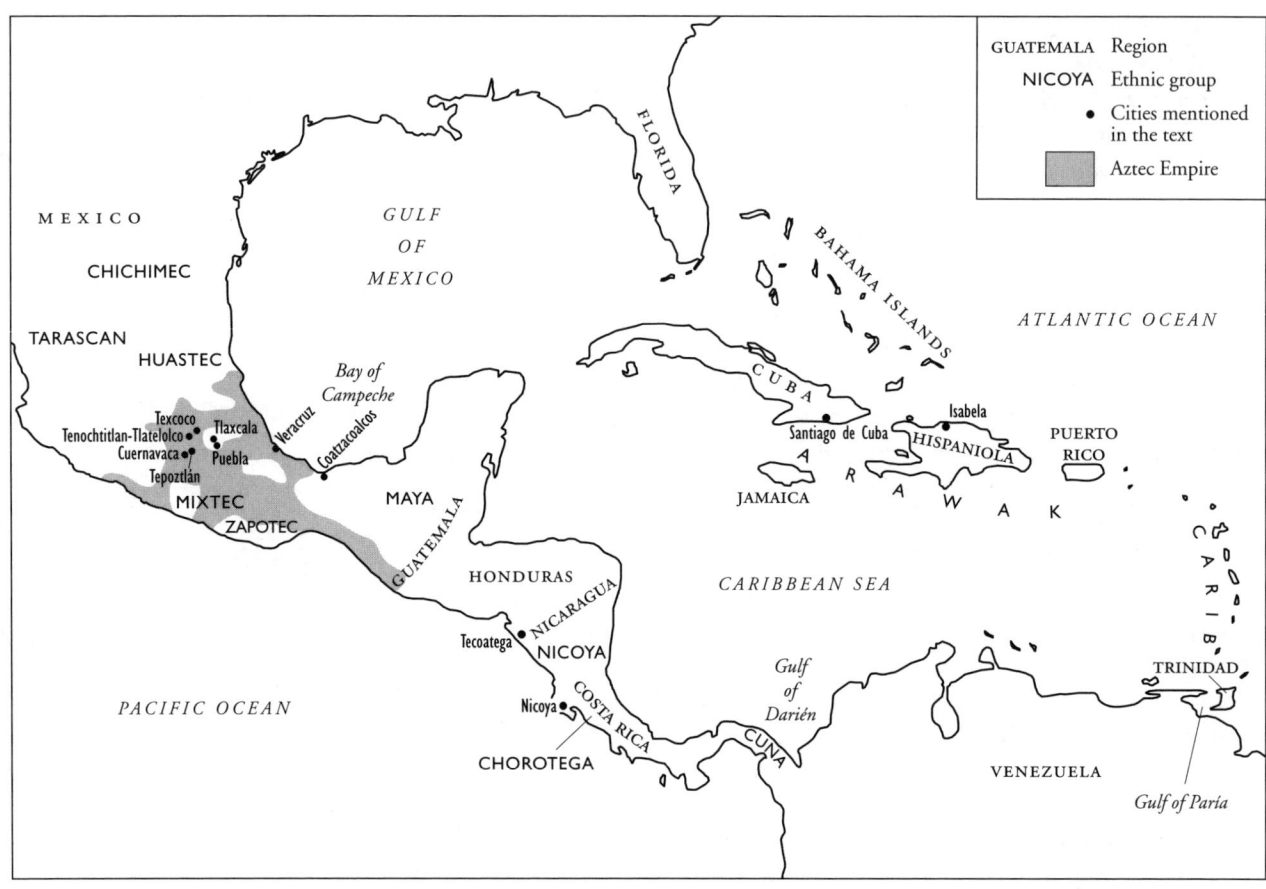

MAP 2 Tenochtitlan and the Ceremonial Precinct (Molly O'Halloran after Townsend).

perched on a *nopal* cactus remains the symbol emblazoned on the modern Mexican flag.)

The city of Tenochtitlan was divided into four quarters (*campan*), an organization that reflected the Aztec conceptualization of a quadripartite universe. At its center was a gated ceremonial precinct that included the massive Templo Mayor (Great Temple), the *axis mundi* of the Aztec civilization. The ceremonial precinct also was filled with palaces, lavishly painted temples, a zoo, gardens, a ball court, and a market district (map 2). The island was connected to the mainland through five main causeways.

The four *campan*, each governed by a ruler (*tlatoani*, or "He Who Speaks"), consisted of smaller districts or neighborhoods (*calpultin*). As with the city itself, Aztec society was highly stratified, with the primary distinction being between nobles (*pipiltin*) and commoners (*macehualtin*). The nobility formed a hierarchy of rulership consisting of a king (*tlatoani*), a primary advisor (*cihuacoatl*), two supreme priests, and lords or dignitaries (*tetecuhtin*) who ruled over the *calpultin*. The rest of the nobility served in various official capacities, as "ambassadors, tax collectors, provincial governors, teachers, scribes, judges, priests, and army generals."[43] The *pipiltin* enjoyed the benefits of rigorous education and military training as well as lavish estates that were maintained by serfs (*mayeque*) and slaves (*tlacohtin*), who occupied the lowest level of the Aztec social order. The *macehualtin* were free citizens that supported the workings of the state through labor, goods, and taxes. They formed a working class of merchants, artisans, farmers, and servants. The children of commoners also were educated. Each *calpulli* had its own *telpochcalli* ("Youth House"), where the male children of the *macehualtin* trained for the military and young girls trained for the domestic sphere.

The elaborate religious and political structure of

the empire relied heavily on two of its most prestigious institutions: the priesthood and the military. According to the *Codex Ramírez*, one in every six Aztec men belonged to the priesthood.[44] And as with all facets of Aztec life, the priesthood was regulated by a stringent hierarchy. From the ritual officiates to the novitiates, priests were the guardians of history and knowledge. They devoted themselves to a rigorous schedule of labor in order to maintain the myriad temples and shrines located throughout the empire as well as to run the *calmecac*, the school for priests, where they trained future generations of religious leaders. They performed private rites as well, including auto-sacrifice and bloodletting, which explains why in the codices priests are often depicted with hair matted with blood and bloodstained skin. Priests were also the custodians of ritual, responsible for procuring offerings, protecting victims, handling masks and regalia, and coordinating music, dance, and chanting, among the other countless details that went into the extravagant festivals. Some of the most sacred rites, such as manipulation of fire and incense, purification ceremonies, wielding the sacrificial knife, and dismembering victim corpses, were restricted to special classes of priests.

The power and wealth of the Aztec empire were based on the strength of its warriors, and for the Aztec, military service was obligatory. Young commoner boys between the ages of fifteen and twenty years of age were trained as warriors at the *telpochcalli*. Their training involved rigorous labor during the daytime hours. By night, they convened in the patio of the *telpochcalli* to play the drums, sing songs of their past, and dance, all in an effort to create a sense of unity through rhythm and a shared history, as well as to maintain physical strength and dexterity. Warriors of noble lineage could ascend into the elite military societies, such as the orders of the eagle (*cuacuauhtin*) and the jaguar (*ocelomeh*), or the most elite ranks of Otomies (*otontin*) or the Shorn Ones (*cuauhchicqueh*). Promotion into these elite military orders was dependent upon a warrior's skill as evidenced by the number of captive enemy warriors he could procure from the battlefield, among other acts of bravery. Aztec military strength ultimately proved to be their downfall. Degraded and exploited by a long history of Aztec military domination, their indigenous enemies throughout Mesoamerica, such as the Tlaxcalans, readily allied with Spanish conquistadors to facilitate the conquest of the Aztec empire.

The level of Aztec ingenuity and discipline dedicated to the spheres of social, political, and religious organization is reflected in Aztec calendars. The Aztec measured time against three calendars. The "counting of the days" (*tonalpohualli*) was a calendar for divination and astronomy. The "counting of the years" (*xiuhpohualli*) was a 365-day solar calendar that organized the annual cycle of the sun (such as equinoxes and solstices) and the agricultural seasons into eighteen "months" of twenty days (*veintenas*) plus five "leftover" days (*nemontemi*). The "bundle of years" (*xiuhmolpilli*) measured cycles of fifty-two years, a period of time for the Aztec that was the equivalent to our century. The Aztec calendars calculated astronomical and agricultural phenomena, and also reflected the beliefs and practices of their polytheistic religion. Aztec gods were associated with specific local, natural forces, and sacred principles and could manifest through animals, humans, dreams, and objects.

Renowned Mesoamerican scholar H. B. Nicholson identified three broad categories within the Aztec pantheon.[45] The first category includes deities concerned with celestial and paternalistic forces, including the primordial, supreme god Ometeotl ("God of Duality")—"the alpha and omega of Aztec religious thought" and his various manifestations; the omnipotent, omnipresent, and polymorphous Tezcatlipoca ("Smoking Mirror"); and the god of fire, Xiuhtecuhtli ("Turquoise Lord"). The second category includes gods of agriculture and fertility, such as the god of rain, Tlaloc; the god of wind, Ehecatl-Quetzalcoatl; the maize god, Cinteotl ("Maize Cob Lord"); and the god of sun, joy, music, and dance, Xochipilli; as well as a range of female fertility goddesses, including the universal mother goddess Teteoinnan ("Mother of the Gods"). The final category encompasses gods related to war, sacrifice, and sanguinary nourishment. These include some of the most powerful gods in the Aztec sacred order, such as the god of the sun, Tonatiuh ("The One that Illuminates"); the solar god of war, Huitzilopochtli; and god of the Milky Way, Mixcoatl ("Cloud Serpent"). The Aztec gods were meaningfully and systematically integrated into Aztec calendars, myths, architecture, and rituals. Temples were dedicated to individual gods, where many elaborate rituals and offerings were made to them. In addition to rituals and beliefs related to the tutelary gods, the Aztec practiced "anthropomorphic supernaturalism," such as witchcraft, magic, and sorcery.[46] These rites were both distinct from and sometimes integrated into the ceremonies connected to the major agricultural festivals.

The sacred, agricultural, and military spheres of Aztec society converged in ritual. The eighteen major "ceremonies" (*ceremonias*) or "feasts" (*fiestas*) were synchronized with the agricultural seasons, yet were also forms of military, sacred, and political theatre. All members of the Aztec social spectrum participated—rulers and priests, nobles and commoners, merchants and laborers, slaves and captive enemy warriors. Rituals were performed in the *calpultin* as well as throughout the main ceremonial center of Tenochtitlan. During these occasions, the city was transformed into metaphorical stages—plazas into battlegrounds, temples into mythical volcanoes, and the marketplace into sacred caves.

One of the distinguishing aspects of these ceremonies was the performance of human sacrifices. To the Aztec mind, blood sacrifices were necessary to repay the tremendous debt they owed to their gods for the creation of the earth, as well as for their continued protection. In most instances, the victims of human sacrifices were consecrated into living representations of the gods. These "representations" were called *ixiptlas*, and were often captive enemy warriors, women from within the empire, children, and/or purchased slaves who went through a ritual purification. It is in the context of these sacrificial spectacles that some of the most compelling Aztec choreographies were performed. Migration accounts, battles, creation stories, and other defining events were in reenacted during the eighteen month–long ceremonies of the Aztec world. Aztec dance was not only a representational practice, but also a means to effect change in the terrestrial world—a performative practice that James Frazer refers to as "imitative magic." Aztec hunting dances, war dances, rain dances, and crop dances are just a few examples of rituals Frazer would have characterized as "magic"—

or as humanity's belief that through dancing they can create conditions to produce desired effects.

This conceptualization of Aztec dance was guided by the belief that movement connected the terrestrial and celestial worlds. Put another way, the Aztec believed that dancing was a vehicle for reciprocal exchanges of energy between the sun and the human body.[47] This principle is suggested by the Nahuatl word *ollin*, which narrowly translates to mean "movement" or "motion" but more broadly means the "dynamic life of the world."[48] It also conveys the idea of social or physical change or transformation. For example, natural phenomena like earthquakes, the sun's trajectory through the sky, or any ongoing patterns of creation and destruction that structure life and death are all forms of *ollin*.[49] While *ollin* does not specifically reference human movement or "dance," it no doubt informs sacred and social principles and practices of Aztec dancing. *Ollin* is one of the twenty day signs that combined with thirteen numbers to designate the 260 days in the Aztec ritual calendar.[50] As with all day signs, *ollin* had divinatory properties that influenced the temperament of those born under it. The *Florentine Codex* tells us that Montezuma revered the day sign "Four Movement."[51] Dominican missionary Diego Durán said that *ollin* was associated with the sun and that all men born under its sign "were thought to be men who would shine like the sun. They were held to be blessed, fortunate, of good fate, blissful. It was considered desirous, well omened, and fortunate to be born under this sign." Women born under this sign, however, had a very different fate. They were to become "stupid, foolish, stubborn, limited in their intelligence, obtuse, and confused" yet they were also destined to become "rich, prosperous and as powerful as men."[52]

The pictogram (or "sign") for *ollin* is "an X-shaped form or twist" that pervasively and intricately appears throughout Aztec codices and sculptures (fig. 0.3).[53] Durán poetically described the symbol as "a butterfly."[54] Some scholars have suggested that the symbol represents the joining of the four quarters of the Aztec universe, whereas others have emphasized the symbol's integration of a "solar eye" made from a precious stone as its distinguishing characteristic.[55] We might combine these two interpretations of *ollin* to say that for the Aztec, dancing was the manner by which the body experienced the convergence of heavenly and earthly forces.

The Aztec distinguished between historical eras as "suns." At the time of the Spanish arrival, the Aztec were living under the Fifth Sun—also known as "4 Movement" (*Nahui Ollin*). Jaguars, wind, fire, and rain respectively had destroyed the first four suns. It has been prophesied that the Fifth Sun would be destroyed by a series of earthquakes—but, of course, the Spaniards destroyed it first.

One of the enduring mysteries of modern history is how a few hundred Spanish soldiers were able to conquer with relative ease and speed such a powerful military culture such as the Aztec. On Good Friday of April 1519, the Spanish noble-turned-conquistador Hernán Cortés led an expedition of Spanish soldiers from the Caribbean island of Hispaniola to the eastern shores of Mexico and founded the settlement of Veracruz (City of the "True Cross"). From this point of arrival, he led his troops into the heart of Tenochtitlan with the help of the Tlaxcalans, the sworn indigenous enemies of the Aztec, and a female Indian interpreter named Malintzin (La Malinche). By November 1519, they had peacefully penetrated Tenochtitlan and sequestered the Aztec *tlatoani* Montezuma. Within thirty months of his arrival in Mexico, Cortés had captured and conquered the mighty Aztec empire, leveling its palaces, temples, and markets to create the foundation upon which New Spain was built. There are many compelling explanations for the Spanish victory over the Aztec: the Spaniards allied with the Tlaxcalans to overwhelm the Aztec; the spread of diseases brought by Spaniards or African slaves to indigenous peoples, decimating them; and the superiority of Spanish weaponry and military strategies over Aztec modes of symbolic warfare.

Dancers figure prominently in several accounts of one of the defining moments in the history of the conquest of Mexico. Allegedly, in May 1520, Mexica nobles were summoned to perform dances to satisfy the curiosity of Spanish conquistador Pedro de Alvarado. Thousands of nobles assembled on the patio of the Templo Mayor to perform the sacred dances associated with the festival of Toxcatl. During the height of the celebration, Alvarado led Spanish soldiers in a surprise attack on the unsuspecting dancers, leaving the ceremonial precinct drenched in the blood of native dancers and spectators. This event, "The Massacre at the Festival of Toxcatl," precipitated a fifteen-month conflict between the Aztec and the Spaniards that left Tenochtitlan and its environs under Spanish control for nearly three centuries, until Mexico won its independence from Spain in 1821.

FIG. 0.3 *Ollin* (movement). *Codex Telleriano-Remensis*, fol. 33r. Courtesy of Bibliothèque nationale de France.

Indigenous and European accounts of the massacre memorialize its unimaginable horror in remarkably different ways, yet almost all writers either justify or condemn its devastating effects by asserting competing ideas about the meaning of dancing—whether the ceremonial dancing of that day was an expression of violence or a symbol of peace. Writing about indigenous survivors of the massacre, the controversial Dominican missionary and "Defender of the Indies" Bartolomé de las Casas wrote: "As long as a few of these people survive, they will not cease to tell and re-tell, in their *areítos* and dances, just as we do at home in Spain with our ballads, this sad story of a massacre which wiped out their entire nobility, beloved and respected by them for generations and generations."[56] Las Casas understood that for native societies in the New World, dance—and performance more broadly—was a vital form of social memory. Indians danced to songs about military victories and defeats, lamentations for their ancestors, and songs in praise of their gods. Aztec dances in particular were a means of embodying history. As such, Las Casas was directing these words to the king of Spain as a thinly veiled warning about native retaliation.

For Las Casas, dance was a palpable threat of political resistance. His words were ironically prescient, for shortly after the fall of Tenochtitlan, surviving Indians were made to perform dances that dramatized their conquest. In church patios and town squares, indigenous performers reenacted the devastating events of the Spanish arrival in dances of conquest (las danzas de conquista) and the aforementioned moros y cristianos. In many instances these dances were part of larger religious dramas Indians were made to perform in and observe, which taught Christian morality and biblical dramas, and sometimes even involved actual baptisms of natives. Dancing was part of a larger umbrella of colonial performance that drew upon indigenous ideas of spectacle to transform conquered Indian masses into colonial subjects.

Las Casas recognized that in indigenous worlds, concepts of historiography and choreography were intimately linked. This connection is also demonstrated by the ancient Aztec codices, the sacred pictorial books. Elizabeth Hill Boone has gone so far as to assert that the codices are "theatrical" in that they stage historical, physical, or social "transformations."[57] We might also say that they are choreographic in that one of the ways they convey historical meaning is through the traces of the body's physical movement in time and space. Footprints traverse the pages of Aztec codices, in most instances to visualize relationships between representations of historical events, such as spatial paths within migration narratives or lines of descendancy in genealogies. In other instances, footprints represent physical motion. For example, a folio from the *Codex Borgia* depicts twelve dancing spirits of women who died during childbirth (*cihuateteo*) (fig. 0.4).

Taken literally, "choreography" is a "writing of dance." Footprints, too, are a type of bodily writing—an impression of the body's movement in time and space. As with the Indian slave's pantomime recounted by Martyr, footprints trace a presence in the material world while simultaneously concretizing an absence. This book is interested in retracing the literal and figurative footprints of movement in colonial discourse. These steps take us from the migratory paths of the Mexica into Aztlán and the accounts of fleeing and transformation that dance helped to make representable.

About This Book

Each of the book's chapters examines a set of related texts and images about dancing in the New World and charts evolving European conceptions of dance through the eras of discovery, conquest, and colonization. The book first covers the earliest writings about dance among the natives of Hispaniola in order to examine the ways that these initial encounters set the foundation for thinking about "Indians" and indigenous dance. The following three chapters focus primarily on the writings about Aztec dance by missionary-ethnographers in Mexico, the next addresses the role of dance in the accounts of the conquest of Mexico, and the final chapter examines writings about the role of dancing in colonial New Spain.

Chapter 1 gathers the earliest references to dancing in the accounts of the New World discovery, including those written by Christopher Columbus, Amerigo Vespucci, and three of the earliest Spanish chroniclers: Peter Martyr d'Anghera, Gonzalo Fernández de Oviedo y Valdés, and Bartolomé de las Casas. These chroniclers referred to indigenous dance by the Arawak (or Caribbean) term *areíto* ("song-dance"). They were convinced that the Spanish terms for "dance" (*baile* and *danza*) failed to convey the significance of the indigenous *areíto*. Although the *areíto* has been studied by musicologists and literary scholars, its choreographic dimensions have escaped critical scrutiny. This chapter examines the chroniclers' competing descriptions and definitions of the *areíto* as a practice of divination, a form of writing, and a means of political resistance. I argue that the early chroniclers went to great lengths to define the *areíto* as a method for memorializing history, and in the process defined it according to their own preoccupations and interests as historians: a mnemonic device for memorializing laws; a means to

FIG. 0.4 *Cihuateteo. Codex Borgia*, pl. 39. Courtesy of Dover Publications.

recall the past and to divine the future; and a type of commemorative performance.

Chapter 2 focuses on the writings of Friar Toribio de Benavente "Motolinía," one of the first of the twelve Franciscan missionaries to arrive in New Spain in 1524. Motolinía understood almost every facet of colonization through the lens of mimesis, for he believed that the Indians' ability to imitate European language and behavior was a sign that they could conform to Christian practices and beliefs, a necessary step to fulfilling his vision of a Christian utopia in America. Motolinía's writings about Aztec dance are no exception. In his *Memoriales* ("Notes"), Motolinía provides one of the earliest accounts of a specific Aztec dance ceremony, which includes unique and rare information about the Nahuatl terms for "dance"; the relation between choreography and music; the process by which dances were composed; and the social context in which such dances were performed. Interestingly, Motolinía's dance writings were among the most copied in colonial discourse—the proverbial whisper in an early modern game of "telephone." This chapter examines how Motolinía's unfaithful imitators appropriated, plagiarized, and repurposed his dance writings. Their "counterfeit" histories claim Motolinía's eyewitness experiences of dance as their own, and in the process refocus his perspective on dance, transforming it from a symbol of a possible Christian future into one of an extinguished pagan past.

It is impossible to overestimate the importance of Friar Bernardino de Sahagún to our understanding of the Aztec world. Between the 1540s and 1570s, Sahagún conducted a systematic study of the Aztec world encompassing all aspects of the indigenous past, through interviews with surviving Aztec nobles, who served as his "informants" and collaborators. These interviews resulted in the *Historia general de las cosas de Nueva España* (*General History of the Things of New Spain*), more commonly referred to as the *Florentine Codex*, a twelve-volume encyclopedic work that covers nearly every facet of the Aztec world: its cosmology, dynastic history, omens, rituals, etc. It is an invaluable source not only because of the breadth of information it contains, but also because the information is largely derived from natives who had firsthand access to such privileged knowledge. Chapter 3 focuses on the second book of the *Florentine Codex* ("The Ceremonies"), one of the earliest texts—and perhaps even the first—dedicated to the systematic cross-cultural study of ritual, dance, or performance. Book 2 contains descriptions of the eighteen major rituals of the Aztec calendar as well as the sacred and political spectacles staged in and around the ceremonial precinct of Tenochtitlan, including the confusing and terrifying rites of human sacrifice that garnered tremendous scholarly and popular attention. Dancing shaped the political, social, and sacred meanings of human sacrifice rituals at almost every phase—from choreographies that purified and displayed human victims to dances with victims' skins, limbs, and hearts. This chapter brings into relief a theory of Aztec representation that is embodied in Sahagún's informants' testimonies about ritual dance.

Perhaps no other performance in human history has held greater historical consequence than the Aztec festival of Toxcatl of May 16, 1520.[58] As mentioned earlier, this massacre of Aztec dancers directly precipitated events that led to the Spanish conquest of the Aztec empire. Chapter 4 examines the configuration of dance in the broad range of sixteenth-century images, reports, and histories that sought to memorialize this defining moment. It compares the competing use of dance imagery in the Spanish, missionary, and native accounts of the massacre and shows how dancers became an ideal figure for memorializing its unrepresentable violence.

Chapter 5 examines the role of dance in the formation of "New Spain." In particular, it demonstrates that colonial and Church authorities closely controlled dancing, especially the "dances of conquest" (dramatic reenactments of the conquest of Mexico) and Church-sponsored festivals (such as Corpus Christi processions, ecclesiastic *entradas*, and missionary dramas). Church authorities had diverging ideas about the syncretic nature of dancing in the young colony—whether dancing was a sign of Christian devotion or a means through which ancient idolatries persisted. To examine this tension, I analyze the writings of Dominican friar Diego Durán and Jesuit missionaries José de Acosta and Andrés Pérez de Ribas, all of whom wrote about Indians dancing in Christian contexts and similarly argued that dancing was both a technique for converting Indians into subjects of the Crown and Church, and a providential sign of that conversion.

The conclusion reflects on the writing of Fernando de Alvarado Tezozómoc (b. 1535), the son of two ruling indigenous lineages and the first full-blooded Mexican to write a post-conquest history of the Aztec. His *Crónica mexicana* (ca. 1598) offers an insider's perspective on the rise and fall of the Aztec empire. Remarkably, Tezozómoc integrated descriptions of dance throughout his narration of epic events. He describes how dance was a diplomatic weapon, a sacred practice, and a form of martial terror. In 1609 Tezozómoc, "the first indigenous historian," finished writing *Crónica mexicáyotl*, a Nahuatl version of his *Crónica mexicana*. His Nahuatl chronicle of the rise and fall of the Aztec empire came nearly a century after the first "official" Spanish history of the discovery of the New World as composed by Peter Martyr.

Dance figures prominently in these landmark histories—and in surprisingly similar ways. One of the anecdotes Tezozómoc tells concerns the Mexica *tlatoani* Itzcoatl ("Obsidian Serpent"), who in 1434 launched a military campaign against Xochitlolinqui, the *tlatoani* of the neighboring pueblo of Cuitlahuac, all because Xochitlolinqui had refused one of Itzcoatl's requests.[59] Itzcoatl demanded that Xochitlolinqui send his daughters and sisters of Tenochtitlan to sing and dance publicly for him at the *cuicayan*, "the place of the song," a patio at the temple of Huitzilopochtli. Xochitlolinqui was astounded by Itzcoatl's request and responded in kind to his messengers: "What do you say, Mexicans? What business have my daughters and sisters over there? Are they going to dance there so that Itzcoatl can laugh at me?" Of course, Itzcoatl's request was really a cryptic warning that he planned to conquer Cuitlahuac, thus giving Xochitlolinqui an opportunity to make peaceful, albeit humiliating, signs of submission and tribute before these were extracted by force. Messengers went back and forth between the palaces trying to ease the escalating tension between the two rulers. Fortunately for Xochitlolinqui, Itzcoatl died before he ever saw his daughters and sisters dancing in "the place of song" for his enemy.

Itzcoatl's desire to see his enemy's daughters and sisters dance for him at the sacred *cuicayan* recalls Peter Martyr's request to see the Indian slave dance at the palace of King Charles V. Both accounts suggest that dancers were valuable within the political, economic, and symbolic economies of empire. Not only were they commodified as tribute, they were also coerced into submission by being made to participate in command performances at symbolic sites of power. Martyr and Itzcoatl's shared impulse seems to indicate that Spanish and Aztec perspectives on dance sometimes converged. They shared an understanding that dance played an important role in the formation, maintenance, and representation of imperial power. This idea undergirds the remarkable network of images and writings about Indian dance, dancers, and dancing that formed in the century between Martyr's "first official history" and Tezozómoc's first Nahuatl chronicle. These representations provide a new way to understand the role of dance in the Aztec empire before the European arrival, during its violent conquest, and during its subsequent colonization—as well as in the experiences of the discoverers, conquistadors, missionaries, and travelers who witnessed these defining moments in world history.

One

on the *areito*

DISCOVERING DANCE IN
THE NEW WORLD

Signs of the New World

On December 26, 1492, during his first voyage to the "New World," Christopher Columbus encountered a *cacique* (Indian "chief") named Guacanagari, whom he invited, along with other Indians, aboard his ship the *Niña*. The Indians allegedly brought pieces of gold to exchange for hawks' bells; they immediately hung the bells on their bodies and began to dance to the chiming sounds they made.[1]

And so we see that one of the first encounters between Europeans and natives in the New World precipitated a dance. In his journal, Columbus mentioned his surprise at learning that Indians had such a fondness for dancing. It may seem curious that such a relatively insignificant detail would have made its way into the admiral's journal and by extension nearly every history attributed to Columbus about his "discovery." But to Columbus, dancing was a sign that the Indians could be easily manipulated, excited as they were to exchange precious gold for bells. Moreover, for Columbus, this dance might have served as a sign that he had reached the Far East. Columbus took with him on his travels a heavily annotated copy of Marco Polo's chronicle *Il Milione* (ca. 1295), which describes the rituals and traditions of cultures that Marco Polo had encountered on his travels to and around Asia during the late thirteenth century. These included several ritual and court dances, such as a shamanic dance of possession in a Chinese province and a performance by temple dancers in the Indian province of Malabar. Marco Polo also recorded the tales about the king of Ceylon, who filled his palace with dancing maidens. No doubt Marco Polo's references to these exotic dances figured into Columbus's expectations of how the Indies would reveal itself to him.

The impromptu dance aboard his ship apparently left an enduring impression on Columbus, for years later, during another of his many encounters, he recalled the Indians' passion for dancing and attempted to use it to his advantage. During his third expedition to the West Indies, in 1498—a journey to explore lands beyond those that he allegedly discovered and mistook for India—he attempted to land his ship along the shores of Trinidad, whereupon he encountered several armed Indians who ventured toward his boat via canoe. He explains how the language barrier forced him to attempt communicating with the natives through signs: "I made signs to them, however, to come nearer to us, and more than two hours were spent in this manner—but if by any chance they moved a little nearer, they soon pushed off again."[2] When the signs failed, he tried to lure them closer with "mirrors, clear and shiny bronze vases, bells and similar objects unknown to them." When he failed to charm them with trinkets, Columbus commanded his sailors to make music and dance, hoping to attract the attention of the Indians, whom he recalled were passionate about dancing. Instead, the Indians mistook the spectacle as a sign of aggression and began to shoot arrows at Columbus and his men. Amidst that barrage of arrows, Columbus made the shocking realization that dancing can mean different things to different cultures.

Dance figures prominently in these two accounts of Columbus's discoveries. In the former, Columbus expresses a sense of wonder and curiosity. He marvels that the Indians were "very graceful in form" and is astounded that they were "tall, and lithe in their movements."[3] However, in the latter account, Columbus stages a "deceptive dance" in an attempt to capture the Indians' attention, the same way one might tame a wild animal. In so doing, he conveys his perception of the Indian as inferior, bestial, savage—the mythical "wild man" of the ancient world.[4] Considered against and alongside one another, these accounts invoke dancing as a sign of both peace and violence, alliance and annihilation, pleasure and fear, humanity and savagery—the constellation of paradoxes associated with the theme of the "noble savage" that runs through early modern writings and images of natives in the New World, wherein Indians are ambivalently portrayed as noble by nature yet seemingly always and already poised to incite danger and violence.

The figure of the dancing noble savage appears in other early references to dance in the discourse of exploration, discovery, and encounter, including writings attributed to Amerigo Vespucci (ca. 1454–1512), one of the most important European explorers and cartographers. Between 1497 and 1504 Vespucci made several expeditions from Spain and Portugal to the South American continent, which now bears his name. In May 1487, Vespucci wrote a letter to his patron and former schoolmate, the powerful Florentine merchant Pietro Soderini, to request financing for his trans-Atlantic expeditions. In his appeal, Vespucci makes two passing yet relevant references to dance in describing his first encounter with Indians, who were walking naked along the coast of Paria (modern-day Venezuela). Like Columbus, Vespucci tried to open pathways for communication by making "signs of peace" and by offerings objects such as bells, looking glasses, and trifles. Like Columbus, Vespucci describes the physical characteristics of the people he encounters as a sign of their moral composure. He notes that they have skins as red as "a lion's" but observes that if properly clothed, "they would be white like ourselves."[5] He takes note of their physical strength and beauty, especially their agility in walking, running, and swimming, which gives them "a very great advantage over us Christians." He assures Soderini that, like Christians, they behaved modestly, such as when they sought privacy to defecate.

In addition to the description of Indians Vespucci had actually encountered, he includes accounts of Indians in "some other places" that perform "barbarous and inhuman" rituals involving dance. He reports:

> Some bury their dead with water and food, thinking they will want it. They have no ceremonies of lights, nor of weeping. In some other places they practice a most barbarous and inhuman kind of internment. This is when a sick or infirm person is almost in the throes of death, his relations carry him into a great wood, and fasten one of those nets in which they sleep to two trees. They put their dying relation into it and dance around him the whole of one day. When night comes on they put water and food enough for four or six days at his head, and then leave him alone, returning to the village.[6]

Although this passage is relatively unremarkable in terms of information about dance, it exemplifies the impulse to link savagery, dance, and death in early reports about the Indians. In this instance, Vespucci qualifies that this "barbarous and inhuman" burial dance was performed not by those whom he had actually encountered, but by Indians "in some other places," out in "the great wood." Here Vespucci conjures the "wild man," the mythical and ancient construct that was "associated with the idea of the wilderness—the desert, forest, jungle, and mountains—those parts of the physical world that had not been domesticated or marked out for domestication in any significant way."[7] It is well documented that the Europeans wrote terrifying accounts about "native" societies they themselves had never seen, but had only learned of through those native groups they actually had encountered. In many instances, the accounts that Europeans heard from Indians about "other Indians" are infused with long-standing interethnic tensions, fears, and stereotypes. These sto-

FIG. 1.1 Vespucci in Paria. Theodor de Bry, *America*, part 10 (1619). Courtesy of the John Carter Brown Library at Brown University.

ries about the "other's other" often involve descriptions of behaviors and rites, including cannibalism, human sacrifice, and other barbaric rituals, such as this burial dance. Explorers' accounts, including Vespucci's, fueled the European construction of an America filled with the "noble savages" they encountered and "wild men" they heard about, persuading readers, especially would-be investors, about both the value and the danger of their expeditions.

The distinction between the "noble savages" Vespucci "discovers" and the "wild men" he hears about is crystallized in an engraving that accompanied the 1619 publication of Vespucci's letter (fig. 1.1). The engraving and the letter appear beside one another in one of the most extensive and popular series of travel books of the colonial era, aptly named *America*, published by Dutch engraver Theodor de Bry. In the foreground a Carib *cacique* offers Vespucci and the Christians his modest and beautiful Indian wives, whom Vespucci tells us he could not refuse.[8] However, in the background there are two related "scenes" that illustrate the burial rite reported by Vespucci. On the right, seven figures hold hands and dance around a body resting in a hammock. This circle of dancing Indians is situated in the untamed world depicted in the engraving's background. The dancers are indistinguishable from the wilderness itself—in fact, their limbs merge with the roots and branches of the trees to form one monolithic entity. On the left, there are six figures lowering a corpse into a grave. These scenes of a barbaric and dangerous ritual serve as a literal and figurative background for the financial, sexual, and political exchanges transpiring in the engraving's foreground.

While dancing represents threats of death and violence in the early descriptions of the New World, it also symbolizes promises of fertility and wealth. Another early reference to dancing in the early encounters comes from a book based upon letters that author Niccolò Scillacio received from Guglielmo Coma, a Spanish noble who reported the stories about Columbus's travels that were flowing into court. Scillacio—known as "the Moor" for his dark complexion—slightly augmented these letters with information he gleaned from independent sources, and published them in *De insulis meridiani atque Indici maris nuper inventis* (ca. 1494). His letters read like early travel brochures, boasting that the colonial settlement of Isabella would "vie with any of the Spanish cities," and asserting, "Many illustrious Spaniards have migrated to this place to become inhabitants of the new city."[9] He falsely promises that gold is readily available in the streams, reporting that one Spaniard struck a mountain with a club and large particles of gold came bursting forth, creating an "indescribable brightness [that] glittered all around like sparks."[10]

Scillacio also describes a dance among women of Cibao, a native province of Hispaniola (now Haiti and the Dominican Republic)—suggesting that women were a readily available natural wonder of the New World, just like the gold bursting forth from the mountains.

> Their manner of dancing is nearly as follows: Several women at once, having hair confined under wreaths and turbans, start off from the same line sometimes with an ambling, sometimes with a slower movement. The plates of metal which they wear attached to their fingers are mutually struck against one another, not merely in sport but for the purpose of producing a tinkling sound. They accompany this sound with a voice not deficient in modulation, and singing that is not wanting in sweetness; and in a gracefully voluptuous manner, through winding mazes execute a languid dance in beautiful order, with multiform involutions, while no one claims a conspicuity above her companions; the whole performance eliciting the admiration of the spectators. Being at last both excited and fatigued by the sport, they hurry forward with equally accelerated steps, and in a more petulant and frolicsome mood, and with voices raised to a higher pitch, finish their dance.[11]

Every detail in this passage participates in conjuring the image of women who are "excited and fatigued" by dancing, and sufficiently disoriented to allow would-be suitors, hunters, or colonizers to possess them.

Vespucci's account of unseen yet threatening savages dancing in the wilderness and Scillacio's account of unseen yet inviting dancing girls may seem to proffer contradictory perceptions of dancing—emphasizing its association with death and violence on the one hand and with fertility and possession on the other. What these writings share, however, is an attempt to capture the reader's "exalted attention" through the discourse of wonder.[12] In his deconstructionist reading of travel accounts written by Europeans in the New World, Stephen Greenblatt reflects on the operation of "wonder" in writing the other. He argues that "wonder effects the crucial break with an other that can only be described, only witnessed, in the language and images of sameness. It erects an obstacle that is at the same time an agent of arousal. For the blockage that constitutes a recognition of distance excites a desire to cross the threshold, break through the barrier, enter the space of the alien."[13] For Columbus, Vespucci, and Scillacio, dancing Indians inspired wonder that either alienated or seduced them into "the space of the alien."

References to dance in the early accounts of discovery and encounter reveal that for Indians and Christians alike, bodily behaviors, gestures, and stances were paramount to their interpretation of each other and to their coexistence in absence of a common language. Accounts of dancing and its potential for deception intensified in the early histories written by the first royal and missionary historians, especially when they concern struggles for territory, gold, and human survival. Many of these accounts reveal that Indians and Christian manipulated each other's trust by dissimulating their intentions through performance. In fact, one chronicler went so far as to say that music and dance rituals were tools of deception intended "to conceal treason."

Throughout these accounts, the early chroniclers ubiquitously refer to native performances of music and dance by the Taíno word *areíto*.[14] Chroniclers used this term in a flexible manner to describe indigenous chants, songs, or poems. Sometimes they used it to describe "dances" or "sung dances" (*bailar cantando*) or "poem-songs." In other instances they used the term to refer to the event at which such performances took place, in a way analogous to the usage of "ritual." Cuban ethnomusicologist Fernando Ortiz examined the early chronicles and developed the following definition based on these formative uses: "The greatest musical artistic expression and poetic of the Antilles Indians was the *areíto*, which was like a *conjunto* (gathering) of music, song, dance and pantomime, applied to religious liturgies, magical rites, and the epic narrations of the tribal histories and the great expressions of the collective will."[15]

In the pages that follow I will argue that the early chroniclers "invented" the term *areíto* to represent an evolving early modern concept of performance as an embodied way of knowing and transmitting knowledge that is distinct from writing. In the meantime, however, I will briefly describe several examples of infamous encounters between Christians and Indians that draw upon the "religious," "magical," and "epic" dimensions of the *areíto*. As Donald Thompson has written, "European writers welcomed the Antillean *areíto* as a ready-made set piece useful as a device for plot development and for also characterizing a tragically doomed people."[16] Through its emphasis on the theatrical nature of these narratives, Thompson's "set piece" recalls Michel de Certeau's description of historical representation as a type of "literary staging."[17] It also summons Diana Taylor's use of the term "scenario" as an alternative to "narrative" in describing schemas of social action ("discovery," "encounter," and "conquest," for example) that connect history, literature, and performance. By thinking about "scenarios" instead of narratives, she argues, we attend more closely to the traces of embodied experience and material conditions that are not always reducible to narrative.[18] These evocative terms—"set piece," "literary staging," and "scenario"—invite us to consider the ways that indigenous performance served as a model for writing history.

One of the most popular "literary stagings" of an *areíto* in Caribbean music and literature is the "Areíto de Anacaona," a nineteenth-century "song-poem" about and attributed to Anacaona ("Golden Flower") (ca. 1474–1503), the legendary Taína chief (*cacica*) of Hispaniola at the time of Columbus's landfall. Anacaona was royal both by birth and by marriage. She was born in Xaragua, one of the five kingdoms of Hispaniola—the "heart and core of the whole island," according to Bartolomé de las Casas—where today stands the Haitian capital Port-au-Prince. She was married to Caonabo, the *cacique* of Maguana, a neighboring kingdom. Xaragua was ruled by her brother, the *cacique* Behechio, until his death, at which point Anacaona seized power and led native revolts against the Christians with whom she had previously established trade agreements. For her resistance, she was ultimately hanged in 1503 at the behest of Nicolás de Ovando (ca. 1460–1511), the first governor in the New World. The "Ariéto of Anacaona" honors her place as a leader of native resistance. Fittingly, the chroniclers tell us that Anacaona "was a very remarkable woman, very prudent, very gracious" and was "reputed to be talented in the composition of *areítos*, that is to say poems."[19]

Anacaona became a symbol of Caribbean identity in the nineteenth century when Cuban composer Antonio Bachiller y Morales wrote a popularized song called "Areíto Antillano." The song spurred decades' worth of debate regarding its lyrics, especially whether some of its seemingly incomprehensible verses were actually fragments of "original" Taíno war songs. Some even held the *areíto* was a vestige of Taíno culture, regarding it as the first Caribbean "poem-song" and thus the source of all Caribbean literature and drama. Ortiz put to rest the debates surrounding the song's authenticity as an *areíto*, persuasively arguing that its lyrics, with their seemingly incomprehensible verses, were in fact Congolese phrases used in Afro-Haitian Voudun ceremonies: "It is neither by Anacaona, nor is it even an *areíto*," wrote Ortiz. "It is a couplet creolized by the black practitioners of Voudou in Haiti, which they summoned in their wars against whites."[20]

The debate surrounding the authenticity of this *areíto* has somewhat overshadowed discussions regarding the relevance of the event it purportedly memorializes, which, as told by some of the early chroniclers, is remarkable not only for the story of Anacaona's resistance, but also because it demonstrates that performance was wielded as a political weapon in early American encounters. Moreover, the debate over lyrics has also eclipsed exploration into the role of dance in the broader scenario of Anacaona's encounter with Europeans.

The story is told in related yet slightly differing accounts (see selections in app. A). In 1496 Bartholomew Columbus, Christopher's brother, was left in charge of Hispaniola and set out on an expedition across the island. In the course of his travels, he encountered Anacaona's brother, *cacique* Behechio, who also was on a conquering expedition. Bartholomew unsuccessfully tried to extract gold from the *cacique*, but Behechio convinced him to accept tributes of cotton and hemp instead. Upon negotiating the trade agreement, Behechio ordered his people to welcome the Christians with "the full panoply of their traditional celebrations" (Las Casas, app. A). One of these traditional celebrations was a dance performed by Behechio's thirty wives. Descriptions of the ceremony linger on the near-nakedness of his dancing wives, their cotton skirts, and loosely bound hair. Their dancing and singing recalled the "splendid naiads or nymphs of the fountains, so much celebrated by the ancients" (Martyr, app. A). By all accounts the women knelt before the Christians, in order to place palm fronds on the ground in front of them in a gesture of submissiveness.

One version of the event insists that the dancers were virgins assembled by Anacaona herself, who directed the young women to perform for the Christians, for she "did not wish that either a man or a married woman, or one who had known a man, should enter into that dance or *areíto*" (Oviedo, app. B). The dance of the virgins took place before Behechio and Bartholomew had made their trade agreement, suggesting that Anacaona leveraged Indian sexuality in her economic negotiations with the Christians.

Following this performance, the Christians were treated to a feast of exotic foods and then offered accommodations in the king's *caney* (great house). The following day the Indians entertained Don Bartholomew and the Christians with more dances and a mock-battle tournament called *juego de cañas* that was "like the wooden-sword fights in Spain" (Las Casas, app. A). As Las Casas describes how the fighting intensified—"as if they were battling their worst enemies"—until four Indians died, so Behechio brought the match to a halt. Bartholomew's men thus were made painfully aware that seemingly innocent diplomatic displays could devolve into violence and never forgot the lethal fury that this particular *juego de caña* aroused.

In 1503, five years after the initial encounter between the Christians and the peoples of Xaragua, Behechio died, leaving Anacaona as their chief *cacica*. Governor Ovando suspected that she had been plotting revolt among the Indians across Hispaniola. To suppress the threat posed by her rule, Ovando sent hundreds of soldiers—seventy on horseback, two hundred on foot—with the intent of murdering her and her elite chiefs and developed a plan involving performance. Allegedly, Anacaona had masterminded a similar strategy. Ovando and Anacaona made a series of amiable yet disingenuous overtures to one another. Anacaona, for example, asked Ovando if the Indians could watch the Christians play a game of *juego de cañas* against the Indians. No doubt Anacaona intended to physically position the Christians before her armed warriors. However, Ovando saw through Anacaona's thinly veiled trap and declined her invitation. Instead, he pretended to be absorbed in a game of *hierro* (horseshoes) with the Christians. Ovando ordered one of his men to sound the trumpet at a predetermined time, as a signal for the Christians to gather the *caciques* into a *caney* and to burn them alive. Anacaona was spared the humiliation of death by fire. As Las Casas laments, "In deference to her rank, Queen Anacaona was hanged."[21]

Just as Anacaona's *areíto* demonstrates the natives' capacity for deception and violence, the following "literary staging" of an *areíto* can be said to dramatize the natives' capacity for peace and submission. The account concerns Hatuey, a Taíno *cacique* who led his people from the island of Hispaniola to Cuba in order to escape the threat of Spanish cruelty. According to Las Casas, in 1511 Hatuey heard that the

Spaniards had followed them to Cuba to broaden their search for land and gold. With nowhere left to escape, the *cacique* gathered his people to explain why the Spaniards were infiltrating their lands:

> He had beside him, as he spoke, a basket filled with gold jewelry and he said: "Here is the god of the Christians. If you agree, we will do *areítos* (which is their word for certain kinds of traditional dance) in honour of this God and it may be that we shall please Him and He will order the Christians to leave us unharmed." They all shouted: "So be it, so be it." And after they had danced before this god until they were dropping from exhaustion . . .[22]

In an astounding set of displacements and resignifications, Hatuey's subjects allegedly performed Taíno dances on foreign soil in order to honor golden trinkets they understood to be the Christian god. In this instance, dancing was not a premeditated lure—as with Anacaona's dancing virgins or the *juego de cañas*—but a last resort of passive resistance. Indeed, Las Casas was sure to tell us that the *areíto* drained their bodies of physical agency and by extension, political will. The story is almost too bizarre to be true, and in all likelihood was significantly embellished by Las Casas, one of the most vocal defenders of the Indians, in order to sympathetically demonstrate the lengths to which Indians went to escape confrontation with the Spaniards while simultaneously conveying the traumatic affects of Spanish imperialism. (Interestingly, Las Casas did not miss this opportunity to highlight the willingness and ease with which the Indians transformed their dance from a means of worshiping their pagan gods into a means of worshiping the Christian god.) Dancing, however, could not save them. Thus, Hatuey instructed his subjects to throw all the gold in the river, knowing that the Spaniards would have killed them for it. He also led them in a guerilla resistance once the Spanish arrived, a resistance that ended with Hatuey's capture and death by fire. Before he was engulfed in flames, a Franciscan missionary tried to convince Hatuey to convert to Christianity. Hatuey refused, explaining that he would prefer to go to hell than see Spaniards in heaven.

In another "scenario," the *areíto* serves as a turning point in a narrative that results in the violent death of Indians. The account takes place on the island of Boriquén (later Saint John, now Puerto Rico) and concerns an Indian uprising of 1511 against Don Cristóbal de Sotomayor, a Spanish officer under the command of Governor Juan Ponce de León. Sotomayor and his men invaded and inhabited a Boriquén village. There he met Guanina, a native princess, and the two became instantly enamored with each other. What kept them apart, however, was Guanina's brother Guaybana, who had vowed to kill Sotomayor and his Christian soldiers. In an effort to protect Sotomayor, Guanina warned him of her brother's determination to kill him, yet Sotomayor paid no attention. Sotomayor was warned again, this time by his translator—*la lengua*—Juan Gonzales, who not only spoke the indigenous language, but also, we are told, could pass as an Indian when properly disguised. One evening Gonzales masked himself in war paint and then infiltrated an *areíto* where Indians were singing songs, one of which involved a plot to rebel against Sotomayor. Gonzales was able to decode Guaybana's plans and in turn warned Sotomayor, but could not convince him to escape. Instead, Sotomayor gathered his Indian servants and set out on an expedition to meet Ponce de León. En route, Guaybana and his fellow Indians executed their plan and killed Sotomayor. They also tried to attack Juan Gonzales, but he escaped. As for Guanina, it was determined that she should be sacrificed, but she had committed suicide and was found dead on Sotomayor's body before they could exact revenge on her for her betrayal.[23]

One of the striking facets of this "scenario" is that it involves the performance of a Spaniard in an *areíto*, albeit a Spaniard disguised as an Indian. Gonzales seamlessly moves between languages and cultures, and between the worlds of the *areíto* and the battlefield, manipulating the world of Indian signs, as did Columbus's dancing sailors. Indeed, throughout these "scenarios" of choreographic encounter, dancing—whether spontaneous or rehearsed—holds the promise of contact and reconciliation, yet routinely results in violence and death. Columbus's deceptive dance, Vespucci's "wild man" funeral, Scillacio's golden dancers, Anacaona's dancing virgins, Hatuey's dance of defeat, and Gonzales's performance of passing form a constellation of scenarios wherein the act of dancing comes to represent the inherent and dangerous ambiguity of crossing the threshold into the space of the alien.

Of course, there is no reliable way to confirm whether these "scenarios" are social facts or historical fictions, though we can calibrate them against early chroniclers' non-narrative reflections, polemics, and field notes about *areítos*. These sources offer descriptions of actual indigenous dance and music performances, and give some elucidation as to why the chroniclers were fascinated by the *areíto* in political, theological, and historiographic terms. Below I focus on the writings of Peter Martyr d'Anghera (Italian humanist, courtier, royal chronicler, and translator), Gonzalo Fernández de Oviedo y Valdés (royal court historian and natural historian), and Bartolomé de las Casas (the controversial "Defender of the Indians"). Although their writings about the *areíto* have been studied in terms of colonial discourse, music history, and literature, the choreographic aspects of their writings have escaped critical scrutiny.[24] To rectify that oversight, the following analysis focuses on the ways in which dance figured into these writers' evolving definitions and interpretations of the *areíto*—all of which, as I will argue, stand on the threshold of recognizing dance as an embodied epistemology, a mode of memorializing history, and a form of political resistance.

"Inventing" the *Areíto*

In 1498, the same year Columbus staged a dance aboard his vessel to attract the attention of the Indians, he received a copy of "the first book written on American soil in a European language," the *Account of the Antiquities of the Indians* by Friar Ramón Pané.[25] Ramón Pané was a missionary of the order of Saint Jerome who arrived in the New World in 1494 as a member of Columbus's second expedition. For four years he lived among different native populations on the island of Hispaniola. His *relación* documents his eyewitness experiences of the first conquests, conversions, and native rebellions in the Americas. It also preserves aspects of native language, myth, and ritual, including one of the first descriptions of an indigenous musical performance. In outlining the rites performed by a *behique* (a "physician" or "healer") Pané briefly describes an instrument called a *mayohabao*—a hollow wooden percussion instrument "in the shape of a blacksmith's tongs" that was hit with an item that "looks like a long-necked squash"—which the Taíno played when they sang their songs, which "they learn by heart."[26] In so doing, he writes the following sentences, which foretell a whole tradition of writing about performance in the Americas: "Indeed, I have seen it in part with my own eyes, although of other matters I have told only what I heard from many people, particularly from the leaders, with whom I have had more contact than with others. In fact, just as the Moors, they have their laws gathered in ancient songs, by which they govern themselves, as do the Moors by their scripture."[27]

Pané's passing reference to this singular musical event presages several enduring preoccupations with indigenous performance in the Americas within the writings of subsequent chroniclers. First, he references the epistemological gap between knowledge that is based on eyewitness experience and knowledge that is derived from native informants. Even though Pané ambiguously qualifies that his own knowledge about the *areíto* is based "in part with [his] own eyes," he establishes a burden of proof for subsequent chroniclers who write about performance in the New World—witnessing was the *sine qua non* of the reliable chronicle. Second, his description makes an explicit reference to the Moors, the Muslims of mixed Arab, Spanish, and Berber origin who in 1498 had only recently been expelled from southern Spain. As such, the passage blueprints a whole discourse on indigenous performance that projects European perceptions, attitudes, and histories concerning the Moors onto the bodies and behaviors of Indians. Indeed, one of the most striking and shared rhetorical impulses among the early chroniclers was to make comparisons between indigenous cultures in the Americas, as well as to compare the Indians with the Moors, the ancient Romans and Greeks, and especially themselves, the Christians. Finally, Pané articulates the idea that performance was somehow linked to history, recognizing that music functioned as a mnemonic device that codified "laws." Although later chroniclers proposed alternative explanations for the relationship between performance and history, their writings manifest a preoccupation with the notion that performance could memorialize or otherwise represent the past. For the chroniclers, men who dedicated their lives to the practice of representing the past, this prospect was both profoundly familiar and terrifyingly foreign. That tension animates their writings about Indian dances.

As a courtier, diplomat, chronicler, translator, and royal tutor to the children of Ferdinand and Isabella, Peter Martyr d'Anghera held positions that gave him unique access to discoverers, travelers, and explorers in the New World. He was appointed to the Council of the Indies in 1518 and as royal chronicler in 1520. Even though he held these important posts regarding the New World, Martyr himself never visited the lands about which he wrote, which created suspicion and resentment among his contemporary chroniclers. His most notable writings about the New World were published in the *Decades of the New World* (*De orbe novo*) between 1493 and 1525.

Martyr gives one of the earliest provisional definitions of the *areíto* based on a report he included in his "Third Decade," which he composed between 1514 and 1516. This report was informed by talks he had with Andreas Morales, a Spanish sailor who had conducted an expedition to Hispaniola. Martyr describes his discussion of the *areíto* as a "digression" from the more pressing issues contained in his report, conveying his sense of "astonishment" that "such uncivilized men, destitute of any knowledge of letters" were able to preserve "for such a long time the tradition of their origin." As a historian, Martyr was fascinated by the historiographic potential of the *areíto* and thus describes it as a kind of history without writing:

> This has been possible because from the earliest times, and chiefly in the houses of the *caciques*, the *bovites*, that is to say the wise men, have trained the sons of the *caciques*, teaching them of their past history by heart. In imparting their teaching they carefully distinguish two classes of studies; the first is of a general interest, having to do with the succession of events; the second is of a particular interest, treating of the notable deeds accomplished in time of peace or time of war by their fathers, grandfathers, great-grandfathers, and all their ancestors. Each one of these exploits is commemorated in poems written in their language. These poems are called *arreytos* [*areítos*]. As with us the guitar player, so with them the drummers accompany these *arreytos* and lead singing choirs. The drums are called *maguay*. Some of the *arreytos* are love songs, others are elegies, and others are war songs; and each is sung to an appropriate air. They also love to dance, but they are more agile than we are; first, because nothing pleases them better than dancing and, secondly, because they are naked, and untrammeled by clothing.[28]

For Martyr, the *areíto* was a type of poem "written in their language" that was performed by choirs to recall a vision of the past. By making an explicit link between Spanish guitarists and Indian drummers, he emphasized that the *areíto* was similar to Spanish poems, songs, and elegies. However, Martyr could not fathom how dancing figured into the *areíto* performance and stops short of making an explicit claim concerning the relationship between its musical and choreographic aspects. He mentions dance, but only as an incidental aspect of *areíto* performance. In fact, whereas Martyr identifies a similarity between Christians and Indians with respect to using language to recall the past, his remarks about dance point to physical and kinesthetic difference, which he couches in patronizing comments about their nature ("they are more agile than we") and custom ("because they are naked, and untrammeled by clothing"). Ultimately, for Martyr, dancing was a pleasurable yet meaningless aspect of the *areíto*.

He explains that songs were composed by "their ancestors" and as such were part of a tradition of transmitting knowledge from wise men to *caciques* and nobles. Elsewhere he stresses the importance of this tradition with an anecdote concerning a native rebellion. He tells us that the Christians threatened the kingdom of a *cacique* named Maiobanex lest he release to them the *cacique* Guarionex, whom Maiobanex had been protecting from the Christians. Maiobanex refused, explaining that he was obliged to protect his fellow *cacique*, who "had taught the *cacique* himself and his wife to sing and dance, a thing not to be held in mediocre consideration."[29] If true, then Maiobanex was risking his own kingdom to protect his dancing master and the sanctity of the *areíto* tradition. Martyr relates this episode to establish the significance of music and dance to the indigenous world.

Martyr also suspected that the *areíto* had divinatory properties. In a digression about the *areíto*, he puts forth the staggering allegation that Indian ancestors had predicted the European arrival and conquest through their *areítos*: "Some of the *arreytos* composed by their ancestors predicted our arrival, and these poems resembling elegies lament their ruin. . . . I really am not very much astonished that their ancestors predicted the slavery of their descendants, if everything told concerning their familiar relations with devils is true."[30] As such, for Martyr, the *areíto* was significant for its capacity to reveal the Indian past and future.

Francisco López de Gómara (1511–ca. 1566), who was the secretary to conquistador Hernán Cortés, repeated and expanded Martyr's claim about the *areíto* as a divinatory rite. He included an account concerning native ancestors who spoke through an elder to warn about the arrival of bearded and clothed men who would devastate the native world. In deference to the power of this prophecy, the Taíno purportedly danced and sang to the elder's words as a rehearsal for conquest.[31]

After Cortés's death in 1547, Gómara wrote a history of the conquest and a general history of the Indies, both published in 1552. Like Martyr, Gómara never traveled to the Americas. His writings were based on secondhand reports, including those he had collected from Cortés. He also relied heavily on other chroniclers, such as Martyr. In fact, it appears that he extracted information about the *areíto* from one of Martyr's lengthier chapters about music and dance in Venezuela, yet Gómara makes a more definitive claim about the role of dance in the *areíto* than Martyr ever did. He reports that dancing was a central part of the *areítos* of Hispaniola and—just as Pané did—likens them to ceremonies of the Moors. Unlike Martyr, Gómara equates the *areíto* to a dance rather than a song, especially the Moorish *zambra*: "*Areítos* are like the Moorish *zambra*, a dance performed to the sound of bagpipes and flutes."[32] Interestingly, Gómara compares the dancing aspect of the indigenous *areíto* to the Moorish *zambra* but its verbal aspect to Spanish *romances* (ballads): "The Indians dance while singing *romances* in praise of their idols and their kings and in memory of victories and notable events of the past, for they have no other historical accounts. Many dance and often in these *areítos* and sometimes all day into the night."[33] Like Martyr, Gómara equated singing with Spanish forms, whereas he associated dancing with the Moors and the Indians.

Gonzalo Fernández de Oviedo y Valdés (1478–1557) was appointed official royal chronicler of the Indies in 1532 by king of Spain and Holy Roman emperor Charles V.[34] In 1514 he traveled to the New World for the first of eleven visits, and thus, unlike Martyr and Gómara, Oviedo had actual eyewitness experience with the phenomena about which he wrote. His experiences of the New World and its wonders are chronicled in his fifty-volume *General and Natural History of the Indies* (*Historia general y natural de las Indias*). His *History* is perhaps best known for introducing Europe to the exotic architecture, flora, fauna, and people of the New World; the work included the first representations of the canoe, hammock, pineapple, tobacco, and prickly pear, as well the most extensive and earliest descriptions of *areítos*. In some instances, Oviedo even provides dates for specific *areítos* he witnessed throughout the Caribbean and Tierra Firme (the Mainland). For example, in 1548 Oviedo wrote a chapter about the dances, songs, and games of the Tierra Firme. In this chapter he mentions that he also had seen *areítos* performed on the island of Hispaniola in 1515. Even though Oviedo quickly dismisses the Caribbean *areítos* as insufficiently noteworthy compared to those he saw along the mainland coast, where he traveled extensively, he believed that dance was a pervasive component in indigenous social organization and made the following generalization: "Their manner of dance and song are common in all the Indies, except in diverse languages."[35]

Despite the qualitative differences Oviedo perceived between the *areítos* of Hispaniola and the performances on the Tierra Firme, he referred to all music and dance performance in the New World by the Taíno word *areíto*. This was in spite of the fact that Oviedo not only acknowledged that the term was specific to the Taínos, but even conceded that the people of the Tierra Firme called their dances *mitotes*, a Nahuatl term for "dance" used primarily in the region of Mesoamerica and a cognate among the Chorotega-speaking peoples about whom he writes.

Oviedo learned of the term *mitote* no later than 1544, which is when he interviewed Juan Cano, a Spanish conquistador who had participated in the conquest of Mexico in 1519–1520. Cano described to Oviedo a *mitote* performed at his wedding to a descendant of the slain Aztec ruler Montezuma. Oviedo used the *areíto* as a category for classifying a broad range of performances throughout the Indies (such as games, dances, or formal ceremonies) despite his apparent recognition that the term was linguistically specific. In fact, Oviedo explicitly acknowledged that there were differences among the indigenous cultures he studied with respect to language, customs, and performance: "As these people differ in their languages and customs, so do they vary in their songs, and dances, and many other things."[36] This statement, of course, contradicts his earlier opinion: "Their manner of dance and song are common in all the Indies."

In terms of content and reliability, Oviedo's writings about *areítos* far surpass those of other chroniclers who wrote from Spain based on secondary sources, but that is not to say that Oviedo's *areíto* is by any means definitive. He went to lengths to test his observations about the performances he saw against the testimony he solicited from local chiefs and elders and tirelessly sought ways of redefining and representing it.

In book 5 (chapter 1) of the *History* (see app. B) Oviedo implicitly qualified Pané and Martyr's descriptions of the *areíto* by suggesting that dancing was an essential component of its performance, at least among the examples he had seen. In so doing he revised Martyr's definition of the *areíto* from a "poem" to a *bailar cantando* (a "sung dance"). By compounding the Spanish words for dancing and singing (*bailar* and *cantar*) Oviedo presumably meant to express the meaningful integration of the musical and choreographic aspects of the *areíto*. However, he never convincingly explains the relation between music and dance, apart from making the observation that the dance steps and verses were "coordinated."

In some passages he distinguishes between singing and dancing as discrete forms of expression, using *areíto* to denote the singing component and *contrapás* to denote the dance component: "Other *areítos* and songs, together with dancing and the *contrapás*, are customary with the Indians, and are of frequent occurrence" (see app. C). The *contrapás* is a "measured and coordinated" step or figure in European dances, such as the *contradanzas* of Spain, which Oviedo points out he previously had seen Spanish farmers perform. The *contrapás* also reminded him of a clog dance called the *panadero* that he had seen in Flanders. Elsewhere he elaborates what he means by *contrapás* by describing a walking pattern that does not go "more than a pace or two one side or the other" or an established and stylized step pattern that moves along a specific pathway, such as a line or a circle, with dancers joined by the hands or linked arms (see app. C). In his description of the *bailar cantando* we also learn that performers are led by either a male or a female "guide" or "dance master" (*guías o maestro de la danza*) in a call-and-response pattern of song and steps. In a prototype for the *Historia* published in 1526, Oviedo identifies the dance leader by the term *tequina*.[37] The leader establishes not only the steps, words, and rhythm, but also the qualitative energy, tone, and pitch. Oviedo also indicates that the composers of the songs and dances were "held among the Indians as discriminating and with great talent in this art" (app. B). Although he offers no additional details about the "composers," we at least learn that the dances were "choreographed" and that there were continual adaptations and additions to the repertoire of dances, presumably to accommodate newly composed songs about ongoing historical events.

Oviedo distinguishes between two different types of the *areíto*: an interpretative, expressive form of performance that commemorated historical or social events and an imitative type of performance that functioned as pastime or diversion. He bases this classification on his knowledge of the ancient world. Citing Livy's *History of Rome* (book 7.2), Oviedo compares the *areíto* to the dance style brought to ancient Rome by the Etruscans in the fourth century B.C. Livy tells us that between 366 and 341 B.C. the Romans were suffering from a plague, so Etruscan dancers (*saltantes*) were sent for to provide diversion with a style of dancing that involved "no words, no mimetic action; they danced to the measures of the flute and practiced graceful movements in Tuscan fashion.[38] Livy compares these mimetic Etruscan dances to the contemporary dances he observed (sometime between 30 and 25 B.C.), which were interpretive in nature and responded meaningfully to the lyrics of the songs that accompanied them. Moreover, Livy explains that Etruscan dancers gained wide appeal, especially among young men, and catalyzed the development of professional performers in Rome.[39] Oviedo takes this information to mean that the *areíto* functions not only as a tool for remembering but also a means of active forgetting: "Livy says that the Etruscans were the first dancers to come to Rome and they organized that their voices and their movements go together. This was done to forget the work and the pestilence and death, the year Camillus died; and this I say must be like the *areítos* or choruses of these Indians" (app. B). Remarkably, Oviedo infers that both forms of dancing in the *areíto* responded to forces of colonization, slavery, and disease wrought by Spanish landfall by dint of their expressive and diversionary functions, similar to the roles that dancing played in the wake of the disintegration of the Camillan state.

Oviedo's writings about the *areíto* exhibit his preoccupation with its capacity to produce, contain, and express knowledge, particularly historical knowledge. He comes to understand that one of the functions of the *areítos* was to take the "place of books" (app. B). Like Pané and Martyr before him, Oviedo describes the *areíto* as a means of recording history as well as a "good and pretty way of recalling past and ancient things," as if to assure his reader that there was nothing savage about his Indian subjects. His reasoning, however, is based on the similarities he perceived between the *areítos* and European forms of performance. Curiously, Oviedo provides not a single example of an *areíto* that "recall[s] past and ancient things," yet makes the assumption about its function on the basis of its resemblance to Spanish *romances* (ballads). The similarity leads him to pose the following rhetorical question, as if encountering the *areíto* surprisingly forced him to consider the significance of Spanish discursive forms: "What else are the *romances* or the songs which are founded on truth, but part and agreement of the past histories?" (app. B). Oviedo ultimately arrives at the conclusion that the *romance* functioned as a form of history for the illiterate people of Spain. He calls the *areíto* an "effigy of history" (*una efigie de historia*), which signals his perception of the discursive dimension of *areíto* performance. Interestingly, Oviedo emphasizes that performance resembles writing by likening the *areíto* to a type of inscription that leaves ideas "carved in memory," evoking the image of the engraver's burin against parchment.

Oviedo's understanding of the *areíto* as a *bailar cantando*, an Etruscan dance, and an "effigy of history" was rooted in his personal experience seeing dances in Europe, his knowledge of the classical world, and his reflection on Spanish expressive forms. As Galen Brokaw puts it: "Europeans approached the New World from an established, rigid Old World perspective attempting to fit the round peg of America into the square hole of Western European knowledge."[40] Indeed, there is a meaningful disparity between Oviedo's learned analysis of the *areíto* and his descriptions of the *areítos* he actually witnessed.

In part 3, book 4, chapter 11 (app. C), Oviedo compiles his field notes on several *areítos* he observed in Nicaragua and Costa Rica during his time there between 1527 and 1529, as well as those he had seen in Hispaniola years prior. The chapter is roughly divided into two parts: the first half positively describes *areítos* performed in the region of Tecoatega; the latter half deals with the "common" and dangerous *areítos* in the region of Nicoya. The implicit comparison between the *areítos* in these regions both clarifies and convolutes Oviedo's thinking about the *areíto*. He begins the report with one of the first European descriptions of *voladores*. The *volador* ceremony (a "flying pole dance") is a Mesoamerican ritual that simulates flight. It involves young boys (*voladores*, or "flyers") who climb a tall pole to a platform that is perched on top. Connected to the pole by cords fastened to their waists, they dive off the platform and masterfully cycle and glide around it and each other as they descend toward the ground. Oviedo notes that dancers in elaborate dress, feathers, and masks (including men dressed as women) circle in silence on the ground around the *volador* pole as the boys make their descent. He describes the ceremony with an acute attention to the quantifiable details. For example, he notes the number of and distance between dancers, the duration of the festival, the height of the pole, the number and age of participants, etc. Curiously, Oviedo does not mention the number of revolutions the *voladores* make around the pole. No doubt he would have been intrigued by the speculation famously made by Franciscan missionary Bernardino de Sahagún that the *voladores* metered out fifty-two revolutions, one for each cycle of the Mesoamerican solar calendar.[41] Oviedo also has an eye for the physical mechanics involved in the ritual, noting that the *voladores* must make carefully coordinated flexions and extensions in order to seamlessly land on the ground. Oviedo paid careful attention to the quantifiable details of this performance, yet ultimately it was the qualitative aspect that most impressed him. He was most pleased by the costumes, feathers, and array, which he emphasizes over the physicality of the flight itself. Indeed, Oviedo was so overcome by a sense of wonder that he was inspired to illustrate the *voladores* (fig. 1.2). His illustration captures the *voladores* somewhat awkwardly suspended midair so as to clearly depict each *volador*, one with a bundle of arrows in one hand and the other with his mirror and fan of feathers. Remarkably, the ceremony also inspired Oviedo to imagine the *voladores* in Europe "or indeed in any part of the world," where he predicted they would have been received well for their beauty.

Following his description of the *voladores*, Oviedo mentions a ceremony that was performed following the death of a *cacique*. He decisively refers to this ceremony as a "dance" and to its performers as "dancers," although it clearly seems to have incorporated elements of a hunting game or a gladiatorial tournament. The ceremony involved the newly installed *cacique* shooting rods at four dancing warriors. One by one, the warriors entered the plaza dancing and walking while intermittently twisting and contorting their bodies so as to both avoid and recover from rods slung at them by the *cacique* from close range (never "more than a pace or two one side or the other"). Three other dancers remain motionless as they wait their turn to become moving targets.

Oviedo asked the *cacique* about the "mysterious significance" of the ceremony. The *cacique* denied that was any, and instead explained that the ceremony was performed to provide an opportunity for young men to prove they were "strong and capable warriors" and thus worthy of a lot of *cacao* beans, which they received for their performance. Oviedo was not entirely satisfied by the *cacique*'s explanation. Apparently, Oviedo suspected that the dance was a type of religious "feast," hunting ritual, or military ceremony, especially since it involved shooting arrows, a technique for sacrificing victims in Mesoamerican societies. Nonetheless, Oviedo leaves the topic with the suggestion that the *areíto* was intended to symbolically establish the power of the new *cacique* in the wake of his father's death.

The latter half of the chapter is dedicated to a description of what Oviedo calls "common" *areítos*, by which he meant *fiestas* that involved heavy drinking and smoking: "It is not so much to dance as to drink that they come together" (see app. C). Oviedo notes that these common *areítos* were performed among "the vulgar and plebian people" in the region of Nicoya, as opposed to the nobles, warriors, and *cacique* he saw perform in Tecoatega. Nambi, the *cacique* of the Nicoya, was baptized Don Alonso, but Oviedo did not trust him, and twice reminds us that in his native language his name fittingly means "dog." Oviedo observed an *areíto* performed in the plaza of Nicoya on August 29, 1528. In one part of a plaza, plebeians gathered to perform a rite. In another part of the plaza, Nambi and his nobles started to smoke tobacco and drink a maize wine called *chichi*. The gathering soon devolved into a drunken revelry (*borracheras* or *beoderas*). Watching the Indians enter into states of inebriation and immobility, Oviedo and his fellow Spaniards began to feel physically threatened. Oviedo describes becoming cognizant of the Indians' animosity toward the Spaniards ("they take no joy in the Christians"), yet also understood the source of their animosity, admitting that the Spaniards had reduced the Indians to slaves and "restrained them in their rites and ceremonies." Oviedo tells us that he and his fellow Spaniards took up weapons to protect themselves from a potential Indian attack, for based on the accounts of the deceptive *areítos* that the first settlers had described, he knew that *areítos* could devolve into violence or be performed "to conceal treason." In fact, Oviedo even reminds us about the entanglement between Sotomayor and Guaybana in Puerto Rico to make his point. However, the terrorizing *areíto* Oviedo encountered tested the limits of classical history to explain the dances of the New World. These dances had nothing to do with

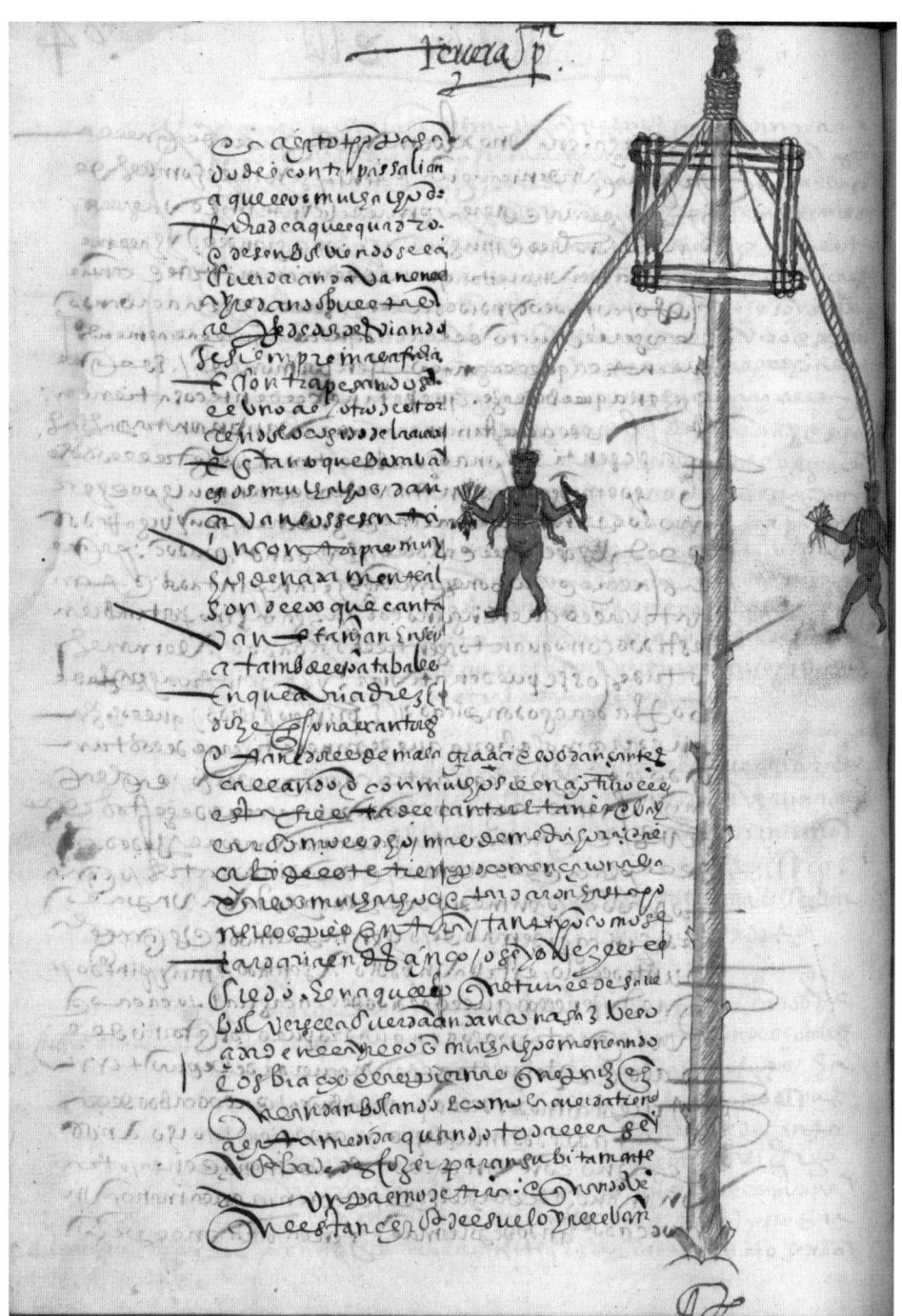

FIG. 1.2 *Voladores*. Gonzalo Fernández de Oviedo y Valdés, *Historia general y natural de las Indias* (Palacio Real II/3042), fol. 84v. © PATRIMONIO NACIONAL.

the Etruscan dances described by Livy, for there was no dance sufficiently distracting for the Indians to forget the perils of disease and slavery. At the *areíto* in Nicoya, Oviedo dramatically experienced the impending threat of resistance to the Christian presence, albeit dissimulated by dancing and singing.

Oviedo's conflicting experiences with the *areítos* of the Tecoatega and Nicoya allow him to reach the conclusion that the *areíto* was both a "good and pretty way of recalling past and ancient things" as well a form of "debauchery" and "treason." One conjures Oviedo's fantasy of beautiful Indians performing for European gentility, and the other compels him to take up arms in defense. Given the radical differences in the performances he encounters, why use the term *areíto* at all?

As a scientist of the natural world, Oviedo experienced "nomenclatorial pressure" to classify his discoveries with great specificity.[42] Yet in some measure, it may be more correct to say that Oviedo "invented" rather than "discovered" the *areíto*. In *The Invention of America*, Edmundo O'Gorman famously argued that the New World was not "discovered" as much as it was "invented" through discourse.[43] Galen Brokaw draws upon this powerful idea to examine the "invention" of the *areíto* in the writings of Oviedo. Brokaw identifies intricate patterns of displacement, substitution, and "ambivalent slippages" amid Oviedo's use of the Taíno *areíto* and various Spanish equivalents, such as *bailar cantando*, *contrapás*, and *romance*. He argues that Oviedo "established a relationship of resemblance or analogy between indigenous and European cultural phenomena based on a perceived common denominator" and deployed "Spanish referents that then displace the unique cultural significance of the indigenous sign."[44] Oviedo's discursive move, Brokaw adds, conveys a type of "ambivalence" that undergirds what Homi Bhabha calls "colonial mimicry": "the desire for a reformed, recognizable Other, *as a subject of difference that is almost the same but not quite*."[45] That is to say, Oviedo readily sought to identify the continuities between Spanish and indigenous performance, yet needed a term that would simultaneously mark a difference between Europeans and Indians.

Oviedo's ambivalent use of the term *areíto* is reflected in the way he names certain dance performances. If we look closely at Oviedo's texts, we see other Spanish words that approximate his idea of an *areíto* yet are not entirely reducible to it. These include "festival" (*fiesta*), "rite" (*rito*), "vice" (*vicio*), and "ceremony" (*ceremonia*). In three instances when Oviedo uses these terms in context of writing about *areítos*, he imposes a distinction between sacred and secular performance. For example, when Oviedo asked the *cacique* in Tecoatega about the "mysterious significance" of the rod-slinging "dance," he inquired whether it was performed on a "feast day" (*si era aquel día fiesta*), as if to ask whether there was religious significance to the dance. The *cacique* responded that the dance was simply a display of strength, as if to deny that there was any sacred meaning to it. Second, Oviedo speculates that the *areíto* that he observed in Nicoya had replaced their "rites, ceremonies, and vices" (*ritos é çeremonias é viçios*), once again distinguishing between the secular *areítos* and the sacred rites that they were prohibited from performing. And third, Oviedo concludes his field notes with a description of a human sacrifice ceremony among the Nicoya. Here he describes preparatory dances wherein men and women performed concentric circles around a temple for over four hours, all the while consuming alcohol. He reports that the dance was followed by a human sacrifice and the consumption of the victim's blood and body.[46] He initially introduces the ceremony as an *areíto* then qualifies it as an *areíto* or rite (*areíto o rito*).

In each of these instances, Oviedo uses terms such as *fiesta*, *rito*, *vicios*, or *ceremonia* to reference ceremonies with sacred significance—rituals of praise, purification, or divination—whereas he uses the term *areíto* to reference the songs and dances he thought demonstrated governance, ingenuity, nobility, and power—such as the dances he encountered in Tecoatega. Thus, in the world of Oviedo's *Historia*, *areíto* denotes performances that are concerned with commemorating history, whereas *fiestas*, *ritos*, *vicios*, or *ceremonias* connote a "mysterious" sphere of sacred idolatry.

For as much linguistic, descriptive, interpretive, and historical specificity Oviedo brings to his invention of the *areíto*, he brings an equal amount of contradiction, generalization, and disregard for the very critical category he himself was so central to "inventing." Oviedo never harnessed the word into a consistent use. Instead, he employed it along with a number of appositives, qualifications, supplements, and disclaimers. For Oviedo, the *areíto* was a song that accompanied a dance, a poem, and an event. It could have meant a choreographed dance just as easily as it could have referred to a martial game, a drinking party, and an acrobatic display. An *areíto* was a mode of faithfully memorializing the past as well as a deceptive tool for enacting violence. It refers specifically to the music and dances of Hispaniola, but was used, however problematically, to index the ceremonies performed both in Tierra Firme and Europe.

The one common denominator to Oviedo's many applications of the term is that in the world of his writings, *areito* always refers to a live, physical, or otherwise performed act. Thus, although Oviedo's use of the *areito* to describe phenomena across linguistic, temporal, and spatial barriers elides differences between indigenous cultures, it also reveals a shared mode of embodying history that takes the "place of books." In that sense, we may say that Oviedo was on the verge of articulating an early modern notion of "performance" as embodied meaning. He implies there is a hierarchy within that category—from the "good and pretty" to the "common" and from the "solemn" to the "debaucherous."

Whereas Oviedo was ambivalent about the *areito* and its significance to Indian identity and the success of Christian conversion, Bartolomé de las Casas (ca. 1474–1566), the self-proclaimed "Defender of the Indians," illustrated Indian humanity through his writings about the *areito*. Las Casas remains one of the most controversial figures in Latin American colonial history for his persistent defense of Indian rights and his theological and legal arguments against Spanish colonialism, slavery, and torture.

Las Casas was not always a defender of the Indians. Quite the contrary, in 1502 he traveled to Hispaniola alongside other Spanish merchants in pursuit of riches and soon became an *encomendero*. However, in 1514 Las Casas experienced a well-documented conversion from Spanish colonist and *encomendero* to Dominican priest and advocate. Las Casas renounced his wealth and began to tirelessly advocate for Indians' rights. Las Casas drew upon his firsthand experiences traveling throughout the Indies, as well as his extensive theological and legal knowledge, to rehabilitate the pervasive image of the "Indian" as a "barbarian" into a studied portrait of human rationality and nobility, qualities he believed made them worthy of Christian salvation. This meant familiarizing rather than exoticizing the Indian to European readers, which he achieved by identifying a myriad of similarities between native and Christian worlds. In fact, Las Casas held that to denigrate Indians customs was tantamount to "spitting in the wind," for pre-Christian European beliefs and behaviors were more similar to those of the Indians than other chroniclers would admit. Writing about the *areito*, Las Casas even argued that the Indian was equal if not superior to the Spaniard.

Las Casas wrote against an overwhelming tide of reports from the New World that depicted the Indians as barbarians. This includes the writings of Oviedo, whom Las Casas called a "looter" for amassing wealth at the expense of the Spanish exploitation of the Indians. Moreover, Las Casas argued, albeit unconvincingly, that Oviedo had never set foot on Hispaniola (or if so, "only at a very late date") and that his information about the island was based on reports from a corrupt sailor named Fernand Pérez.[47] As we will see, Las Casas's writings about the *areito* are a direct response to Oviedo's writings on the subject. He directly refutes several of Oviedo's statement, including his claims that Indians practiced human sacrifice, cannibalism, and sodomy. He also expresses his indignation with a series of admonitions, including the fastidious remark that one should pronounce *areíto* by accenting the "long *i*"—*la i letra lengua*—ostensibly correcting Oviedo's own spelling of the word as *arreyto*.[48] (Friar Motolinía later insulted Las Casas regarding his own particular use and abuse of the term.)

Despite the meticulousness Las Casas exhibited regarding the term's pronunciation, his writings about the *areíto* convey a strategic vagueness. In his *Historia* he dedicates a chapter to the dances and songs "widespread throughout the Indies" but surprisingly provides little substance about how they were performed (app. D). He generalizes about the *areíto*, often eliding distinctions between *areítos* performed for different ceremonies (coronations, funerals, weddings) and in different locations within the Indies and the Tierra Firme. In this chapter he offers a generic description of a ceremony as it was performed in Venezuela, yet presents it as an example of the songs and dances performed not only throughout the Indies, but also, he adds "in the same way that they existed in the ancient nations of both Jews and gentiles."

Las Casas was noticeably less concerned with structural and formal performance elements of music and dance. While he acknowledges, *pace* Oviedo, that the Indians perform music and dance "just like our people often do in Spain" (app. D) and that their songs and dances are tied to history, he was more interested in the broader significance of performance to indigenous social life. Las Casas took a more comprehensive view of the indigenous *areíto* as a complex event involving drinking, feasting, pantomimes, and alleged sacrifices, and paid less attention than Oviedo to its constitutive choreographic elements. Even when Las Casas actually describes musical and dance aspects of the *areíto*, as he briefly does in another chapter, it is to render a portrait of a disciplined yet lighthearted performance:

> They like their dances. To the sound of the songs and harsh drums made of wood, made without skin nor with any other attached thing. It was something to behold their coordination in the voices as well as the steps because there were three or four hundred, all with their arms on each others shoulders, and their feet were so perfectly aligned, never off by more than a head of a pin. And this was for all of them. Women by themselves danced with the same rhythm tone and order by themselves. The lyrics of their songs made reference to the old things and sometimes childish things like "that little fish was captured in this way and escaped." And others like that, as far as I was able to understand from them in those times.[49]

For reasons I develop in the following chapter, I am confident that Las Casas plagiarized this meager description of an actual performance, most likely from writings about Aztec dances by Franciscan missionary Friar Toribio de Motolinía. Were Las Casas so attentive as to appreciate the alignment and precision of the Indians' footwork, he would have likely provided more compelling description of the music and choreography. Arguably, Las Casas was never very interested in the *areíto* as a performance practice per say, but rather in what the *areíto* allowed him to express about the devastating affects of Spanish colonialism.

In his *Apologetic History* (*Apologética historia sumaria*), Las Casas dedicates a series of chapters to an extended comparison between the *areítos* of the New World and the *bacanales* of ancient Greece and Rome, the mythical ancient festivals dedicated to Dionysius and Bacchus, the gods of wine. By comparing *areítos* to the *bacanales*, Las Casas uses performance as evidence to substantiate his broader theological argument against the conquest and slavery. In particular, Las Casas persistently argued that the Indians could be successfully converted into Christians, an argument that ran contrary to popular belief. Oviedo, for example, was an outspoken proponent of the view that the Indians were incapable of becoming Christians—an opinion he shared with the Council of the Indies, which readily adopted his formal recommendation to keep the Indians under Spanish subjugation.[50] Las Casas, however, argued otherwise, basing his statements partially on the observation that the Indians, whose rituals resembled those of ancient culture, could be converted just as the ancient Greeks and Romans had been. He supports this argument by declaring that the *areítos* were less "unpleasant and dishonest" than the *bacanales*—or "orgies," as he often refers to them. Citing Aristotle and Saint Augustine, he disparages the ancient *bacanales* as "most vile, ugly, dirty, lascivious, dishonest and shameless and with the greatest violation of natural reason and of human diffidence."[51] He notes that the Christian forebears once existed in a state of chaos, naked but for some animal skins, and that "Roman matrons, maids, widows, married and single women" went about, covering only their privates with grape vines, while jumping, making gestures and faces, singing and falling atop of one another as if drunk. He especially points out "the most dishonest dances and representations before all of the town" for the Roman goddess Flora.[52] He emphasizes Livy's claim that Roman women would go so far as to murder their husbands in order to gain freedom to experience the ecstasy aroused by *bacanalia*. Thus, Las Casas's "apology" for Spanish cruelty comes in the form of a confession that the ceremonies of antiquity were themselves once more barbarous than those of the Indies.

To argue that the *areítos* were relatively less corrupt than the *bacanales*, Las Casas had to dispel the notion that the *areítos* necessarily led to cannibalism, sacrifice, and sodomy—a claim made by Oviedo in his writings about the *areítos* of Nicaragua. To that end, Las Casas cites the testimony of a Spanish writer he identified as Diego de la "Tobilla." According to Tobilla, cannibalism and sacrifice were myths, as were the reports about cross-dressing sodomites. Las Casas dismisses the association between cross-dressing and sodomy by speculating that if there were cross-dressed men at an *areíto*, they were likely to have been performing the domestic duties of women and thus were not necessarily sodomites. Las Casas emphasizes Tobilla's claim that Spaniards unleashed dogs to destroy and eat the cross-dressers. As if to convey that the Indians had their own disciplinary practices, Las Casas assures his reader that if there had been sodomites, Indian women would surely have killed them.[53]

Las Casas's "defense" was based not only on Indian behaviors, but also on Indian "nature." In the *Apologetic History* he says that their appreciation of the arts and their capacity to improvise demonstrate their inherent reason and "sanguinity": "Indians are sanguine. All of these people are very happy, from childhood on; they are friends of music-making, dancing, and singing unaccompanied when they lack instruments. They did have certain instruments with which they made sounds for dancing and stirred themselves to joy and gaiety."[54] In a related chapter about the beauty of the Indians, he makes a similar claim about the mirroring relationship between Indian physiology and temperament, noting that their physical movement was a sign of their noble nature: "As for the bodily disposition and beauty and for the modesty, constraint, purity, maturity, composition, mortification, sanity, and the other acts and exterior movements that they show in themselves and of themselves even from childhood, which are innate and natural, it is clear that nature has provided them and their Creator has endowed them naturally with aptitude and capacity for good reason and good understanding."[55] With these statements, Las Casas argues that the beauty, grace, and sanguinity of Indian movement and physicality are expressions of a God-given nature.

Ironically, for Las Casas, it was precisely the Indians' sanguine nature that rendered them vulnerable to conquest. He states that "the magnitude of cruelty, injuries, afflictions, labors, and continuing persecutions" precipitated by the Spanish overwhelmed the Indians' capacity to reason and created conditions for disease.[56] Moreover, he claimed that their vulnerability was both physiological and emotional, noting that the Indians experienced sadness more acutely than other vanquished peoples "because of the delicacy of their bodies and limbs, and because of their noble temperament, which causes anything injurious to be more painful to them than to others."[57] Las Casas intensified Oviedo's observation that the *areítos* performed in the wake of Spanish conquest reflected the Indians' experience of the dehumanization, injustice, and pain they endured at the hand of the Spanish. In fact, Las Casas says that the *areítos* were performed by Indian bodies weakened by conquest, exploitation, and disease. Their songs of misery even referenced the terrifying sounds of the dogs and horses that were commonly unleashed on them. They performed songs of lament until they reached a state of exhaustion, for the *areíto* was the only means the Indians had to memorialize the violence they had suffered at the hands of the Spaniards.

Las Casas repeated this provocative statement about the power of the *areíto* in his description of a major massacre during the conquest of Mexico, the Massacre at the Festival of Toxcatl. About the survivors of this massacre, Las Casas wrote: "As long as a few of these people survive, they will not cease to tell and re-tell, in their *areítos* and dances, just as we do at home in Spain with our ballads, this sad story of a massacre which wiped out their entire nobility, beloved and respected by them for generations and generations."[58] For Las Casas, the *areíto* was both a spectacle of domination and a threat of retaliation.

How are we to understand Las Casas's persistent efforts to demonstrate that the *areíto* and dancing in particular were expressions of Indian humanity, especially given his disinterest in or unfamiliarity with its actual content and form? One possible answer to this question is that for Las Casas, upholding the *areíto* as a form of history counterbalanced his rational estimation that the Indians were in fact "natural slaves." Las Casas defended the Indians' humanity at almost every turn of phrase, yet he also accepted Aristotle's claim that men without a written language were "barbarians" and thus "natural slaves." Las Casas made this concession in his most public and impassioned defense of the Indians during his appearance before a junta organized by King Charles V at the debates of Valladolid of 1550–1551. In this pivotal debate, Las Casas argued against Dominican Juan

Ginés de Sepúlveda, a staunch defender of Spanish colonialization and of the idea that Indians were "natural slaves." In part, Sepúlveda's claim that the Indians were "natural slaves" was based on the perception among missionaries and colonial administrators alike that the Indians "lacked" a written language. This perception was famously expressed in a 1558 letter to Philip II from missionary Pedro de Gante, which called Indians "people without writing, without letters, without written characters and without any kind of enlightenment."[59] Of course, it was self-serving for missionaries to disregard the indigenous painted histories, divinatory manuals, horoscopes, ritual calendars, and auguries as forms of "writing," for acknowledging such would have undermined their justification to evangelize and to teach Spanish and Latin to indigenous nobles. In some measure, Las Casas's characterization of the *areíto* as a form of performed history ("they will not cease to tell and re-tell, in their *areítos* and dances") was meant to compensate for the perception that the Indians lacked a written history—the chink in Las Casas's defensive armor against the arguments about Indian barbarianism. For Las Casas, the *areíto* was proof of the Indians' humanity. Not only did the *areíto* guarantee that the Indians had a past, but it also evidenced the likelihood that they could have a Christian future.

One would think, given the importance that Las Casas assigns to these dances, that he would have been moved to describe them, to record them, or at least to explain the important histories they purportedly told. Yet it seems unlikely that Las Casas had any direct experiences with the dances he so passionately discussed. He wrote virtually nothing about the choreography, movement, or physicality of the *areíto*, though he provided ample description of the *bacanales*. In fact, the Indian dancing body is entirely absented by his attention to the rituals of antiquity and by his own polemics. Ultimately, for Las Casas, the indigenous *areíto* was a means to express his own theological arguments. The Indian dances emerge only as reason, apology, and explanation—not necessarily for what they could prove about the indigenous world, but instead for what they could reveal about the Christian world: its own barbarous past, its cruel effects on the natives, and its prospects for taking hold in the New World.

Conclusion: Embodying History

From Columbus's landfall in the Indies in 1492 to Las Casas's "defense" of the Indies at the debates of Valladolid in 1550–1551, dancing played a significant role in the accounts of the first encounters between Europeans and Indians in the New World. Far from dismissing dance as an insignificant pastime, the early chroniclers attempted to understand it as a sphere of knowledge production, a mode of political resistance, and an expression of the sacred. In so doing, they legitimized dance as a locus of investigation for subsequent chroniclers, missionaries, and travelers. These representations of their encounters convey contradictory perceptions of dance as a source of both wonder and terror, a threshold for fertility and death, and an act of humanity and barbarianism. In the fifty years of writing following the "discovery" of the Indies, these contradictory perceptions intensified to such a degree that by the mid-1550s, the *areíto* was both a sign that the Indians were worthy of Christian salvation and freedom from Spanish enslavement, and proof that Indians were incapable of transcending their savagery.

Each of the early chroniclers placed his unique stamp on the evolving definition of the *areíto* as a site of both identification and difference. They differently "invented" the *areíto* in the likeness of Spanish expressive forms and reconciled its alterity by referencing a litany of other Spanish "others." For Pané and Martyr, the *areíto* recalled the ceremonies of the persecuted Moors; for Oviedo, the pagan Germans and devastated Romans; and for Las Casas, the barbaric ancient Greeks and Romans. It should not surprise us that these early chroniclers were concerned with the *areíto* as a form of historical knowledge. As both historians and students of history, they defined the *areíto* in light of their own historiographic practices, though they recognized the crucial distinction that the *areíto* was a means of embodying and not writing the past. For Pané, the *areíto* was a mnemonic device for memorializing laws; for Martyr, a means to recall the past and to divine the future; for

Oviedo, an "effigy of history"; and for Las Casas, an embodied form of history that would recall Spanish atrocities.

Moreover, their preoccupation with the *areíto* as a form of historiography partially eclipsed their discussion of the different functions of the *areíto*, such as its role in rites of passage, healing ceremonies, and divinatory rituals. The few exceptions include Pané's brief reference to a song that formed part of a shaman's ritual, Oviedo's account of a dance in a human sacrifice, and Las Casas's dubious account of Hatuey's dance for gold in Cuba. It is as if the sacred aspects of the *areíto* escaped their notice altogether, or that the *areíto* was "invented" as a historiographic and political phenomenon so as to disavow the deeper sense of difference that indigenous cosmologies inspired among the first Christian chroniclers. It should be no surprise that the sacred significance of the *areíto* became an ardent interest among the Spanish missionaries who wrote in the decades following the early chroniclers. Their attempt to understand the significance of New World dances is the subject of the chapters that follow.

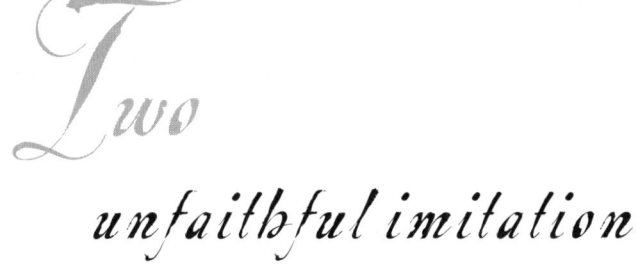

Two
unfaithful imitation

FRIAR TORIBIO DE BENAVENTE "MOTOLINÍA"
AND THE "COUNTERFEIT" HISTORIES OF DANCE

On January 25, 1524, Friar Toribio de Benavente (ca. 1490–1569) joined a delegation of eleven other Franciscan missionaries and left Spain for the New World. They arrived near Veracruz, Mexico, on May 13, and shortly thereafter traced the steps of the conquistadors to Tenochtitlan, where they arrived on June 18. Along the way, Friar Toribio had a life-defining conversion. When natives saw the barefoot friar in threadbare clothes, they purportedly shouted "*motolinía*" at him. Learning that *motolinía* in Nahuatl means "poor" or "unfortunate one," Friar Toribio declared: "That shall be my name for my entire life."[1]

Given that Indians were forced to adopt Spanish names upon being baptized, taking the name "Motolinía" was a reverse baptism of sorts. Indeed, by adopting a Nahuatl name, Motolinía hoped to bridge the Old and New Worlds in religious terms. For instance, the anecdote about his name recalls that of Saint Francis of Assisi, the thirteenth-century founder of Motolinía's missionary order. Saint Francis's father, a merchant, affectionately changed his son's name from Giovanni to Francesco ("the French one"), in hopes that his son would return to the land where he had made his wealth. In a similar gesture, though with an opposing connotation, Motolinía took a foreign name to embolden his vow of poverty. Furthermore, according to Motolinía, the twelve friars departed on January 25, the feast of Saint Paul's conversion. Thus, by taking the name "Motolinía," he became the embodiment of both Saint Paul and Saint Francis in the New World, which he hoped to convert into "a new Jerusalem in America."[2]

Motolinía traveled widely throughout New Spain, Guatemala, and Nicaragua. Between 1524 and 1527 he was the guardian of the monastery of San Francisco in Tenochtitlan, a position he would later hold in Texcoco and Huejotzingo. In 1536 he was appointed guardian in Tlaxcala, where for six years he performed an investigation into native religion and customs. His research primarily consisted of gathering oral histories from native elders and, when possible, consulting with indigenous pictorial codices. Motolinía mentions that he had seen five different types of pictorial books, each dealing with a different aspect of indigenous history, divination, or ceremony. His research also relied on that of Andrés de Olmos (ca. 1480–1568), a missionary who had arrived in the New World in 1528 along with Friar Juan de Zumárraga, the first appointed bishop of New Spain. In 1533 Sebastián Ramírez de Fuenleal, the president of the second *audencia* of New Spain, ordered Olmos to study the ancient customs of the indigenous communities of Tenochtitlan, Texcoco, and Tlaxcala, an order that Baudot calls the "birth certificate of the Mexican chronicles."[3] Based on these multiple streams of research, Motolinía wrote two works now extant: *History of the Indians of New*

Spain (*Historia de los indios de la Nueva España*) (ca. 1536–1541) and *Memoriales* (ca. 1556–1560), preliminary "rough drafts" or "notes" for another volume.[4]

Concurrent with conducting his ethnographic investigation, Motolinía actively taught, preached, and administered the sacraments of confession and baptism. His mission was fueled by a millenialist fervor that had gripped the Franciscan order in the New World, where their writings and actions were distinguished by a "radical primitivism, messianic militancy, apocalyptic reformism, and medieval mysticism."[5] Franciscan friar Géronimo de Mendieta (ca. 1528–1604), a disciple of Motolinía's, characterized the Franciscans' dream as a wish to convert the New World into a Christian utopia wherein the Indians would become "the purest Christians and the best behaved in the whole world."[6] Motolinía shared this vision. By 1526, he had begun to administer the sacrament of confession to the Indians. In fact, he instructed Indians to write or draw their sins on paper so that he could avoid spending time translating their verbal confessions. By one account, during his lifetime Motolinía baptized "more than four hundred thousand, not counting those he might have forgotten," many in defiance of a 1537 papal bull that restricted the number of baptisms friars were able to perform.[7]

He defends his methods and the results of his evangelism by demonstrating how well the Indians could imitate Christian rituals and behaviors, which he understood as signs of providence. For example, Motolinía tells us that on Easter Sunday in 1536, he came across a young Indian woman who carried a woven cloth that depicted the crucifix. Marveling at its "double-sidedness," Motolinía notes that "when you looked closely, one side seemed more like the right side than the other."[8] One could imagine Motolinía inspecting the weaving, flipping it from side to side, measuring its accuracy, and, ultimately, expressing his awe that he could not discern the difference between the two sides. Motolinía was amazed not only by the skill required to weave such an object—a skill that he claims rivaled that of European tapestry makers—but also by the colonial subject's ability to perform activities in service of a Christian vision. When describing the natives' acquisition of Spanish reading and writing skills, he notes, "They learned to write in a short time, for after writing only a few days they can at once make an exact copy of the material that their masters give them."[9] For example, he goes on to describe how a young boy from Texcoco copied a papal bull with such precision that there was "no difference between the model and the other writings."[10]

Motolinía also claims that the Indians' desire to become Christians was expressed through the way they readily adopted Christian rituals and participated in religious processions, dances, and dramas. In turn, Motolinía used performance as a method of evangelization. By all accounts Motolinía was a principal architect of the missionary theatre, the Church-sponsored presentations of religious plays, or *autos*, based on the Bible or Christian history. Motolinía was responsible for organizing and writing several of these plays.[11] In *History*, he gives a perspective into the process and performance of three such productions in 1539.[12] It was through his ethnographic investigations and his participation in the mendicant theatre that Motolinía became familiar with the principles and practices of Aztec dance.

Motolinía references dance throughout his *History*, almost exclusively in the context of describing Aztec sacred ceremonies that were held prior to the conquest. In *Memoriales* he dedicates two brief yet profoundly influential chapters to dance. In these chapters, Motolinía expresses his utter frustration with the term *areíto* and its misapplication to the dances of the Indians of New Spain: "Spaniards call these dances 'areítos,' which is a term from the islands, but up to now I have never known anyone who could account for or explain, in writing or in speech, the words of that island language" (see app. E). He even disparages Spaniards who misuse the term, going as far as to compare their misuse to the broken Spanish spoken by black slaves who had recently arrived in Mexico (*los negros bocales*).[13] Bartolomé de las Casas was in Tlaxcala at the time Motolinía was conducting his investigations and writing. Given the well-documented tension between the two missionaries concerning the role of the mendicant orders in the New World, especially Motolinía's zealous administration of the sacrament of baptism, it is plausible that Motolinía's intentionally degrading comparison was aimed at Las Casas, who liberally used the term to describe performance across the Indies. That said, Motolinía was evidently familiar with Fernández de Oviedo's writings as well, and thus might have meant to disparage both Oviedo and Las Casas.[14]

With his outright rejection of the term *areito*, Motolinía effectively cleared the space for new thinking and writing about dance in New Spain. In the following sections, I examine Motolinía's two chapters about Aztec dance in order to understand their debts to Oviedo's writings about the *areito*. Then I examine the influence of Motolinía's dance writings on subsequent chroniclers who copied and appropriated them, essentially fabricating "counterfeit" dance histories that present the embodied experience of witnessing registered in Motolinía's texts as their own, often to wildly different ends.

Converting "Dance"

Two consecutive and complementary chapters in Motolinía's *Memoriales* focus on the language and performance of dance. Chapter 91 (app. E) provides a description of an Aztec music and dance gathering (or *fiesta*) that includes unique information about Aztec choreography, the social world of the *fiesta*, and the relationship between music and dance. In the very beginning of the chapter, Motolinía establishes that dance was both widespread throughout and pervasive within native worlds. He says dance was a "principal thing" that was "made much of" and that was "everywhere." Unfortunately, his remarks are tied to neither a specific time nor place, so his description may refer to a *fiesta* that he attended in Tlaxcala between 1536 and 1542, an event he saw in Tenochtitlan while compiling his "notes," around 1556–1560, or a composite of the many *fiestas* he had seen throughout New Spain. What is certain is that his description of dancing at an Aztec *fiesta* is based on Oviedo's description of *areitos* in Hispaniola and the Tierra Firme.

There are far too many correspondences between Oviedo's and Motolinía's structure and diction within their writings on dance to allow us consider these coincidental. For example, Motolinía tells us that dances took place during ceremonies for "victory . . . marriage of a noblewoman, or some other notable event" (app. B). This directly mirrors Oviedo's claim that *areitos* were performed during festivals "such as celebration of a victory or defeat of their enemies, or the marriage of the *cacique*, or chief, of their province, or for other causes which brought pleasure to everyone." Moreover, Motolinía uses the word *contrapás* to characterize the dancing, which seems a very revealing choice given that Oviedo not only uses the same term but also explains that he had seen several *contradanzas* in Europe. Motolinía makes no mention of his previous exposure to dancing in Europe. In fact, nowhere in his writings does Motolinía explicitly claim that he directly witnessed the dances about which he writes, except for a very oblique reference that the quality and unison of the Indian dances "astonishes good dancers from Spain when they see it, and they greatly esteem the dances of these natives and the great coordination and feeling they have put into them." However, it is possible that Motolinía counted Oviedo among the "good dancers from Spain" for his apparent expertise in dance.

The differences between their texts are equally revealing, as Motolinía likely changed some of Oviedo's points of reference, even when making similar critical gestures. Whereas Oviedo compares the *areito* to the performances of the Moors and the Greeks, Motolinía unsurprisingly compares Aztec dances to those mentioned in the Bible. Apart from his reference to *memorativas* ("signifying gestures"), Motolinía does not address the historiographic dimension of Indian dances in the way Oviedo characterizes the *areito* as an "effigy of history." If anything, Motolinía believed the dances were meaningless, joyous events. These points of difference and similarity between Motolinía and Oviedo's texts are relevant insofar as they suggest that one of the earliest and most influential writings about Aztec dance was actually based on the dances of the Indies and the Tierra Firme about which Oviedo wrote.

Motolinía also provides unique information about the creation and performance of dance among the Indians of New Spain. For example, he tells us that Indian nobles patronized talented "composers of dances and songs," ensuring a continuously evolving repertory of ceremonial and social songs and dances. He also describes that these rites were performed in specific ceremonial spaces, such as "chapels" in nobles' homes or the plazas of each *calpulli*, or district.

In terms of describing actual Aztec performance, Motolinía emphasizes the Indians' seemingly endless ability to imitate, apparently to demonstrate the Indians' capacity to adopt Christian behaviors and practices. He writes: "Their entire bodies, the head as well as arms and hands, are so synchronized, measured, and ordered that they do not differ from one another or come apart for even half a measure" (app. E). His description emphasizes not only the dancers' ability to keep time, but also the "astonishing" way the dancers, musicians, and drummers synchronize. For example, he is attentive to the way an outer circle of dancers must cover more space and dance with more speed in order to maintain "synchronicity" and "unison" with both the inner circle and the music. He is equally impressed by how dancers can enter and exit a dance without disrupting the dance's momentum. Even when describing the "jesters" who perform at the end of feasts, he notes that their humor is borne from an ability to "disguise their voices, imitating people of other nations, altering their speech."

Essentially, Motolinía's account flattens the Aztec dance-circle into a linear narrative of Christian progress. In his care, the Indians' dances no longer tell native histories, but instead march to the rhythm of Christian time. This operation happens most clearly in chapter 92 (app. F), wherein he provides a linguistic analysis of two Nahuatl words for "dance": *macehualiztli* and *netotiliztli*. Motolinía describes *macehualiztli*, "the principal name of the dance," as a form of sacred, or "meritorious," dancing, and *netotiliztli* as a type of secular dancing, or a "dance of rejoicing," that was performed at social rites of passage at court, such as weddings, funerals, and coronations. Motolinía likens the *macehualiztli* to the *areíto*—as a "solemn festival" that both honors gods and serves as a repository of military and social history. These dances, he specifies, were performed to songs that supplemented the history recorded in their "books and manner of writing," referring to the Aztec codices.

Motolinía also describes the intense physical exertion involved in the *macehualiztli*: "Not only did they call and honor and praise their gods with songs of the mouth, but also with the heart and gestures of the body . . . by the movements of their heads, arms, and feet, and with their entire bodies . . . raising their hearts and feelings to their demons and to serving them with all the humors of the body."

In his study of Motolinía's writings on music,[15] Scott Metcalfe offers the illuminating insight that the description of the Aztec *macehualiztli* recalls descriptions of dancing in the Old Testament, such as Miriam's triumphant song and dance in Exodus (15:20–21) or in Psalms (149:3): "Let them praise his name in the dance: let them sing praises unto him with the timbrel and harp." As Metcalfe also points out, the chapter title explicitly suggests that Motolinía intended to compare the *macehualiztli* with "the dances and songs performed upon the victories which God granted to the fathers of the Old Testament" (app. F). However, this promise was left unfulfilled. Motolinía may even have intended to propose that the similarity between Christian and Indian dances meant that the Indians were descendants of a lost tribe of Israel—and so support his claim that the Indians were worthy of Christian conversion.

Motolinía's desire to create a Christian utopia in the New World was all-encompassing, even extending to his translations of the Nahuatl words for "dance." What follows is an analysis of Motolinía's reflections on the language of dance, particularly his refutable yet fascinating translation of the Nahuatl word *macehualiztli*, which effectively "converts" Indian dancing into a form of Christian devotion.

Motolinía notes that *macehualiztli* narrowly means "merit," based on its similarity to the verb *macehualon* ("to merit") and its derivative *tlamacehualo* ("to do penance or confession"). To support this claim, he calls upon his own perception of actual performances of the *macehualiztli*, which required intense physical and emotional exertion as a form of "penance," "labor," "service," and "work." Thus, he interprets *macehualiztli* to mean "the laborious care devoted to raising their hearts and feelings to their demons and to serving them with all the humors of the body, and that work of persevering all day and a large part of the night" (app. F).

Motolinía's definition of *macehualiztli* as "merit" corresponds with those of two sixteenth-century authorities on "classical" Nahuatl (which was spoken around the time of the conquest). Franciscan friar Alonso de Molina's 1555 *Vocabulario en lengua caste-*

llana y mexicana, the first Spanish–Nahuatl dictionary, defines *macehualiztli* as "dance" (*dança o baile*). It also provides three entries for *macehua*: "to dance" (*bailar, o dançar*); "to acquire or merit what one desires" (*conseguir, o merecerlo desseado*); and "to do penance" (*hazer penitencia*).[16] In the *Florentine Codex*, Friar Bernardino de Sahagún equates the *macehualiztli* with the *areíto*: "Their *danzas o bailes* . . . that by another name they call *areítos*, in their language are called *macehualiztli*."[17] However, it is likely that Molina and Sahagún corroborate Motolinía's definition of *macehualiztli* as a form of penitential dancing because they based their own definitions and interpretations on Motolinía's.

Having established an association between "dancing" and "making penance," Motolinía goes on to link *macehualiztli* to *macehual*, a Nahuatl word for "commoner" or "laborer." He explains that from the verb *macehualo* ("to work or to earn merit," or "work of merit") comes *macehuali*, which means "laborer," and, in the plural, *macehualtin*, or "laborers." However, contemporary Nahuatl scholars refute the associations between *macehualiztli* ("dance"), *macehua* ("to do penance"), and *macehual* ("commoner") on linguistic grounds. The spoken language of Nahuatl contains "glottal stops"—voiceless sounds in speech that create phonetic and semantic differences between words with similar morphology. Unfortunately, many missionaries were not sensitive to glottalization when transcribing Nahuatl, which led them to misidentify the roots of compound words. Thus, some words may appear morphologically similar when phonetically transcribed into the Latin alphabet, even though they do not share a common root.

For instance, Motolinía's definition of *macehualiztli* is based on an understanding of the word as composed of the root verb *macehua*, meaning "merit, recompense, or fortune," and the nominalizing suffix "-liz-tli." However, the constitutive roots of *macehualiztli* are *ma-* ("hand, arm") and *cehualli* ("shade"), which when combined are "associated with various meanings having to do with coolness, resting, etc."[18] Indeed, according to J. Richard Andrews the term *macehua* (*ma-cehua*) means "to rest the hands" or "to dance," as in a dance without gesture.[19]

Even though the association Motolinía makes between "dancing" and "commoner" is linguistically refutable, it is still revealing insofar as it expresses his desire to "convert" Aztec dancing into the practice of a penitent "commoner," just as he himself "converted" to "Motolinía" ("the poor one"). To further compound the association, Motolinía explains that the plural form of the Nahuatl *macehual* (*macehualtin*) was Hispanicized by adding the plural nominalizing suffix (*-les*): "The Spaniards say 'los macehuales,' that is, 'the common laboring folk.'" With this circuit of linguistic associations, Motolinía effectually performs a linguistic baptism that converts Aztec sacred dancing (*macehualiztli*) into a form of penance (*macehua*) performed by Hispanicized commoners (*los macehuales*).

Motolinía also achieves this result with direct substitution. In his writing about the *areíto*, Oviedo refers to the dance leader in secular terms such as "guide" or "dance master" (*guía* or *maestro de la danza*) and by the Taíno word *tequina*. Motolinía recasts the role of the "guide" with the Spanish term for "subcantor" (*sochantre*) (app. E), the ecclesiastic official charged with directing the singing during the Christian liturgy—thus "converting" the Indian dance master into a Christian cleric.

Motolinía completes this linguistic baptism by erasing the sacred and historical significance of the native dances. In *History*, Motolinía makes the disingenuous claim that he knows little about the sacred ceremonies of the preconquest world: "These people had many other festivals and great cruelties which I do not remember well enough to write the truth about them, although I lived for six years amongst them and heard and learned many things. I did not, however, inform myself so as to be able to write about them."[20] Given that Motolinía includes several references to dance throughout his writings, his claim that he does not "remember well enough" and "did not inform" himself is outright deceptive. Motolinía elsewhere proves that he went to great lengths to "inform" himself about native rituals and remembered them quite well. However, by conveniently choosing to forget, Motolinía completes his "conversion" of *macehualiztli* into a Hispanicized and "common" form of Christian penance that is unfettered by its pagan past.

Unfortunately, Motolinía's writing contains too

many false starts, disruptive pauses, lapses of memory, and changes in direction for it to convey either a compelling explanation about the role of dance in Aztec society or a convincing comparison between Aztec dances and the *areítos* of Hispaniola and the Tierra Firme. Ultimately, Motolinía's "notes" on dance amount to little more than borrowed impressions, fragments of descriptions, linguistic reflections, and rhetorical gestures, yet they exerted a profound influence on subsequent chroniclers, who readily appropriated his refutable claims about the performance and language of Aztec dance and in the process validated them as accepted "facts" about Aztec reality. We now turn to an examination of that process and its detrimental consequences for the study of Aztec dance.

Discursive Charades

Motolinía's writings were the proverbial whisper in an early modern game of telephone. As with many topics he covered, his writings about dance are echoed in those of subsequent chroniclers, who promiscuously borrowed, stole, or otherwise "fed happily" on his texts.[21] Of course, Motolinía himself avidly compiled, copied, and repeated information from a variety of sources. Copying was a hallmark of sixteenth-century intellectual culture and the chroniclers "used (or abused)" each other's research without necessarily attributing their sources or explaining reasons for their redactions or revisions.[22] While most chroniclers intended to perfect, clarify, or expand knowledge by compiling and copying information, in many instances they created the misunderstandings, ambiguities, and errors that inevitably arise from such successive retellings.

In the century or so after Motolinía wrote *Memoriales*, several chroniclers wrote chapters about dance that are nearly identical to his in terms of structure, syntax, and diction. Some meaningfully build upon Motolinía's ideas, whereas others liberally appropriate swaths of his text in ways that transformed their original significance. Almost all are "counterfeit" histories of dance, in that their authors fraudulently claim the experience of witnessing embodied within Motolinía's text as their own.

Consider the following. About the *netotiliztli*, Motolinía exclaims, "It was certainly something to see (*Cierto hera muy cosa de ver!*)." Although an exclamatory statement, this sentence is riddled with ambiguity. On the surface, it is a straightforward expression of the fact that Aztec dance was both significant and spectacular. However, it also reads as a confession. Written in the past tense, it begs the question as to whether Motolinía ever saw the dance that he insists "was something to see." In fact, the exclamation might not necessarily be Motolinía's at all. It is altogether possible that he transcribed it from Olmos's now-missing chronicle or intensified Oviedo's claim that dancing was a "good and pretty way of recalling the past." Whatever the case, the statement implies an experience of seeing that was not necessarily Motolinía's. The significance of his exclamation that dance "was certainly something to see" would not matter, however, were it not for the fact that subsequent chroniclers repeated it, often with slight variations, and thus perpetuated the disembodied experience of dance it indexes. For example, about Aztec dancing Spanish chronicler Francisco Cervantes de Salazar claims "that it was something to see (*que es cosa bien de ver*)." Mendieta also exclaims that "certainly it all was something to see (*cierto ello todo era cosa de ver*)." Diego Muñoz Camargo says "that it is a great thing to see (*que es cosa muy de ver*)" and that "there was nothing in the world more worth seeing (*no había en el mundo más que ver*)." Francisco López de Gómara, who was never in the New World and admits that he never saw the dances about which he wrote, instead remarks, "Everyone who has seen this dance says it is a fine thing to watch (*Todos los que han visto este baile dicen que es cosa muy digna de ver*)."[23]

These slight variations on Motolinía's ambiguous claim that dance is a "certainly something to see" shall serve as a point of departure for understanding the deeper imitations of discourse and dance in the counterfeit histories. This analysis requires a critical strategy akin to playing a game of discursive charades, wherein one must identify the sources of texts based on their imitations of movement.

Francisco López de Gómara (1511–ca. 1566) never set foot in the New World. He was secretary and chaplain to Cortés during the final years of the conquistador's life, which he spent in Spain. Gómara wrote a biography of the conquistador, *The Con-*

quest of Mexico (*La conquista de México*) as well as a history of the discovery and conquest of the New World, *History of the Indies* (*Historia de las Indias*), which were published together in 1552. Gómara's *History* is largely based on Cortés's *Letters*.[24] In one of the most renowned sections of his "Second Letter" to the king of Spain, Cortés describes the exotic world of Aztec emperor Montezuma—his palace, treasures, animals, and clothing. He explains some of the palace rituals, such as Montezuma's lavish feasts. Cortés also mentions some of the specialized rooms in the palace, including several dedicated "to many deformed men and women, dwarfs and hunchbacks and others with other deformities; and each manner of monstrosity had a room to itself; and likewise there were people to look after them."[25] Cortés implies that these "monstrosities" were court entertainers, as he follows this description with the following statement:

> I shall not mention the other entertainments which he has in this city, for they are very many and of many different kinds.... The forms and ceremonies with which this lord was attended are so many and so varied that I would need more space than that which I have at present to recount them, and a better memory with which to recall them, for I do not think that the sultans nor any of the infidel lords of whom we have heard until now are attended with such ceremony.[26]

By his own admission, Cortés needed a "better memory" in order to recall the range of rituals he had observed. To fill the gaps in Cortés's account, Gómara turns to Motolinía's *Memoriales*.

In his *History*, Gómara's dedicates a chapter to the "Dances of Mexico"; it fuses information from Cortés's account of a banquet at Montezuma's palace with Motolinía's description of a local dance ceremony, which may have taken place in Tlaxcala or Tenochtitlan. He effectively transforms Motolinía's generic description of a ceremony hosted by a local lord into a "very good, long, and public" postbanquet performance held in the seat of Aztec imperial power. We learn nothing of the humpback entertainers that Cortés faintly recalls in his *Letters*, but instead about the *netotiliztli* that Motolinía vividly documents in his *Memoriales*.[27] In fact, Gómara's compressed chapter mirrors the content and structure of Motolinía's chapter about a generic festival.

He even draws upon Motolinía's linguistic analysis to specify that the dance performed at the palace was a *netotiliztli*. Furthermore, like Motolinía, Gómara describes the *teponaztli* and *huehuetl* drums and mentions that eight or ten men whistle to cue the dancers. (Motolinía tells us there are three or four.) He also repeats Motolinía's "unique" observations about choreography—the dancing guides, the synchronicity between the circles of dancers, and the entertaining buffoons who follow.

However, Gómara's chapter departs from Motolinía's in meaningful ways. For example, he adds that the dancers wore "head coverings made of feathers or masks made in the form of heads of eagles, tigers, and alligators, or other wild animals." In all likelihood, he knew about these masks from the array of objects that Cortés had brought to Seville in 1528, which he would have seen. Also, whereas Motolinía compares the *netotiliztli* with the dances of the islands, Gómara compares it to the Moorish *zambra*, a dance that would have been more familiar to his Spanish readers. In fact, he goes as far as to make the baseless comparison that the *netotiliztli* was "better than the *zambra* of the Moors, which is the best dance that we have here." Gómara undercuts this compliment by claiming that although the Indians' dances are of high quality, their voices are not. Motolinía makes a similar observation, noting that the Tlaxcalans were able to learn songs with the same alacrity and speed with which they learned to write, yet argued that their voices were weak, a characteristic "caused by their going about barefoot, with their chest ill-protected"[28] Finally, Gómara sexualizes the comparison between the *netotiliztli* and the *zambra* by making the off-topic claim that women perform the *zambra* better than men and the baseless claim that Mexican women did not dance in public.

Gómara's variation on Motolinía's description of a *netotiliztli* was later adapted further in the *Crónica de la Nueva España* (*Chronicle of New Spain*) by Cervantes de Salazar (ca. 1514–1575). Born in Toledo, Cervantes de Salazar left for New Spain in 1551 to assume the position of chair of rhetoric at the newly formed University of Mexico. By 1554, he had begun work on his *Crónica*, drawing upon a wide range of written and oral sources, including Motolinía's *Memoriales* and Gómara's *Historia*, as is evident from the way he explicitly references Motolinía throughout the text to "correct" Gómara.[29] *Crónica* includes two chapters that allude to dancing, one of which draws upon Motolinía's writings about the *netotiliztli* through the prism of Gómara's *Historia*.[30] "About the *danzas y bailes* that were performed in Mexico (*De las danzas y bailes que en México se hacían*)" transposes the *netotiliztli* to Montezuma's palace and conspicuously refers to the ceremony as a *sarao*, which according to sixteenth- and early seventeenth-century Spanish dictionaries was a dance event often associated with nobles and kings or the hall where such events took place.[31] Clearly, Cervantes de Salazar wanted to emphasize the regal nature of the *netotiliztli*—or as he says, the *sarao*—noting that dance was enjoyed by nobles in all known parts of the world. Moreover, he mentions that European instruments, such as the sackbut, trumpet, and horn, were part of the musical accompaniment to the Aztec *saraos*, which by 1554 may have been the case.

Major Chronicler of the Indies of the Royal and Supreme Council of the Indies Antonio de Herrera y Tordesillas (1549–1625) used Cervantes de Salazar's writings as a source for his *General History of the Castillians in the Islands and Mainland* (*Historia general de los hechos de los castellanos en las islas y tierra firme del mar Océano*), an eight-volume work published between 1601 and 1615. In fact, Herrera's account of the Aztec *netotiliztli* is a near-verbatim transcription of Cervantes de Salazar's writing—which itself was based on Gómara's after Motolinía's—apart from a few minor changes, of which the most significant was the redaction of the word *sarao*. Nearly a century after its publication, in 1707 Herrera's *Historia general* was translated into Dutch and compiled in *Naaukeurige versameling der gedenk-waardigste zee en land-reysen na Oost en West-Indiën*, a monumental collection of twenty-eight travel books concerning European voyages to the East and West Indies between the thirteenth and seventeenth centuries. Published by Pieter van der Aa, a leading international bookseller based in Leiden, *Naaukeurige versameling* included an engraving to illustrate Herrera's lifted passage about the *netotiliztli* (fig. 2.1).

Pace Gómara and Cervantes de Salazar, Herrera stages the *netotiliztli* at the palace of Montezuma. The engraving that accompanies his text depicts Montezuma perched at the edge of his throne, poised as if ready to stand up and join the dance. Exaggerating Gómara's claim that the dancers dressed as wild animals, it also portrays dancers in headdresses fashioned from fish tails, bull horns, bird legs, and even a jaguar head. Given that the engraving was created approximately one hundred fifty years after Motolinía wrote *Memoriales*, and was based on a text four times removed from its original, it is relatively significant that any of Motolinía's observations endured the test of time, imitation, and translation. The engraving does capture some of his distinguishing details, such as the approximate shape and position of the drums and mat, as well as some elements of the costumes and props.

It is important to note, however, that none of the actual choreographic information gathered by Motolinía survived the discursive trajectory between his book and this engraving. For example, Motolinía underscores the intense synchronicity of Aztec dance and the precision of the concentric rings of dancers who perform *comemorativas* and *contrapases*. Instead the engraving's dancers perform their own unique movements and postures. Although the engraving distinguishes between two "classes" of dancers (those who wear animal headdresses on the right side of the engraving and those with feathered headdresses on the left), it does not preserve an observation repeated by virtually every chronicler, namely, that the dancers were ordered according to their rank. Moreover, the engraving makes no reference to the women who also performed in the *netotiliztli*, nor does it include the buffoons who imitated different nationalities. Ultimately, the profound communal dimension of the *netotiliztli* that Motolinía describes is effectively erased by the engraving's portrayal of male individuality, wealth, and power.

Naaukeurige versameling features another engraving of Aztec dance, this one of the sacred *macehualiztli* (fig. 2.2). Though Motolinía writes about the *netotiliztli* and *macehualiztli* in the same chapter, his copyists parsed and repurposed his writings, which created distinct historical paths for the two styles of Aztec dancing. Whereas the *netotiliztli* endured in writings about dances among Aztec nobles, descriptions of the *macehualiztli* were inserted into accounts of the Massacre at the Festival of Toxcatl, the 1520

FIG. 2.1 *Netotiliztli*. Pieter van der Aa, *Naaukeurige versameling...*, vol. 9, part 1 (1707). Courtesy of the John Carter Brown Library at Brown University.

Spanish siege on unsuspecting Aztec dancers that precipitated the conquest of Mexico. Both Gómara and Cervantes de Salazar extract Motolinía's writing about the *macehualiztli* and insert it into their accounts of the siege, as if to emphasize that the nature of the dancing was sacred and not social. In his recounting of the events leading to the massacre, Cervantes de Salazar shares the idea that dances, like *areítos*, could conceal the natives' plans for armed assault. He drew upon Motolinía's distinction between the *macehualiztli* and the *netotiliztli* to emphasize the sacredness of the dancing performed in the temple in the moments prior to the Spanish attack, as if to justify the massacre. Cervantes de Salazar even goes as far as to compare the *macehualiztli* dancers to *matachines*, which he explains were similar to Roman *gesticulatores*, or dancers "that speak without talking."[32]

In the sixteenth century, the term *matachines* had connotations that ranged from "buffoon" to "swordfighter."[33] Quite possibly Cervantes de Salazar ascribes this term to the *macehualiztli* dancers to foreground the martial dimension of their dance and, once again, to justify the Spanish attack.

By most accounts, the dance that led to the massacre took place in the patio of the Templo Mayor and not within Montezuma's palace. However, the engraving situates the ritual in a Baroque hall. The architecture resembles that of a cathedral, perhaps a reference to the National Cathedral of Mexico, on which construction had begun in 1573 and whose footprint borders the patio of the Templo Mayor where the siege was staged. The central action of the image takes place in a nave-like atrium, with two side aisles, a chandelier, vaulted ceilings, columns, and

52 DANCING THE NEW WORLD

FIG. 2.2 *Macehualiztli*. Pieter van der Aa, *Naaukeurige versameling* . . . , vol. 9, part 2 (1707). Courtesy of the John Carter Brown Library at Brown University.

carved facades. The five-sided domes within the engraving obliquely reference the rectilinearity of Aztec architecture. The dancers cavort throughout the space in their elaborate costumes, as if awaiting the whistling cue from the dance leaders. They wear large insignias of gold around their chests and their diadems of feathers. As mentioned in the text, some Indians play instruments such as the drums, the coronet, and rattles. In the foreground's left (and farther afield in the engraving) there are two clusters of Spaniards who watch the proceedings, whispering to each other, as if hatching the plan to attack.

This engraving brings into stark relief the subtle anachronisms and anatopisms within the chroniclers' "counterfeit" histories. Motolinía mentions that the *netotiliztli* and the *macehualiztli* had their own periodicity: performed "every twenty days" or "when there had been some victory in war or when they elevated a lord" (see app. E). However, Motolinía's copyists eliminate this detail, effectually taking time away from the Aztec other. In the counterfeit histories, dancing is transformed from a ritualized behavior to an essentialized aspect of Indian identity. Untethered by time (and timing) and space (Motolinía says that dancing is "everywhere"), images of dancing Indians are transported from the "grand patios" of lords and nobles to the battlefield, the palaces, and ultimately a European cathedral. Similarly, the *macehualiztli* and the *netotiliztli* are likened to ancient Jewish dances mentioned in the Bible, Roman *gesticulatores*, Moorish *zambras*, and *areítos* of Hispaniola and the Tierra Firme—and, through that association, exiled to the cognitive periphery of the Spanish empire.

The counterfeit chroniclers and artists took liberties when representing dance, though not necessarily to deceive or confuse their readers. Most were confident that by compiling and synthesizing multiple sources they were clarifying, extending, and deepening knowledge. However, the "counterfeits" produced unintended outcomes. Rather than dismissing the various anachronisms, time reversals, spatial displacements, and acts of deterritorialization as superficial accidents or acceptable contingencies of sixteenth-century intellectual and artistic culture, we might consider their dehumanizing effects.

In *Time and the Other: How Anthropology Makes Its Object*, Johannes Fabian argues that in the process of writing, ethnographers manipulate time, with the effect of "distancing those who are observed from the time of the observer." He characterizes this impulse within ethnographic discourse as "the denial of coevalness . . . a persistent and systematic tendency to place the referent(s) of anthropology in a Time other than the present of the producer of anthropological discourse."[34] The denial of coevalness leads to a type of allochronic discourse, or "a science of other men in another time."[35] Fabian developed this idea in relation to ethnographic writing within modern anthropology, but the proto-ethnographical writings of sixteenth-century chroniclers of the New World similarly demonstrate this latent impulse, wherein "the other's empirical presence turns into his theoretical absence."[36]

Reading the "counterfeit" histories of dance, one notices the accretion, repetition, and manipulation of empirical details: the size and shape of drums, the variety of headdresses and masks, the dimensions of performance spaces, and the words for "dance" and "dancers" (*sarao, matachine, mitote*). The texts accumulate an arsenal of empirical details that efface any sense of subjectivity that Motolinía's original text might suggest. Indeed, the Indian's body, movement, and physical presence progressively recedes within these histories.

One of the most dramatic portrayals of how "the other's empirical presence turns into his theoretical absence" is a widely contested point of fact that runs throughout the counterfeit histories: the number of dancers who performed the *macehualiztli* and *netotiliztli*. Motolinía establishes that "no small number . . . about a thousand, and at other times more" performed. Gómara reports "as many as a thousand dancers, or at least four hundred." Cervantes de Salazar challenges that modest estimate with "not one thousand as Gómara says, but more than eight thousand" and sometimes "more than ten thousand dancers." Milanese traveler and historian Girolamo Benzoni relativizes "two or three hundred, or even three or four thousand . . . according to the population of the province." Spanish court physician Francisco Hernández casts a wide net with his approximation of "three thousand, sometimes four thousand, and sometimes even more men."[37]

How does one count bodies one has never seen? How do eight thousand dancing bodies look different from ten thousand? What problem does such empiricism resolve? What curiosity does it satisfy? What intellectual, ethical, or historical impulse guides the chronicler to quantify the unimaginable?

These figures are body counts—not necessarily of dancers, but of corpses. They represent the chroniclers' attempts to quantify the incalculable demographic trauma wrought by the conquest. This much is made clear by the fact that several chroniclers specifically account for the dwindling number of dancers who continued to participate in the *fiestas* after the conquest. Motolinía estimates that "since the conquest, half as many" participate in the dancing *fiestas* and that "the number was steadily diminishing and shrinking." Mendieta similarly observes, "In olden times, before the wars, when they celebrated their *fiestas* with freedom, in the big pueblos they would gather three or four thousand or more to dance, but now as the population has diminished and lessened, there are few that gather to dance." Muñoz Camargo confirms that the declining number of dancers was also the result of the fact that "all of this [dancing] has been forbidden on account of the propriety of our Christian religion."[38]

What Motolinía most admired about the dances of New Spain was their synchronicity—the simultaneous convergence of bodies with music in time and space. Over the course of approximately one hundred years, the "counterfeit" histories begat from Motolinía's *Memoriales* transformed a single moment of affirming synchronous dancing into a whole diachronic history of difference and death.

Conclusion: *Una fiel imagen*

Francisco Hernández (ca. 1515–1587) was a court physician who traveled to New Spain in 1570–1577 to study its natural history and antiquities. To that end, he consulted many available sixteenth-century sources, including Motolinía's *Memoriales*. Like Motolinía, Hernández dedicated an entire chapter to Aztec music and dance. "About the *Netoteliztli* (*Del netoteliztli*)" shares several distinguishing characteristics with Motolinía's urtext.[39] However, Hernández includes unique information that is independent of Motolinía's writings. Curiously, Hernández does not mention the *macehualiztli* at all. Instead, he reports the names of over a dozen *netotiliztli* songs and dances associated with wedding and war ceremonies, and ancestors, such as the *nenahuayzcuicatl* ("song of the embraces"), *cococuícatl* ("song of the turtledove"), and *tlacuiloltepecáyotl* ("song of the painting").[40]

Hernández does not identify Motolinía as one of his sources, and his is in no way a "counterfeit" history. In fact, Hernández changes the tone of the chroniclers' resounding echo that dance *was something to see*. He concludes his chapter about the *netotiliztli* with the following assurance to his reader: "We present an accurate representation of the majority of these things so that they can be known and seen by the Spaniards and by all other nations, as much as that is possible to do." With this statement, Hernández acknowledges that "the majority of these things" are subject to misrepresentation, and thus offers a narrow but meta-critical point of entry into the relationship between imitation, dance, and historiography. In promising an "accurate representation"—*una fiel imagen*—of dances, Hernández acknowledges the power that writing has over the production of knowledge and history, as if to condemn the unfaithful imitations of the counterfeit chroniclers who preceded him.

The first two chapters of this book have traced some of the earliest writings about dance in the New World. These writings largely reflect the physical and ideological perspectives of the chroniclers and not necessarily any social reality around indigenous dancers or dancing. An obvious yet important observation is that chroniclers rarely attempted to represent the experience of dancing, native explanations of dances, or the indigenous function of dance in general.[41] All the chroniclers wrote about Indian dances is what the dances reflected back about their own experiences, fantasies, or interpretations: as acts of historiography, as emblems of conversion, and even as symbols of death and extinction.

In 1529, five years after Motolinía's arrival, another Franciscan missionary, Bernardino de Sahagún, reached the shores of New Spain. Following nearly two decades of proselytizing and teaching natives, Sahagún embarked on a systematic study of indigenous culture that involved interviewing natives and giving them a voice to narrate their own memories and experiences of the preconquest world. These memories include dancing. Through Sahagún's pioneering research, natives' experiences, ideas, and subjectivities, as well as a vast and deep archive of knowledge pertaining to Aztec dance, began to emerge from "theoretical absence" within colonial discourse and to create a different empirical presence.

Three
the sacrifices of representation

DANCE IN THE WRITINGS OF
FRIAR BERNARDINO DE SAHAGÚN

It is impossible to overestimate the importance of Franciscan missionary Bernardino de Sahagún (1499–1590) to our understanding of the Aztec past. In the mid-sixteenth century, Sahagún embarked upon a systematic study of the Aztec world that culminated in several manuscripts, most notably the *General History of the Things of New Spain* (*Historia general de las cosas de Nueva España*), more popularly known as the *Florentine Codex*.

The *Florentine Codex* is arguably the most important colonial source for the indigenous world, not only because of the breadth and depth of the information it contains about Aztec history and culture, but also because of the origin of its information. For this project Sahagún extensively interviewed a select group of elite native "informants" regarding nearly every aspect of the Aztec world. Along with his four native assistants, Sahagún compiled, edited, and translated the informants' testimony to form the twelve volumes of the codex, each of which is dedicated to a specific aspect of Aztec thought and culture: the origins of the gods, dynastic history, rhetoric and moral philosophy, astronomy and nature, and the conquest, among other topics. The codex includes the most extensive information we have about Aztec ritual and dance. Scholars have examined countless topics covered within the *Florentine Codex*, yet until now there has been no study of the role of dancing in the text or in the Sahaguntine corpus at large, which is curious, given that Sahagún's informants reference dance at least as often as, and by some measure more than, they do other aspects of Aztec ritual, including human sacrifice, a topic that has dominated popular and scholarly writing about the Aztec. This chapter will redress that oversight by examining the visual and written representations of dance in the *Florentine Codex* and related texts.

Dance is a topic touched upon in almost all of the twelve books of the *Florentine Codex*. In the course of their interviews, the native informants discussed the role of dance in relation to the Aztec gods and their origins (bk. 1, "The Gods," and bk. 3, "The Origins of the Gods"); its role in divination and omens (bk. 4, "The Soothsayers"); the configuration of music and dance in riddles (bk. 6, "Rhetoric and Moral Philosophy"); its place in astronomical rites (bk. 7, "The Sun, Moon, Stars, and the Binding of the Years"); dance as a factor in the Aztec social world, especially among the ruling and merchant classes (bk. 8, "Kings and Lords," and bk. 9, "The Merchants"); comparisons of foreign dances (bk. 10, "The People"); and the role of dance in the Spanish conquest (bk. 12, "The Conquest").[1]

Not surprisingly, the most extensive verbal and visual descriptions of dance appear in book 2, "The Ceremonies," one of the earliest cross-cultural studies of ritual. Sahagún described its subject as the "calendar, festivals, and ceremonies, sacrifices, and solemnities that these natives of New Spain made in honor of their Gods."[2] As the list of overlapping yet distinct topics indexed by its title suggests, the book casts a wide net to capture the complex range of rites that constituted the primary topic of the book, the eighteen month–long Aztec ceremonies—the elaborate sacred spectacles staged in and around the Aztec ceremonial center of Tenochtitlan. Each of these ceremonies involved sacrifices to a specific god, often in the form of human victims serving as "payment" for continued divine protection from the persistent threats of annihilation.

Some of the most compelling yet confusing descriptions of dance emerge in the informants' accounts of these human sacrifice rituals. This is especially true of the choreographies involving *ixiptlas*—human "representations" of Aztec deities. Most *ixiptlas* were slaves or captured warriors who were forced to represent specific Aztec gods via ritual dress, masks, props, speech, and dance, and then ritually sacrificed by ceremonial priests. The informants indicated that dancing was an essential component in the creation and destruction of these living representations. Dancing was involved in the selection of victims, the transformation of victims into gods, and in the sacrificial act itself. In some instances, even after *ixiptlas* were sacrificed, their bodies kept dancing, in that ceremonial priests integrated the victims' decapitated heads, detached limbs, shorn hair, and flayed skins into subsequent ritual choreographies.

Although it is evident that dancing played a significant role in Aztec rituals of human sacrifice, the nature of that significance remains somewhat of a mystery. Sahagún's informants gave no general explanation as to the meaning or function of ritual dances. Instead, their testimony is limited to observable facts: the placement of the dance within the broader emplotment of ritual; the social identity of the performers; the location and time of the dances; the dancers' raiments, masks, and props; and the relationship between music and dance.

The empiricism of their testimony is likely a result of the fact that Sahagún and his assistants based their interviews on a set of questions carefully devised to elicit information that would help missionaries to determine whether continuing indigenous practices and behaviors were secretly expressing pagan beliefs. Understanding the sacred significance of the rituals was less of a concern to them than identifying the signs of its expression. As such, many questions about the significance of ritual dances went unasked and unanswered. Moreover, Sahagún's interviews were modeled after the Christian sacrament of penance, which implicated the native informants in an asymmetrical "confession-generated" ethnographic process.[3] Thus, the resultant testimony is limited not only by the parameters established by Sahagún's questionnaire (to say nothing, for the moment, about his editing process) but also by the informants, who might have testified with the desire to please, confuse, and perhaps even terrorize their confessors. Thus, the seemingly objective descriptions of dance in the *Florentine Codex* are actually a result of a highly mediated process that was conditioned by the memory of the informants, the experience of the interview process, and the compiling and translation of the informants' testimony. Although Sahagún attempted to make the *Florentine Codex* a scientific and authoritative encyclopedia of Aztec culture and history, it is ultimately a text riddled with strategic omissions, partial confessions, and distorted secrets.

Understanding dance in the Aztec empire means closely reading the *Florentine Codex* for what the informants confessed—and reading it even closer to decipher what they concealed. This chapter examines the role of dance in the Aztec empire as described by indigenous informants to Sahagún and his assistants. It also interrogates the patterns of silence surrounding the meaning and function of dance as a locus for understanding the significance of Aztec rituals, especially rituals of human sacrifice. In so doing, it considers what might be considered the "sacrificial quality" of the *Florentine Codex* itself. That is to say, the text's verbal and visual representations of dancing bodies are types of offerings. For Sahagún, representing dance was a way to purify and exorcise the Aztec past; for the informants, representing dance was a means to atone for their pagan ways and in the process placate Sahagún. Thus, this chapter explores the dynamic between two related and dependent "sacrifices of representation"—the choreographed creation and destruction of *ixiptlas*, or "living representations," in Aztec rituals of human sacrifice and the necessary discursive sacrifices made to represent them in the *Florentine Codex*.

Sahagún and the *Florentine Codex*

Bernardino de Ribeira was born in 1499 in the town of Sahagún in Leon, Spain. He entered the order of Saint Francis at Salamanca. Little else is known about his life until he joined nineteen other monks to cross the Atlantic for New Spain, where he arrived in 1529, only eight years after the conquest of Tenochtitlan.

During his first three decades in New Spain, Sahagún was primarily dedicated to teaching Latin, especially at the Colegio Imperial de Santa Cruz de Tlatelolco, a school established in 1536 to educate the descendants of indigenous nobles. During this time, Sahagún developed a mastery of Nahuatl and began to write sermons and listen to confessions in the native language. His ability to communicate in Nahuatl equipped him better than any other missionary for the task of writing the history of the ancient world, an opportunity that came in 1558 when his Franciscan superior, Friar Francisco de Toral, officially commissioned him to undertake a formal comprehensive study of "the things of New Spain."

Sahagún began this project in earnest between 1558 and 1561, when he relocated to the Franciscan monastery at Tepepolco, a provincial town on the outskirts of Mexico City. He brought with him four assistants (*indios ladinos,* or "Hispanicized Catholic natives") whom Sahagún himself had trained at the Colegio Imperial. His assistants were "trilingual," conversant in Spanish, Nahuatl, and Latin.[4] Together they interviewed the local *señor,* Don Diego de Mendoza, and ten or twelve respected elders (*principales ancianos*). The visual and testimonial material they collected from these informants became the basis for a preliminary text for the *Historia* that later became known as the *Códices Matritenses* (Madrid Codices) or *Primeros memoriales* (First Memorandum).[5] In 1561 Sahagún returned to the Colegio Imperial and repeated his interview process with another group of local noble informants, who confirmed and augmented the information Sahagún had collected from his interviews in Tepepolco.

Between 1565 and 1568, Sahagún lived at the convent of San Francisco de México, where he organized and translated all the material he had compiled. One of the versions of this document was confiscated sometime between 1577 and 1578, owing to a policy change ordered by the Council of the Indies and the Holy Office of the Inquisition that would "ban future and suppress extant works in native tongues by missionaries, as possibly heretical and dangerous to true conversion."[6]

He returned to the project of writing his encyclopedic history between 1578 and 1580, when, going against orders from Madrid to cease work on such projects, he supervised the creation of a massive, richly illustrated version of the text and his translations. This version comprised twelve books in three volumes, and contains more than 1,210 leaves and more than 1,800 illustrations, many painted in color, as well as decorative embellishments.[7] Each folio has two columns: one on the right with the informants' testimony in Nahuatl, and one on the left with Sahagún's edited transcriptions, paraphrases, and translations of the Nahuatl passages in Spanish. Sahagún gave this version of the manuscript to Friar Rodrigo de Sequera, a commissioner in the Franciscan order, who brought it to Spain. By means that still elude historians, the manuscript reached the Biblioteca Medicea Laurenziana in Florence sometime around 1588. It is this version of the *Historia general de las cosas de Nueva España* that has become known as the *Florentine Codex* (*Códice Florentino*), named after the city where the manuscript continues to reside.[8]

Sahagún's investigation was primarily a theological enterprise undertaken with the intent to supplant indigenous belief systems and to assist in the indoctrination of Christianity. He envisioned that *his monumental work* would help missionaries to better evangelize the Indians. Sahagún notoriously compared Mesoamerican belief systems to "illnesses," Christian preachers and confessors to "physicians of the soul," and knowledge as a type of great medication.[9] However, he sought his religious ends through scientific means. Sahagún's systematic approach to conducting interviews with native informants, his attentiveness to linguistics, and his attempts to independently verify information were nothing short of pioneering. For his remarkable efforts, modern scholars have enthusiastically claimed Sahagún as the founder of the modern social sciences: "the first true ethnologist," "the first great historian," the "Father of Modern Ethnography," and—most passionately though less reliably—the "First Anthropologist."[10] In a more sobering tone, Walden Browne places Sahagún at the threshold of medieval and modern epistemologies for having integrated a "medieval" way of knowing (that knowledge is preexisting, revealed through God, and protected through memory) with an emerging "modern" sensibility (that recognizes the role of the subject in the production of knowledge).[11] The tension stemming from these two encroaching epistemologies created a "crisis of representation" for Sahagún. J. Jorge Klor de Alva identifies this crisis in Sahagún's pioneering methodology: "[Sahagún's] tireless editing of native assistants' texts, and his continual experimentation with philological, hermeneutic, and methodological approaches suggest that he did not assume a simplistic objectivist epistemology founded on a naive belief that the representation of the other was not problematic."[12] Sahagún's "crisis of representation" is reflected in his preface to the *Historia*, where he gives the following caveat concerning the legitimacy of his life's work: "I have not had all these fundamentals to prove what I have written in these twelve books, nor do I find other sources to vouch for my assertions; all I can do is to put down here an account of the efforts I made to find out the truth of all there is contained in these books."[13]

Book 2 ("The Ceremonies") is partially based on information about and illustrations of the ceremonies that Sahagún had elicited from his informants at Tepepolco and that appear in the *Primeros memoriales* text. "The Ceremonies" is organized in thirty-eight chapters: two chapters dedicated to each of the eighteen *ceremonias* (a preliminary summary and a longer description) and two additional chapters dedicated to the "moveable feasts" (those ceremonies that were not fixed by the monthly calendar). The book also includes appendices with information regarding ritual buildings, ritual paraphernalia, ritual actions, songs, and the role of women.

As previously mentioned, Sahagún devised a questionnaire to guide the interviews with his informants. Based on the patterns of information found in book 2, Alfredo López Austin infers that the following five questions were those crafted by Sahagún's to prompt his informants to relay details about the rituals and about the illustrations of the ceremonies that they had created:

1. What is the name of this feast (in reference to the rectangle containing the drawing)?
2. Why is it called that (when the name arouses his curiosity)?
3. What human sacrifices or offerings were made for this feast?
4. How was the ceremony performed?
5. On what dates of the Julian calendar did this month [feast] fall?[14]

These questions were specifically designed to elicit empirical information that would enable missionaries to easily identify whether the natives were continuing to perform their sacred rites. When Sahagún repeated the interview process in Tlatelolco, he abandoned the questionnaire format, allowing his informants to narrate their knowledge of Aztec rituals with "freedom of exposition," although it seems evident from some of the digressions within the text that Sahagún interjected some questions of clarification.[15]

Before delving into the wealth of information contained in the *Florentine Codex*, we must acknowledge some of its frustrating yet ultimately fascinating deficits. Despite the remarkable and unique information it offers about Aztec ritual, the text manifests surprising omissions concerning the rules of ritual engagement. Most notably, virtually no background is given on the training and preparation that went into the rituals, except for some brief remarks about Aztec youth learning songs and dances at schools. Similarly, there is no explicit explanation about the roles and responsibilities of performers and audiences. By and large, the informants focused their testimony on ritual actions and objects, and thus gave little to no attention to the experiences of either the celebrants or their audiences. Moreover, the material that it does contain has been filtered through the memories and experiences of elite informants whose access to ritual knowledge is left unqualified. The informants never disclosed whether their knowledge of the rituals was based on participation or learned secondhand from their teachers at the *calmecac*, where Aztec nobles were taught the traditions of ritual and divination. Although there are instances in the text that suggest that the informants held a deep knowledge of ritual, the nature of their experience and participation is left entirely unspoken. It is also impossible to ascertain whether their descriptions were based on a single or multiple experiences of the ceremonies. Nowhere do the informants give any indication of whether the ceremonies evolved over time.

Apart from the limitations to our understanding of Aztec ritual imposed by the content of the informants' testimony, the structure and form of the *Florentine Codex* impose their own unique restrictions. Sahagún edited his informants' testimony into quasi-narrative accounts that imply but do not necessarily deliver narrative coherence. Although the informants' descriptions follow a chronological sequence, there is rarely any suggestion of the significance or consequence of any given ritual act. Although presumably multiple informants contributed testimony about the rituals, the text is edited as if a single informant had delivered it. Sahagún's translations and paraphrases do not always elucidate, either. In fact, in his Spanish transcriptions of the rituals Sahagún confesses that the wealth of detail burdened his editing process. "In order not to tire the reader," he significantly redacted portions of the informants' testimony in his Spanish translation.[16]

There is little balance to the pacing and proportion of information in the ritual accounts. For example, in one instance several folios are dedicated to describing the ideal physical characteristics of a victim for human sacrifice, whereas in a different account the description of the victim's selection, execution, and disposal is given in less than a paragraph. The barrage of details can disorient a reader, too. Ritual objects, actions, and array are described with an overwhelming attention to detail. However, the quantity of the descriptions does not necessarily reflect the depth of their meaningfulness.

In his "Prologue," Sahagún explains that his investigation was partially designed as a linguistic enterprise. To that end, he prompted his informants to express ideas in multiple ways, which partially accounts for the many redundancies found within the Nahuatl text. As such, when reading the *Florentine Codex*, one must be keep in mind that the quality and quantity of description may reflect Sahagún's interest in drawing out linguistic variation more closely than the significance of the topic at hand. It is Sahagún's interest in language that accounts for why the *manuscript* provides a virtual lexicon of dance-related terms for specific dances, steps, and styles of dancing. That said, Sahagún consistently translated specific Nahuatl dance terms into generic Spanish terms such as *bailar* and *danzar*. Sometimes he used the Taíno term *areíto* to indicate a form of dance-song performance,[17] while at other times, he altogether omitted his informants' references to dancing in his Spanish glosses of their testimony.

The creation of the *Florentine Codex* was an enormous and unprecedented enterprise. No other colonial source possesses its depth and breadth of information about the indigenous world. That dance figures so prominently in the text's visual and verbal grammar alerts us to the significance that dance held for the Aztec—and quite possibly for Sahagún as well. The following sections provide an examination of the text's unique representations of Aztec dance, calibrated against the text's patterns of omissions, translations, and erasures of dance-generated knowledge.

Dancing in the *Florentine Codex*

The *Florentine Codex* relays remarkably little information about the origins of Aztec ritual. For that, we need to turn to the work of Friar Gerónimo de Mendieta (app. G), who explains that music and dance were brought to humankind for the express purpose of worshiping gods. According to his account, music and dance were stolen from the "House of the Sun," a celestial paradise (or a "place of joy," according to Sahagún) where "men who died in battle lived, and who accompanied the Sun in its daily journey from the east" and "women who died giving birth to their first child accompanied the Sun on its nightly journey from the west."[18] Together these spirits were entrusted with guiding the Sun's eternal trajectory. The mastermind behind the robbery was Tezcatlipoca, the "Smoking Mirror God," who sent one of his devotees to perform the task. The devotee had been wandering the shores of Mexico in search of Tezcatlipoca, carrying with him the god's masks and mantles, for the Aztec believed that their "dead gods" had left their raiment behind as vestiges of their power. Tezcatlipoca appeared to his devotee and sent him on a pilgrimage to the "House of the Sun" equipped with an irresistible song. On a bridge made of a turtle, a mermaid, and a whale, the devotee entered the paradise to seduce some of its musicians with his captivating tune. The Sun, suspecting the devotee's sinister plan, warned his court and servants to turn a deaf ear to his charming song, but some were unable to resist its melody and responded in turn. The devotee took those who had succumbed to the power of his melody, as well as their *huehuetl* and *teponaztli* drums, and thus, "they say, was the beginning of the festivities and dances that they make for their gods: and the songs they sing in those *areítos* they consider to be prayers, performing them in concert with a particular melody and choreography, with much concentration and gravity, without any disagreement in the voices or in the dance steps."

As indicated by this myth, dance and music formed bridges between the celestial and terrestrial realms, the present and the past, and the human and the divine. This is true of other rites central to Aztec ritual, including the circulation, display, and offering of objects such as precious stones, featherwork, and ceramics; the array of dress, masks, and insignias that indicated a celebrant's position within the Aztec social order; symbolic and actual competitions, from innocent chases among the youth to fierce gladiatorial contests among warriors; manipulations of fire, smoke, and incense; feasting and fasting; and a broad range of discursive performances, such as speeches, songs, prayers, swearing, and curses. These rites took place at the regimented times and places in and around the ceremonial center of Tenochtitlan, conspiring to synchronize and orient corporeal bodies with agricultural, political, and astral patterns of time and space. The rituals were governed by a concept of sacrifice known as "debt payment" (*nextlaoailli*). The Aztec believed they needed to repay a great debt to their gods, who sacrificed themselves to create the universe. During their eighteen month–long ritual cycle, the Aztec made offerings in the form of dance, song, animals, food, and precious objects.

Several gods preferred to be compensated in human lives. Book 7 of the *Florentine Codex* contains an account of the origins of the "Fifth Sun" (a measure of time tantamount to an "era") that serves as a partial explanatory device for Aztec ritual violence. In this myth, the gods were enshrouded in darkness at the ancient site of Teotihuacán ("Place Where They Become Gods") when two gods, Nanauatzin ("The Pimply One") and Tecuciztecatl ("The Wealthy Lord of Snails"), answered a call to self-sacrifice by throwing themselves into a pit of fire. Their auto-sacrifices had a transformative effect: Nanauatzin transformed from a "pimply" lord into the mighty Sun, and Tecuciztecatl into the Moon. However, once they were projected from the pit of fire into the heavens, they realized they needed movement: "They could only remain still and motionless. So once again the gods spoke: 'How shall we live? The sun cannot move. Shall we perchance live among common folk?'"[19] In awe of their sacrifice, the other gods gathered at Teotihuacán performed auto-sacrifices in order to create the necessary movement to send the Sun and Moon on their celestial paths. These godly sacrifices established a tremendous debt, which the Aztec repaid through ritual sacrifice, a practice called *teomiqui* ("to die like gods"). Sacrifice was necessary to heavenly movement, and, as we will see, human movement was necessary to the practice of sacrifice.

DANCE IN TIME AND SPACE

The festivals were organized within three multiple and interlocking cycles of time: an annual solar calendar (*xiuhpohualli*), a ritual and divinatory calendar (*tonalpohualli*), and a fifty-two-year calendar round (*xiuhmolpilli*). Although the *Florentine Codex* focuses on those rites associated with the month-long ceremonies of the *xiuhpohualli*, with each chapter dedicated to the ceremony of a specific "month," there were distinct ceremonies attached to each of these calendars. The "counting of the days" (*tonalpohualli*) was a 260-day divinatory and astronomical calendar. The *tonalpohualli* was recorded in an almanac called a "book of days" (*tonalamatl*), which was consulted to determine the "influences that affected people's lives, and recording the historical events of the world."[20] This involved having sages or diviners who were expert readers of these calendars interpret information about a child's fate, offer advice for choosing marriage partners, or select dates for conducting commerce, war, or traveling.[21] The *tonalpohualli* was related to the body, and its cycle lasted a gestational period. This calendar was organized by means of thirteen day numbers that combined with twenty day symbols to create twenty thirteen-day cycles known as *trecenas*, over each one of which one or more deities presided.[22]

It is certain that there were rituals, dances, ceremonies, and processions associated with the *trecenas*. However, the *Florentine Codex* gives more information regarding the ceremonies attached to the 365-day solar calendar (*xiuhpohualli*, or "counting of the years"), which organized the recurrent cycles of seasons. This calendar was divided into a "year" (*xihuitl*) composed of eighteen twenty-day "months." Although "months" were called *metztli* (moon) in Nahuatl, they were closely associated with the various movements of the sun (equinoxes and solstices) and thus linked to agricultural events. The earliest chroniclers referred to *metzli* as *meses* (months) and later chroniclers referred to them as *veintenas* ("twenties"). Each *veintena* was associated with a specific deity that reigned over the month. And while there was a main festival during each *veintena*, there were numerous preparatory rites that were initiated during prior months, forming a sequencing that Johanna Broda aptly characterizes as "a fugue," in which "a web of ceremonies was created which spanned the whole year and led from one celebration to the next."[23] The exception to this general pattern came during the *nemontemi* (five extra days at the end of a year), when no ceremonies were held.

Given the exacting attention to time that guided the Aztec ritual cycle, it is not surprising that Sahagún's informants almost always described dancing in relation to a measure of chronological, narrative, or physical time. Sometimes the informants tell us when dances transpired in relation to the other ritual acts: "And then they danced . . ."; "before they danced . . ."; "while they danced . . . ." Descriptions include information about a dance's duration, especially when dances were notably long, such as during all-night vigils or, in some cases, when dances stretched out several days. For example, during the festival of Tecuilhontli ("Small Feast of the Lords") "the captives danced all the night," and during Panquetzaliztli ("The Raising of the Banner") men and women gathered for twenty consecutive days to dance every afternoon until "nearly ten o'clock."[24] The informants also invoke time to express the singularity of a given performance. For instance, during one of the ceremonies a "captives' dance" was performed: "It was only at the time that one warmed them in the sun; it was only at the time that one danced the captives' dance."[25]

The informants were even more specific when describing the time of day that certain dances were performed. Aztec days were organized in four parts: sunrise to midday, midday to sunset, sunset to midnight, midnight to sunrise.[26] The informants' descriptions of dances observe these measures, implying that the sun's heat, intensity, and color were essential dramaturgical aspects of the ritual choreographies. For example, the informants tell us that during a festival of maize in the month of Tecuilhuitontli, "while yet there was sun, while it yet shone, then they began to dance."[27] During a flower festival in the month of Tlaxochimaco, "when there was an end to the dancing, there was only a little sun; already the sun was about to set."[28] During the celebrations for the month of Izcalli, they performed a dance, "and when the singing and dancing were begun in the temple, it was noon."[29] During the feast of Ochpaniztli, when the "hand-waving dance began, it was already late afternoon."[30] These measures of time are expressed both literally ("the hour of nine") and metaphorically ("when the eyes are blinked").[31]

The Aztec were sensitive to the character of the sun's energy, for the sun radiated *tonalli*—an animistic force similar to the Western concept of "soul" or "spirit." *Tonalli* corresponded to the timing and dynamics of Aztec dance.[32] The codex also gives a surprising amount of detail regarding the presence of fire, indicating the presence and position of torches and braziers during all-night vigils. Fire was essential to illuminating, augmenting, and multiplying dancing bodies by casting their shadows against temples. The informants' keen attention to the use of fire during the marathon ceremonial dances might also suggest that the Aztec attempted to manipulate the circadian rhythms of dancers, forcing them to endure the demands of seemingly endless dances, some of which lasted in excess of four days.

The *Florentine Codex* informants also emphasize the relationship between movement and space by identifying the specific locales of certain dances—in front of temples, in courtyards, on rooftops, in houses, or even in the marketplace. Moreover, the informants mention how dances were adapted to the spaces where they were performed: some dancers encircled temples, flower poles, and sacrificial victims, while others formed processions into and out of temples or houses. They describe the movement of priests and victims up and down temple stairs and the preparatory rites the priests performed on the sacrificial altars, often while dancing. These spatial indicators are relevant not only for understanding how sacred dance took place in space, but also how dance consecrated Tenochtitlan itself.

Tenochtitlan's architecture and organization formed an *imago mundi*, a representation of the cosmos on the ground.[33] The layout of the city mirrored the Aztec idea that the universe had four cardinal directions: east (Tlapallan, "the place of light"), west (Cihuatlampa, "the place of women"), north (Mictlampa, "a region of the dead"), and south (Huitzlampa, "the place of spines"). In addition to a horizontal plane with four cardinal directions, the Aztec universe was comprised of a vertical plane consisting of thirteen levels of heaven and nine levels of underworld. The horizontal and vertical planes intersected at its sacred pivot, the ceremonial precinct of Tenochtitlan, which was centrally situated in the island city. The 400-meter precinct contained some of the most important and monumental buildings, temples, and plazas in the Aztec empire, all of which were enclosed by a *coatepantli* (a "serpent wall").[34] An appendix to the second book of the *Florentine Codex* lists seventy-eight buildings and sites specific to the ceremonies. These include the *teocalli* ("god houses"), shrines dedicated to gods, the *temelcatl* ("stone of gladiatorial sacrifice"), priest quarters, and the ball court, the site of the infamous Aztec ballgame. At the very center of the ceremonial plaza—and by extension the Aztec world—stood the Templo Mayor, the most sacred monument in the city and a ritual stage for many Aztec rituals and sacrifices. Modeled after the mythic volcano of Coatepec, the site of one of the founding myths of the Aztec empire, the Templo Mayor's shrines and platforms were "metaphors for the surrounding mountains' volcanic shapes and the plateau for the lake" and functioned as ritual stages for reenacting mythical or cosmic events.[35] For example, during a *trecena* ceremony dedicated to the sun god, Nauholin ("Four Motion"), a "Messenger of the Sun" ascended the steps of the Temple of the Sun "little by little, pausing at each step" so as to "illustrate the movement of the sun . . . imitating [the sun's] course here upon earth."[36] The messenger was not only a human timekeeper—a "hand of the clock"—who traced the edge of the sun's shadow as it was cast along the temple stairs, but also a type of celestial mechanic whose walk ensured the sun stayed entrenched in its orbit. In this instance, the moving body was at once controlling the heavens and a reflection of them. The Messenger's body was a pivot where the cosmic and the terrestrial converged and his movement communicated equally to both realms.

Perhaps better than anyone else, Davíd Carrasco has elucidated the dynamic relationship between performance and space in Aztec ritual. Carrasco argues that Tenochtitlan's symbolic geography gave meaning to ritual actions, just as ritual action sacralized the city, particularly through the manipulation, circulation, and exchange of bodies and objects between the city's center and periphery: "The Aztec vision of place was directed not only toward founding and maintaining a magnificently ordered cosmos held firmly in the capital through miniaturization of religious archetypes but also directed through the expansion of these archetypes, toward controlling peripheral communities by integrating them forcefully within the Aztec world."[37] He demonstrates this dynamic with an analysis of one of the major celebrations in the Aztec calendar, the New Fire Ceremony.

Every fifty-two years the *xiuhpohualli* and *tonalpohualli* converged, forming a "bundling of years" (*xiuhmolpilli*) that demarcated a measurable occurrence tantamount to a "century." To observe this concurrence, and to soothe the great distress stirred in the people by the prospect of an apocalypse, the Aztec performed a rite known as the New Fire Ceremony (*toximmolpia*).[38] As a transitional moment, the "bundling of years" was a time of danger and fear that the city would be destroyed; in fact, during this time women were sequestered, in fear that they might transform into man-eating beasts. In anticipation of the ceremony, all fires in the city of Tenochtitlan were extinguished and all images, pottery, and stones were hidden from view. In utter darkness, priests would "walk like gods" (*teonenemi*) in a procession toward a distant hill on the eastern bank of the lake, where they awaited the sign of the Sun's return as signaled by the Cabrillas (a constellation of stars known to us as the Pleiades). Upon the appearance of the constellation at the central meridian, a priest removed the heart of a captive warrior with a flint knife. Once the heart was removed, the priest used his "Fire Drill" to immolate the captive warrior's chest and ignited torches with the fire emanating from his chest.

Meanwhile, the people of Tenochtitlan sat atop their rooftops, anxiously awaiting the sign of the new fire. This sign came in the form of a mystical choreography of fire, as runners and priests carried great torches with flames ignited by the victim's immolated body. From all four directions, the fire was carried across the lake back to Tenochtitlan and to the temple of Huitzilopochtli, to announce the impending return of the Sun and the successful transition into the new century. The fires were brought to the people in their neighborhoods, where they directly encountered the flame's heat and let it blister their skin, literally allowing the sign of the Sun to inscribe itself on their bodies. The flame also fueled a fire in a special altar in which fifty-two reeds were ceremonially burned as a symbol of the end of the last bundle.

The New Fire Ceremony linked not only the past with the future bundle of years, but also the ceremonial center of Tenochtitlan to its periphery.[39] The ceremony literally and figuratively illuminated the connections between the four cardinal directions and the celestial and terrestrial worlds, and in the process renewed the Templo Mayor as its sacred center.

DANCE AND THE SOCIAL ORDER

We will now see that in describing the ceremonies, Sahagún's informants gave as much attention to social identity as they did to time and space. Participants came from all strata of the Aztec hierarchy: priests and warriors, nobles and merchants, laborers and artisans, commoners and slaves.

Johanna Broda and Burr Cartwright Brundage refer to groups of devotees of specific divinities and ritual practices as "cults."[40] Each "cult" was led by a specialized priest called a *teohuatzin* ("Keeper of the God"), who was guardian of the temple dedicated to a specific deity. The priests were the primary custodians of ritual knowledge and instrumental to the performance of the ceremonies. As "keeper" of a temple, each priest was responsible for ritual training and the preparation of specific ceremonies. Some larger temples had sacerdotal staffs and some were attached to a school (*calmecac*) that prepared children of nobility to assume roles as priests and rulers.[41] The *calmecac* functioned as a "priestly dormitory, a repository for cult paraphernalia, and a center of discipline and learning."[42] Under the guidance of the priests, students at each *calmecac* were taught to perform rituals, to read the Aztec calendars, and to interpret divinatory books. Book 2 of the *Florentine Codex* lists the various "keepers" and describes their duties and responsibilities, which included procuring offerings and ritual paraphernalia (such as flowers, branches, bells, and pulque), selecting and guarding victims, keeping sacred fires stoked, and directing participants in songs and dances. Other ceremonial rites were performed by specialized priests, such as the *tlenamacac* ("fire sellers"), who were charged with performing human sacrifices.

Aztec youth were trained in ritual song and dance by veteran soldiers known as "masters of youth" at the "Houses of Youth" located in each district.[43] The students of the *telpochcalli* observed a disciplined routine of arduous labor. They were prohibited from drinking and from socializing, although they were permitted to dance and sing after sunset as a form of exercise and presumably as a means of refining their coordination, speed, strength, and agility for the battlefield. The youth gathered each evening to participate in a ritual that involved bathing themselves, then blackening their faces, adorning themselves with feathers, precious metals, and shells, and starting a fire and dancing in the patio of the *cuicacalli* ("House of Song"). "Everyone danced until the half division of the night passed, until midnight passed. And in those times no one covered himself with anything. All thus danced, wrapped only in netted capes, not a little as if indeed they went naked."[44] The "masters of youth" directed their students, who performed their dances in many of the ritual ceremonies.

FIG. 3.1 Aztec dancers and musicians. *Florentine Codex*, book 8, chapter 14. Florence, Biblioteca Medicea Laurenziana, Ms. Med. Palat. 219, c. 338v.

Priests and teachers were not the only custodians of rituals. Each city-state within the empire had a *tlatoani* (ruler), whose functions and responsibilities involved dancing. The *Florentine Codex* contains several passages about the role of dance in the life and duties of the rulers, especially regarding the "Great Ruler" (*huey tlatoani*), Montezuma. The text stipulates that dancing was part of the ruler's responsibility "to perform well their office and their government" and as such "the ruler was greatly concerned with the dance, the rejoicing, in order to hearten and console all the peers, the lords, the noblemen, the brave warriors, and all the common folk and vassals."[45] For example, book 8 ("Kings and Lords") offers a glimpse into the ritual lives of the noble and warrior classes and lists stewardship of dances among their many responsibilities, which also include the appointment of judges and administrators to the court, command and protection of the warriors, and interaction with his subjects. Sometimes these responsibilities were related, such as when the ruler "commanded that rulers of the youths, the brave warriors, and all the youths, each day, at night, should sing and dance, so that all the cities which lay around Mexico should hear."[46] A *tlatoani* had to know how to use music and dance to assert his political presence, while at the same time, he had to be able to allow music and dance to flourish as one of the many pastimes and entertainments performed by and for the court.

The book also describes spaces connected to the palace that were significant to dance, including the "House of Song" (*cuicacalli*) and the "House of the Cloud Serpent" (*mixcoacalli*), where musicians and dancers consorted, composed works, and prepared for performances.[47] The *Florentine Codex* conveys little about this process, aside from an illustration of these royal dancers and musicians (fig. 3.1).

Sahagún's informants gave a great deal of attention to the quality and care put into the dance array of the rulers. An entire chapter of book 8 is dedicated to the manner in which "the rulers were arrayed when they danced."[48] The informants lavishly described and illustrated the instruments and array accompanying the *tlatoani* when he danced—his headdress, lip pendants, necklaces, sandals, and other accessories made of leather, crystal, gold, and

FIG. 3.2 Instruments and equipment for the dance. *Florentine Codex*, book 8, chapter 14. Florence, Biblioteca Medicea Laurenziana, Ms. Med. Palat. 219, c. 280r.

symbol of beauty and nobility: "There were flowering trees, which were to be seen in the palace courtyard; for it was the ruler who was to dance."⁵⁰ Although the *tlatoani* staged himself amid symbols of nobility, beauty, and wealth, his performance was anything but a spectacle. In fact, the *Florentine Codex* informants alert us that the *tlatoani*'s entourage shielded his body from the gaze of his court: "When the ruler went forth, in his hands rested his reed stalk which he went moving in rhythm with his words. His chamberlains and his elders went before him; on both sides, on either hand, they proceeded as they went clearing the way for him; none might come forth before him; none might look up at him; none might come face to face with him."⁵¹

The *Códice Carolino* contradicts the above passage, in that it claims that Montezuma actively sought out the attention of women when he danced. It describes how Montezuma saturated himself in the perfume of the *poyomatli* flower when he danced in public so that he could attract a woman from among his spectators.⁵² While the *Florentine Codex* offers no comment on the king's sexuality (it is reticent about Aztec sexuality in general), the suggestion that the king danced to court women seems plausible in light of the text's overall insistence that the king used danc-

shells (figs. 3.2 and 3.3). Elsewhere we learn that artisans and feather workers from Amantlan, a district of Tlatelolco, created the royal raiment. The informants praise the skill of these feather workers, who were charged with outfitting the king's accoutrement for dancing: "When a feast day came they displayed for him, they made attractive to him, whatsoever he may want in which to dance."⁴⁹ The raiment was created with feathers from quetzal birds, troupials, red spoonbills, parrots, and hummingbirds. Feathers were a luxury item in the Aztec empire and often served as a form of tribute to the king, and as such the king danced with insignias, diadems, fans, shields, and other objects covered with the spoils of his power. These items were kept in a special large basket that was closely protected by artisans when the ruler danced.

The *tlatoani* prepared to dance by performing a ritual of investiture while adoring his reflection in a special mirror. When he danced before his court, his body was staged in a courtyard of flowers, an Aztec

FIG. 3.3 The *tlatoani*'s dance array. *Florentine Codex*, book 8, chapter 14. Florence, Biblioteca Medicea Laurenziana, Ms. Med. Palat. 219, c. 283v.

ing as an opportunity to experience and display both pleasure and power.

In most instances, the informants describe the *tlatoani*'s dancing as a volitional and exceptional act. Their references insist that the *tlatoani* maintained his power while dancing and that neither ritual nor social expectation burdened his performance. For instance, the *tlatoani* decided how he wanted to appear before his court: "The *majordomos* gathered together all the ruler's dancing array which he requested, and which he might exhibit; whatever he might desire to dance in, in which he would show himself to the people."[53] We also learn that his participation was subject to his mood, for "sometimes he came not forth; it was only as his heart felt"[54] and "when there was a dance, the ruler [decided] the day."[55] His participation did not necessarily need to adhere to ritual or precedent: "But only Montezuma in his own heart knew—[for] no one [else] determined—for how many days he established his dance."[56]

These few yet revealing references to dance convey the power the *tlatoani* wielded in his performance. He also exercised a similar power as a spectator. The *tlatoani* dispensed punishment to those who made mistakes while performing music or dance in the palace: "And if the singers did something amiss—perchance a two-toned drum was out of tune, or a ground drum; or he who intoned, marred the song, or the leader marred the dance—then the ruler commanded that they place in jail whoever had done the wrong; they imprisoned him, and he died."[57] This type of punishment was memorialized in an image of a careless musician who is imprisoned in a cage, then beaten with a *macana*, a club spiked with obsidian blades.

Book 2 also describes Montezuma's participation in several *veintena* rituals. He danced at the festivals of Huey Tecuilhuitl ("Great Festival of the Lords") and Tlacaxipeualiztli ("Feast of the Flayed God"). During the festival of Ochpaniztli, he led a hand-waving dance. During Izcalli ("Growth" or "Sprout"), the last of the eighteen *veintenas*, there was a festival for the fire god Xiuhtecutli ("The Fire God") in which celebrants gathered to make offerings of tamales, incense, and music. Every four years at this ceremony, there was a mass sacrifice of men and women dressed in the likeness of the fire god. Following their ritual deaths, Montezuma graced the ceremony with his presence and performed a "princely dance" on top of the temple dedicated to the fire god.[58] The *Florentine Codex* informants identify the dance as "the dance of the lords" (*netecuitotoli*), not only because the rulers performed it, but also because they dressed in turquoise, a symbol of Xiuhtecutli, who was also known as the "Turquoise Lord."[59] Montezuma led the procession wearing a turquoise miter, a symbol of his rulership, and was followed by the dancing lords decked in turquoise-studded tunics, nose rods, and ear plugs. "Thereupon they came down [from the temple]; they came dancing."[60] They filled the courtyard, and then performed the "serpent dance," winding around the temple four times: "There is lordly dancing; the lords dance the lordly dance. It was the privilege only of the rulers that they should dance the lordly dance."[61]

Although the informants refer to the "dance of the lords" as a particular type of "serpent dance," they use the term "serpent dance" or "winding dance" (*necocololiztli*) to describe a broad range of processional dances performed by the whole spectrum of Aztec society. One description of the serpent dance emphasizes that the Aztec social hierarchy was reflected in the file and rank of its various segments. As a refection of the Aztec social order, the dance was both closed and impermeable: "Nowhere did the line break; nowhere were hands loosed. They went in order [. . .] None disturbed, none intruded, none encircled, none broke in."[62] The serpent dance is the most referenced dance in the *Florentine Codex*. In fact, it is the only dance that is listed among the official rites in an appendix to book 2. The serpent was a sacred symbol in the Aztec world and is mentioned more than any other animal in the *codex*. It appears in Aztec architecture, sculpture, and codices. It emerges in the central narratives of origin, and especially in the legendary account of the Mexica arrival in Tenochtitlan, which held that the migrant Mexica knew to settle in Tenochtitlan upon seeing the sign described to them by Huitzilopochtli: an eagle perched on a cactus and devouring a snake. Many accounts of Quetzalcoatl, the "Feathered Serpent God," involve his magical transformations between human and serpent state. The serpent's ability to shed its skin no doubt influenced Aztec ritual practices concerning the adornment and layering of skin with leather, feather, and masks as well as the removal of skin through flaying. The serpent dance reflected the importance of the symbol to Aztec identity.

The informants most often describe the "serpent dance" as a winding procession around temples, poles, or sacrificial victims.[63] However, each description gives slightly different impressions of the dance. Based on the divergent descriptions, functions, and performers of the serpent dance, it seems plausible that it was a vehicle for displaying bodies in—and as—a social order. One description suggests that it was performed by pairs of dancers arranged in two lines that braided and wound around each other: "And hence it went, being called the serpent dance. It was because they went back and forth, they went from side to side, they met one another face to face, they went holding one another's hands as they danced."[64]

Another description emphasizes the quality of movement of the dancers. Not only did the dance follow the serpent's winding path, but dancers also imitated its slithering efficiency. The passage below describes this quality through its dissimilarities to other types of Aztec dance:

> And as they danced, they did not keep leaping nor did they make many great dance movements; they did not go making dance gestures; they did not go throwing themselves continually about, they did not go dancing with any arm movements, they did not continually bend their bodies, they did not continually go whirling themselves, they did not keep going from side to side, they did not keep turning their backs.
>
> It was quite quietly, quite calmly, quite evenly that they went dancing. Very much as a serpent goeth, as a serpent lieth, was the dance.[65]

In contrast to the solemn aspect of the serpent dance described above, the informants also convey the dangerous, chaotic quality the dance could inspire. For instance, after a midday banquet during the Xocotl Huetzi ("Feast of the Falling Fruit") there was a rousing performance of the serpent dance that induced chaos: "The courtyard was well filled, it was well crowded, it was well packed. No longer was there coming forth among the people. There was much jostling." Even after the music had stopped, the crowds made it difficult to disperse, causing "shouting," "continual trampling, "hurrying," and a "press of people."[66] During Panquetzaliztli, the slaves (or "bathed ones") performed a serpent dance in preparation for their sacrifice. The following passage conveys a sense of the erratic energy of the ritual, its relentless progressiveness embodied by the serpent's mobilization through ongoing constriction.

> And hence was it said that the serpent dance was danced: they took one another's hands; they were ranged in line. . . . The bathed ones went trotting among [the other]. Much did they run; they continually hopped; they kept hurrying. It was as if they hastened, as if they were breathless. They kept winding about; they did not sing, they did not sing at all.
>
> And the old men of the *calpulli* kept beating the drums for them; and only they sang. Some looked on; they marveled at [the dance]. And it was much admired; much was the fasting respected. Indeed everyone abstained, especially the bathers. No [man] lay with a woman, nor did any [woman] lie with a man.[67]

During the festival of Atamalqualiztli ("The Eating of the Water Tamales") the serpent imagery took on a more active presence, with dancers performing the serpent dance while devouring live snakes. During the festival, an image of Tlaloc, the rain god, was placed in a pool of water filled with serpents and frogs. Celebrants danced near the pool, then lunged headfirst into the water and fished out the serpents with their teeth. They then swallowed their catch alive and whole, and next preceded to dance around the nearby temple. Folio 254r of *Primeros memoriales* depicts this scene (fig. 3.4). The action is enclosed by footprints, which most likely indicate the pathway of the procession around the temple. It also depicts the dancers performing what the *Primeros memoriales* identifies as the "Dancing of the Gods," which comprises a procession of performers dressed as "hummingbirds, butterflies, honeybees, flies, birds, black beetles, dung beetles; in the guise of these the people appeared when they danced."[68]

The informants convey glimmers of insight into how dance reflected the social order within Mexica society. They also express how dance figured into Mexica perceptions of other indigenous social

FIG. 3.4 Atamalcualiztli. Bernardino de Sahagún, *Primeros memoriales* (II/3280), fol. 254r. © PATRIMONIO NACIONAL.

groups throughout Mesoamerica. In book 10 ("The People") Sahagún's informants describe the characteristics of more than a dozen different Mesoamerican societies and in three instances reference dance in their depictions of their indigenous allies and enemies. For instance, the informants recognized the Tolteca as the "wise, learned, experienced" original inhabitants of Mexico, as well as the discoverers of peyote, a hallucinogenic mushroom, and the ecstatic dances and songs that ingesting peyote inspired. In a gesture of respect, the informants memorialize the Tolteca's time-honored gatherings in the desert, where "they danced, they sang all night, all day" under its influence.[69] Similarly, the informants report that the northern nomadic tribe called the Totonaque (Totonaca) led a "human, civilized life" distinguished by their skills in various arts: "They were quite skilled in song; they were very able in the dance."[70] By contrast, the informants claim that the Chichimeca (Maçauaque) were "not well reared." To illustrate this point the informants make an ambiguous yet assertive criticism of the perplexing way the Chichimeca used their rattles in their dances.[71] These references to the dances among other indigenous societies suggest that the informants perceived dancing as a meaningful expression of a culture's relative civility. Their remarks about other cultures' dances might even suggest that the informants were aware of how their descriptions of their own dances conveyed Mexica power, courage, and ingenuity to Sahagún and his assistants.

Throughout the manuscript, dancing is linked to social identity, especially to the rights and responsibilities of priests and rulers. However, merchants, laborers, slaves, women, and children also performed specific and significant rites that were intimately tied to their social identities. To understand their roles in Aztec ritual—and their participation in ritual dance in particular—we need to plunge deeper into the testimony of the *Florentine Codex*, into the beating heart of Aztec ritual—human sacrifice.

DANCE AND HUMAN SACRIFICE

The intricate constellation of ritual places, people, times, actions, and objects were coordinated to serve Aztec principles and practices of sacrifice. In Nahuatl, the concept of *tlamacehua* embodies the notion of penance through sacrifice. According to Aztec scholar Miguel León-Portilla, *tlamacehua* was the "primary," "essential," and "reciprocal" relationship between human beings and the gods.[72] Aztec ritual was the mechanism to engender, reaffirm, represent, and fulfill that relation. In many instances, the Aztec paid their debt to the gods for the creation of their world and for their continued protection through blood sacrifice (*nextlaualli*).[73] To that end, they performed a spectrum of sanguinary rites. At one end of this spectrum were auto-sacrificial acts such as self-mutilation, threading, bloodletting, and cutting. At the other end were some of the more elaborate and infamous "modes in which blood was shed"—human sacrifice, dismemberment, decapitation, heart extraction, and cannibalism.

The subject of rituals of human sacrifice has dominated popular and scholarly writings about the Aztec world, which is a likely consequence of the intense attention it received from the sixteenth-century missionaries and conquistadors who recounted tales of human sacrifice to justify their roles in the conquest, colonization, and evangelization of the New World. To refocus the long history of writing on sacrifice away from the moral outrage of the sixteenth-century writers, some scholars have compared Aztec sacrifice to other forms of political theater. Clendinnen, for example, stoically refers to Aztec rituals of human sacrifice as "killing performances" tantamount to the Roman circus and sixteenth-century public executions in Europe. Mesoamerican scholars emphasize that sacrificial violence occurred in highly controlled and ritualized contexts, as if to minimalize sixteenth-century impressions that human sacrifice was arbitrary or borne from Aztec bloodlust. This approach does not necessarily justify its undeniable violence, but instead focuses attention toward the underlying ideas about representation, performance, and identity that undergird rituals of human sacrifice.

This highly ritualized dimension of human sacrifice is best evidenced by the ceremonial figure of the *ixiptla*. An *ixiptla*—or a *teotl ixiptla*—was a person or an object that was ritually transformed into an image of a deity, and through such resemblance was able temporarily to manifest the sacred powers of a god, only then to be systematically sacrificed or otherwise destroyed. Following Dibble and Anderson's English translation of the *Florentine Codex*, modern scholars of Aztec ritual variably translate *ixiptla* as "an image, a likeness," "stand-in," "deputy," "representation," "impersonator," "lieutenant," "proxy of the gods," or "delegate." The barrage of English terms used to approximate the Nahuatl *ixiptla* bespeaks the complex manner in which the figure represented the sacred. Some *ixiptlas* were effigies of vegetable, mineral, stone, and wood. The most valued of the "living images" were captured enemy warriors whose blood was an ideal offering for the Sun. For warriors, offering a captive was a means of gaining social prestige. Other living *ixiptlas* were slaves purchased by nobles or merchants and then ritually purified or "bathed" before being offered as part of their religious and social obligation. Some were painted white and dressed in the array associated with the god in accordance with the Aztec notion that the gods had left their clothing so that their memory could be reanimated through song and dance, in the manner Tezcatlipoca was said to have instructed his devotee.

Brundage describes the *ixiptla* as "a theatrical invention of the highest intensity," for through dress, discourse, display, song, and dance, they represented specific gods.[74] Some *ixiptlas* held an elevated status for an entire year and enjoyed the veneration and honorific treatment afforded to gods. Sometimes they interacted with other *ixiptlas*, dramatizing mythic struggles or engaging in mock-battles that strengthened Aztec notions of identity. However, for almost all *ixiptlas*, a time came when their role transformed from living as a god to dying as one. Almost all of the *ixiptlas* were ceremoniously sacrificed. First they were brought to the platforms of temples and placed on a sacrificial stone, whereupon priests excised their hearts, offering them to the Sun as nourishment. The corpse of the sacrificed *ixiptla* continued to irradiate divine energy from its head, skin, and limbs, which in turn were integrated into other performances: cannibalistic rites, processions with limbs, and dances with flayed skins. The rites that followed sacrificial death spectacularized the power of regeneration and rebirth.

It is also easy to imagine a political purpose served by these violent displays of power. Ritual provided a way for the Aztec to satisfy what Carrasco has characterized as an obsession with a "structured nearness of death."[75] The methodical creation and destruction of human *ixiptlas* not only reflected the human life cycle, but aspired to control the cycle of life and death in the agricultural field and on the battlefield.[76] Through the creation and subsequent destruction of the *ixiptla*'s body, the Aztec sought to control the terrorizing forces that governed human life, vegetation, and political expansion. *Ixiptlas* were integral to the fulfillment of Aztec sacred order—and dance was integral to the performance of the *ixiptlas*.

To best appreciate how central dance was to Aztec principles and practices of human sacrifice, we need to consider several passages from book 9 ("The Merchants"), which explain how merchants and slave dealers came together at the market to auction slaves. Dealers dressed their slaves like gods and forced them to dance to their beating drums, demonstrating their ability to perform sacred choreographies associated with the rituals of sacrifice so as to negotiate a better price for them. The level of dance activity in the market was so intense that Spanish conquistador Bernal Díaz del Castillo mistook it as a district dedicated to dancers.[77] The *Florentine Codex* corroborates this impression with a description of slaves who demonstrated their ability to perform the role of victim, which sometimes meant dancing while intoxicated. Women, too, were forced to dance to the drumbeats of the slave dealer: "They took pains that they should dance well there in the marketplace."[78] Indeed, a slave's selection and price were partially determined by his or her ability to dance well:

> And one who would buy a slave very carefully considered which one he would take. He sought one who was of good understanding; who sang well; who made his dance accompany [the beat of] the two-toned drum [*teponaztli*]; and who was pleasing of countenance, of sound body, very clean, without blemish; nowhere scarred [nor] swollen bruises, [nor] shuffling of feet, afflicted by wens [or] depressions of the forehead, etc., one who was well disposed in body, who was very healthy, slender, in all parts like a round, stone column. Thereupon [the buyer] reached an agreement with the slave dealer on how much the price of his slave would be.
>
> If he were not highly skilled as a dancer, his price was thirty large capes. But if he danced well, if he were clean of body, his price was forty large capes.[79]

As mentioned, not all *ixiptlas* were purchased slaves. In fact, the most valuable victims were enemy warriors plucked from the battlefield. Their lives were temporarily spared (or their deaths interminably prolonged, depending on how one sees it) by forcing them to perform in the *veintena* ceremonies. Other sacrifices involved women, who in some instances valiantly resisted their roles through dances performed before the sacrificial altar. Children also were ceremonially killed. For example, during Atlcaualo ("The Ceasing of Water") there were several types of sacrifices made in honor of Tlaloc, the god of rain, including the sacrifice of young children who were born with cowlicks and on a certain day-sign. Their parents either sold or relinquished their children to priests, who became their custodians. Then, as the time of the festival neared, the children were ornately adorned with feathers, flowers, and paper wings. Thus they were called "human paper streamers." These children—"the most precious debt-payments"—were carried on litters by priests and taken in procession to specific locales (at the foot of a mountain, at the top of a hill, in the center of the lake), where one by one they were sacrificed. Priests helmed this terrifying procession, "playing [musical instruments], singing, and dancing before them" while onlookers watched in terror.[80] "There was much compassion. They made one weep; they loosed one's weeping; they made one sad for them; there was sighing for them." Then priests danced for these children in order to terrorize them, for their tears guaranteed the rains: "It was stated, 'It will surely rain.'"[81]

Of the many questions about the practice of human sacrifice, perhaps the most pervasive concerns the state of mind of the victims, especially regarding their level of awareness and willingness to participate in the rites. The informants make contradictory statements about the physical and mental condition of the victims. In some instances, the informants describe the great honor and courage of the captives who went forth on top of the temple to confront their fate. In other instances, they describe the victims' resistance to the sacrificial stone. Victims were physically forced and coerced through terror to perform their *ixiptla* roles. Priests administered mind-altering substances to them to lessen their resistance. Friar Diego Durán confirms that priests forced victims to drink "divine wine" (*teooctli*), or fermented juice of the maguey plant, which was just one of the mind-altering substances used in ancient Mexico.[82] These substances would have both intensified and numbed the victims' experience of terror, pain, and pleasure during the dances performed in the moments leading to their sacrifice. Though the text does not fully explain the role of hallucinogenic drugs, mushrooms, and alcohol in inducing altered states of consciousness in the rituals, in book 9 there is a reference to a banquet wherein warriors consumed mushrooms as they danced. These mushrooms had both animating and sedative effects on their dancing: "When the mushroom took effect on them, then they danced, then they wept. But some, while still in command of their senses, entered [and] sat there by the house on their seats; they danced no more, but only sat there nodding."[83]

Descriptions of dance appear with more frequency and detail in the accounts of human sacrifice than anywhere else in the *Florentine Codex*, or any other colonial source for that matter. The following two sections examine the informants' verbal and visual references to these sacred dances and to the experiences and responses that dancing evoked among their participants and spectators. Collectively, these descriptions reveal that choreography was used to control the cycle of creation and destruction, especially as it manifested in the primary spheres of Aztec imperial expansion: war and sexuality. This should be of little surprise, given that Aztec dance and music were believed to have originated in the "House of the Sun," the celestial realm inhabited by the spirits of warriors slain on the battlefield and the spirits of would-be mothers who died during childbirth. Dancing in the *veintena* ceremonies not only represented the encounters with death endured by warriors and women, but also created a space for participants and spectators alike to experience the physical pain and emotional terror associated with their sacrifice.

Captivating Dance:
Dance in the Feast of the Flaying of Men

The "Feast of the Flaying of Men" (Tlacaxipehualiztli) was celebrated during the second *veintena* of the

Aztec ceremonial calendar, which fell during the dry season, sometime approximately between February and March.[84] The festival honored Xipe Totec, the "Flayed Lord" of vegetation, sickness, and war, who is most often depicted as a warrior dressed in a suit of flayed human skin to represent the husk peeling from an ear of corn. The festival of Tlacaxipehualiztli drew heavily upon imagery of skins, husks, and membranes. In fact, its principal event centered on captive enemy warriors who were ritually transformed into *xipeme* or *tototecti*—living representations of Xipe Totec—by forcing them to wear the flayed skins of human sacrifice victims. Like the god they honor, *xipeme* are represented wearing masks and suits of flayed skin, usually with a rectangular opening across the chest to indicate that the victim's heart had been excised. They are often depicted in states of ecstasy as if to capture the paradoxical sense of vitality that the victim's skin endowed its temporary wearer. The *Florentine Codex* illustrations draw attention to the *xipeme*'s gruesome masquerade by accentuating the extra pairs of hands and feet that dangled off the limbs of the skin suit (fig. 3.5). With their tailored yet porous garments of skin, the *xipeme* beg the question whether the festival dramatized the virtue of keeping one's enemy close or exposed the threats of the enemy within.

Throughout the course of this ritual, victims were literally and figuratively transformed from subjects of complete alterity (purchased slaves) into symbols of Aztec sacred ideals (a living representation of a god). Once sacrificed, their lifeless bodies were used in ritual choreographies and then buried beneath a temple. About Tlacaxipehualiztli, Carrasco writes: "The Feast of the Flaying of Men is a story of the metamorphosis of the body of the captured warrior as it moved throughout the ceremonial landscape, a landscape marked and linked by the passage and contact with charismatic objects associated with war, conquest, sacrifice, and transcendence."[85] His compelling interpretation is based on the observation that throughout the course of the ceremony, the bodies of the *xipeme* traverse the city—from the terrain beyond Tenochtitlan to its very center, the temple of Huitzilopochtli, and then to local *barrios*—disseminating their "charisma," or divine energy, across geographical terrains. Carrasco argues that this

FIG. 3.5 Tlacaxipehualiztli. *Florentine Codex*, book 2, chapter 21. Florence, Biblioteca Medicea Laurenziana, Ms. Med. Palat. 218, c. 74v.

transmission was achieved through the technique of synesthesia, the controlled manipulation of sensory experience to convey political and moral messages.

Dancing was an integral component in the synesthetic experience. The *Florentine Codex* and *Primeros memoriales* recount six individual dances performed during the festival that collectively form a larger choreography that integrated (and disintegrated) the captives into the Aztec social body. These included a "captives' dance" that symbolically linked captives to their captors, a rain dance, a procession of *xipeme* in flayed skins, a choreographed combat between captives and captors, a "dance of the severed heads," a court pageant led by Montezuma, and a public dance to celebrate the festival's end. Dance was involved at every stage of this festival as a means of dramatizing the evolving physical and social "metamorphosis" of the captives.

The first dance of Tlacaxipehualiztli was fittingly called the "captives' dance" (*momalitotiana*). Sahagún broadly translates this dance as a "solemn *areíto*" (*un muy solemne areíto*), yet the descrip-

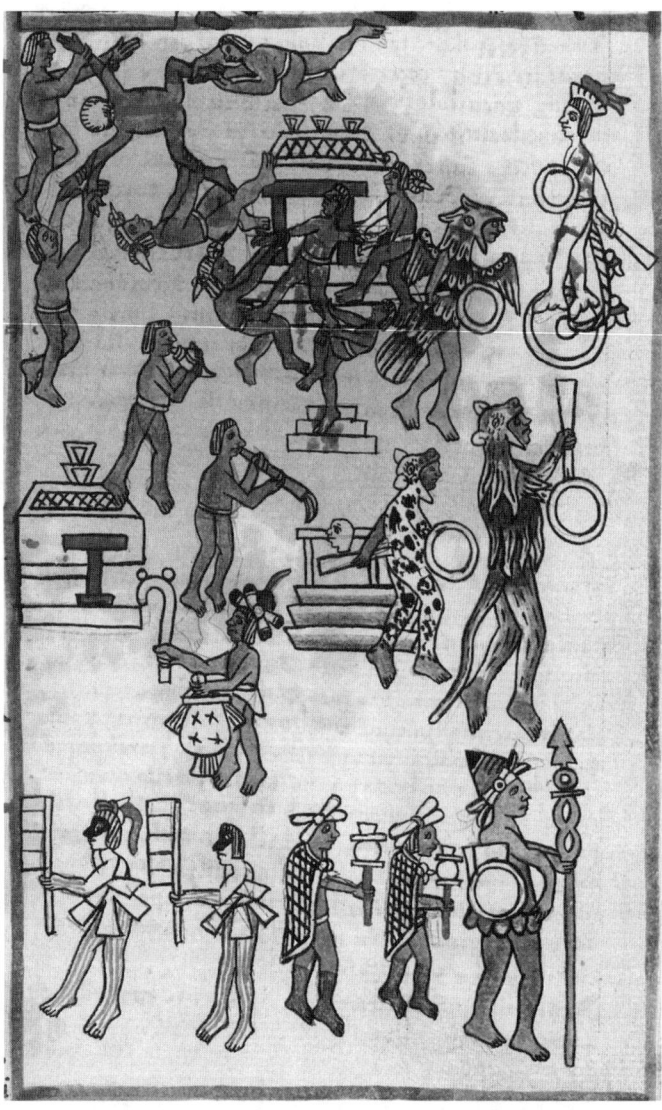

FIG. 3.6 Tlacaxipehualiztli. Bernardino de Sahagún, *Primeros memoriales* (II/3280), fol. 250r (center). © PATRIMONIO NACIONAL.

tion of the dance suggests a more sinister design.⁸⁶ The captives' dance was a choreographed encounter between captors and their captives. The dance was not merely a set of steps and sequences, but an event, a social process, and a style of performing. It took place "when the sun had passed noon" and was at its most intense. The captives were ritually prepared during an all-night vigil. First their hair was shorn, a sign of their transformation from warrior to "striped one"—a particular type of captive whose enslavement was symbolized by red longitudinal "stripes" along his body, created either by paint or by shallow yet bloody incisions into the captive's skin. This was the first stage in a longer striptease of the captive's body. The captors similarly prepared themselves by painting their bodies with ochre and covering their torsos with feather down and their limbs with white turkey feathers. Then they joined in the dance: "It was only at the time that one danced the captives' dance. One only appeared with them; one only was seen with them; one only vaunted himself with them; one was with them only at the time it was a feast day; with them one only made known to men that his captive was a striped one."⁸⁷ The dance was a means of publicly establishing the association between the "vaunted" captor and his captive, to have it "made known to men that his captive was a striped one."⁸⁸ The informant repeats several times that this dance was meant to convey the unique relationship between captor and captive ("one only . . . one only . . . one only . . .") and the exceptional character of their dance ("it was only at the time . . . it was only at the time . . ."). Sahagún's Spanish translation of the informants' accounts of this dance inexplicably omits its name and description.

From the *Primeros memoriales* we learn that the following dance was called the "Sowing of the Rattles," a rain dance named for a seed-filled rattle (*chicahuaztli*) that the performers danced with to produce the sound of rain. During this dance, the *xipeme* struck the ground with his rattle, making divots in the earth so that it could hold the awaited rains: "And his shield went with him; it went resting on his arm. With it he went bending his knees. And his rattle stick went with him; he went rattling his rattle stick. He went planting the rattle stick forcefully [on the ground]; it rattled; it jingled."⁸⁹ *Primeros memoriales* references a related dance wherein "Everyone, all the noblemen and commoners, danced with their rattles; and in the market all the commoners, everyone who gathered there, danced with their rattles."⁹⁰ Whereas the *Florentine Codex* illustrates the *xipeme* on display, the *Primeros memoriales* depicts the *xipeme* leading a procession of dancing commoners (fig. 3.6).

On the following day, specialized priests forcibly led the captives toward their death: "They went taking them by [the hair of] their heads . . . they made them climb to the top of the temple. . . . And when some captive lost his strength, fainted, only went continually throwing himself on the ground, they just dragged him."[91] Once led to the top of the temple, they were killed by the priests, who then removed their hearts. "Afterwards they rolled them over; they bounced them down. They came breaking into pieces; they came head over heels; they came headfirst; they came turning over and over. Thus they reached the terrace at the base of the pyramid."[92] The old men of the *calpulli* removed the bodies from the base of the pyramid and returned them to their respective *calpulcos*, where they dismembered them and "portioned" them to eat. The victim's thigh bone was first offered to Montezuma. The rest of the victim's body was prepared in a stew of dried maize.

With the next day came more captives and more sacrifices, upwards of one thousand a day, Durán estimated. This time, at the Temple of Tecanman, rows of captives arrayed in skins were exhibited in a rite called the "Placing upon Straw," during which time dried grass was strewn about to form a stage upon which they exhibited the "flayed ones." There the captives were taunted and teased into a fighting mood for the central rite: a form of gladiatorial combat between the *xipeme* and eagle and jaguar warriors known as *tlahuahuanaliztli*.

Sahagún referred to the fight as a "game" (*un juego*), but the description of the battle suggests something otherwise. "Game" implies that there were evenly matched opponents, yet here captives were tethered to a gladiatorial stone by a "sustenance rope" around their waists and handed a war club decked with feathers to defend themselves from skilled warriors who were armed with clubs of obsidian blades. The "game" was more of a choreographic encounter, a sequence of martial attacks, recoveries, and escapes. The *Florentine Codex* mentions that the *xipeme* were forced to rehearse this dance of death before they actually experienced it during Tlacaxipehualiztli. Their rehearsed performances of resistance were perceived as a type of dance: "No longer did they delay. As they were turning to the rear at once they came forth. They came *dancing*; they each went turning about. They went as if stretched out to the ground; they each went on the ground; they each went stretched flat; they went looking from side to side; they each went leaping upwards; they each went fighting.[93]

The informants describe a similar choreography of defeat during the festival of Izcalli. Every four years at this festival there was a great sacrifice of men and women who were *ixiptlas* of Ixcozauhqui ("Yellow Face") or Xiuhtecutli, one of the oldest gods in Mesoamerica. Like the *xipeme*, they were harnessed by a rope around the waist: "And when it had dawned, then once again they were adorned. Thereupon they went there where they were to die; they were in order. When they reached there where they were to die, thereupon they danced, they sang; they made an effort. It was said that [they sang until] their voices cracked; it was said that they were hoarse."[94] As with the *xipeme*, dancing prepared the victims by forcing them into a state of exhaustion, deadening their will to resist while simultaneously dramatizing the futility of physical resistance.

The eventual death of the *xipeme* on the gladiatorial stone left a strong impression on the captor, who was awestruck by his captive's choreographed defiance. Clendinnen remarks that in this moment, the captor watched "his mirrored self on display."[95] However, the text instructs us that the captor was not only watching, but also dancing: "And the captor, when he had gone to leave his captive on the round stone of gladiatorial sacrifice, thereupon went away; he stopped where he had been standing; *he stood dancing*; from where he was he stood watching; he stood looking at his captive."[96] The captor's moves may have been a way to imitatively sympathize with his captive's gestures of pain. Alternatively, their mirrored dance may have been a conduit for transferring the sacred powers that the *xipeme* had accrued during his battle with death.

In this dance, the captor–captive relationship was transformed: no longer his possession, the captive became the captor's very being. This much is suggested by the following rite. After a priest sacrificed the captive and fed his blood to the Sun, the captive's body was returned to the *calpulco*, where it was dismembered and flayed. The flesh was then offered to the captor, who refused to eat the skin and gave the following explanation: "'Shall I perchance eat my very self? . . . He is as beloved as my son.'"[97] The informants assure us that the feeling had been mutual, as the captive had once referred to his captor as "my beloved father." The captor may have refused to eat his captive, but made use of his corpse for other choreographies once it had been ritually slaughtered and flayed:

> And when this was done, when they had finished with the striped ones, then they danced, they went in procession about the round stone of gladiatorial sacrifice. All the impersonators [of the gods] and those who had done the striping went in their array. Thus did they who did the slaying go ending [the ceremony]. All severally took with them the head of a captive, of a striped one; with them they danced. It was said: "They dance with the severed heads."[98]

In the "dance with the severed heads," "the people" dressed in the skins of the sacrificed captives and paraded about with their heads. The dance lasted for twenty days, captivating the attention of the commoners who "came out [and] saw."[99] According to Durán, it was common for beggars to wear the *xipeme* skins to strengthen their appeals for food and alms, for one could not refuse gifting the wearer of the *xipe* skins. The beggars shared their spoils with the captors.

The *Primeros memoriales* tells us that at the end of this twenty-day period, the skins "stank, were black, abominable, nauseating, and ghastly to behold."[100] Amidst the choreography of decay and putrescence, revelers came forth to mobilize the signs of growth and prosperity: "They adorned themselves, they danced in quite mixed things, quite various arrays: butterfly nets, fish banners, clusters of maize ears, coyote heads made of amaranth seeds, S-shaped tortillas, thick rolls covered with a dough of amaranth seeds which they covered on top with toasted maize, and red amaranth (only it was red feathers), and maize stalks with ears of green or tender maize."[101] The decaying human skin came in contact with seeds, feathers, and unripened maize, creating a sense of regeneration or rebirth, a reminder of the constant paradox of life and death. According to Durán, at the end of the twenty days of dancing, the skins were buried at the foot of the temple of Xipe so as to contain their sacred power, as well as their menacing stench.

Following the burial of the skins, Montezuma held a ceremony at the palace that involved yet more dancing in enemy skins. For this event, he summoned guests from other cities—the Nonoalca, Cozcateca, Cempoallans, Mecateca—who were forced to watch dances performed in the skins of other enemies. Montezuma staged this dance to terrorize his enemies, who were made to bear witness to a fate that could have been their own. The text registers the response of Montezuma's traumatized guests: "There was witnessing, there was wonder; then consequently there was breaking up, there was dispersal."[102]

Durán's account of Tlacaxipehualiztli corroborates the notion that the festival fulfilled a terrorizing function. He explains that the festival was originally established by Tlacaelel, an advisor (*cihuacoatl*) to the *tlatoani* Axacayatl (r. 1469–1481), after the Aztec defeat of the Matlatzincas. "And the motive for this, Tlacaelel said, is to invite these people to see if they obey us and come to our call, because if not, we will have reason to make war on them and to destroy them. This is my intention."[103] Durán notes that the dignitaries who came to watch that first Tlacaxipehualiztli left "horrified" and so "frightened that they dared not speak."[104] Their speechlessness says volumes about the trauma they experienced watching the dances.

Following this ceremony, in which dance was used to threaten foreign enemies, rulers from the twin cities of Tenochtitlan and Tlatelolco gathered in Montezuma's palace to restore the bonds between allies:

> Thereupon the Tenocha [and] the Tlatelolca joined, paired. The Tenocha formed two rows; also the Tlatelolca formed two rows. They went facing each other. Very slow was the dancing; very much in harmony went the dancing. There was emerging through the palace entrance; there was stopping. Montezuma brought them forth; he went dancing. Two great rulers, Neçaualpilli of Texcoco [and] Totoquiuaztli, ruler of Tepaneca land, came each following him, went facing him. Great solemnity reigned while there was dancing.[105]

This stately dance primarily consisted of mirroring movements performed in rows. The informants were careful to point out that the movement was "very slow" and that "there was stopping," which gave the rulers an opportunity to see and be seen. The passage seems to deliberately distinguish this diplomatic dance from the combative and frenzied dances associated with the *xipeme*, especially the mirroring dance between captors and captives, as if to convey that social order had been healed of its momentary porosity.

With the threat of the enemy temporarily extinguished and the bonds between the Tenocha and Tlatelolca restored, there was one final celebratory dance. Participation was both inclusive and voluntary.

> And when night fell, when it was going dark, there was dispersal; then began the singing and dancing [with interlocked hands]. There danced the rulers of the youths, the leaders of the youths, who had gone to take one [or] two. And also these were called leading youths. And also the rulers danced. And also women danced with them (they were called mothers), only of their own accord, they were not made to. And likewise pleasure girls, who amused themselves.[106]

This celebratory dance temporarily resolved the tension between the self and other that powered all the dances associated with the Feast of the Flaying of Men. The power accrued by the captive's encounter with death on the gladiatorial stone was disseminated across the social spectrum—to the victim's captor, to priests, to commoners, to beggars, to the *tlatoani*, and ultimately, back to enemy warriors. Moreover, the *Florentine Codex* highlights how this cycle of violence captivated audiences: captors, while dancing, watched in awe as their captives danced to their deaths; commoners were enchanted by beggars who danced in the flayed skins of the captives; and enemies watched in shock and terror as priests danced in the skins of their fallen warrior brothers. Watching the *xipeme*, spectators saw a body dancing as well as a body being danced, a body in the throes of death as well as a corpse striving for resurrection. By describing these dances, and the reactions of those who had seen them, the informants unwittingly attempt to give language to the persistent struggle between self and other. For the Aztec, that language was dance. The dances of the Feast of the Flaying of Men dramatized the painful reality that possessing a sense of self was dependent upon possessing the body of the other.

Maternal Terrors:
Women, Sacrifice, and the Dancing Body

Although men performed some of the most significant ritual acts, women played a prominent role in several Aztec ceremonies, especially as *ixiptlas* of goddesses. Women accounted for nearly a third of the victims of human sacrifice performed during the *veintena* ceremonies, and when Aztec women were not the victims of sacrifice, they were intimately linked to the preparation, execution, and dissolution of the bodies of women victims. These ceremonies of human sacrifice involved women of every age and station—noble women and commoners, healers and soothsayers, virgins and "pleasure girls."

Writing about the sacrifice of women in the *veintena* ceremonies, Carrasco notes that "while women play important roles in the sacrifices of women, men direct them, seduce them, insult them, sacrifice them, and wear them."[107] Looking specifically at the references to dancing in the *Florentine Codex*, we can also say that men danced as women, watched women dance, and sometimes even danced inside their skins, all in an attempt to absorb the power that women's bodies contained. This power was revealed through choreographed displays of fertility, chastity, and abstinence, and, most pervasively, in spectacles of terror and pain associated with parturition. Aztec sacrificial dances required that women represent, indeed reenact, some of the most distressing ideals and taboos of Aztec womanhood for the benefit of men, who in turn displayed, manipulated, and controlled women's bodies in hopes of redirecting the force of female sexuality toward the battlefield, the maize fields, and the heavens. Through these choreographies, the terrestrial, political, and spiritual spheres of the Aztec world converged on and through the female dancing body.

For example, the eighth festival of Huey Tecuilhuitl was held during the rainy season and coincided with the first signs of the sprouting maize ear, a precarious time in the agricultural cycle.[108] To avoid the devastation of a failed crop, the Aztec performed various rites to guide the sprout to its maturation and made offerings to Xilonen, the goddess of the tender green maize ear, including a sacrifice of an *ixiptla* in her likeness. During this festival women performed a sequence of dances that integrated maize imagery. More nearly, through these dances, women's bodies became substitutes for the maize itself, and as such were subject to the attention, protection, and cultivation of men.

The festival began with a feast for the lords at the *cuicacalli*. At this feast, young warriors danced with "pleasure girls" (*auianime*), who were chosen to live in the "youth houses" to train in ceremonial songs and dances and to be sexually available for the warriors. The dance began at sunset under the illumination of large braziers carried by youths who had fasted for twenty days. In the patio of the *cuicacalli* they formed a large circle that served as a stage for the "pleasure girls": "And when this was done, then there was issuing from the house of song. They came singing, they came dancing. Between each pair [of men] came the women, the courtesans, the pleasure girls, the best ones, the chosen ones, those set apart."[109] The women joined the ranks of valiant men "worthy of honor," who were arrayed with signs of their warriors status—their shorn hair, lip plugs, pelts of skin, and feathered ornaments. Many warriors were painted black and others striped in a manner befitting their station. And as these women danced, they loosened their hair from the braids that crowned their heads, perhaps in a gesture that summoned the image of the goddess Cihuacoatl ("Serpent Uterus"), who was associated with childbirth and who was depicted with hair flowing like maize silk.[110] And then they danced, among the warriors and the braziers, as if weaving through a maze of maize:

> And they whirled about repeatedly; they went passing by the braziers; they went passing among them; they went entering into all the rows of braziers. When they had gone to reach where [the space] ended, once more they circled back; they returned [whence they had started].[111]

Apart from this brief reference to the pleasure girls weaving through the braziers and displaying themselves for the warriors, the informants focus their remarks not on the dancing, but on the role of the brazier holders, who were charged with protecting the women from unwanted advances: "They did not dance; they did only one thing, they only provided people light. And they kept watch, they kept a close watch on the people."[112] The brazier holders created a stage for sexual display as well as a system of sexual surveillance. They meted corporeal punishment to anyone caught "mak[ing] eyes at the women, in case anyone should go jesting there," especially among the warriors or lords of lower rank. These brazier holders guarded the women, punishing anyone caught dishonoring them by beating them with flaming pine boughs and leaving them to die. In the *Florentine Codex* the image that accompanies the informants' description of this dance illustrates the brazier holders punishing those who transgressed the rules of participation (fig. 3.7). That the informants represented the ceremony with the image of corporal punishment instead of the performance itself seems to suggest that the dance was as much a test of the warriors' discipline and order as it was a demonstration of their courting abilities.

The warriors did not need to work too hard at courting, for the pleasure girls were freely given to them as "gifts." The warriors' seductive gestures on the dance floor were more likely meant to symbolize a farmer's careful tending of his maize stalks until they flower, or in this case, until the pleasure girls unfurled their silken hair. At the end of the dance, some pleasure girls accompanied warriors back to their quarters, where they "ate in secret," a euphemism for a sexual encounter. The rest were "assembled . . . grouped . . . hunted . . . rounded up" and chaperoned back to the *telpochcalli* in order to protect them from any "perverse youth" who would try to take a woman home with him.[113] Those pleasure girls who accompanied warriors back to the living quarters of the *cuicacalli* were certain to leave "well into the night," for the discovery of a sexual liaison would have likely meant social alienation for the couple. The informants emphasize that any couple who violated this rule would be ostracized and prohibited from performing in dances at the *cuicacalli*: "Nevermore was he to sing and dance with the others. . . . Nevermore was she to sing and dance with the others; nevermore was she to hold others by the hand."[114]

It was within this context of rehearsed sexual discipline that the main sacrifice of the *veintena* took place. On the tenth day of the month—the "real feast day," as stipulated by the informants—they sac-

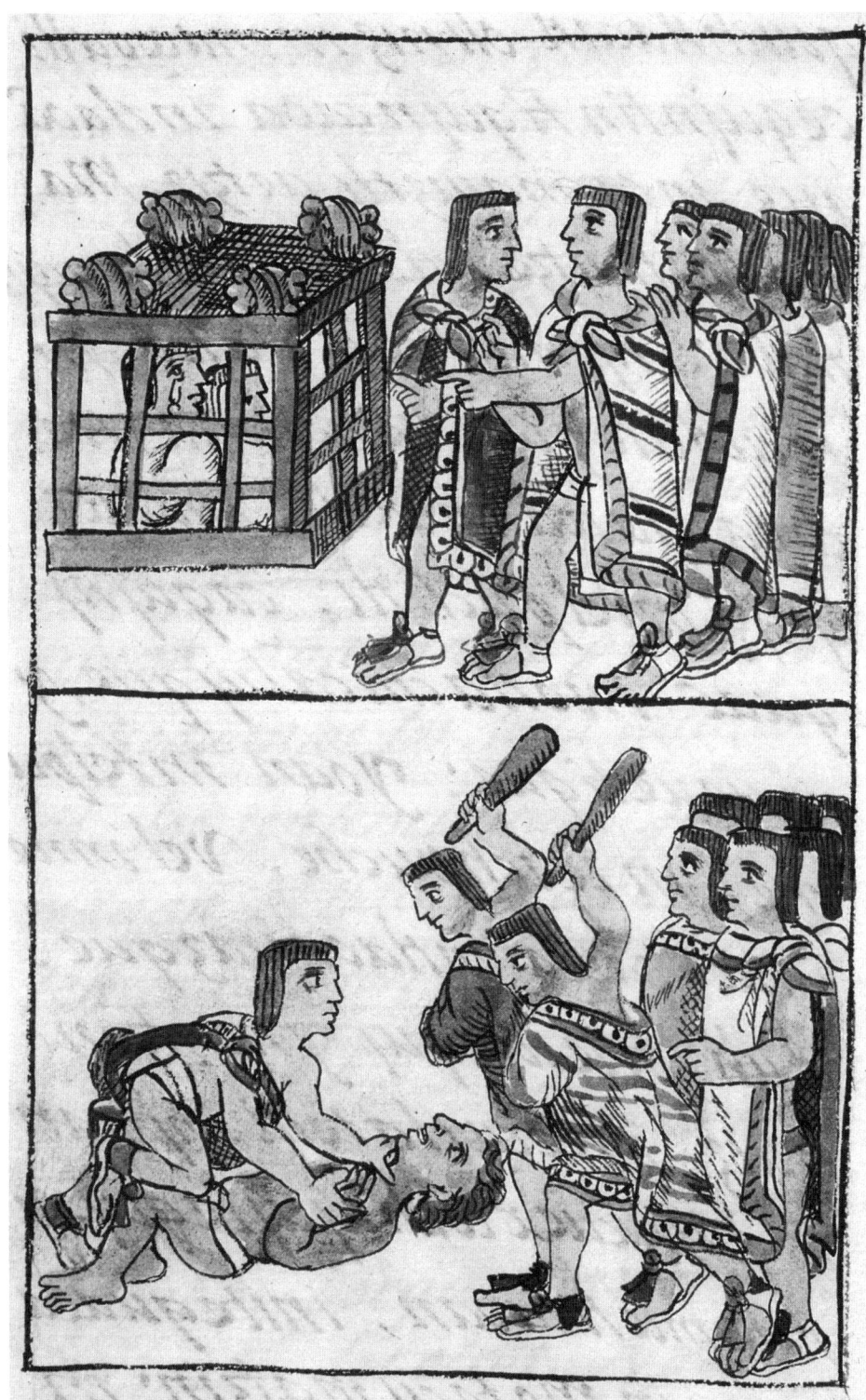

FIG. 3.7 Discipline during Huey Tecuilhuitl. *Florentine Codex*, book 2, chapter 27. Florence, Biblioteca Medicea Laurenziana, Ms. Med. Palat. 218, c. 112v.

rificed a woman made up in the image of the green maize ear goddess Xilonen. The *ixiptla* of Xilonen was arrayed in a manner that foretold her death. Her face was painted yellow about the lips and chili-red on the forehead. She wore obsidian sandals and carried quetzal feathers, a shield, and a rattle stick. The informants are careful to clarify that men and women "mingled not" but danced "apart," continuing with the festival's theme of rehearsed abstinence. A consort of offering priestesses gathered to hold a vigil for the goddess. They were called "the hanging gourd" because they went along beating a two-tone drum from which hung a water gourd. "They went encircling [the likeness of] Xilonen; they went enclosing her."[115] These "hanging gourds" danced and drummed in order to disorient Xilonen as she moved around the temple platform. Men played instruments and cast powdered marigold seeds at her as she passed by them. Then a fire priest took her to a temple platform and prepared her for her death. However, instead of splaying her body across a sacrificial stone, as was customary in rituals of human sacrifice, he laid her across the back of another priest in a curiously inverted sexual position, ostensibly to eliminate the threat of a sexual connection. Following her sacrifice came a celebration of all things virginal. They held a feast of tortillas and cane made from unripened corn while virgins danced: "And when it was Huey Tecuilhuitl, there was dancing which was the particular function of women: old women, maidens, mature women, little girls. The maidens, who had looked upon no man, were plastered with feathers; their faces were painted."[116]

But what precisely could the informants have meant by their assertion that dancing was the "particular function" of women? What was the "function" of women in the broader sequence of ritual choreographies performed during Huey Tecuilhuitl? If one thing is clear, it is that the informants were attentive to the ways that dancing brought men and women into and out of physical contact with one another. They describe how women danced around, away, and separate from men: pleasure girls weaved through torches while displaying themselves to warriors; "hanging gourd" priestesses encircled the goddess, separating her from the men; and virgins danced among women, both old and young. Even at the moment of sacrifice, the sacrificial priest encountered his victim in a manner that denied even the slightest threat of sexual intimacy. In their descriptions of the Huey Tecuilhuitl dances, the informants describe spatial configurations between men and women that convey the manipulation of sexual energy at the heart of the *veintena* celebration. Considered against and alongside each other, these dances formed a rite of purification that began with the sexual danger presented by pleasure girls, continued with the preparation and sacrifice of the Xilonen, and concluded with a dance of virgins. The "particular function" of women within this "great festival of the lords" was to perform a sequence of dances that dramatized the purification of women's dangerous sexuality as a means to restore the field's fertility, which, depending on the success of the dance, would have returned in a few months' time.

Considered against other *veintena* choreographies, the dances performed during Huey Tecuilhuitl were chaste. During other ceremonies women victims performed terrifying dances in the moments leading to their sacrifice, most often emphasizing the victim's choreographed expressions of physical resistance and submission to her impending death. For example, Quecholli ("Precious Feather") was the fourteenth *veintena* and a celebration dedicated to the god of hunting, Mixcoatl ("Cloud Serpent"). Fittingly, the major rite involved an offering to the god in the form of slaves who were tied by their hands and feet as if they were captive deer. They were brought to a sacrificial altar atop a sacred mountain, where the male captives danced and bravely faced their sacrifice: "And thus did they die: they climbed up purely of their own will; of their own accord they ascended. Then they went straight to the offering stone and then they died there at [the Temple of] Tlamatzincatl."[117] The text does not clarify how the slaves moved of their own free will while bound as a captive deer. In all likelihood, the informants overstated the voluntarism and courage of the male captives as an example against which to compare the women slaves, who approached the altar with a paradoxical mix of resistance and acquiescence to their fate: "And the women died when it was indeed still dawn.... When they ascended, they went singing lustily. Some went dancing. Some indeed wept. And the escorts went holding them by the hand."[118] This brief description reflects the tension between submission and resistance to death that informs almost all of the writings about sacrificial dances of women.

This is true of a sacrificial dance performed during the seventh *veintena* of Tecuilhuitontli ("Small Feast of the Lords"), which also involved the sacrifice of a woman, this time an *ixiptla* of Huixtociuatl, the goddess of salt and the salt makers, and elder sister of the rain gods. The *ixiptla* of Huixtociuatl performed a distinctive dance that involved the goddess's martial moves: "When she danced, she kept swinging the shield around in a circle; with it she crouched around. . . . When she danced, she walked leading into it, she walked thrusting it into the ground. She went marking the dance rhythm with it."[119] However, after ten days of preparing for her death, the *ixiptla* of Huixtociuatl unwillingly performed her dance for the last time. A consort of women had to physically force her to dance: "And as the [impersonator of] Huixtociuatl danced, the old women held her; they went holding her as they made her dance. Likewise captives danced all night, those who were to be the first to die . . . whom they would make her fundament."[120] At dawn, Huixtociuatl followed captives and the priests in a climb up a temple, where she was sacrificed. The informants make a conspicuous reference to the presence of "common folk" who witnessed Huixtociuatl's dance and sacrifice, drawing attention to the intrinsically public aspect of her dance of death: "And all the common folk who looked on, all carried, each one, their flowers . . . each one their artemisia flowers."[121] In contradistinction to some of the sacrifices of victims that took place among relatively intimate audiences of priests, warriors, and lords, the death and sacrifice of female *ixiptlas*, such as Huixtociuatl, was necessarily public. The expression and display of resistance, fear, and pain was not ancillary to the dance, but its very choreographic end. That is to say, these preparatory dances of women victims were not only techniques for confusing, disorienting, and distracting the victim from her fate, but also allowed the victim to evidence terror, resistance, and submission to her ultimate sacrifice. Women's expressions of terror in rituals of sacrifice were intimately linked to the experience of childbirth.

The associations between childbirth, dancing, and death converge most clearly in the figure of the *cihuateotl*—the supernatural spirit of a woman who died in childbirth. In the Aztec world, women were warriors in the battlefield of reproduction. In fact, the informants tell us that at the time of childbirth, women "gave war cries, which meant that the little woman had fought a good battle, had become a brave warrior, had taken a captive, had captured a baby."[122] Women who died during childbirth, like men who died on the battlefield, held a special and complementary role in the cosmological order. It was believed that the spirits of slain warriors carried the sun from the underworld to its zenith and that the *cihuateteo* (pl.) escorted the sun on its western descent to the underworld. The *cihuateteo* resided in the western sphere known as *cihuatlampa*, "a realm of darkness, death, and ill-omen," yet appeared in the terrestrial world to haunt, demonize, and sometimes inflict disease, especially paralysis.[123] They were most closely associated with Itzpapalotl, the "Clawed Butterfly," the first woman to die through sacrifice, and were most often depicted with "claws at elbow and knee" to represent their power to "cripple movement."[124] In myths, they were thought to appear at crossroads, where they controlled the flow of movement. They were also associated with the *tonalpohualli* ritual calendar, particularly one of its feasts in which mothers fiercely protected their children from the deadly female spirits, who were wont to descend to the earthly realm to inflict disease and palsy. To stave off these inflictions, mothers made offerings to the spirits and hid their children from them, lest they be "violently possessed, their lips twisted and withered, their eyes crossed and cloudy, their noses crooked, etc."[125] They were also thought to incite adultery.

In book 6 ("Rhetoric and Moral Philosophy") we learn that when a woman died during childbirth, her family ritually bathed and dressed her body, then closely guarded it from thieves who would pluck "relics" from her corpse, such as a strand of hair or an arm, as her body had accrued sacred power in its struggle with death.[126] The immobilizing power contained by the bodies of the would-be mothers was paradoxically reanimated through dance. For example, the *temacpalitoti* was a specific brand of thief who danced with the forearm of a woman who had died

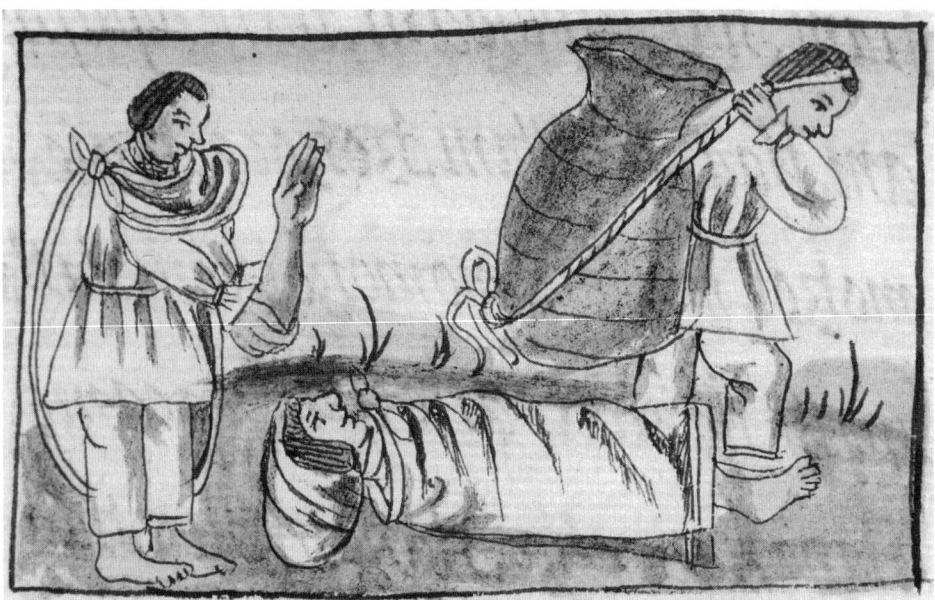

FIG. 3.8 Thief dancing with forearm. *Florentine Codex*, book 10, chapter 11. Florence, Biblioteca Medicea Laurenziana, Ms. Med. Palat. 220, c. 29r.

during childbirth.[127] His dance transported the immobilizing energy of the relic onto his intended victim, who, upon seeing his dance, would "faint" or "swoon." "[While his victim sleeps] he dances, beats the two-toned drum, sings, leaps about."[128] Once his victim lost consciousness, the *temacpalitoti* fled, taking his victim's goods, most often a sack of maize. The *Florentine Codex* includes an illustration of the *temacpalitoti* dancing with the dead woman's forearm and then taking off with the loot as his victim lies in a somnambulistic state, seemingly paralyzed by the power contained within the woman's lifeless limb, which had been re-energized through the thief's dance (fig. 3.8).

The power of a *cihuateotl* had a similar immobilizing function on the battlefield. Thus, a warrior might wield a finger or hair plucked from a woman's corpse to use against enemies during combat. Her lifeless body worked as both a shield and a sword "in order that they might act boldly in war, and in order that they might overpower, might seize many of their enemies."[129] If childbirth was like a battle and women were like warriors, then it was also true that warriors were like women, in this instance using women's bodies to protect life on the battlefield. These two spheres of the Aztec world were united through dancing *ixiptlas* in two of the most significant *veintenas*: Tititl and Ochpaniztli.

Tititl ("The Stretching") was a ceremony of the seventeenth month of the Aztec calendar and was dedicated to Ilamatecuhtli ("Old Lady"), a goddess associated with fertility and death.[130] During the ritual dedicated to her, a slave girl bought by tribute stewards (*calpixque*) was made to represent the "Old Lady" as an *ixiptla*. Once ceremonially bathed and displayed in the raiment of the goddess, the slave girl was sacrificed. However, between the ceremonial preparation of her body and its sacrifice, the informants tell us, there was an important intermediary ritual:

> And before she died, she danced. The old men beat the drums for her; the singers sang for her; they intoned her song. And as she danced she could weep for herself, and she sighed; she felt anguish. For indeed it was only a short time, only so much time, only a brief time until she was to give her service when she would bring an end to earthly things.[131]

As with the women slaves in the festival of Quecholli and Tecuilhuitontli, the Ilamatecuhtli *ixiptla* expressed the paradoxical state of submission and resistance through the progressive and simultaneous acts

82 DANCING THE NEW WORLD

of dancing and crying (*andando bailando lloraba*).¹³² This passage stands out among descriptions of human sacrifice, for the informants describe her emotional state; the female *ixiptla* wept as she danced because she feared death. Of course, the slave cried because she was terrified, but her dancing and crying may have also expressed the terror and pain associated with childbirth, an association underscored by the fact that she danced and cried among male performers masked and adorned as *cihuateteo*:

> This was also the time of "Ilamatecuhtli's Leap" [*illamatecuhchocholoya*], when [priests] assumed the likenesses of the *cihuateteo* [and] danced wearing masks. And two days later there was a procession; the temple was circled [by] all the devils mentioned above. After the temple was circled, they took their gods to their homes. Once again they made them dance there. It was said that when the gods danced, their feet were washed.¹³³

The slave's tears may have been an expression of the terror she faced, a reenactment of childbirth, or both. Whatever the source of her anguish, through her choreographed resistance she accrued the power of a warrior, which was not wasted on mere display. The sacred energy she came to embody through her struggle with death was then transferred onto men, just as the male priests drew upon the power of death in their impersonations of *cihuateteo*. Following the dance of "Ilamatecuhtli's Leap," the *ixiptla* was taken to the top of a temple, where they "cut open her breast." Then they severed her head and gave it to a male priest, who was also adorned as the goddess Ilamatecuhtli. He took the victim's head and with it led a procession of the masked *cihuateteo*:

> He took it with him; in his right hand he went grasping it; he went dancing; with the severed head he went making dance gestures. . . . And when he thus danced, it was said: "Ilamatecutli backeth away." And they put on him a mask; it looked in two directions. It had large lips, it had huge lips; it had big, round protruding eyes.¹³⁴

Interestingly, Ilamatecuhtli is most often depicted lipless and with her teeth protruding from her jaw, yet here the priest dances with a two-faced mask with "huge lips" while dancing around and holding the head of the slain slave girl. He went dancing as if falling backwards (*baile de reculada*), qualifies Sahagún: "And the impersonator, the likeness of Ilamatecuhtli, thus danced: he kept stepping back; he raised his legs up behind him; and he kept supporting himself upon his cane."¹³⁵ There among the dancing *cihuateteo*, a male *ixiptla* of the "Old Lady" danced while wearing the skin of a female slave and carrying her head. He locomoted back and forth ("as if falling backwards") and up and down (performing "Ilamatecutli's Leap") while looking side to side (through his two-faced mask). His movements animated the vertical, horizontal, and sagittal dimensions, as if tracing the "crossroads" where the *cihuateteo* resided.

Like Tititl, Ochpaniztli was a festival that involved the sacrifice of a female victim as a dramatization of the reciprocal relation between life and death. The eleventh *veintena*, Ochpaniztli ("Sweeping") was a ritual of purification and was dedicated to Toci ("Mother of the Gods—Our Grandmother"), the patroness of healers (*titici*), midwives, soothsayers, sorcerers, and witches. The five days leading up to the festival were a sacred time when "nothing more was done; only silence still prevailed." A "hand-waving dance" called *nematlaxo* signaled the end to this nothingness. This dance was performed on eight consecutive days, from late afternoon until sunset, during the transition from one *veintena* to the next.

Whereas many descriptions of Aztec dances emphasize the coordination between singing, dancing, and drumming, this particular dance, the informants insist, was performed in silence, even without the *teponaztli* drum: "They did not sing; none called out; they went in complete silence."¹³⁶ In silence men and women waved branches of flowers—most likely a physical reference to the ceremony's theme of "sweeping." With this gesture they symbolically purified the roads for Toci's divine arrival, sweeping away chaos with order. This is also exemplified by the formations in which dancers performed their gestures of cleansing:

> And thus was the hand-waving dance danced: there was the arrangement of various rows; four rows were formed; there was the forming of four rows. Thus they danced: they only went walking; they kept circling about. Their hands each went filled with flowering tagetes branches. They went grasping them in their hands at both sides. . . . On both sides they went

FIG. 3.9 Ochpaniztli. *Florentine Codex*, book 2, chapter 30. Florence, Biblioteca Medicea Laurenziana, Ms. Med. Palat. 218, c. 127r.

circling their arms. They only went in rows; they only went as one. None broke ranks; none turned another aside; none went astray.[137]

According to the *Primeros memoriales*, everyone performed this entrancing dance: "the god-keepers, and the rulers, the lords, the seasoned warriors, the offering priests, and the women."[138] The only visual representation of the Ochpaniztli festival in the *Florentine Codex* depicts this dance (fig. 3.9). In the image, two loinclothed men sweep with the flowers. Curiously, the image does not convey a sense of the order or repetition inferred by the written description of the dance, but instead represents improvisatory and perhaps even sensual gesticulations with the flowers.

Following the eight days of hand-waving dance, there were four days in which a "mock battle" took place between female physicians, maidens, and pleasure girls who gathered before the *cuicacalli*. The "battle" was waged between two teams, who pelted each other with balls made of matted reeds, grass, flowers, and insects. This battle was staged for the benefit of the victim "in order to amuse her and thus prevent her from crying, because they considered it a bad sign if the woman who was to be killed became sad or cried."[139] Her tears were an omen that many warriors would die on the battlefield or that women would die in childbirth. Thus, the battle ensued for four days so as to avoid the unbearable misfortune her tears would have wrought. On the fourth day they took the slave to the marketplace for a final visit. There, women physicians encircled her in a rite called "She Tramples on Her Marketplace" before returning her to the temple to face her death.[140] The women tried once again to console the victim, this time with a sexual promise: "'My dear daughter, now at last the ruler Montezuma will sleep with thee. Be happy.'"[141] With this promise, they sufficiently deceived Toci and led her "unaware" to the temple, where she was subsequently sacrificed, beheaded, and flayed. Her body's various parts were then surrendered to a priest named Teccizquacuilli who dressed himself in the *ixiptla*'s flayed skin and thereby assumed the role of Toci. The informants deliberately describe Teccizquacuilli as "a very strong [man], very powerful and very tall," as if to emphasize the paradox of gender at play: the body of a young woman with the spirit of a divine mother embodied by a very "strong," "powerful," and "tall" man. The informants subsequently refer this "strong man" as "Toci."

Toci was then joined by an *ixiptla* of her son Cinteotl ("Young Lord Maize Cob"), another priest who danced while wearing a mask made from the skin of the sacrificed victim's thigh, evoking the image of a child nestled in his mother's womb. Together, mother and son paraded about, empowered by the suits of flesh they wore. Priests and warriors were terrified by this power and approached the mother and son with bloodied brooms and shields, surrounding them and striking at them. They called this ritual skirmish "They fight with grass." In stark contrast to the frantic sparring of the bloodied brooms, the divine embodiments of Toci and Cinteotl walked with deliberation toward the Temple of Huitzilopochtli: "They did not run; it was only at their leisure that they went along."[142] They joined together on top of the temple, where "Toci" then "raised her arms, she spread her arms at the foot of [the Temple] of Huitzilopochtli. She placed herself facing [the god]; then she turned about; she placed herself by her son, Cinteotl."[143]

The following day "Toci" and her "son" sacrificed four captives, which led to more festivities, including a reprise of the "hand-waving dance," this time led by Montezuma: "And in this manner was the hand-waving: they went in various rows as hath been said; they moved like flowers. They indeed went in glory. They kept circling the temple."[144] Toci, the women physicians, and Huaxtecs then gathered en masse to sing in a falsetto voice—"like a mockingbird"—behind dancers who performed yet another dance of death. The informants say nothing about the dance but that it elicited a feeling of mourning, especially among the mothers of warriors who watched. In fact, the informants cite the ritual laments of mothers of warriors, for whom the dance inspired a sense of anticipatory mourning for their sons who were soon to go into battle.

> And all the onlookers, the beloved old women, all the beloved women, raised a tearful cry; their hearts were compassionate.
>   They said: "These are our beloved sons whom we see here. If in five days, in ten days, the sea, the conflagration are announced, that is war, will they perhaps come returning? Will they perhaps come making their way back? Verily, they will be gone forever!"[145]

Dancing in the festivals of Ochpanitzli and Tititl dramatized inverse maternal terrors: respectively, the death of a child on the battlefield and the death of a mother in the battle of childbirth. In both instances, dancing induced tears of anguish, terror, and loss. Women's tears, as with their skins, arms, heads, hair, blood—and even the limbs of their cadavers—were trafficked into sacred choreographies that were meant to empower men: pleasure girls and virgins danced for warriors; thieves danced with the postpartum, postmortem parts of women to attain wealth; men danced as spirits of dead mothers; and priests draped themselves in the skins of "Our Mother," all in order to impregnate themselves with female powers of creation and destruction.

Conclusion: The Secret of Magical Dancing

Nearly three decades after the conquest of Mexico, Sahagún gathered trilingual indigenous assistants and native informants to document Aztec *veintenas*. His informants described a broad range of dances: serpentine processions, diplomatic pageants, celebratory dances of youth, and a monarch's choreography of investiture, among others. They described these dances with scrupulous attention to the identities of the performers, as well as to the times and spaces of their performances, as if to convey that the idea that dancing enacted a vision of the Aztec social order.

However, in their accounts of human sacrifice rituals, the informants also describe dances that seem to have upended that order: the display and manipulation of bodies and their parts, dances of resistance, staged conflicts of physical and emotional endurance, and embodiments and disembodiments of mythic and social identities. Dancing in the human sacrifice rituals effectively blurred distinctions between human and the divine, astral and agrarian, terrestrial and material, warrior and mother, captor and slave. Indeed, it even blurred distinctions between the dead and the living, as bodies danced (and were danced with) in various degrees of consciousness, duress, and stupefaction and in various states of destruction, decay, and disintegration. Moreover, these dances were performed within an unrelenting system of surveillance. The *Florentine Codex* offers fleeting glimpses into the human responses to these dances of death, not enough to substantiate a persuasive theory of spectatorship, but sufficient to at least suggest that among performers and spectators alike, sacrificial dances incited experiences of terror and wonder that were central to the sacred fulfillment of sacrifice.

At the outset of this chapter I suggested that Aztec ritual dances and the representations of them in the *Florentine Codex* perform similar and related "sacrifices of representation." In the *veintena* ceremonies, dancing was an integral component of the willful creation and destruction of *ixiptlas*. Narrating sacrificial rituals required that informants reference dance, even though the text ultimately leaves unexplained the meanings and/or functions of the undecipherable gestures, actions, and movements it describes. That is to say, the text makes no reference to the pattern of imagination or belief that made dancing meaningful to performers or spectators. In that sense, we may say that the *Florentine Codex* sacrifices the meaning of dance. Given the seemingly significant role that dancing played in Aztec sacrificial rites, the lack of explanation about its significance in the manuscript appears as a deliberate act of discursive sacrifice, performed either by Sahagún, his assistants, his informants, or any combination thereof.

It is entirely possible that Sahagún's assistants never asked their informants about the meanings of their dances, given that the chroniclers were primarily interested in gathering descriptions of idolatrous behaviors so that they could recognize if and when Indians continued to perform them. It is also plausible that the assistants asked about the cosmological significance of the rituals and that the informants answered, but that Sahagún redacted their explanations in a compromising gesture that honored the prohibitions that the Crown had imposed regarding the documentation of indigenous belief systems and practices. As we have seen, Sahagún had a tendency to withhold names and descriptions of dances from his Spanish translations of the informants' testimony. Moreover, the encyclopedic structuring of information within the *Florentine Codex* leaves little space for representing the experience of performers and spectators. Another possibility is that the assistants asked about the significance and/or functions of their dances, yet the informants curtailed their responses in an act of deliberate or unintentional defiance. It is easy to imagine that the informants would have been careful not to implicate themselves too deeply in the esoteric knowledge of their ancestors.

These are all plausible and practical explanations for the "sacrifice of representation" in the *Florentine Codex*. However, rather than regarding the absence of explanation as an obstruction to understanding the significance of Aztec ritual dance, it is worth contemplating that the absence of explanation is itself meaningful to an understanding of the significance of dance, as well as to an understanding of the representations of dance in the *Florentine Codex*. To make appear what is essentially not there—or what may have been made to disappear—brings us to the topic of magic.

Sir James Frazer's theories of magic profoundly shaped twentieth-century perceptions of "primitive dance." In his influential comparative study of ancient rites and myths, *The Golden Bough* (1890), he puts forth his theory about the role of "imitative magic" in primitive worlds, including its role in dance. Frazer contends that primitive dances can be classified by two types of magic. The first form he calls "sympathetic magic," which describes when "the magician infers that he can produce any effect he desires merely by imitating it" ("like produces like" or "effect resembles its cause"). The second he calls "contagious magic," which is when "the magician infers [that] whatever he does to a material object will affect equally the person with whom the object was once in contact, whether it formed part of his body or not."[146] Working with a variety of sources from myth, folklore, and nineteenth-century ethnography, Frazer describes the "magic of dance" in cultures across time and place. He emphasizes the magical quality of dances in ancient Greece, including those mentioned in Homer's *Iliad*, such as Ariadne's Dance (or the "Game of Troy"), wherein youths and maidens imitated the paths of a labyrinth. He questions:

> May not, then, Ariadne's dance have been an imitation of the sun's course in the sky? And may not its intention have been, by sympathetic magic to aid the great luminary to run his race on high? We have seen that during an eclipse of the sun the Chilcotin Indians walk in a circle, leaning on staves, apparently to assist the laboring orb. In Egypt also the king, who embodied the sun-god, seems to have solemnly walked round the walls of a temple for the sake of helping the sun on his way. If there is any truth in this conjecture, it would seem to follow that the sinuous lines of the labyrinth which the dancers followed in their evolutions may have represented the ecliptic, the sun's apparent annual path in the sky.[147]

Frazer wrote a chapter about Aztec rituals of human sacrifice based largely on the *Florentine Codex*, although he did not write specifically about the role of dancing within them. However, the questions he posed about the relationship between magic and dance within other "primitive" societies are relevant to Aztec ritual dances, which similarly demonstrate the desire to insert human agency into the workings of the supernatural and physical worlds. The Chilcotin Indians, of whom Frazer writes, "walk in a circle, leaning on staves" in a manner that recalls the dance of Huixtociuatl, who danced with her staff while "marking rhythm." Both of these celestial timekeepers metered the orbit of the sun. His reference to the Egyptian king's walk around the temple similarly recalls the myriad references to Aztec priests who processed around temples and altars to consecrate spaces for sacred sacrifices. And Ariade's dance, too, seems to resemble the dance of Nauholin, the "Messenger of the Sun," whose pathway along the temple's stairs was not merely a reflection of the sun's orbit, but a guide for the sun's trajectory in the cosmos. This is to say nothing of the myriad rain dances, war dances, and hunting dances described in the *Florentine Codex* that attempt to create rains, victories, and successful hunts through the art of sympathetic magic.

Aztec ritual also involved dances that Frazer would have characterized as "contagious magic." For example, during the festival of Atlcaualo ("The Ceasing of Water"), priests performed dances to terrorize the child *ixiptlas* of Tlaloc, the god of rain, forcing them to spill tears and so bring the rains. Certainly, the dance of the *temacpalitoti* also meets Frazer's criteria of contagious magic: When the thief dances with the arm of a *cihuateotl*, he reanimates the power the limb had accrued during the pregnant woman's confrontation with death. In turn, that power was used to paralyze enemies on the battlefield as well as unsuspecting merchants. Thus, dancing was a means to transmit death's contagiousness from the pregnant woman's body to that of the thief, and in turn, to unsuspecting merchants or warriors on the battlefield who were immobilized by the power contained in the limbs of the *cihuateteo*. A similar contagious circuitry of power animates the dance performed during the Feast of the Flaying of Men, when ceremonial priests danced in the skins and with the severed heads of the *xipemes* following their spectacular defeat in gladiatorial battles with warriors. In their choreographed confrontations with death, the bodies of the *ixiptla* accrued and then disseminated power.

Frazer's notion of magical dance offers a compelling explanation for several Aztec choreographies. Almost all of the *ixiptla* dances produced physical or social transformations through acts of imitation, association, or contact. However, less persuasive is the significance Frazer attaches to societies that perform "magical dancing." In fact, many of Frazer's ideas have been rejected outright, mostly because they were meant to support a broader evolutionary argument about the primitive mind. For Frazer, magic was practiced by those with "crude intelligence not only of the savage, but of ignorant and dull-witted people everywhere."[148] A "spurious system of natural law," magic was never performed by "conscious agents," but instead by those who could not reflect "on the abstract principles involved in [their] actions."[149] For Frazer, magical dancing was a sign of the moral and intellectual inferiority of the "primitive" humans compared to the individual of science or religion. Thus, as Frazer crudely puts it, the primitive magician, and the primitive dancer by extension, performs his magic in a state of ignorance, "just as he digests his food in complete ignorance of the intellectual and physiological processes which are essential to one operation and the other."[150]

Frazer alludes to the *Florentine Codex* throughout his *Golden Bough*, even though he did not specifically write about the *veintena* dances. His opinion that primitive dance was an act of "ignorance" may have been partially based on the fact the Sahagún's work does not provide any rationale, explanation, or interpretation of the dances it describes. I would suggest, however, that there is a far more complex relationship between dancing and knowing in the *Florentine Codex* than Frazer admits, which becomes evident especially when we consider the function of these dances within the broader context of sacrificial ritual.

In *Violence and the Sacred*, René Girard posits a theory of sacrifice that helps to explain the meaning of magical dancing in Aztec ritual and the lack of explanation for it in the *Florentine Codex*. For Girard, violence is the "secret soul of the sacred" that ritual sacrifice helps to keep.[151] Without ritual sacrifice, violence born from human antagonism would overwhelm human relations. Thus, ritual sacrifice is a necessary means for mediating relations between men as well as between men and their gods, often by reenacting an "original" violent episode around which a culture organizes its identity and by using sacrificial surrogates—objects, animals, human victims—to represent that which was originally sacrificed in formative scenes of religious terror. This "sacrificial substitution" must perform the difficult task of creating a resemblance between that which is sacrificed (the sacrificial object or victim) and its referent while simultaneously concealing the process as an act of mimesis, or what Girard calls an "act of transference."[152] The act of transference must be maintained as an illusion that keeps secret the violence that is at its core: "Celebrants do not and must not comprehend the true role of the sacrificial act."[153] Thus, for Girard, imitation transforms otherwise criminal acts into sacred ones.

Like Frazer, Girard referenced Aztec rituals of human sacrifice, yet he never made a concerted effort to test his theory against actual Aztec ritual practices. Instead, he primarily developed his idea about violence and the sacred based on Judeo-Christian myth and ritual and secondarily on ethnographic literature from Africa. That said, his theory of sacred violence illuminates some aspects of Aztec ritual. In Aztec rituals of sacrifice, *ixiptlas* were "substitutes" par excellence. They were "representations," "surrogates," or "imitations" that were created for no other reason than to be sacrificed. Following Girard, we can say that *ixiptlas* mediated relations between humankind and their gods, for not only were *ixiptlas* representations of gods, but they were also sacrificed in their honor. *Ixiptlas* also mediated relations between humans, especially in the sense that the entire Aztec social body had a role in the process of their creation and destruction. Dancing had an important role in almost every stage of that process: from the selection of slaves, to the performances of terror, to the distribution and display of body parts. Dancing was a means of achieving the many necessary "acts of transference" that effectively blurred the distinction between victims and gods, and by extension, between social terror and sacred violence. Dancing was a means for marshaling the sacred terror in service of maintaining social order. The episodes of choreographed violence in the *veintena* ceremonies powered and legitimized social identities and ideals, especially regarding the masculine sphere of the battlefield and the feminine domain of sexuality and reproduction.

While Frazer claims that "magical" dances reflect the "primitive" human's ignorance and inability to think abstractly, Girard asks us to imagine that such acts of confusing and violent imitation were meant to strategically produce states of confusion, terror, and wonder among its performers and spectators. If, as Girard suggests, violence was the secret soul of the sacred, then dancing was the means by which the secret was both revealed and concealed. In fact, there are a few significant descriptions of subjective experiences within *veintena* rituals that alert us to the possibility that sacred rituals were illusions for social violence. Interestingly, these responses to ritual emerge in the context of dance. For example, in the *Florentine Codex*'s account of the Feast of the Flaying of Men, when enemy guests left Tenochtitlan in a state of stupor after having witnessed a cautionary performance of sacrifice, the informants made certain to tell us that "There was witnessing, there was wonder."[154] Similarly, during the festival of Tititl, the Ilamatecuhtli *ixiptla* goes about dancing and crying to express her "anguish" over her impending death. In their account of the "hand-waving dance" in the festival of Ochpaniztli, the informants stress that mothers of warriors experienced anticipatory mourning for their sons while watching dancers. What is significant about these responses to dancing is that they are not necessarily responses to the divine. Instead, they are human reactions to very real threats of physical violence, which minimally suggests that performers and spectators were aware that choreography was a technique for acting out the unspeakable secret that the Aztec social order was maintained through violence.

The brief references to the subjective experiences in these episodes of choreographic violence not only suggest that dance was central to the sacred fulfillment of sacrifice, but also give us a clue regarding the discoursing of violence in the *Florentine Codex*. According to Girard, there is a contagiousness between rituals of violence and their textual representations: "The narrative [of sacred violence] itself, then, might be said to partake of a sacrificial quality; it claims to reveal one act of substitution while employing this first substitution to half-conceal another."[155] Girard illustrates this point with the biblical story of Isaac. Nearing death, Isaac, a blind man, orders his elder son, Esau, to sacrifice venison in exchange for his final blessing. Jacob, Isaac's younger son, overhears his father's request and decides to offer a sacrifice to his father before his brother has the chance to make his own. Ultimately, Jacob tricks his blind father into giving him his blessing by offering a sacrifice in the form of lamb while wearing the lamb's skin, hoping that if his father were to touch him, Isaac would mistake Jacob for his more hirsute brother Esau. Girard emphasizes that there are two related substitutions at play in this narrative: the substitution of brother for brother and the substitution of animal for man.

Girard also insists that narratives of sacrifice reveal an awareness of the sacrifice as an illusion or deception: "The narrative does not refer directly to the strange deception, nor does it allow this deception to pass entirely unnoticed."[156] Indeed, the narrative offers a "fleeting, sidelong glimpse into the process" by which the deception is conceived and executed. In the narrative of Isaac and his sons, the reader is made privy to the substitution as deception through Jacob's plot to mask himself. In fact, we even learn that Jacob's mother, Rebekah, participated in his act of substitution. Rebekah not only had slaughtered the kids that Jacob offered to his father, but she also suggested that Jacob disguise himself in the lamb's skin when presenting the savory dish, which she also prepared. The emplotment of Jacob's deception within the narrative of sacrifice ensures that we receive a "fleeting, sidelong glimpse into the process" of substitution.

The *Florentine Codex*'s accounts of sacrificial dance abide by a similar discursive logic. Just as the Bible exposes Jacob and Rebekah's plan to deceive Isaac with the sacrificial lamb, the *Florentine Codex* exposes a "fleeting, sidelong glimpse into the process" by which *ixiptlas* were methodically prepared and offered as sacrificial substitutes to deceive its spectators. To ensure that such acts of substitution did not "pass entirely unnoticed," the *Florentine Codex* embeds performers' and spectators' responses to sacrificial dances. The references to bewildered enemy warriors, to "dancing and crying" women victims, and to mourning mothers of warriors indicate that neither performers nor spectators were entirely tricked by the magic of dance.

Whether as a result of Sahagún's editing process, his assistants' interview techniques, the reticence of the informants, or some combination thereof, the *Florentine Codex* superficially withholds the secret of dance's significance to sacrifice. However, the absence of explanation might not necessarily mean that dancing was always or only an act of magic, as Frazer would have us believe. Instead, the absence of explanation might suggest the degree to which the meanings and functions of Aztec ritual dance were protected, either by a Franciscan friar whose mission was to erase the meaning of the "ancient rites" or by indigenous nobles who could not or chose not to reveal their ritual knowledge, but whose descriptions of those very dances alert us to the complex modes of knowing they instantiated. In that sense, we may say that Aztec dancers were sacrificial lambs—not only within the *veintena* ceremonies but also as subjects within the text of the *Florentine Codex*. The dancing body was an instrument with which the Aztec negotiated the sacred and secular worlds, and representations of dancers in the *Florentine Codex* were bodies of knowledge through which indigenous informants both revealed and concealed the secrets of the Aztec world in their testimony to the agents of the burgeoning empire of New Spain.

Four
dances of death

THE MASSACRE AT THE FESTIVAL OF TOXCATL

Huitzilopochtli ("Hummingbird from the South") was the Mexica god of the sun and war. Conceived immaculately by his mother, Coatlicue ("The One with the Skirt of Serpents"), Huitzilopochtli was deified over the course of several hundred years, a history that parallels the imperial rise of the Mexica culture itself. Huitzilopochtli guided the Mexica on their mythic migration from their fabled homeland of Aztlán ("The Place of Whiteness") to their arrival in Tenochtitlan in 1325. Wherever Huitzilopochtli established temporary residence on this journey, his followers erected a temple in his honor. He once led the Mexica to the site of his birth, "Snake Mountain," and there he built a ball court, a skull rack, and a gorge, and then danced and sang to celebrate his return to his birthplace.[1] But when his subjects challenged him, he unflinchingly destroyed it all and led them to new locales.

Finally they settled in Tenochtitlan, where they erected the Templo Mayor and dedicated one of its crowning temples to Huitzilopochtli. The Mexica paid their debt to their patron god during several of its eighteen annual rituals, especially the festival of Toxcatl, the fifth month of the Mexica calendar (a period spanning late April and May). Toxcatl fell during the precarious time between the dry season and the rainy season. In fact, Toxcatl means "dry thing," and most ceremonies performed during this *veintena* were supplications for rain. Whereas the first ten days of the month were dedicated to Tezcatlipoca, the trickster god, the final ten days of Toxcatl focused on rites dedicated to Huitzilopochtli. The *Florentine Codex* describes a series of intense ritual choreographies unique to this final stage of ceremony and provides more information about the variety of dances and processions associated with Toxcatl than it does for any other of the eighteen rituals.[2]

The rites began with the Mexica making an anthropomorphic figure of Huitzilopochtli from amaranth seed dough, which they dressed in a "sleeveless jacket painted with representations of human limbs with severed heads, the palms of hands, hip bones, ribs, tibias, lower arm bones, footprints," a netted cape, and a headdress of feathers. Mexica youth and their masters went dancing and singing in procession with the figure, carrying it between temples, perhaps to reenact the many migrations that Huitzilopochtli had helmed. They raised the figure onto a platform and began to sling arrows at it. Then Montezuma initiated another rite by squeezing the head off of a quail and throwing its decapitated body at the Huitzilopochtli figure. Soon all the commoners joined in, throwing their feathered offering amid what must have been a spectacle of blood, feather, and sound.

They followed this with offerings of fire and incense, letting smoke and flame set the stage for some of the fiercest Mexica choreographies. The masters of youth began "in the fashion of women" by dancing "the Toxcatl Leap" (*toxcachocholoa*) a choreography specific to this festival. To the beats of drums, turtle shells, and gourd rattles, a priest and the masters of the youth leapt in a circle surrounding an inner circle of seated women holding each other's hands. The women painted their faces, pasted themselves with red feathers, and carried canes with paper streamers. Then, all the men danced the serpent dance (*mococoloa*): "They went from side to side, they met one another face to face, they went holding one another's hands as they danced." As the men linked together and coiled around the plaza, young maidens went mingling between them, performing the "popcorn dance" (*momomochiitotia*). They resembled stalks of maize and danced around like corn kernels toasting and exploding in the heat and friction of the ceremony. Following this dance, they joined the men to perform a dance called the "Kiss of Huitzilopochtli," about which we know nothing but for the fact that all the coiling, winding, and popping must have created serious sexual tension. Men were closely watched to make sure no woman's honor was compromised. Those who misbehaved were violently punished in public: "They dragged them; they kicked them; they stepped on them."

They danced into the night and immediately again the next morning in preparation for the festival's final rite: the sacrifice of Ixteucale, an *ixiptla* of Huitzilopochtli. A human version of the dough figure, Ixteucale was smeared with black resin ("smoke from the mirror") and adorned with clothes made of paper, eagle feathers, a mesh cape, a maniple of animal skin, and bells fastened to his legs. Ixteucale led yet another performance of the serpent dance until he decided it was time to sacrifice his life to Huitzilopochtli. At a moment of his choosing, he surrendered, yielding himself to the priests, who then stretched his body across a sacrificial stone, cut into his chest, extracted his heart, and held it up as an offering to the sun. They beheaded his corpse and strung his skull on the *tzompantli*, a rack designed for displaying skulls—some human, others made of stone. At the moment of sacrifice, priests went among the spectators to cut the skin of their stomachs, breasts, and arms, most likely in a gesture of solidarity.

This bloodletting rite had an ironic and tragic outcome when it was performed at the ceremony of Toxcatl on May 16, 1520. By that time, Spanish conquistadors had occupied the Mexica capital of Tenochtitlan for several months, and on that fateful date nearly a hundred of them allegedly stormed the sacred patio of the Templo Mayor and initiated an attack on the unsuspecting celebrants. The chronicles of the conquest of Mexico are replete with visual and written descriptions of the ensuing violence that the Spanish enacted on the Mexica dancers, musicians, and spectators. They describe how Spanish soldiers surrounded the sacred patio and began to murder the celebrants, dismembering dancers as if they were the ears of corn they meant to honor and stopping the rhythm kept by the *huehuetl* and *teponaztli* drums by chopping off the drummers' hands. The Spanish then chased and hunted down the thousands of Mexica nobles who had been watching this most important ritual and filled the temple patio with their blood, guts, and gore. Several sources describe how the Spaniards then divested the Mexica corpses of jewelry of precious metals and stones. Those who escaped the sword tried to hide or feign death, but no one, the sources insist, was safe. This particular performance of the Toxcatl ceremony concluded not with a carefully choreographed sacrifice of an *ixiptla* or ceremonial bloodletting, but with a bloodbath drawn by the Spanish sword.

No other dance in human history has set into motion events that have had such devastating and enduring historical and cultural consequences. The Massacre at the Festival of Toxcatl, as this violent episode has come to be known, figures prominently in virtually all histories of the conquest of Mexico as one of its most defining moments. The massacre precipitated a fifteen-month physical conflict between Spaniards and the Mexica for control of the largest and wealthiest indigenous empire in the New World. Although the conquistadors had already encountered, massacred, and in some cases allied themselves with indigenous rivals of the Mexica en route to Tenochtitlan, sixteenth-century writers often memorialize this particular encroachment on Mexica dancers and musicians as a turning point in the larger narrative of the conquest of Mexico, which is worth summarizing here so as to contextualize its significance.

In February 1519, Spanish explorer-turned-conquistador Hernán Cortés departed Cuba for Mexico with a small army, an enterprise originally sanctioned then later condemned by Diego Velázquez de Cuéllar (ca. 1465–1524), governor of Cuba and protector of the Castilian empire's interests in the New World. Cortés ostensibly set out on a trade expedition, but was primarily lured by tales of limitless Mexican wealth, land, and labor. With an army of several hundred men and sixteen horses, Cortés initially landed on Mexico's Yucután Peninsula, where he sought out and eventually found Gerónimo de Aguilar, a Spaniard who had been marooned during a prior expedition. Soon thereafter, Cortés defeated a local native community and was given as tribute a young indigenous female slave who spoke the indigenous languages of Maya and Nahuatl. Her name was Malintzin (ca. 1501–1550), though she later became known as "Doña Marina" or "La Malinche." Cortés made her his interpreter and advisor, and later his mistress. With Aguilar (who spoke Spanish and a Maya language) and Malintzin (who spoke a Maya language and Nahuatl), Cortés created a linguistic chain that allowed him to communicate in Nahuatl, the predominant language of the Aztec empire.

Armed with his interpreters, Cortés and his army both pillaged and allied indigenous cities, such as Tlaxcala, whose people had endured constant threats from the powerful Mexica. The Spaniards and Tlaxcalans joined forces, with the shared goal of making the Mexicas' wealth and power their own. The Tlaxcalans helped steer Cortés's expedition inland toward Tenochtitlan in hopes of meeting its infamous ruler Montezuma, a fierce conqueror himself. Cortés and Montezuma first began to communicate through messengers, but on November 8, 1519, the two men and their armies met in person at one of the causeway entrances to Tenochtitlan. Many accounts claim that at this meeting, Montezuma invited Cortés and his army into the city and willingly subordinated himself to the Spaniards in a gesture of defeat, an act of disillusionment, or perhaps a calculated step to disarm the stranger. For over six months, Cortés ruled Tenochtitlan through Montezuma. The Spaniards lived within the city, experiencing the inner rhythms of its temples, marketplaces, palaces, and rituals.

In late April 1520, Cortés learned that Pánfilo de Narváez (ca. 1478–1528) had arrived on the eastern shores of Mexico with orders from Velázquez to bring him back. Cortés left Tenochtitlan for the seacoast to fight off Narváez and entrusted Pedro de Alvarado (ca. 1486–1541), one of his captains, with the command of a hundred Spanish soldiers and native allies, who stayed in Tenochtitlan to guard Montezuma and his treasures.[3] During Cortés's absence, Alvarado suspected that Mexica warriors were gathering under the pretense of celebrating the Toxcatl ceremony—a ceremony Cortés ostensibly had authorized before his departure—but in fact were organizing a rebellion against the Spaniards to liberate Montezuma. Alvarado acted upon this perceived threat by attacking the Mexica at the height of the festival and slaughtering the warriors and nobles who were among the performers and spectators. The attack incited Mexica retaliation, which raged for weeks. Mexica warriors surrounded the palace of Axacáyatl, where the Spaniards sought refuge and had been holding Montezuma hostage.

Upon hearing of the massacre, Cortés left the coast for the besieged Tenochtitlan, arriving on or about June 20, 1520, to find a city in revolt.[4] For ten days, Cortés implored Montezuma to command his enraged warriors to stop their retaliation. Montezuma addressed his subjects from the palace rooftop, where he was killed in a manner that remains a mystery. After spending days hidden in the palace, the Spaniards devised a plot to escape Tenochtitlan. On June 30, 1520, the Spaniards attempted to flee during the night without arousing the attention of the Mexica warriors but were sighted. The Mexica subsequently chased Cortés and his troops, many of whom were killed upon leaving the city. Most drowned in the city's canals, weighed down by the treasures they had stolen from Montezuma's palace. That night has come to be known as the *Noche Triste*, or the "Sad Night."

The Spaniards who survived the bloody exodus retreated to areas outside the city, where for several months they waited for the wounds to heal and built brigantines, all in preparation for reconquering Tenochtitlan and retrieving the treasures they had reluctantly left behind. Meanwhile, in Tenochtitlan, the Mexica suffered an epidemic of smallpox introduced by the Spaniards, which claimed countless lives. In January 1521, the Spaniards and their allies attempted to reconquer the embattled and disease-ridden city. Following the brief reign of Montezuma's brother, Cuitlahuac, Cuauhtémoc (ca. 1495–1522), a cousin of Montezuma, had become *tlatoani* and taken over the leadership of the Mexica. However, the Spanish swiftly captured him during his attempt to escape their return. Cuauhtémoc surrendered the empire to Cortés on August 13, 1521, whereupon the conquistadors razed the Mexica temples, houses, palaces, and markets.

One of the first historians of the conquest of Mexico, Francisco López de Gómara, described the conquest as "the greatest event since the creation of the world, excepting the Incarnation and Death of Him who created it."[5] A historian who never set foot in the New World, Gómara was amazed that a few hundred Spaniard soldiers were able to conquer one of the world's largest civilizations in under two years. Whether or not the conquest is the "greatest," it is certainly one of the most revised. The historiography of the conquest—the *history of the history* of the conquest—has also been subject to multiple revisions. In the nearly five hundred years since that "greatest event" took place, it has been recorded in the chronicles of "eyewitnesses," manipulated into a cautionary tale of Spanish cruelty within the "Black Legends" disseminated by Northern Europeans, and used as fuel for the dramatic epics of nineteenth-century historians, in addition to inspiring emerging discourses of *indigenismo* during Mexico's eras of revolution and independence.

In the past thirty years, the field of Latin American colonial history has encouraged yet another revision by taking a linguistic turn and exerting critical energy on the discursive dimensions of colonial sources. This has meant looking at the "greatest event" as a series of discursive events, each with its own claims to authority, narrative idiosyncrasies, and symbolic logics. In describing the discursive dimension of historical narratives, Hayden White explains that "events are *made* into a story by the suppression or subordination of certain [story elements] and the highlighting of others, by characterization, motif representation, variation of tone and point of view, alternative descriptive strategies, and the like—in short, all of the techniques we would expect to find in the emplotment of a novel or a play."[6]

In his foundational study on the writings of the New World, Stephen Greenblatt goes even further, by characterizing many explorers and conquerors as "frequent and cunning liars" whose flagrant distortions of reality make it difficult to parse fact from fiction.[7] Similarly, Inga Clendinnen points to the "story-making predilection" of the Spanish sources of the conquest accounts and posits that by attending to the necessarily "fictive" dimensions of conquest narratives, "it might be possible, with patience and time, to clear some of the drifting veils of myth and mistake that envelop the encounters of the first phase, or at least to chart our areas of ignorance more narrowly."[8]

In this chapter I apply my own "patience and time" to clearing the "drifting veils of myth" enshrouding one of the "greatest events" in the history of the conquest: the Massacre at the Festival of Toxcatl. Throughout the sixteenth century there was a proliferation of visual and written representations of the massacre by conquistadors, royal and mestizo chroniclers, missionaries, and natives that present both competing and complementary visions of it. Most of these accounts were written many years after the massacre; only one was written by an actual eyewitness. Thus we can say that these accounts are replete with willful remembrances, boastful forgettings, hostile corrections, conspiracy theories, and wistful laments about almost every aspect of the massacre—its date and location, the identity and number of Spanish assailants and besieged Mexica performers and spectators, its instigating causes and incontrovertible effects.

Many questions remain unanswered about some of the episode's most basic details. For instance, exactly when and where did the massacre take place? (Some sources say May 6 or 7 whereas others claim that the massacre took place during the final days of Toxcatl, sometime around May 17. Although most reports insist that the massacre occurred in the ceremonial courtyard of the Templo Mayor, some indicate that there were concerted attacks in squares throughout Tenochtitlan.) Was the Toxcatl performed with or without the permission of the Spaniards? (Whereas some reports tell us that Cortés authorized the ceremony on the condition that it was performed without human sacrifice, others suggest that the nobles gathered to perform the dances at the request of Alvarado. Several Spanish sources claim that the Mexica gathered at the Templo Mayor under the pretense of performing the Toxcatl rites but in fact intended to stage a rebellion against the Spaniards during Cortés's leave.) Which dancers did the Spaniards kill? (The dancers of the Toxcatl ceremony, Montezuma's court dancers, or both?) How many performers and spectators were there? (The body count ranges from two to eight thousand.) How many and which Spanish soldiers participated in the siege? (There is no doubt that Alvarado led the massacre, but the sources are curiously reticent about the identity of the Spanish soldiers who participated.)

Further research into the massacre narratives is not likely to yield reliable answers to these questions, but it can at least clarify the questions and bring into relief the stakes in their answers. In the pages that follow I address the bewildering discrepancies between accounts, not necessarily to resolve them, but on the contrary, to illuminate the significance that rests in their contradictions. Thus I approach the massacre less as a "greatest event" in the sense Gómara meant and more as what Fogelson has described as a "nonevent" or an "epitomizing event," which is relayed through "narratives that condense, encapsulate, and dramatize longer-term historical processes." In so doing, I intend to demonstrate Fogelson's contention that "such events are inventions but have such compelling qualities and explanatory power that they spread rapidly through the group and so take on an ethnohistorical reality of their own."[9] By characterizing the massacre as a "nonevent" I mean neither to dismiss nor deny that the massacre occurred. However, that the massacre specifically targeted dancers does not fully explain the significance of the multiple configurations of dance, dancers, and dancing within its various accounts. I contend that sixteenth-century interlocutors were "choreographing history" insofar as they deployed Mexica dancers as a way of organizing, interpreting, and expressing their visions of the massacre and the conquest by extension. Images and descriptions of slain Mexica dancers endow the massacre accounts by both the victors and the vanquished with an "ethnohistorical reality" in that they represent an otherwise unrepresentable violence.

First I examine the accounts of dance in the histories, depositions, and letters of Spanish conquistadors and chroniclers concerning the Toxcatl massacre, which were informed more by economic, political, and religious interests than by actual encounters with dance. I will demonstrate that these chroniclers, inspired by the romances of chivalry, invoke "violent" Aztec dancers in order to memorialize their heroic presence in the New World and to justify the conquest of Tenochtitlan. I then consider the massacre accounts of Bartolomé de las Casas and Diego Durán, two Dominican missionaries in the New World, whose massacre accounts I argue were informed by the *dance of death*, a medieval European literary, artistic, and performance tradition. These missionary accounts stage the conquest as a *dance of death* between two contesting forces: greedy and torturous Spaniards and innocent and noble Indians. In turn, these visions of the conquest inadvertently supported the "Black Legends," Protestant critiques of Spanish imperialism. Finally, I examine the complex configurations of dance in indigenous accounts of the conquest and argue that the principles and practices of human movement give the Toxcatl massacre a "mythistorical" significance. I posit that it is through imagery of the Aztec dancing body that native and mestizo chroniclers situate the European conquest of Mexico within a broader narrative of Aztec world un/making.

"Dancing in a State of Peace":
Spanish Accounts of the Festival of Toxcatl

In 1529 the *audencia* of Mexico, the highest royal tribunal in the viceroyalty of New Spain, leveled thirty-four charges against Pedro de Alvarado. These ranged from petty accusations (such as a complaint that in his youth Alvarado had worn the robe of the Order of Santiago that belonged to his father) to explosive indictments (such as the charge that he withheld from the Crown its rightful "royal fifth" of the money and jewels he had purloined from his various exploits).

One of the charges explicitly accused Alvarado of crimes connected to the Massacre at the Festival of Toxcatl (app. H). The *audencia* reasoned that Alvarado's attack on the Mexica was an act of insubordination because Cortés had authorized the Mexica to perform the Toxcatl festivities before leaving for the coast to fight Narváez. The charge specifies that "Montezuma asked permission of Cortés to hold certain feasts and dances which his people were accustomed to celebrate at such time of the year and the said Cortés gave the requested permission." The charge then radically broadens from insubordination to murder, a legal turn that pivots on the invocation of dance: "All of which is a charge against Pedro de Alvarado because he killed Indians who were dancing in a state of peace by license of the said Cortés." Of course, the *audencia* was not necessarily concerned with convicting Alvarado for his attack on "peaceful" Mexica dancers. By making the seemingly empathetic yet wildly disingenuous claim that the Mexica were "dancing in a state of peace" the *audencia* hoped to win favor with the Crown by alleging that Alvarado had defiled the chain of military command, exerted unauthorized and senseless force that directly led to a mass murder that collaterally took the lives of countless Spaniards, and disabused the Crown's trust by having both lost and withheld some of its riches.

Royal counselors entertained any witness who would testify against Alvarado so as to bolster the *audencia*'s charges. Of the Spanish soldiers who testified, none claimed to have been present at the Templo Mayor at the time of the massacre, for most of the "witnesses" readily admitted they were not in Tenochtitlan at the time of the event, but at the eastern coast of Mexico with Cortés fighting Narváez. As such, the only direct eyewitness account of the massacre comes from Alvarado himself, whose version of the massacre is reported in his formal response to the *audencia*'s charges (app. I).

Alvarado's response to the *audencia* of Mexico expresses a combination of moral outrage and political contempt. In the same year the *audencia* scripted its charges against him, Alvarado returned to Spain, where he was knighted, given the title "Adelanto," and appointed governor and captain general of Guatemala, where, following his exploits in Mexico, he led conquest and settlement expeditions.[10] Alvarado never denied that he murdered dancers at the Templo Mayor. In fact, he openly admitted to having killed many more Mexica at the palace of Axacayatl, where the Spaniards imprisoned Montezuma. His justification for murder is rooted in his perception that the performance was actually a violent gathering: "since in the *areítos* and dances they gather together a large number of people . . . since it is very usual among them that when they want to perform sacrifices or some harm or evil, they have the aforesaid festivals." He contends that the Mexica gathered under the pretense of celebrating a festival, but in fact were executing a "wicked plan" to kill him and liberate Montezuma.

He corroborates this assertion by saying that the Tlaxcalans, his native allies, explained to him that the Mexica used captured enemies as victims in their rituals of human sacrifice. This is a lesson that the Tlaxcalans knew well, for they had routinely witnessed the Mexica feed the hearts of fallen Tlaxcalan warriors to their bloodthirsty gods. According to his account, Alvarado even rescued one of the captives from certain sacrifice. In turn the captive allegedly confirmed Alvarado's suspicions of a Mexica rebellion. (Alvarado never explains how he communicated with the captive, let alone how a captive slave would have known the intentions of Mexica warriors.) Fueled by such suspicions, Alvarado describes the *areíto* as one of the many "signs" of an imminent Mexica revolt against the Spaniards: the drowning of an Indian servant working for the conquistadors, the readying of stakes to carry the heads of slain Spanish soldiers, and a gilded club hidden beneath Montezuma's bed.

Alvarado's charge and his response embody contradictory perceptions of Aztec dance as either "peaceful" or "violent"—and of the *areíto* as either a sanctioned ceremony or a deceptive insurrection. Below I explore the ways in which these tensions animate six "official" accounts by Spanish conquistadors and royal historians.

The conquistador accounts of the Massacre at the Festival of Toxcatl are memorialized in almost all genres of early colonial discourse. Several massacre narratives are contained within "letters of account" (*cartas de relación*), "the name given to the official report, witnessed and authenticated by a notary, which every royal officer in the Indies was expected to provide of his activities."[11] They also appeared in "proofs of merit and services" (*probanzas de mérito y servicios*), which were "perfunctory, usually disingenuous" documents that conquistadors filed about the services they rendered to the Crown and to God.[12] Spanish soldiers were required to file these reports in order to justify the Crown's continued financing of such expeditions. Most often, they were thinly veiled appeals for land, labor, money, and leadership positions within the young colony. By legitimizing their service to the empire, conquistadors justified their claims to the spoils of the conquest, especially to *encomiendas*—"the official consignment of groups of Indians to privileged Spanish colonists," who benefited from indigenous labor and tribute.[13] Moreover, as God-fearing Christians, the conquistadors had to strategically minimize or justify their involvement in acts of violence, torture, and murder in their self-interested accounts of heroism. In addition to the *relaciones* and *probanzas*, conquistadors testified about the massacre in legal depositions submitted to judicial panels, such as those that bolstered the *audencia*'s charges against Alvarado. Conquistador accounts also appear in the official histories written by royal court historians, who relied on "eyewitness" reports from the field. Through these different forms of discourse, conquistadors engaged in narrative warfare, manipulating their versions of the massacre in attempts to explain or distance themselves from it, and to castigate others for what already had been judged to be one of the major tactical errors of the conquest.

One of the few surviving eyewitness accounts of the massacre is also one of the earliest, related just a few months afterward, in June or July of 1520, perhaps even before the temples and buildings of Tenochtitlan were fully razed. During this time the governor of Cuba, Velázquez, was in Santiago de Cuba mounting a legal case against Cortés, who had recently thwarted Narváez's mission to arrest him on the shores of Mexico. Velázquez intended to seek retribution by putting Cortés up on charges against the Crown. He ultimately submitted to the Council of the Indies a series of charges that included withholding the "royal fifth," waging unjustified wars against Indians, mistreating Narváez, abandoning the coastal settlement he had founded, and condoning cannibalism.

To bolster these claims, Velázquez deposed nine "witnesses," including Juan Álvarez, who had been with Cortés since his arrival in Mexico. Álvarez was in Tenochtitlan at the time of the massacre, but he was among those Spaniards guarding Montezuma at the palace, and therefore not at the scene of the Toxcatl massacre. According to Álvarez, on the eve of the festival, he entered the market to observe the Mexica make their ritual preparations for the Toxcatl ceremony and to look out for potential signs of rebellion against the Christians.[14] There Álvarez witnessed some of the Toxcatl *areítos*. He describes seeing a procession led by two men who were tied by cords to an image of Huitzilopochtli, a description of the festival's choreography that is nearly identical to those of native informants. He claims to have observed Mexica celebrants placing swords and shields on the Huitzilopochtli figure, which he interpreted as a potential sign of aggression. In a defensive maneuver, he captured the two Mexica celebrants, who represented the gods Huitzilopochtli and Tezcatlipoca, and brought them to the palace where Montezuma was imprisoned. According to Álvarez, Pedro de Alvarado interrogated the two celebrants about the *areíto*. When Alvarado could not successfully coerce them into revealing a Mexica plan to rebel against the Spaniards, he tortured them, only to set them free, but not without having threatened to kill them in the near future.

Juan Álvarez next contends that Francisco Álvarez, "an authority among the Christians," insisted that Alvarado make a preemptive strike against the Mexica—a suggestion that Alvarado acted upon by ambushing the performers and spectators at the Templo Mayor. Although Álvarez makes it clear that he did not participate in the massacre, he claims to have witnessed its immediate aftermath. He explains that while he was collecting food for the Spaniards, he saw Alvarado and other Spanish soldiers chased by visibly wounded Mexica warriors from the Templo Mayor toward the palace. He reports that the Spaniards secured themselves within the palace, thinking they were safe because they believed they had killed almost all of the Mexica—two or three thousand of them, in Alvarado's estimation. But Alvarado observed armed Mexica arriving at the palace. They surrounded the palace and attempted to infiltrate it in order to seek revenge. At that point, Alvarado brought Montezuma onto the roof, pulled out a knife and threatened to kill their beloved ruler. According to Álvarez, the standoff between Spaniards and Mexica endured until Cortés returned to Tenochtitlan.

There is little in Álvarez's testimony that would have bolstered Velázquez's charges against Cortés, except perhaps the subtle suggestion that Alvarado was the true military mastermind of the conquest: "He who commits the first act, prevails," shouted Alvarado to Álvarez while fleeing from the massacre. What is relatively unique about Álvarez's testimony among Spanish accounts of the massacre is his description of a torture scene involving Alvarado and the two Mexica celebrants. Álvarez portrays Alvarado as frustrated, and perhaps even paranoid about the meaning of the *areítos* and "about why they partake in such merriment." Alvarado individually interrogated these two dancers about the performance, but when he could not elicit a satisfying response about the meaning of their *areíto*, he tortured them. As with many other encounters with dance in the New World, here Alvarado's anxiety about the dance's meanings drove him to violence.

Conquistador Bernardino Vázquez de Tapia reports on a similar torture scene in his testimony about the massacre that formed part of the 1529 hearings by the *audencia* of Mexico designed to incriminate Pedro de Alvarado.[15] Compared to Álvarez, Vázquez de Tapia was decidedly more critical of Alvarado—no doubt a position he developed in the intervening decade between the massacre and the time he gave his testimony, during which he was involved in an ongoing financial dispute with both Cortés and Alvarado.[16] Vázquez de Tapia was a staunch ally of Cortés, and his testimony reflects his partiality. For example, in his formal response to the charges leveled by the *audencia*, Alvarado claims he rescued two captives from certain sacrifice, presumably referring to the two celebrants in Álvarez's account. Vázquez de Tapia details how Alvarado tortured them with burning logs in order to coerce them into revealing their alleged intentions to kill the Spaniards. Vázquez de Tapia goes farther than Álvarez in describing Alvarado's cruelty by claiming that Alvarado tortured the native celebrants, then threw their bodies from the roof of the palace. With this detail, Vázquez de Tapia seems to make an ironic twist on a Mexica ritual practice wherein priests ceremonially cast the corpses of sacrificial victims from the top of the Templo Mayor. In his account, Vázquez de Tapia claims that the Spaniards threw the bodies of the captive *ixiptlas* from the top of the palace. Thus, these *ixiptlas* fulfilled their ritual destiny, albeit via the choreography of Spanish warfare and not that of Mexica ritual.

Vázquez de Tapia compounds the theatricality of Spanish warfare in his description of the actual massacre. He claims that the Spaniards attacked the Mexica on two fronts: those who fought three thousand ritual celebrants in the temple courtyard and those who killed four hundred members of Montezuma's court at the palace of Axayácatl. Vázquez de Tapia's testimony is ambiguous as to whether he was among the soldiers with Alvarado at the temple or among those who safeguarded Montezuma and his nobles at the palace. To confuse matters further, his testimony suggests that he was at both places at the same time. Based on the level of detail he provides about the massacre, it seems that Vázquez de Tapia witnessed the massacre. He describes how when Alvarado arrived at the temple of Huitzilopochtli with his soldiers, he came upon a dance with "three to four hundred Indians, all lords, connected by the hands and more than two or three thousand seated to watch." His attention then abruptly turns to Alvarado's own choreography of violence and to the immobilizing response of Mexica dancers in turn: "Although they saw Pedro de Alvarado and his armed soldiers, none of the Indians made a movement. They stayed still as Alvarado surrounded them, placing ten men at each gate to the courtyard. Then they closed in on the dancers, attacking them and shouting, "Die!" Vázquez de Tapia implicitly dramatizes Alvarado's role in the massacre by depicting him as a dramaturgical warrior who conquered by manipulating the symbols, settings, and actions of Mexica ritual. He concludes his testimony with a final "verdict"—that Alvarado "was the cause of the violence."

The most popular sources for the history of the conquest of Mexico are the *relaciones* of Hernán Cortés.[17] Between 1519 and 1526, Cortés wrote six letters to the Spanish king about his discoveries and conquests in the New World, all of which were published soon after they had reached Spain. Through his second letter to the king—dated October 30, 1520, several months after the massacre—we get a different perspective on the events. Cortés makes no specific mention of the massacre itself, but his omission speaks volumes. Cortés's *relación* had to legitimate his use of force, so he may have chosen to omit the information of an alleged festival and the alleged permission he gave Montezuma to conduct the festival so as to avoid having to explain the circumstances that led to the resulting massacre. He may have just as easily decided that the fact that Indians were dancing at the time of the attack was an irrelevant detail or one that would depict his soldiers as unnecessarily violent and thus raise doubts about his own leadership. It is hard to imagine that Cortés was unaware of the story of the festival, given that many accounts report an alleged conversation between Cortés and Montezuma before his departure from Tenochtitlan, as well as a conversation between Cortés and Alvarado upon his return.

Cortés's omission transformed speculation about the massacre into outright doubt, especially for Gonzalo Fernández de Oviedo y Valdés. As we have seen, from 1532 to 1557 Oviedo served as the official royal chronicler of the Indies for the king of Spain and Holy Roman emperor Charles V. In that role he had access to all official reports and met almost every major figure in the conquest of the New World, as during trips to and from Europe these men invariably stopped on the island of Hispaniola, where he was stationed. On September 8, 1544, years after completing his *General and Natural History* (1535), Oviedo met and interviewed Juan Cano de Saavedra, the Spanish-born conquistador who was a member of Narváez's May 1520 expedition to Mexico to arrest Cortés, but who changed allegiances and subsequently fought alongside Cortés in the conquest of Tenochtitlan. For his participation in the conquest, Cortés gifted Cano one of Montezuma's daughters, Doña Isabel, whom he married and thereby became Montezuma's son-in-law. A covert indictment of Cortés, Oviedo's interview with Cano covers topics such as the legitimacy of his marriage, the story about Montezuma's death, and the rationale behind the massacre.[18]

The question Oviedo poses to Cano about the massacre reveals the historian's distrust of earlier accounts, perhaps even those of Álvarez and Vázquez and certainly that of Cortés, which had been published years prior. Oviedo frames the interview as a search for the "truth" about the massacre, distinguishing himself as a historian and distancing his account from those of the conquistadors. Oviedo asks: "Your Grace, Señor Juan Cano, tell me: why did the Indians of Mexico rise up as soon as Hernán Cortés left that city to find Pánfilo de Narváez, and left Montezuma as a prisoner in the power of Pedro de Alvarado? I have heard much about these things, and I would like to write the truth, may God save my soul."[19]

Cano's response starts with a disclaimer that the "truth" of the massacre is beyond knowing: "Few who dwell on the earth will be able to explain, although the matter was most notorious and the injustice done to the Indians obvious."[20] Cano contributes to the doubt surrounding early Spanish reports when, speaking of another massacre, he admits that stories had been circulated by people who "either did not see [what happened], or know the truth, or wanted to conceal it."[21] As a member of the Narváez expedition that came to imprison Cortés, Cano was not present at the massacre but rather was fighting on the coast, so his version of events, too, was based on hearsay. However, his account brought an important element to the thickening Spanish discourse about the massacre: the Aztec dancer as fetishized object.

One of the enduring explanations given by Cano for Alvarado's decision to strike the dancers is his lust for the riches displayed on the dancers' bodies: "Six hundred Indians, all of them lords, naked, and adorned with much gold jewelry, beautiful plumes and precious stones, men as handsomely adorned and gallant."[22] As such, Cano claims that Alvarado, "impelled by greed" and not self-defense, attacked the dancers "at the precise moment when they were most absorbed in their rejoicing" and proceeded to strip their bodies of the jewels, stones, and precious metals with which they were adorned.[23] Cano summons the image of Alvarado divesting precious objects from the corpses of Mexica dancers to symbolize Alvarado's greed for native lands and wealth.

Moreover, Cano condemns Alvarado's attack, stressing that Spaniards were at "no risk" while the Mexica, "bearing neither offensive nor defensive weapons, danced and sang and celebrated their *areíto* and festival according to their custom."[24] Cano further dramatized the horror of the attack by intensifying images of space and time: Alvarado's men blocked the entrances to the patio where the dance was held, "not pardoning even one." All this, Cano notes, occurred in under an hour. He then justifies the armed resistance of the Mexica, who retaliated with "more than enough cause" in response to this abuse of trust.[25]

Like Oviedo, Gómara was suspicious of early accounts of the massacre. Gómara was Cortés's secretary and biographer, and as such wrote a history of the conquest that accentuates Cortés's heroism. His *History of the Indies* (*Historia de las Indias*) was first published in 1552 and was among the first of the conquest histories to have a significant readership in Spain. As discussed in chapter 1, it was based on a variety of sources, including Cortés's *relaciones*, the author's talks with Andrés de Tapia, a captain among Cortés's soldiers, and Motolinía's *Memoriales*.[26]

Gómara's relatively lengthy account of the massacre indirectly exalts Cortés's ability as a leader by linking the massacre to Cortés's absence. To clear Cortés of any association with the massacre, Gómara places the blame on Alvarado. His near panegyric descriptions of Aztec dance serve to dramatize Alvarado's failings and in the process herald Cortés's leadership.

> Any one of these things could have caused the rebellion, let alone all of them together; but the principal one was this: A few days after Cortés had left to encounter Narváez, there was a solemn festival, which the Mexicans wished to celebrate in their traditional fashion. They begged Pedro de Alvarado (who had stayed behind to act as warden and Cortés's lieutenant) to give his permission, so that he would not think they were gathering to massacre the Spaniards. Alvarado consented, with the proviso that they were not to kill men in sacrifice or bear arms. More than six hundred (some say more than a thousand) gentlemen, and even several lords, assembled in the yard of the main temple, where that night they made a great hubbub with their drums, conches, trumpets, and bone fifes, which emit a loud whistle. They were naked, but covered with precious stones, pearls, necklaces, belts, bracelets, jewels of gold, silver, and mother-of-pearl, wearing many rich plumes on their heads. They performed the dance called *macehualiztli*, which means "reward through work" (from *macehualli*, "a farmer").[27]

Gómara's version of events maintains that Alvarado gave his permission for the Mexica to hold their festival on the condition that they neither bear arms nor perform human sacrifices. Gómara's telling suggests that Alvarado had manipulated the Mexica into attending the Festival of Toxcatl unarmed and gathered in one controllable spot.

Interestingly, at the height of Gómara's narrative of the violent "encounter" between Spaniards and Mexica, he goes off tangentially into a discourse on dance. Gómara paraphrases and inserts Franciscan missionary Toribio de Benavente Motolinía's writings about two different forms of Aztec dance: *netotiliztli* (a type of social dance) and *macehualiztli* (a type of sacred dance).[28] He draws upon this distinction to insist upon the "peaceful" (or in his words, "solemn") quality of the dance so as to intensify Alvarado's crime as well as to discount the "preemptive strike" justification proffered by Álvarez and Vázquez.

Gómara's account attempts to minimize the damage to Cortés's legacy by distancing him from the massacre. In fact, in Gómara's care, the massacre was another opportunity to depict Cortés as the ultimate mediator. He explains that upon Cortés's return to Tenochtitlan, he managed to control his anger at Alvarado and his men because he needed them to complete the larger mission: "Cortés, who must have felt badly about the affair, dissembled his feelings so as not to irritate the perpetrators, for it happened at a time when he had need of them, either against the Indians, or to put down trouble among his own men."[29]

In *Books of the Brave*, Irving A. Leonard argues that the popular literary genre of chivalric *romances* shaped the imaginations of fifteenth-century and early sixteenth-century Spanish chroniclers. As "the melodrama of their age," the chivalric *romances* were "novels . . . of the impossible exploits of knightly heroes in strange and enchanted lands inhabited by monsters and extraordinary creatures, and they presented a highly imaginative, idealized concept of life in which strength, virtue, and passion were all of a transcendent and unnatural character."[30] Several major *romances* gained unprecedented popularity in the decade preceding the conquest of Mexico, which allowed for the "mutual interaction between the contemporary historical events and creative literature, the imaginary influencing the real and the real the imaginary."[31] There is little doubt the *romances* shaped the conquistadors' experiences and representations of discovery and conquest. For example, we know that several conquistadors, including Cortés, recited passages from chivalric *romances* to one another to incite both courage and caution.[32] Chivalric *romances* provided a model for the conquistadors' tales of heroism and estrangement against a backdrop of threatening Aztec rituals of dance, human sacrifice, and cannibalism. None of the conquistador accounts better demonstrates the influence of the *romances* of chivalry than that of Bernal Díaz del Castillo, who, upon seeing the city of Tenochtitlan for the first time, exclaimed, "It was like the enchantments they tell of in the legends of Amadís," referencing *Amadís de Gaul*, the most popular Spanish chivalric *romance*.[33]

Bernal Díaz del Castillo (ca. 1495–1584), a foot soldier in Cortés's expedition, wrote his own version of the conquest, *The True History of the Conquest of New Spain* (*Historia verdadera de la conquista de la Nueva España*). One of the longest and most popular *relaciones*, the *True History* is a thinly veiled petition for land that the then-elderly conquistador wrote between 1552 and 1557 while living in Santiago de Guatemala. Díaz also wrote his *True History* to remedy what he perceived as inaccuracies in Gómara's account.[34] In particular, his account highlights the significance of the Spanish captains in Cortés's expedition, a facet of the conquest that Gómara's paean to Cortés failed to register. Instead, Díaz focuses his account on the heroism and bravery of the captains who fought for "God, gold, and glory."

The *True History* involves several encounters with dance. Díaz first describes Aztec dancers, acrobats, and "humpbacks" at the court of Montezuma, where he regards the court performers with both disdain and wonder: "Sometimes at meal-times there were present some very ugly humpbacks, very small of stature and their bodies almost broken in half, who are their jesters, and other Indians, who must have been buffoons, who told him witty sayings and others who sang and danced, for Montezuma was fond of pleasure and song."[35] Díaz also describes Aztec dancers to convey Montezuma's wealth and excessive tastes. For example, in describing the palaces and markets of Tenochtitlan, he comments on "the great number of dancers kept by the Great Montezuma for his amusement, and others used stilts on their feet, and others like *matachines*. . . . There was a district full of these people who had no other occupation."[36] Moreover, he gives a painstakingly detailed description of Montezuma's meals and his post-banquet tradition of watching dancers and singers while inhaling smoke from tobacco and herbs through ornately painted and gilded tubes.

Bernal Díaz mentions little about the Massacre at the Festival of Toxcatl, for he, too, was with Cortés on the coast fighting Narváez. However, he does give an impression of how the news of the massacre was first reported. He recounts that Montezuma's messengers from Tenochtitlan arrived at the coast "with tears streaming from their eyes," explaining that "for no reason at all" Alvarado had slain the Mexica nobles.[37] As such, he characterizes Cortés's return to Tenochtitlan as a mission to rescue the Indians from Alvarado. Díaz memorializes their return to Tenochtitlan on June 20, 1520, through an exchange between Cortés and Alvarado in which Cortés "very angrily" admonished Alvarado for having made "a great mistake." He recalls that Cortés said to Alvarado: "'But they have told me that they asked your permission to hold festivals and dances'; [Alvarado] replied that it was true, and it was in order to take them unprepared and to scare them, so that they should not come to attack him, that he hastened to fall on them."[38] Immediately following the description of this exchange, Díaz signals to the reader his own disbelief regarding Alvarado's explanation, cynically noting that some "stories were told by Alvarado alone."[39]

Alvarado's defense—that Mexica music and dance were signs of impending violence—receives its full expression in Díaz's care. In fact, in one of the defining episodes of his chronicle, he seems determined to rival all previous narratives of danger, violence, and wonder in the discourse of conquest. This episode involved dance, and his account comes in his lengthy description of the Spanish reconquest of Tenochtitlan, wherein he arduously describes the actions and experiences of the Spaniards during their return to the embattled city in the face of Mexica resistance. Here he treats the Spaniards' offensive and defensive military moves as if they were dances set to the rhythm of "terrifying" Mexica drums: "The dismal drum of Huitzilopochtli and many other shells and horns and things like trumpets and the sound of them all was terrifying drums." This sense of terror instilled by Aztec war songs and dances is corroborated by the chronicle of the Anonymous Conqueror, who observed, "During combat they sing and dance and sometimes give the wildest shouts and whistles imaginable, especially when they know they have the advantage. Anyone facing them for the first time can be terrified by their screams and their ferocity. In warfare they are the most cruel people to be found."[40]

But Díaz also had occasion to describe the Spaniards' martial dance: their timing, methods for covering space, and performance values, such as masking intentions through bodily stance. Bernal Díaz, Alvarado, and other Spanish soldiers were regrouping during a momentary rest in their camp on the city's outskirts—"where javelins and stones could no longer reach." There they saw one of the most remarkable and horrifying performances imaginable, involving the Mexica and Spanish soldiers they had captured.

> We all looked toward the lofty *Cue* (temple) where they were being sounded, and saw that our comrades whom they had captured when they defeated Cortés were being carried by force up the steps, and they were taking them to be sacrificed. When they got them up to a small square in front of the oratory, where their accursed idols are kept, we saw them place plumes on the heads of many of them and with things like fans in their hands they forced them to dance before Huitzilopochtli, and after they had danced they immediately placed them on their backs on some rather narrow stones which had been prepared as places for sacrifice.[41]

Díaz claims to have witnessed Mexica warriors force captured Spanish soldiers to dance themselves to death. In fact, he describes a scene wherein fallen Spanish conquistadors performed as if they were *ixiptlas*, the human "representations" of gods in Mexica ritual. Following in the paces of Ixtecuale, the *ixiptla* of the Toxcatl ceremony, the captured conquistadors were adorned in ritual array, forced to dance, and then sacrificed. Then the Mexica kicked their bodies down the steps of the temple to where priests were waiting to dismember and flay their skin. He prolongs the connection between terror and dance by detailing how the Mexica flayed the faces from the corpses of the Spanish soldiers and fashioned them into masks "like glove leather with beards on" to use in their future festivals. In so doing, Díaz conjures the images of Aztec gods being represented by dancing Spaniards and Spanish bodies being animated by dancing Indians. To pile horror on horror, he explains that the Mexica warriors ambushed the Spanish camp and threatened to force-feed the Spaniards and their native allies the roasted limbs of their "brothers."

In this compressed account, dancing sets into motion a constellation of terrorizing embodiments and incorporations—human sacrifice, possession, cannibalism—that comes to represent the transformation of an Aztec empire into a Spanish colony. Díaz stages acts of reciprocal possession by summoning the threat of dancing Indians possessing Spanish bodies as Spanish soldiers seize possession of Aztec territories.

Although Bernal Díaz undoubtedly saw bloodshed and various forms of Spanish and indigenous violence, the aforementioned scene was more likely a figment than a fact. To defend his own "true account," he emphasizes his physical proximity to the massacre: "It should be noted that we were not far away from them, yet we could render them no help, and could only pray God to guard us from such a death."[42] No doubt Díaz sought here to emend any characterization of Spanish weakness or defeat, or at least to give it context. Moreover, he revealingly expresses his disappointment with native and other chroniclers' representations of Spanish warfare, noting that they perhaps unjustly represented the Spaniards "badly wounded and streaming with blood." His description of the ritual sacrifice of Spaniards suggests a type of choreographed retribution for the Massacre at the Festival of Toxcatl. It presents eyewitness "proof" of the danger and violence inherent in Aztec ritual that in his estimation no other account of the Toxcatl massacre reliably delivered.

Apart from Alvarado, none of the "witnesses" claimed to have directly seen the Toxcatl massacre: Álvarez witnessed only its aftermath; Vázquez de Tapia describes its brutality but does not confirm his whereabouts; and Cortés and Cano were not even in Tenochtitlan. These accounts are riddled with overt and implicit expressions of doubt concerning Alvarado's intentions leading up to the massacre and almost every conceivable circumstance surrounding its execution. The intensity of these doubts is expressed through the shifting significance and changing roles of the Mexica dancers in their accounts: as victims of torture who withheld intelligence, as obedient nobles performing at the request and with the permission of the Spaniards, as irresistible symbols of wealth, and as violent "possessors" of Spanish soldiers. The representation of Mexica dancers within the conquest accounts ranges from a generic sign of native "peace" and "violence" to a complex symbol of the sacrifice the self makes in taking possession of the other.

Dancing the Black Legend: Missionary Accounts of the Massacre

If the conquistadors' accounts of the Massacre at the Festival of Toxcatl reveal increasingly elaborate attempts to explain and justify Spanish violence during the conquest of Mexico through the configuration of Mexica dancers, then those of the missionaries reveal a persistent indictment of it by similar means. In particular, the writings of the Dominican missionary Bartolomé de las Casas, the self-proclaimed "Defender and Apostle to the Indians," simultaneously decry Spanish imperial violence and defend "Indian" humanity in the decades following the conquest. Las Casas's writings fueled the "The Black Legend"—a form of Protestant propaganda against Spanish Catholicism expressed through a constellation of visual and written representations of the Spanish empire as "inquisitional, intolerant, and fanatic."[43] Ironically, Protestant indictments of Spanish imperialism were largely informed by the accounts of Spanish missionaries in the New World who criticized Spanish imperialism for its atrocious treatment of natives.[44] The Black Legend reflected deeper hostilities between the Dutch and Spanish empires, especially long-standing religious tensions born of the Protestant Reformation (1517) and the Eighty Years' War (1568–1648), which began as a Dutch revolt against King Philip II's control of the Dutch lowlands. The Black Legend's criticism of Spanish abuses of power abroad was a form of propaganda designed to inspire resistance within Protestant Europe. Las Casas' writings of the New World inadvertently fueled that resistance with an arsenal of condemnatory reports of Spanish cruelty, some of which involved dance.

Las Casas was one of the most controversial figures of the colonial era for his fierce defense of Indians in the New World and his vociferous denunciation of Spanish cruelty as exemplified by the *encomienda* system.[45] Las Casas articulated his quasi-legal, theological "defense" in two lengthy treatises, *Defense of the Indians* (ca. 1548–1550) and *Apologetic History of the Indies* (*Apologética historia sumaria*) (ca. 1551).[46] These books encapsulate the central legal and theological defenses that Las Casas made at the debates of Valladolid (1550–1551) in Spain, which addressed the treatment of Indians and the justifications for conquest. At the debates, Las Casas confronted Juan Ginés de Sepúlveda, a Spanish philosopher and theologian. Sepúlveda drew upon the Aristotelian notion of "natural slavery," as well as biased if not altogether fabricated reports from the New World about native savagery, in order to claim that Indians were naturally inferior to Christians and thereby justify the Spanish conquest and enslavement of Indians. (Aristotle argued that Greeks could not enslave from among their own, but could enslave those from other ethnic or racial groups.) They argued before a council appointed by King Charles V comprised of jurists, theologians, and members of the Council of the Indies. Las Casas took five days to deliver his rebuttal to Sepúlveda. Vociferously refuting Sepúlveda's claims that the Indians were irrational, natural slaves, or otherwise unfit for government, Las Casas tried to convince the jury and subsequently his readers that the Indians were equal to Spaniards.

Las Casas's defensive position toward the Indians informed his *A Brief Account of the Destruction of the Indies* (*Brevísima relación de la destrucción de las In-*

dias). Published in 1552, a year after the great debate at Valladolid, *A Brief Account* was his most widely read text and the only one to be published during his lifetime.[47] It is less a formal history than an impassioned petition to the Spanish Crown to reform its policies and practices in the New World.[48] In order to convince the Spanish Crown of the Indians' humanity and of the atrocities inflicted upon them, Las Casas had to challenge the diabolic representations of them disseminating from the New World and circulating within Spain, including Sepúlveda's claims, which Las Casas characterized as groundless lies.

In place of these countless misrepresentations, Las Casas offered his own revisionist account of the conquest of the Indies, methodically bringing into relief a pattern of unprovoked Spanish assaults on native peoples in the Americas. As Anthony Pagden argues, Las Casas privileges his own version of events over other Spanish accounts by insisting upon his status as a "witness" to Spanish cruelty, even though he had not actually witnessed many of the events he describes, including the Massacre at the Festival of Toxcatl. For Las Casas, witnessing was more than a rhetorical strategy to validate his authority; it was a model of historiography. To wit, *A Brief Account* portrays the conquest as a series of dramatically violent performances as if witnessed by an unwilling spectator.

Dance and dancers figure prominently in Las Casas's account of the conquest of Mexico, although his version of the conquest departs significantly from those of the conquistadors and Spanish historians, even from those sources upon which he based his work. It is widely accepted that *A Brief Account* is fraught with exaggerations and selective about details. Las Casas's imaginative orchestration of fact and fiction takes on epic proportion in his treatment of the Toxcatl massacre. Although Las Casas describes a massacre involving Mexica dancers, he mentions neither the Templo Mayor nor Toxcatl—arguably, two of the defining indices of the massacre in conquistador accounts.[49] In Las Casas's version of the unidentified, yet clearly recognizable Toxcatl incident, Mexica dancers were not celebrating the ritual of Toxcatl, but were providing entertainment to the imprisoned Montezuma and protesting the Spanish occupation.

All the local citizens, great and small, as well as all the members of the court, were wholly taken up with entertaining their imprisoned lord. To this end, they organized *fiestas*, some of which involved staging traditional dances every afternoon and evening in squares and residential quarters throughout the city. These dances are called in the local language *mitotes* (those typical of the islands being known as *areítos*); and since these dances are the principal form of public entertainment and enjoyment among the people, they deck themselves out in all their best refinery. And the entertainments were organized with close attention to rank and station, the noblest of the citizens dancing nearest the building where their lord was being held. Close by this building, then, danced over two thousand youths of quality, the flower of the nobility of Montezuma's whole empire.[50]

By portraying the gathering as a form of entertainment and perhaps even a type of political protest, Las Casas emends the conquistadors' claims that the massacre was a justified preemptive strike against an alleged Mexica uprising. Furthermore, by framing the gathering as a social rather than religious event, he circumvents the necessity of dealing with the actual bloody, confusing rites of Toxcatl. Instead, he describes the organization of the danced gathering, emphasizing that such practices were intelligible by name (*areítos*, *mitotes*), were established traditions, and were performed with reason and intent. Perhaps even more importantly, Las Casas emphasizes that the dancers were youthful nobles. He refers to them as the "flower" of the nobility—borrowing the term "flower" (*xochitl*), a Nahuatl metaphor for "noble." Las Casas paints the entire ritual as a demonstration of Mexica rationality and governance, as exhibited by the hierarchical arrangement of the dancing nobles.

Describing the moments leading to Pedro Alvarado's attack, Las Casas writes:

The Spanish captain made his way, accompanied by a platoon of his men, under pretense of wanting to watch the spectacle but in fact carrying orders to attack the revelers at a prearranged time, further platoons with identical orders having been dispatched to the other squares where entertainments were being staged. The nobles were totally absorbed in what they were doing and had no thought for their own safety when the soldiers drew their swords and shouting: "For Saint James, and at 'em, men!" proceeded to slice open the lithe and naked bodies of the dancers and to spill their noble blood. Not one dancer was left alive, and the same story was repeated in the other squares throughout the city.[51]

In this passage, Las Casas characterizes the Spanish choreography of conquest as premeditated, calculated, and deceitful, whereas he depicts the Aztec celebrants as so "absorbed" in their own naked dancing bodies, that they were defenseless—or, as he says, "without thought"—against the reasoned strategies of the Spanish soldiers. In his attempt to dramatize the horrendous acts of the conquistadors, Las Casas inadvertently elides native innocence and irrationality with dancing, an elision that reveals itself in his contradictory claims that the dancers were both adorned in their "refinery" and "naked." Thus, Las Casas makes it seem as if the Mexica were victims not only of deceitful Spanish military tactics, but also of their own uncontrollable desire to dance. This account is certainly ambivalent, for while it attempts to "defend" the Mexica as a noble people, it also depicts them as unthinking slaves to dance.

Following his description of the attack, Las Casas warns that dancing will prove to be a form of Mexica resistance equal to physical retaliation: "As long as a few of these people survive, they will not cease to tell and re-tell, in their *areítos* and dances, just as we do at home in Spain with our ballads, this sad story of a massacre which wiped out their entire nobility, beloved and respected by them for generations and generations."[52] With this thinly veiled threat, Las Casas reveals his own understanding of dance's capacity to memorialize multiple interpretations of history. Appealing to the Spanish king's preoccupation with his place in history, Las Casas warns that future Mexica dances will commemorate the violence imparted by the Spanish sword.[53] Ultimately, for Las Casas, performance serves both as an explanatory device for the Mexica demise as well as a threatening symbol of Mexica retaliation. For Las Casas, dancing makes "Indians" both vulnerable and resistant to Spanish violence.

Following its 1552 publication in Spain, Las Casas's *A Brief Account* was translated into multiple languages and published in Antwerp in 1578, Paris in 1579, London in 1583, Amsterdam in 1607, and Venice in 1630.[54] None of these publications fueled the Black Legend as much as the 1598 edition published in Frankfurt that included the famous copperplate engravings of Dutch bookmaker Theodor de Bry (1528–1598).[55] Between 1590 and 1634, de Bry and his sons published several hundred engravings in *Grands Voyages*, a thirteen-volume series of books that depicts defining moments in the discovery and conquest of the New World. These engravings—and the many copies in sixteenth- and seventeenth-century travel books they inspired—were among the first realistic visual images of the New World made available to Europeans.[56]

Dancers and dancing figure prominently in the de Bry corpus, including three engravings that depict the discovery and conquest of Mexico.[57] Two of these appeared in the 1598 publication of Las Casas's *A Brief Account*. These are among seventeen engravings that illustrate Las Casas's descriptions of Spanish techniques of murder—gruesome portrayals of Spaniards burying, hanging, and dismembering Indians alive. The first of the conquest engravings depicts a moment leading up to the initial "encounter" between Montezuma and Cortés at the gates of Tenochtitlan (fig. 4.1). The image illustrates Las Casas's description of the Mexica procession that set out to greet Cortés with gifts and entertainment. The procession is led by several men bearing gifts of gold, vessels, and shields. At the tail end of the procession Montezuma sits on a litter carried on the shoulders of his four favorite advisors.

The very next engraving, which occupies the same position on the consecutive page in the 1598 edition, shows a traumatic "reversal of fortune."[58] It illustrates Las Casas's description of the massacre of the Mexica nobles performing for Montezuma (fig. 4.2). The engraving takes us inside the palace, where the imprisoned Montezuma sits upon a pillow, physically unscathed yet visibly traumatized by the execution of dancing nobles in front of him. The engraving embodies Las Casas's "witness as historian" approach in that it stages Montezuma as a "spectator" to the violence surrounding him, as if he were watching a dance performance. In fact, what is dramatized here as much as the enactment of violence is the trauma of witnessing. Writing about such images, Conley observes: "On a broader scale the engravings appear to be asking if violence, like death itself, can be grasped

FIG. 4.1 First encounter between Cortés and Montezuma. Bartolomé de las Casas, *A Brief Account of the Destruction of the Indies* (1598), published by Theodor de Bry. Courtesy of the John Carter Brown Library at Brown University.

through visible representation."⁵⁹ By staging the violence as—and during—a performance, this particular engraving seems also to ask whether the trauma of *witnessing* violence can be visually represented.

A related engraving of the massacre also depicts a scene of traumatic witnessing (fig. 4.3). In part V of de Bry's *America* (1595) there is an engraving based on Milanese historian Girolamo Benzoni's *History of the New World* (*Historia del mondo nuovo*) (1565). Benzoni, like Las Casas, did not concern himself with the sacred aspects of the Toxcatl ceremony or the Templo Mayor. Instead, he distilled the encounter into a spectacle of Spanish greed: "One day, while they were looking at a great number of Indians of all ranks dancing and singing, the Spaniards seeing that in honor of this feast the Indians were adorned with a great variety of jewels, they were seized with such an unconquerable rage for plunder, that, without any fear of shame, Alvarado with a party of his men assailed them, and most cruelly killed a great many, and tore off the jewels they were wearing."⁶⁰ Taking Benzoni's text to its visual conclusion, de Bry situates the Spanish assault on Mexica dancers in "nature," in surroundings devoid of "culture," with the exception of a modest thatched-roof hut in the upper-left corner of the landscape. The engraving freezes the mo-

FIG. 4.2 Montezuma watches as conquistadors attack his court dancers. Bartolomé de las Casas, *A Brief Account of the Destruction of the Indies* (1598), published by Theodor de Bry. Courtesy of the John Carter Brown Library at Brown University.

ment at which the conquistadors rush the open field where the Mexica dance. It captures the transformation of dancers' gestures of celebration and praise into the flailing chaos of distress and desperate attempts to escape.

De Bry illustrates the dancers in various states of awareness and duress. In the background of the composition, dancers attempt to escape from Spanish conquistadors who threaten them with raised swords and grasp at the jewels adorning their bodies. A solitary corpse occupies the engraving's foreground, an ominous yet modest symbol of the inevitable massacre that ensued. The right side of the engraving is lined with musicians, who continue to beat the *teponaztli* drum, blow conch shells, and strike the tambourine as if not yet aware of the threat that surrounds them. Among the musicians is a group of Mexica women, who look at the violent assault from behind men who shield them from attack. In this specific engraving, women not only were seemingly protected from the Spanish sword, but also acted as witnesses to the military mastery of the Spanish and the brutal massacre of their fellow Mexica. This is not the case in other de Bry images, in which women

106   DANCING THE NEW WORLD

FIG. 4.3 The Massacre at the Festival of Toxcatl. Theodor de Bry, *America*, part 5 (1595). Courtesy of the John Carter Brown Library at Brown University.

are equally subject to violence. For example, one of the most gruesome depicts pregnant Indian women thrown into a ditch. However, this particular depiction of the massacre shies away from explicit representations of violence. Although violence is certainly implied, de Bry does not depict the Spaniards penetrating the Mexica with their swords. Instead, the engraving stages the women as spectators to a traumatic scene and thus depicts the massacre not only *during* but also *as* a performance.

As with de Bry's depiction of the massacre in Montezuma's palace, this engraving includes figures who witness violence as choreography. Montezuma and the Mexica women are spectators within these engravings who function as stand-ins for the Protestant viewer, in whom de Bry sought to inspire a sense of moral outrage and superiority toward both the Spaniards and the Indians. De Bry's audiences would have looked on with ambivalence at the two equally reprehensible forces dramatized in these engravings: the Spaniards, whose greed led them to perform unimaginable acts of torture, and the Indians, whose naked, immoral dancing invited and precipitated their own demise.

Contemporary viewers of de Bry's conquest engravings would have been familiar with the allegorical associations between death and dance, as the imagery strongly resonates with the *dance of death*, a visual and literary theme that runs throughout fifteenth- and sixteenth-century European art. Also known as *le danse macabre*, *der Totentanz*, or *la danza de la muerte*, the dance of death was a *memento mori*, a creative work meant to remind the living of their mortality. In most dance of death paintings, murals, engravings, poems, and songs, a dancing skeleton represents the omnipresence of death amidst the living. The dance of death theme allegorizes the indiscriminate power of death itself through a Death figure whose dancing has the power to seduce or coerce unsuspecting mortals into their final steps. The Death figure indiscriminately chooses a member of society—regardless of station or age—so as to dramatize the capricious nature and power of death itself. He is a sardonic figure, who often mocks mortals when they invariably attempt to escape his grip. Everyone was equal before the figure of Death—the emperor and child, the knight and the merchant, the martyr and the slave. In that sense, the dance of death was a form of social commentary in that it lampooned the conceits of social hierarchy and social mores as little more than a "comedy of manners."[61]

The dance of death emerged in Europe as early as the fifteenth century. As Paul Binski notes, "Dance, like death, was itself becoming an allegorical form in the fifteenth century, a way of explaining and categorizing things."[62] Paradoxically, dancing could represent social chaos as easily as it could represent social control—a symbol for a body regulated by or resistant to social and moral codes. Referring to the "massive demographic change and social transformation" that marked medieval societies throughout Europe, Binski claims that the dance of death expressed "a new anxiety of social control."[63] That anxiety is often directed toward the Church and its powerlessness to protect society from rampant disease.

The critical dimension of the dance of death reaches parodic heights in the woodcuts of Hans Holbein the Younger (ca. 1497–1543), who produced some of the most famous works of the genre. Although the dance of death theme appeared in church murals as early as 1424, by the late fifteenth-century,

FIG. 4.4 The knight dances with Death. Hans Holbein, *Dance of Death* (1538). Courtesy of Dover Publications.

printmakers had begun to reproduce the images in engravings and woodcuts and thus further popularized the imagery.[64] Holbein's collection of forty-one woodcuts was first published in Lyon in 1538; several of these depicted a dancing figure of Death antagonizing religious orders.[65] In one engraving, a priest preaches before a kneeling congregation, unaware that Death stands behind him, holding a jawbone over his head, attempting to upstage the priest for the attention of his flock. But not only the religious suffer. The nobility is also a target of Death's dance. "The Knight," for example, attempts to avenge Death by arching backward to strike uselessly at his attacker, yet Death seems only to delight in his vain attempts at resistance (fig. 4.4).

Arguably, Las Casas and de Bry were both drawing upon a popular tradition of allegorizing death through dance, and their audiences understood how to read the political and religious critique embedded in its iconography. For example, the most distinguishing choreographic feature of the dance of death was its "arrangement of characters by estate; carefully graduated in rank they are passed in review, each one with an appropriate vice."[66] This detail recalls Las Casas's insistence that the Mexica were dancing at the palace "with close attention to rank and station, the noblest of the citizens dancing nearest the building where their lord was being held." In effect, Las Casas's description of the Toxcatl massacre was a dance of death staging. De Bry's engravings seem especially influenced by the dance of death, given that they stage moral and political critiques via bodies in various states of dancing and dying.

Dances of death were also expressed in literary form, most often as a dialogue in which the living plead with the Death figure for salvation. Although pictorial representations of the dance of death did not flourish in Spain, a fifteenth-century poem entitled *Danza general de la Muerte* (or *Códice del Escorial*) was published and gained general recognition throughout the peninsula. Most literary scholars concur that the Spanish poem was written by a Benedictine monk.[67] The poem was certainly adapted for a Spanish public, as is evident from its inclusion of characters such as *el Alfaquí* (a Muslim wiseman), a Jewish rabbi, and a Santero (a custodian of a sanctuary).[68]

The *Danza general de la Muerte* likely influenced Michael de Carvajal's *The Complaint of the Indians in the Court of Death* (1557), the first known published Spanish play about the conquest of America.[69] Structured as a dance of death, the play casts the Spanish king as the Death figure who negotiates with Indians who came to his court to appeal for better living conditions. It is unclear whether the play was ever performed, and if so, whether dance was ever a part of its staging. However, Carlos Jáuregui suggests that the play was conceived as a "staging" of Las Casas's indictment of the Spaniards, given that *A Brief Account* was published five years before the play was written.[70] Audiences would have also related this fictional setup to the actual arrival of Indians in the Spanish court in 1528, when Hernán Cortés returned to Seville.[71]

Of course, the fictional Indians in *The Complaint of the Indians* perform a whole different variety of drama. They come to court not to entertain, but rather to plead their arguments for freedom from the tyranny of colonialism. Some of the appeals in the play eerily reference the prevailing topoi of the massacre accounts, including Alvarado's uncontrollable desire for gold. In fact, in a stunning discursive maneuver, the Indians are blamed for being too beautiful, wealthy, and rich, and thus for the Spaniards' inability to control their greed. Christians accuse the Indians of adorning themselves with precious metals to lure helpless Spanish to indulge in their avarice. "Another Indian," one of the characters in the play, makes the following appeal:

> To snatch away golden rings
> What fingers did they not sever?
> What ears did their knives not slash
> For the sake of golden earrings?
> What arms did they not break?
> What wombs, amid cries of woe,
> Did they not pierce with their swords?
> What were they thinking, doing this?
> That our Indians hid their treasure
> Within the vessel of their bodies?

Carvajal's Indians abide by their own modesty and will in the face of unbridled Spanish greed. "Another Indian" claims: "We are quite happy to know just this: / To know that we are in control / Of our wants and of our will."[72] Yet this "control" results only in more death. "Another Indian" appeals to the character of Death:

> It only remains to be seen
> If by this honorable court
> A judgment could somehow be found
> To wrest away control
> From these human beasts of prey
> And if there's no remedy here,
> Let us live not one more day,
> And rather, Death, if you will,
> Better carry us away
> And free us from such tyranny.

To the pleadings of "Another Indian," Death chillingly concedes: "Oh, how very right you are."[73]

The play stages the plight of the Indians, but it only offers death, disappearance, and submission as a remedy to the colonial project. Carvajal's Indians are made to contribute to the discourse of colonialism by inviting their own annihilation as an alternative to political tyranny. At another point in the play "Another Indian" states that he would prefer to see his children and by extension his entire race die rather than become a sinful Spaniard:

> How much better it would be
> To see our children while young
> Slashed, severed, or killed
> Than have them take in and learn
> So many insults and evils!

This counterintuitive reasoning, meant to convey Indian contempt for Spaniards, actually reveals the ambivalence at the center of the Black Legend tradition. Its representations of excessive violence are meant to make violence available for critique, yet they are simultaneously complicit with an "imperialist fantasy of colonial submission."[74] The configurations of dance in the narratives, images, and plots of Black Legend texts are equally complicit with and critical of Spanish justifications of conquest and colonization.

Carvajal's *Complaint of the Indians*, like Las Casas's *A Brief Account* and de Bry's engravings, may not be about dance per se, but its underlying dance of death structure undergirds the representation of oppositional forces at work, which necessitates the dramatization of native submission. In fact, it is only through death, pain, submission, and dancing that the Indians' humanity is represented. Their experiences of violence and death enter into historical discourse on the condition that they are represented through dance—as a performance that produces a traumatic witnessing.

No sixteenth-century chronicler of the Massacre at the Festival of Toxcatl goes as far to dramatize it as an encounter between Spanish cruelty and indigenous naïveté as does Dominican friar Diego Durán (ca. 1537–1588).[75] Durán wrote two related accounts of the massacre, one in each of his two extant books: *The Book of the Gods and Rites* (1574–1576) and *The History of the Indies of New Spain* (ca. 1581). Neither of these accounts is narrowly a Black Legend text. However, like Black Legend texts, Durán's accounts depict the massacre as a contest between Spanish greed and native submission—forces that animate the dance of death. Like Las Casas, Durán was determined to redress conquistador accounts of the conquest, which he perceived to be full of strategic omissions, exaggerations, and silences. About the Toxcatl massacre, Durán laments: "But as all of them deny other things that have always been obvious, and remain silent about them in their histories, writings, narrations, I am sure they would also deny and omit this, one of the worst and most atrocious acts committed by them."[76]

Durán's accounts of the massacre certainly deliver a counternarrative, yet his unconditional sympathy for native victims of Spanish violence often reduces Indians to little more than defenseless primitives with an unlimited capacity to endure and express pain, like those in Carvajal's play. Durán's determination to deliver a Christian critique of Spanish cruelty emerges in an iconographic image in the *History of the Indies of New Spain* (fig. 4.5). Whereas de Bry's engravings of the massacre mediate the violence through spectators positioned within the composition, the painting from Durán's *History* forces the viewer to directly confront the brutality of the attack, exposing dismembered Mexica dancers and musicians in the temple courtyard. Here the violence is physical, not psychological. The *History* image makes no attempt to suspend the moment right before the violence. Instead, it languishes in its material, bloody aftermath. Furthermore, unlike de Bry's classical rendering of space, the Durán image embodies two perspectives: an aerial view (which tries to represent the dimensionality of the courtyard) and a head-to-toe view (which represents soldiers and performers). These simultaneous, and perhaps competing, perspectives may or may not be a function of the fact that there are at least two historical perspectives operating in the account.

Durán's writings about Aztec culture and its conquest integrate the perspectives of both conquistadors and natives. He liberally manipulates both to assert his own theological and historical ideas. Durán went to great lengths to corroborate information from Spanish sources by consulting Friar Francisco de Aguilar (ca. 1479–1572), a conquistador who had traveled to Mexico with Cortés and later become an *encomendero*. In 1529 Aguilar released his Indian slaves and gave up his land to enter the Dominican order. At more than eighty years of age, Aguilar recorded his memory of the conquest in *Brief Report on the Conquest of New Spain* (*Relación breve de la con-*

FIG. 4.5 The Massacre at the Festival of Toxcatl. Diego Durán, *History of the Indies of New Spain* (ca. 1581), fol. 211r. Courtesy of Biblioteca Nacional de España.

quista de la Nueva España).[77] Durán's account of the massacre in *The Book of the Gods and Rites* is partially based on Aguilar's memories. Durán first addresses the Massacre at the Festival of Toxcatl in his dissertation about the Aztec god Huitzilopochtli, for whom Toxcatl was celebrated. Durán describes Huitzilopochtli, his festival, and his temple, invoking the massacre only in order "to give a clear idea of the magnitude of the courtyard of the temple."[78]

> When [the marqués] Cortés entered the City of Mexico with his men, the Indians were celebrating the feast of their supreme god. When the marqués discovered this, he begged Montezuma, monarch of the land (since the feast of their god was taking place), to give orders to all the lords, braves, and captains to appear, to celebrate and perform the usual dance, for he wished to take pleasure in the magnificence of the kingdom.... Thus all the flower of Mexico appeared for the dance—great, valiant brave men. In a painted picture I calculated them to be eight thousand six hundred men—all of high birth or captains of great valor.[79]

Interestingly, Aguilar's own *relación* makes no mention of the Toxcatl celebrations. Aguilar claims that he was with Cortés in Veracruz fighting off Narváez when he received a message that Alvarado and his men were in danger and that the Mexica had already killed a Spaniard.[80] He was not, as Durán claims, with Alvarado at the massacre where "with his own hands [he] murdered many natives within [this courtyard.]"[81]

Moreover, whereas Aguilar contends that Montezuma ordered an indigenous uprising against Alvarado and his men, Durán suggests that Cortés himself instigated the siege. In fact, he suggests that the celebrants were convened in Cortés's honor. This assertion, which historians disregard as a naïve error on Durán's part, is actually a kernel of a borderline conspiracy theory. Years later, in *The History of the Indies of New Spain*, Durán contradicts all other testimonial evidence by claiming that Cortés was not only at Tenochtitlan at the time of the massacre, but also commanded the performance and subsequently led the attack on its participants. In *History*, Durán postulates that the Tlaxcalans incited Alvarado into thinking that the Mexica were going to attack. In turn, Alvarado sent a dispatch to Cortés in Veracruz informing him of the danger that awaited him in Tenochtitlan, intentionally misleading Cortés to make him believe that Alvarado and his soldiers were under attack and directing Cortés to come prepared to stage a defense. According to Durán, upon his return to Tenochtitlan, Cortés asked Montezuma "to explain to him the meaning of those dances and ceremonies."[82] Although several sources mention various types of responses Cortés made upon his return, none suggests, as Durán's does, that Cortés's concern was with the significance of the dances. He recreates the conversation to proclaim and reinforce Montezuma's innocence: "Montezuma, who was naïve and sincere and did not suspect malice, nor did he realize that such treachery was being planned, called together his dignitaries and told them that the Spaniards wished to enjoy the spectacle of the grandeur of Tenochtitlan and its nobility."[83] By contrast, Cortés manifested the superiority of Spanish tyranny by manipulating the power dynamics of the festival.

> The day of the festivities having arrived, some eight or ten thousand men of the highest order and purest lineage appeared, wearing all their refinery as we have said, and formed a great circle in the temple courtyard. While they were dancing, all with contentment and pleasure, Cortés, instigated by Alvarado, ordered ten soldiers to be placed at each of the four gates of the courtyard so that no one could escape. He sent ten others to stand next to those who were beating drums where the most important lords had gathered. The soldiers were told to kill the drummers and after them all those who surrounded them. In this way the "preachers of the Gospel of Jesus Christ," or rather, disciples of iniquity, without hesitation attacked the unfortunate Indians, who were naked except for a cotton mantle, carrying nothing in their hands but flowers and feathers with which they had been dancing. All of these were killed; and when the other Aztecs saw this and fled to the gates, they were slain by the soldiers who were on guard there. Others tried to take refuge in the rooms of the temple, fleeing from those ministers of the devil. As they were unable to do so, all were slain and the courtyard was drenched with the blood of those wretched men. Everywhere were intestines, severed heads, hands and feet. Some men walked around with the entrails hanging out due to knife and lance thrusts. Verily it was a terrible thing to behold, the saddest thing one could imagine, especially when those dreadful screams and lamentations pierced the air! And no one there to aid them.[84]

Durán contends that amidst the chaos of the embattled Tenochtitlan, the Spaniards—"disciples of iniquity"—gained strength from the example of Nero, the Roman emperor who fiddled while Rome burned and blamed Christians for the city's destruction. According to Durán, the conquistadors sang the following ballad with indifference while performing acts of violence:

> From the Tarpeian Rock
> Nero watched Rome on fire.
> Not even the tears of women
> His pity did inspire . . .[85]

Durán portrays the Spaniards as flaunting their power through song, as they arbitrarily kill Indians who appeal for their salvation, unfazed and perhaps bemused by the pain they cause, much like the figure of Death in the dance of death tradition. Durán describes a tragically sympathetic people and city. He laments that the Indians were "the saddest thing one could imagine" and that "they have done nothing to deserve this fate" and that even "stones burst from pain and pity." Ultimately, for Durán, the Massacre at the Festival of Toxcatl was "the most atrocious act ever committed in this land."[86]

Durán's and Las Casas's massacre accounts, de Bry's engravings, and Carvajal's play represent the encounter between Spaniards and Indians through elements of the dance of death structure: a choreographed seduction, a physical struggle between opposing yet unequal forces, and a victor who is indifferent to the vanquished. These Black Legend texts attempted to redress accounts of the Massacre at the Festival of Toxcatl by Spanish conquistadors and royal historians, which justified Spanish violence as a response to terrorizing, threatening, and unintelligible Mexica dances. However, on the opposite end of the same scale of exaggeration, these texts represent the Mexica as little more than naïve, unthinking, and submissive slaves to dance. They express uncompromising sympathy for the conquered, but seemingly only to dramatize Spanish greed, violence, and godlessness through the figure of Mexica dancers and their endless capacity to express physical and emotional pain and suffering.

The Fall(ing) of Empire: Aztec Accounts of the Massacre

The Tlaxcalans admired Pedro de Alvarado. In fact, because he had a handsome face, a graceful disposition, and golden blond hair, they thought he was the sun and accordingly addressed him as "Tonatiuh." This is according to the mestizo historian Diego Muñoz Camargo (1529–1599), the son of a conquistador and a Tlaxcalan noble woman. Muñoz Camargo raises the point of Alvarado's mistaken identity to justify the Tlaxcalan alliance with the Spaniards that led to the Toxcatl massacre.[87] Of course, the Spaniards had imposed their alliance with the Tlaxcalans through military force. Plus, in joining forces with the conquistadors, the Tlaxcalans hoped to loosen the economic and military grip that the Mexica had held on them for generations. So even though Alvarado's mistaken identity makes a compelling explanation for the pact between the Tlaxcalans and Spaniards, we also have to recognize it as an *a posteriori* rationale for the Tlaxcalan submission to the Spanish.

Drawing on Muñoz Camargo's conquest account, William Prescott makes exaggerated claims about Alvarado's misrecognized godliness in his classic *History of the Conquest of Mexico* (1843). He reports that during the Noche Triste, Alvarado attempted to escape from encroaching Mexica warriors by crossing the causeway that connected Tenochtitlan to the mainland. However, the Mexica already had strategically destroyed the causeway as a measure to trap the Spaniards. Facing no alternative, Alvarado performed a choreographic feat that Prescott describes in epic terms:

> [Alvarado] was a man of powerful frame, and despair gave him unnatural energy. Setting his long lance firmly on the wreck which strewed the bottom of the lake, he sprung forward with all his might, and cleared the wide gap at a leap! Aztecs and Tlaxcalans gazed in stupid amazement, exclaiming as they beheld the incredible feat, "This is truly the *Tonatiuh*,—the child of the Sun!"—The breadth of the opening is not given.

But it was so great, that the valorous captain Diaz, who well remembered the place, says the leap was impossible to any man. Other contemporaries, however, do not discredit the story. It was, beyond doubt, a matter of popular belief at the time; it is to this day familiarly known to the inhabitants of the capital; and the name of the *Saltado de Alvarado*, "Alvarado's leap," given to the spot, still commemorates an exploit which rivaled those of the demi-gods of Grecian fable.[88]

According to Prescott, "Alvarado's leap" amazed the natives—"*quedaron maravillados*."[89] Tlaxcalans and Mexica alike were mesmerized by Alvarado's physical prowess, and so, as was custom among the Aztec upon encountering the divine, they started to eat handfuls of dirt and grass.[90] Alvarado's spectacular traversal proved that he was indeed Huitzilopochtli.

A similar myth of misrecognition explains Montezuma's willingness to surrender to Cortés. According to various sources, Montezuma purportedly mistook the conquistador for the Aztec god Quetzalcoatl, the "Feathered Serpent," who was portended to return to earth in the year 1519—or One-Reed of the Aztec calendar. Similarly, the *Florentine Codex* informs us that the Mexica foretold the arrival of the Spaniards from a series of omens: a comet, a fire, lightning, bubbling waters, the birth of monsters, a bird with a diadem, and a drunken soothsayer. Another native prophecy portends that one sign of the apocalypse was the appearance of two-headed men. The Mexica had never seen horses before, so they mistook the sight of armored conquistadors on horseback as a sign that the world was to end and were convinced that resistance would be futile.

These misidentifications are part of a larger constellation of myths, omens, and prophecies that circulate in chronicles of the conquest and whose explanatory force continues to power contemporary interpretations of the conquest. For example, Tvetzan Todorov's *The Conquest of America* makes the compelling yet controversial argument that the Spaniards were able to defeat the natives more with their ability to manipulate signs than by military force. Matthew Restall convincingly argues otherwise, noting that conquistadors and missionaries themselves created and circulated these "native" omens and myths, often to explain the conquest as an exercise of Spanish military genius and divine providence over indigenous religious disillusionment.⁹¹ Even Prescott suspected that reports of Alvarado's leap were fabricated by his heirs in an attempt to add to the conquistador's list of "good deeds" and possibly buy them political favor.

Clendinnen, by contrast, acknowledges that indigenous peoples participated in the circulation of these myths. She characterizes early indigenous efforts to chronicle the conquest in the following way: "What the informants offer for the most of the first phase is unabashed mythic history, a telling of what 'ought' to have happened (along with a little of what did) in a satisfying mix of collapsed time, elided episodes, and dramatized encounters as they came to be understood in the bitter years after the conquest."⁹² The Massacre at the Festival of Toxcatl is certainly one of the "unabashed mythic histories" or "dramatized encounters" to which Clendinnen refers. Native accounts of the Toxcatl massacre are memorialized in several sixteenth-century pictorial and alphabetic texts, almost all of which were created by descendants of indigenous nobility or native scribes at the behest of Spanish missionaries. While none of these sources provides direct eyewitness testimony on the massacre, they all offer a glimpse into the evolving influence that it held on indigenous perspectives in the "the bitter years after the conquest." The visual and written representations of the massacre in native sources willfully blend myth and history to make order of a new political reality, yielding accounts that Dennis Tedlock characterizes as "mythistory."⁹³ Not surprisingly, these sources also express native perspectives on the conquest through the symbolism of ritual and dance.

The *Annals of Tlatelolco* (*Anales de Tlatelolco*) is one of the earliest extant indigenous accounts of the conquest.⁹⁴ The 1528 document was written in Nahuatl with Latin characters and relates the accounts of anonymous informants from Tlatelolco, the thriving "twin" city of Tenochtitlan, which the Spaniards famously destroyed despite their professed admiration for the massive market it housed. The Spaniards imprisoned Itzcohuatzin, the *cacique* of Tlatelolco, along with Montezuma. The *Annals* commemorates Tlatelolcan solidarity with the Tenochca by establishing the Tlatelolcan presence at the Templo Mayor at the time of the massacre:

For this reason, our warriors were on guard at the Eagle Gate. The sentries from Tenochtitlan stood at one side of the gate, and the sentries from Tlatelolco at the other. But messengers came to tell them to dress the figure of Huitzilopochtli. They left their posts and went to dress him in his sacred finery: his ornaments and his paper clothing.

When this had been done, the celebrants began to sing their songs. That is how they celebrated the first day of the *fiesta*. On the second day they began to sing again, but without warning they were all put to death. The dancers and singers were completely unarmed. They brought only their embroidered cloaks, their turquoises, their lip plugs, their necklaces, their clusters of heron feathers, their trinkets made of deer hooves. Those who played the drums, the old men, had brought their gourds of snuff and their timbrels.

The Spaniards attacked the musicians first, slashing at their hands and faces until they had killed all of them. The singers—and even the spectators—were also killed. This slaughter in the Sacred Patio went on for three hours. Then the Spaniards burst into the rooms of the temple to kill the others: those who were carrying water, or bringing fodder for the horses, or grinding meal, or sweeping, or standing watch over this work.⁹⁵

The description of the massacre emphasizes that the celebrants were unarmed, contradicting the notion that the festival was a covert attempt to kill the Spaniards. This sentiment is reiterated in the text by way of the alleged protestations that Montezuma and Itzcohuatzin made to Alvarado during the massacre: "Our lords, that is enough! What are you doing? These people are not carrying shields or *macanas*. Our lords, they are completely unarmed!"⁹⁶ In that regard, the *Annals* reads like a denial of—or at least a defense against—the conquistadors' accusations that the Mexica had gathered to stage their own attack.

The *Códice Aubin* goes one step further, denying that Toxcatl was a "disguised" revolt.⁹⁷ Interestingly, the codex utilizes an indigenous mode of record keeping that assigns "glyphs," or symbols, for names, dates, and locations associated with historically significant events, which in turn Aztec sages (*tlamatine*) interpreted in their verbal recitations of history. The "glyph" for the Toxcatl massacre discreetly depicts a Spanish conquistador and a Mexica warrior squaring off in the courtyard of the Templo Mayor, while

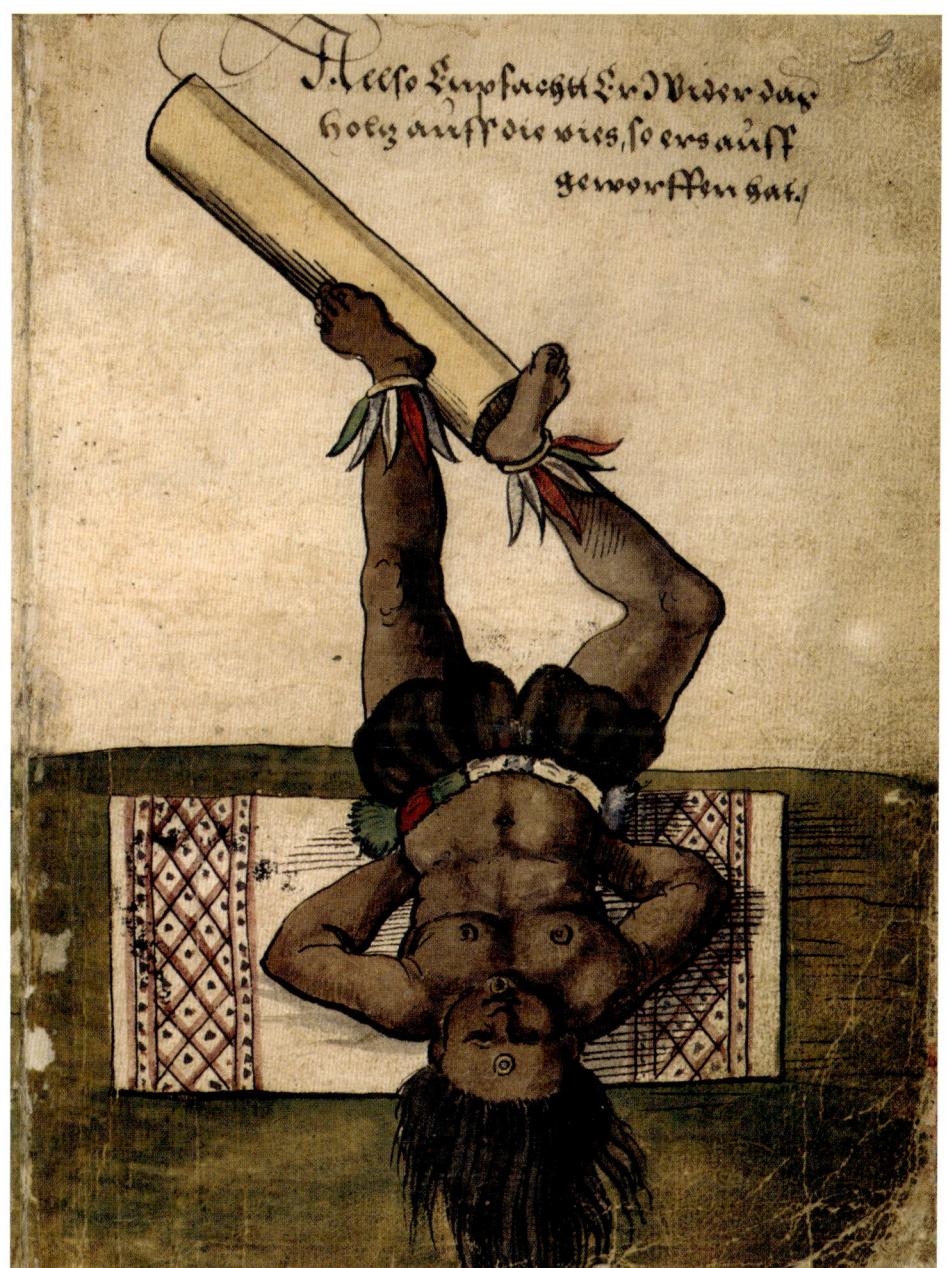

FIG. 0.2 Aztec acrobat in Spain. *Das Trachtenbuch des Christoph Weiditz* (1529), fol. 9. Courtesy of Germanisches Nationalmuseum, Nürnberg.

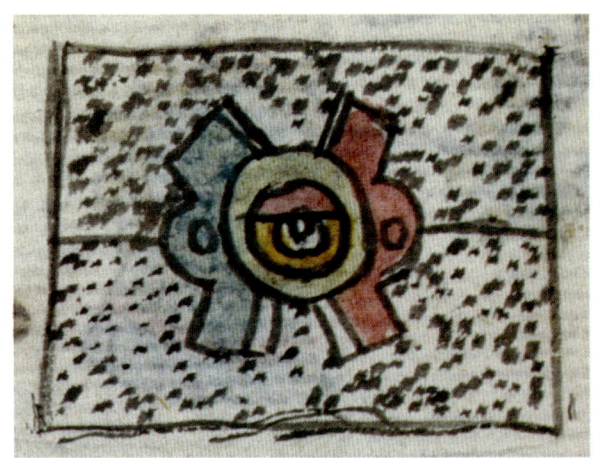

FIG. 0.3 *Ollin* (movement). *Codex Telleriano-Remensis*, fol. 33r. Courtesy of Bibliothèque nationale de France.

FIG. 0.4 *Cihuateteo. Codex Borgia*, pl. 39. Courtesy of Dover Publications.

FIG. 3.1 Aztec dancers and musicians. *Florentine Codex*, book 8, chapter 14. Florence, Biblioteca Medicea Laurenziana, Ms. Med. Palat. 219, c. 338v.

FIG. 3.4 Atamalcualiztli. Bernardino de Sahagún, *Primeros memoriales* (II/3280), fol. 254r. © PATRIMONIO NACIONAL.

FIG. 4.5 The Massacre at the Festival of Toxcatl. Diego Durán, *History of the Indies of New Spain* (ca. 1581), fol. 211r. Courtesy of Biblioteca Nacional de España.

FIG. 5.3 Dancing at the *cuicacalli*. Diego Durán, *Book of Gods and Rites*, fol. 305r. Courtesy of Biblioteca Nacional de España.

FIG. 5.4 Xochipilli, "The God of Dance." Museo Nacional de Antropología, Mexico City. Photograph © John Bigelow Taylor.

FIG. 5.6 Xochipilli drumming and Huehuecoyotl dancing and singing. *Codex Borbonicus*, fol. 4. Courtesy of ADEVA, Akademische Druck-u. Verlagsanstalt, Graz, Austria.

FIG. 5.8 Dance of the Emperor. *Crónica de Michoacán*, v. 18. Courtesy of the Archivo General de la Nación, Mexico.

FIG. 5.9 Dance of the Emperor Montezuma. Joaquín Antonio de Basarás y Garaygorta, *Origen, costumbres, y estado presente de mexicanos y philipinos* (1763), lam. 3, 118. Courtesy of the Hispanic Society of America, New York.

a single drummer plays the *huehuetl* in the center of the precinct (fig. 4.6).

The accompanying text documents the alleged dialogue between Montezuma and Cortés, via Malinche, regarding the Toxcatl festivities, emphasizing that Cortés authorized the performance of the ceremony:

> Montezuma said to Malinche: "Please ask the god to hear me. It is almost time to celebrate the *fiesta* of Toxcatl. It will last for only ten days, and we beg his permission to hold it. We merely burn some incense and dance our dances. There will be a little noise because of the music, but that is all."
>
> The Captain (Cortés) responds: "Very well, tell him they may hold it."
>
> The Aztec captains then called for their elder brothers, who were given this order: "You must celebrate the *fiesta* as grandly as possible."[98]

This humble exchange between Cortés and Montezuma insists that the Mexica had permission to hold the festival and planned to do so with the noblest of intentions, contesting Alvarado's defense that the Mexica had planned to attack Alvarado and his soldiers. It is revealing that the exchange reduces the larger tension between the Mexica and the Spaniards to the contention that the Mexica received Cortés's "permission" to "dance [their] dances." As if to refute the Spanish claims of Mexica aggression toward the Spaniards, the exchange unconvincingly portrays the Mexica as both naïve and utterly subservient to Cortés's command.

One of the other truly exceptional ways that the *Códice Aubin* emends European accounts of the massacre is by naming one of the murdered Mexica dancers: "Then the songs and dances began. A young captain wearing a lip plug guided the dancers; he was Cuatlazol, from Tolnahuac. But the songs had hardly begun when the Christians came out of the palace."[99] Cuatlazol must have been a high-ranking warrior to have led the dance and to have worn a lip plug, an adornment reserved for priests and warriors. The *Códice Aubin* tells us too that he is from "Tolnahuac," which most likely means he was a ranking member of the cult of the temple of Tolnahuac, one of the sacred temples in Tenochtitlan. Alternatively, he may have been a descendant of the Tolnahuac, one of the city's four founding clans, or a warrior from the district within Tenochtitlan named for that clan. By naming an individual dancing warrior, the *Códice Aubin* established its link to an eyewitness source, however removed, who was either present at the siege or who had access to ritual knowledge in the highest echelons of Mexica society. In its own modest way, the codex works against the dehumanizing effect of the Spanish chronicles, wherein dancers are depicted as a violent and anonymous mass that seemingly only existed as a foil to the threatened yet brave conquistadors.

The lengthiest and most detailed native version of the Toxcatl massacre comes in book 12 of Spanish missionary Bernardino de Sahagún's *Florentine Codex*, "The Conquest."[100] The account is based on the testimony of native informants from Tlatelolco who were interviewed by Sahagún and his native assistants.[101] In general, its narrative of the conquest is similar to those of the conquistadors and missionaries. However, whereas the accounts of conquistadors draw from chivalric *romances* and missionary accounts draw from the dance of death tradition, the account in the *Florentine Codex* draws upon native ritual for its explanatory framework. For example, two mirroring Nahuatl passages in the *Florentine Codex* use the imagery of dance to convey a native interpretation of the massacre. The nineteenth chapter in Book 12 offers a final representation of the Mexica, just moments before the siege on the city, and this is a description of a Toxcatl dance:

> All hastened and ran, as they made their way toward the temple courtyard, in order there to dance the winding dance. And when all had assembled, then the start was made; then began the chanting and the winding dance. And those who had fasted twenty days, and those who fasted a year, stood aside facing the others. Those who hemmed in [the dancers had] their pine cudgels; whosoever tried to leave [the dance] they menaced with the pine cudgels. But one who would [leave to] urinate took off his net cape and his forked heron feather ornament. But one who did not at once obey, who would not be excluded, or who was mischievous, they soundly beat his back therefore, [or] his thighs, [or] his shoulders, and thrust him outside. They cast him out by force; they threw him on his face—he went falling on his face; he fell forth on his ear. No one in their hold took his leave.[102]

FIG. 4.6 Drummer, Conquistador, and Aztec Warrior at Templo Mayor. *Códice Aubin*, fol. 42r. Courtesy of the British Museum.

This entry celebrates the centrality of dance to the maintenance of Mexica culture and details the degree of dedication and discipline ritual choreographies required of celebrants. The passage reveals nothing less than the making of the Mexica world and its subjects. By contrast, a passage in the following chapter, which follows the first by only a few short paragraphs, reveals the unmaking of that world through a description of the very same ritual dance as it was performed on the day of the massacre:

> Thereupon they surrounded those who danced whereupon they went among the drums. Then they struck the arms of the one who beat the drums; they severed both his hands, and afterwards, struck his neck, [so that] his neck [and head] flew far away. Then they pierced them all with iron lances, and they struck each with the iron swords. Of some they slashed open the back, and then their entrails gushed out. And one who tried to go out, there they stuck and pierced him. But some climbed the wall, and so succeeded in taking flight. Some entered the various tribal temples, and there escaped. And some eluded [the Spaniards] among the dead; they went in among those who had died, only feigning death, and were able to escape. But one who stirred, when they saw him, they pierced.[103]

The description of the massacre hauntingly echoes that of the ritual dance: both passages make references to dancers' necks, shoulders, and backs as well as to the instruments of violence to which those bodies were subjected. However, in the description of the massacre, backs were split open with iron swords, rather than disciplined with pine cudgels. The similarities between and position of these mirroring passages in the *Florentine Codex* poignantly expresses an implicit indigenous Aztec lamentation about the conquest. Through the imagery of dancing, it symbolizes the making and unmaking of political realities.

The *Florentine Codex* also imparts a native perspective on the conquest through its many drawings, most of which are graphic depictions of terror and violence. For example, one image shows a drummer with one hand still on the *huehuetl* drum, and the other lying on the floor, severed by a Spaniard who is poised to strike his sword yet again (fig. 4.7).

One of the most complex images in the *Florentine Codex*'s series of massacre depictions illustrates two Mexica warriors plunging from the platform of

FIG. 4.7 Conquistadors dismembering Aztec drummer and decapitating Aztec dancer. *Florentine Codex*, book 12, chapter 20. Florence, Biblioteca Medicea Laurenziana, Ms. Med. Palat. 220, c. 440r.

the Templo Mayor as two conquistadors watch. One of the conquistador's arms is raised, as if to indicate that he had made the fatal push that sent the warriors falling to their impending death (fig. 4.8). Images of warriors falling from the Templo Mayor, which appear in several native codices, memorialize the "fact" that conquistadors rushed the temple pre-

FIG. 4.8 Falling from the Templo Mayor. *Florentine Codex*, book 12, chapter 22. Florence, Biblioteca Medicea Laurenziana, Ms. Med. Palat. 220, c. 446v.

cinct and killed ritual celebrants. However, they also express a comment on that violence by referencing one of the distinguishing characteristics of Mexica ritual: the ceremonial casting of sacrificial victims' bodies from a temple platform.

The *Codex Azcatítlan* is a late sixteenth-century pictorial manuscript that details the history of the Mexica, from their mythic migration to Aztlán to their eventual conquest. Its depiction of the massacre spans four pages (fig. 4.9). The first page shows the conquistadors and their Indian allies approaching the Great Temple. The final page depicts the Mexica under attack—either massacred, retaliating, or continuing to drum or dance. There is one figure falling from the temple stairs, his body symbolizing the fall of the empire itself.

The *Lienzo de Tlaxcala* is a pictorial manuscript composed around 1550 that memorializes the role of the Tlaxcalans in helping the Spanish to conquer indigenous towns throughout the valley.[104] Tlaxcala provided a ready source of victims for Mexica ceremonies of human sacrifice, and in one of the linens from the *Lienzo*, we see the lifeless body of a Mexica warrior fall from the top of the Templo Mayor, tracing the path of many Tlaxcalans who had fallen before him. As such, the *Lienzo* documents a reversal of power within Aztec culture: the fall of the Mexica at the hand of the Tlaxcalans and their Spanish allies.

These images of dancers and warriors falling from the Templo Mayor are significant not only because they symbolize the fall of the Aztec empire, but also because they do so in choreographic terms—via the ritual and mythical symbolism of falling bodies. To best understand the significance of the fall of the Aztec empire, we need first consider its "mythistorical" rise.

In the winter of 1978, a crew performing routine electrical maintenance in central Mexico City discovered a large carved stone buried beneath the city's street. As the crew members knew that they were working close to the archeological zone near the Cathedral of Mexico City, where the Templo Mayor once stood, they immediately notified authorities about their accidental finding. In time, archeologists and art historians identified the stone as the relief disc of the goddess-warrior Coyolxauhqui ("The One with Painted Bells") (fig. 4.10). The stone represents a dismembered Coyolxauhqui, whose fatal fall is central to narratives of the Aztec empire's rise.

The myth of Coyolxauhqui's fall is recorded in the *Florentine Codex*. According to Sahagún's native informants, Coyolxauhqui's mother, Coatlicue ("The Lady of the Serpent Skirt"), had been miraculously impregnated by a ball of feathers that had fallen from the sky. Disgraced by her mother's pregnancy, Coyolxauhqui incited her four hundred brothers to join her dancing army and to slay their mother. Along with Coyolxauhqui, these brothers, also known as "stars" (Centzonuitznaua), approached Coatlicue with the precise and vigorous choreography of warriors: "in order; in columns; in armed display, moving with deliberation" to assassinate her.[105] However, before dying, Coatlicue gave birth to a son, Huitzilopochtli, who avenged his mother's death by decapitating Coyolxauhqui, thrusting into his sister with a *xiuhcoatl*, a flaming serpent, and throwing her body from the mountain Coatepetl ("Serpent Mountain"):

> Then with it he pierced Coyolxauhqui, and then he quickly struck off her head. It came to rest there on the slope of Coatepetl. And her body went falling below; it went crashing in pieces; in various places her arms, her legs, and *her body kept falling*. And [Huitzilopochtli] then arose and pursued the Centzonuitznaua, and went among them, and pounced upon them, and scattered them from the top of Coatepetl.[106]

As a result of his miraculous birth and subsequent act of revenge, Huitzilopochtli became the reigning deity of the Aztec. His domination over and mutilation of his sister, a goddess associated with older fertility gods, symbolized this transference of power. However, in order for that power to be maintained, the cult of Huitzilopochtli had to ensure that "her body kept falling." Sacrifice was a constant necessity for achieving this new balance of power, for Huitzilopochtli was the Sun and needed blood to maintain his domination over his sister, the Moon.

The Coyolxauhqui Stone keeps the goddess's body in a perpetual state of falling. Its carved relief entombs the goddess, immortalizing her body's crash into the earth. Indeed, the stone was stationed at the foot of the Templo Mayor, and thus most likely served as a fatalistic warning to the victim who performed ritual choreography on the temple's platform. Hers was the last image that sacrificial victims saw as they performed their dances on top of the temple platform. Once sacrificed, their bodies were intentionally cast from the temple stairs, symbolically tracing the pathway of Coyolxauhqui's world-making fall.[107]

Coyolxauhqui's fall recalls other Aztec myths of creation, especially the cosmogony of the Fifth Sun. The Aztec numbered historical eras as "suns"; at the time of the Spanish conquest, the Fifth Sun—also known as "Five Movement"—was in effect. The seventh book of the *Florentine Codex* contains a myth about the creation of the sun and moon that involves falling bodies. At the end of the era of the Fourth Sun, the gods gathered at the ancient city of Teotihuacán to figure out how to reanimate the sun and moon, which had been extinguished. The gods called upon two men to sacrifice their lives by casting themselves into a pit of fire and transform themselves into the sun and the moon. Tecuciztecatl ("The Wealthy Lord of Snails") was the first to accept the invitation: "Upon this, he went [forward] to cast himself into the flames. And when the heat came to reach him, it was insufferable, intolerable, and unbearable; for the hearth had blazed up exceedingly, a great heap of coals burned, and the flames flared up high. Thus he came terrified, stopped in fear, turned about, and went back."[108] He made four attempts at leaping into the fire, but each time fear immobilized him.

His failure gave an opportunity to the physically deformed Nanauatzin ("The Pimply One") to seek deification. Despite his unprepossessing appearance and cheap offerings, Nanauatzin unexpectedly rose to the challenge:

> And Nanauatzin, daring all at once, determined—resolved—hardened his heart, and shut firmly his eyes. He had no fear; he did not stop short; he did not falter in fright; he did not turn back. All at once he quickly threw and cast himself into the fire; once and for all he went. Thereupon he burned; his body crackled and sizzled ... And when this was done, when both appeared [over the earth] together, they could, on the other hand, not move nor follow their paths. They could only remain still and motionless. So once again the gods spoke: "How shall we live? The sun cannot move. Shall we perchance live among common folk? [Let] this be, that through us the sun may be revived. Let all of us die."[109]

Transformed into the sun and propelled by the wind, Nanauatzin rose skyward from the pit of fire, catapulted into a trajectory of perpetual movement. His mythic fall and recovery establish a relationship between corporeal and heavenly bodies that Aztec ritual dances continually reaffirmed.

The third book of the *Florentine Codex* details a myth of cultural destruction that bears a striking similarity to that of Coyolxauhqui and Nanauatzin's falls. The myth concerns the destruction of Tula, the ancient city of the Tolteca, the native ancestors of the Mexica. According to the myth, a "demon sorcerer" enchanted the Tolteca with his singing, drum-

FIG. 4.9 Encounter at the Templo Mayor. *Codex Azcatítlan*, fol. 22v and 23r. Courtesy of Bibliothèque nationale de France.

ming, and dancing, inspiring them to dance in turn: "Thereupon there was dancing; they went as if leaping. There was the grasping of hands, there was the taking hold of each other from behind."[110] Having cast his spell, the sorcerer led the Tolteca to a canyon, where he set a trap:

> And when there was dancing, [as] there was the greatest vibrancy of movement, [as] there was the greatest intensity of movement, very many threw themselves from the crags into the canyon. All there died. Then they were turned into rocks.
> And [as for] the others at the craggy canyon, the demon then broke the bridge. And the bridge was of stone. Indeed all fell there where they crossed the water. All were turned into rocks.[111]

Those who did not willfully leap into the canyon met a similar fate through different means. The demon sorcerer sabotaged them by destroying the stone bridge upon which they traversed the deadly canyon. They, too, fell and were transformed into stone: "When there was [this] falling, the Tolteca verily destroyed themselves."[112] This myth of Tolteca destruction resembles not only the symbolic landscape of the myths of Coyolxauhqui and Nanauatzin, but also that of the dance of death. Like the Death fig-

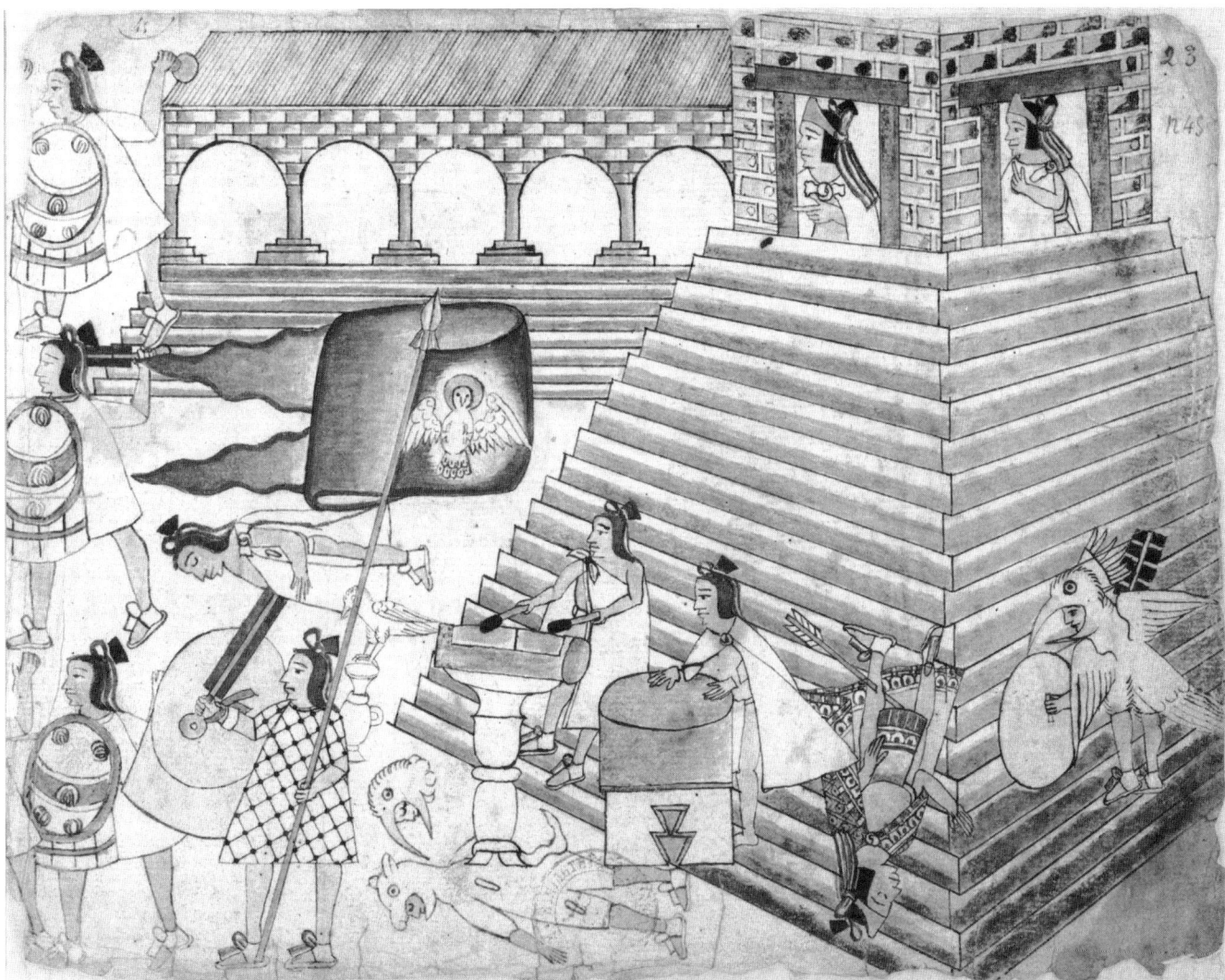

FIG. 4.9 (continued)

ure in the dance of death, the demon sorcerer uses dance to entrance, seduce, coerce, and ultimately lure others into death: "the Tolteca died . . . as they danced."[113]

As Todorov notes, "The Aztecs' entire conception of time favors the cyclical over the linear, repetition over difference, ritual over improvisation."[114] This is evidenced by the many interreferential falling bodies within Mexica myths of cosmogenesis. The mythical, sacred, and portentious falls of Coyolxauhqui, Nanauatzin, and the Tolteca dramatize the cycle of creation and destruction so central to Aztec conceptions of the universe. Falling is never an accident in Aztec myth, sculpture, or ritual, but is instead the result of a highly choreographed act that attempts to suture the crags, chasms, and lacunae between past, present, and future. In native accounts, the Toxcatl massacre is represented through the prism of the mythic past by way of falling bodies. These accounts cope with the shock of the Fall of Tenochtitlan and absorb its impact by understanding the European presence in the New World as yet another political transformation. Thus, native representations of the Toxcatl massacre bear witness to Spanish violence, but do not necessarily admit Mexica defeat. Instead, they offer mournful laments, proclamations of innocence, and discursive acts of resistance expressed through ritual and dance, especially the rich network of mythical, sacred, and political associations set into motion by falling bodies.

Conclusion: Dancing on Graves/Engraving Dancers

This chapter has examined various European and Mesoamerican accounts of the Massacre at the Festival of Toxcatl. While no examination of these sources could yield a "true" account of what transpired in early May 1520, scrutinizing the configurations of dance, dancers, and dancing within them reveals the range of competing and complementary meanings that conquistadors, chroniclers, missionaries, and natives brought to and drew from the massacre.

For the conquistadors and early chroniclers, one's perspective on the role of dance in the Toxcatl massacre—to praise, to entertain, to deceive, or to resist—mattered insofar as it conveyed one's position within broader legal and ethical debates and in some instances determined political and economic consequences. Spanish missionaries' accounts of the massacre drew upon the theme and structure of the dance of death tradition, which allowed them to simultaneously critique the evils of Spanish colonialism and depict the Indians as savage yet noble beings worthy of Christian salvation. For the native chroniclers, representing dance in the accounts of the massacre was a way of memorializing trauma. Their accounts attempt to integrate the Spanish conquest with Mexica ideas of change and transformation, especially through the "mythistorical" symbols of falling.

Collectively, the accounts of the Massacre at the Festival of Toxcatl crystallized an association between dancing and Mexica culture that endured for centuries. The image of Indians dancing at the Templo Mayor gained near iconic status in colonial representations of Tenochtitlan. In fact, during the three

FIG. 4.10 Coyolxauhqui Stone. Museo del Templo Mayor, Mexico City. Reproduced with permission of the National Institute of Anthropology and History (INAH), Mexico.

hundred years following the conquest, a series of approximately fifty related images of dancing Indians at the Templo Mayor were published in various English, German, French, and Dutch travel books.[115] Most were copies of an original woodcut that was first published in Friar Diego Valadés's *Rhetorica christiana* in 1579, the first book written by a mestizo to be published in Europe. Seen against and alongside each other, these images of the Templo Mayor progressively intensify their focus on the dancer as symbol of a Mexica past.

One of the earliest copies was published as a frontispiece to the second volume of Franciscan missionary Gerónimo de Mendieta's *Historia eclesiástica indiana* in 1595 (fig. 4.11). Like the nearly identical Valadés woodcut upon which it is based, the image offers a bird's-eye perspective on the Templo Mayor and its ceremonial precinct, surrounded by exotic plants, houses, and other scenes of daily life, which are identified in Spanish or Nahuatl words. As indicated by its title, "Print of the sacrifices which the Indians savagely made in the temples of their Demons," the engraving depicts an elaborate Mexica sacrificial ritual, complete with priests extracting a victim's heart on the temple platform.[116] The scene also shows the ceremonial courtyard occupied by nine dancing couples. Marking the spot where the Massacre at the Festival of Toxcatl took place, the image displays the Latin words "Saltatio Indorum" (Dance of the Indians).

More than a half-century after the publication of Valadés's woodcut, an engraving entitled "The Great Temple of Mexico" was published in J. Fuller's *The American Traveller* (1741) (fig. 4.12).[117] This vision of preconquest Tenochtitlan focuses even more on dancers, eliminating the architectural and agricultural elements depicted in the Valadés woodcut and the Mendieta engraving. It also uncouples the dancers and shows them with a greater range of movement, all of them balancing on one leg. The ceremonial precinct is also more explicitly defined. Unlike the Mendieta engraving, in which dancers appear to dance in a ditch, the Fuller image fully renders the gated serpent wall (*coatepantli*) that surrounded the ceremonial precinct, which is referenced throughout the massacre accounts.

Created a century after the Valadés original and nearly fifty years after the Fuller engraving, "The Rejoicing of the Mexicans, at the Beginning of the Age" was published in John Hamilton Moore's *A New and Complete Collection of Voyages and Travels, Vol. 2* (ca. 1785) (fig. 4.13). The engraving telescopes into the ceremonial precinct, displacing the Templo Mayor in favor of dancers as the *axis mundi* of the Mexica universe. The engraving takes a sidelong view into the ceremonial precinct, thus illustrating the eastern vantage Alvarado had when he arrived to execute the massacre. In the foreground, a group of men and women performs a linked dance near drummers. In the background, another group dances on the temple platform. They make offerings to priests and perform dances to welcome the rising sun. At close range, the dancers appear more human than they had hitherto been depicted in European books. We can also see their facial expressions, distinctive shapes and poses, and the detail of their costumes, jewelry, and ornaments. As its title suggests, the engraving captures the Indians expressing the pleasure, joy, and ecstasy of dancing and endows the dancers with a previously unrepresented subjectivity.

Inasmuch as these postconquest images attempt to restage preconquest Tenochtitlan, they are haunted by the Toxcatl massacre by way of their references to the "dance of the Indians" in the Templo Mayor courtyard. As these three engravings suggest, over time, dancing was an increasingly important vehicle for imagining the preconquest past. No doubt the differences between these engravings reflect shifting tastes and artistic sensibilities in the travel book market. These images also purify the crime scene by imaging Mexica "dancing in a state of peace" while simultaneously erasing the hand of the Spanish sword that had made these dancing bodies such a powerful symbol of the Aztec world to begin with. To conjure Tenochtitlan moments before its destruction, the engravings simultaneously exorcise and resurrect slain Mexica dancers, who literally and figuratively dance on their own graves.

A poignant passage in the *Florentine Codex* defuses the fantasy of resurrection enacted by these engravings. Of all the accounts of the Toxcatl massacre, only the version found in the *Florentine Codex* memorializes its traumatic aftermath. The text describes how at the moment when the conquistadors

stormed the sacred courtyard, the Mexica made desperate attempts to escape, either by scaling the patio wall or by feigning death. The text also explains what happened to those who were unable to escape. Sahagún's informants elegize the slain Mexica dancers by describing how their corpses were cremated on the day following the massacre:

> And thereupon there was the bringing forth, the taking out, the identification of each of the brave warriors who had died. And their mothers, their fathers raised a cry of weeping; there was weeping for them; there was weeping. First they had taken them, each one, to their homes; then they took them forth to the temple courtyard; they brought them together. There they burned them together.[118]

Dance was a powerful figure for representing complex relations to the conquest. However, this passage reminds us that the massacre was not merely a discursive event or a field of representation. While it is important to continually rethink the massacre in terms of myth, allegory, symbol, and all the other manners in which meaning is constructed, represented, and perpetuated, there is a material reality to political violence that ought not to be neglected.

This chapter has focused on the ways in which the legacy of the conquest endured through representations of dance in visual and written texts. The following and final chapter will examine how that legacy endured through actual dances and bodies.

facing page

FIG. 4.11 "Dance of the Indians" at the Templo Mayor. Gerónimo de Mendieta, *Historia eclesiástica indiana*, book 2 (1595). Courtesy of Nettie Lee Benson Latin American Collection, University of Texas Libraries, the University of Texas at Austin.

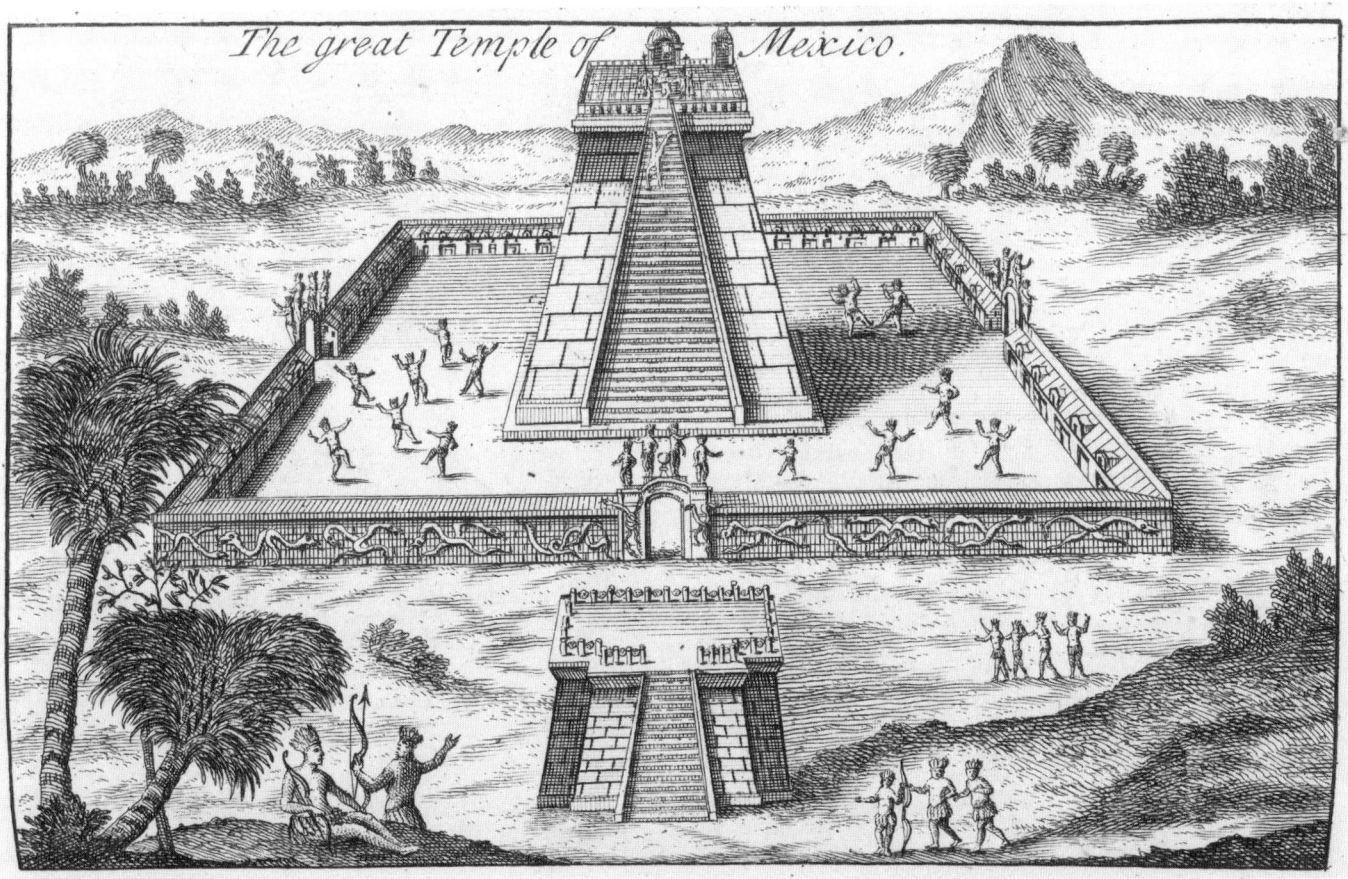

FIG. 4.12 "The Great Temple of Mexico." J. Fuller at the Dove in Creed-Lane, *The American Traveller* (1741). Courtesy of John Carter Brown Library at Brown University.

FIG. 4.13 "The Rejoicings of the Mexicans, at the Beginning of the Age." John Hamilton Moore, *A New and Complete Collection of Voyages and Travels*, Vol. 2 (ca. 1785). Courtesy of John Carter Brown Library at Brown University.

Rather than focusing on the dancer as a discursive figure, it treats dancing as an embodied practice. In particular, it examines various dances of conquest (*danzas de conquista*), the choreographed reenactments of the conquest of Mexico. In dramatizations at official state ceremonies and on the stages of missionary plays, natives were forced to perform their subjugation for decades following Massacre at the Festival of Toxcatl. As such, the final chapter charts a history of the dancing body that runs parallel to—and sometimes intersects with—the portrayals of the "dance of the Indians" (many based purely on imagination or hearsay) that circulated in the travel books and histories throughout the colonial era. The practices of and prohibitions against dancing in colonial New Spain meaningfully calibrate the relationship between choreography and encounter this book has thus far brought into view.

Five

the mystery of movement

DANCING IN COLONIAL NEW SPAIN

Steps of Conquistadors

In 1522, upon hearing of the final conquest of the Aztec, Charles V appointed Hernán Cortés governor and captain general of New Spain. Within the next few years, Cortés continued his military campaigns until the Spanish colony was almost double the size of the former Aztec empire. Bernal Díaz del Castillo tells us that in 1524 Cortés set out on yet another expedition to amass even more wealth and land. As he made his journey toward South America, he passed through various towns, where he was welcomed with "great reception and *fiestas*." For instance, in the gulf city of Coatzacoalcos, Indians greeted Cortés with "dances of Moors and Christians and other great rejoicings and cunning diversions."[1]

Moros y cristianos are staged reenactments of military battles between Moors and Christians. The tradition developed in Spain, but Spaniards brought it to the New World in the sixteenth century, where it quickly became popular, especially in New Spain. These scenarios incorporated dance and dialogue to represent the military defeat of the Christians (almost always led by Saint James, the patron saint of the Spanish army) over the Moors (often led by Pilate). Spaniards participated in some of the New World *moros y cristianos*, but for the most part Indians played Christians and Moors alike, which not only symbolically integrated Indians into a history of Spanish domination, but also literally forced natives to repeatedly and publicly affirm their own subordination.[2]

According to Arturo Warman, Bernal Díaz's reference to the *moros y cristianos* at Coatzacoalcos is the first in the chronicles of the New World, although it certainly is not the last. In June 1530 Cortés returned to New Spain after a two-year sojourn in Spain. Díaz tells us that Cortés, by then the "Marqués del Valle de Oaxaca," was again fêted by Spanish cavaliers and natives alike when he arrived in Texcoco. Indians assembled in their best dress, and armed as warriors, filled the lake with their canoes; "the dancing continued in every street during the day, and at night the city was illuminated with lights at every door."[3] We know of another historic performance of *moros y cristianos* from the *relación* of Álvar Núñez Cabeza de Vaca, the renowned explorer who survived a fatal shipwreck off the shores of Texas, from where he made a nine-year journey on foot to New Spain. Cabeza de Vaca tells us that his arrival in Mexico City on July 23, 1536, coincided with the feast of Santiago and that the viceroy, Don Antonio de Mendoza, and Cortés celebrated his rescue and arrival with the presentation of a bullfight and a performance of *moros y cristianos*.[4]

In 1538 Charles V of Spain and Francis I of France brokered a peace treaty. When news arrived in New Spain, Spaniards and Indians alike celebrated by transforming the plaza in Mexico City into a metaphorical City of Rhodes and reenacting the series of battles that led to the Christian liberation of the island from the Turks. Hernán Cortés himself allegedly performed the role of the Christian commander and Indians played newly arrived Dominican missionaries. The audience largely consisted of the conquistadors' wives, who watched the action from windows that lined the Great Plaza.

One section of the *Códice de Tlatelolco* commemorates a celebration of the 1556 coronation of King Philip II of Spain (fig. 5.1).[5] The scene depicts the archbishop, Alonso de Montúfar, and other colonial administrators (seated on the central platform) and the *caciques* of Tenochtitlan, Tlacopan, and Texcoco (seated on their thrones between the warriors and the colonial officials). Beneath them, Mexica eagle and jaguar warriors perform a military *danza*.

Though this particular ceremony is not a *moros y cristianos* per se, it is an example of the types of militarized dances that formed what Richard C. Trexler has influentially called "military theatre." These military reenactments were performed on special occasions, to commemorate events in Spanish royal history as well as for viceregal or clerical *entradas*. As rituals of "humiliation," colonial military reenactments shared a dramaturgical morphology of a "greeting, battle, and submission" through which Indians repeatedly performed their subordination for the benefit of the colonial gaze.[6]

Military theatre was just one of the many varieties of performance that the Spaniards deployed to create and represent New Spain. For generations scholars have examined the role of performance in the political and religious conquest of the Americas. Some of the most generative research has come from the retrieval, translation, and critical interpretation of Nahuatl dramas, mostly seventeenth- and eighteenth-century transcriptions of sixteenth-century plays. Scholarship concerning the role of music in the evangelization of the Indians, especially the translation and teaching of liturgical psalms in the Christian missions, has also been extremely important to understanding the way embodied practices contributed to the evangelization of indigenous society.[7]

Interestingly, within this deep and dynamic field of colonial performance studies, the role of dancing as a technique of political and religious conversion has escaped critical scrutiny. This oversight is somewhat understandable given that dance leaves little material trace. However, references to dancing in colonial chronicles, missionary ethnographies, municipal and church records, and postconquest codices give us a glimmer of the distinctive role that dancing held in the formation of New Spain. While dancing was a welcomed part of military events and the missionary theatre, it raised its own unique set of problems and possibilities for colonial and Church authorities. Dance was paradoxically both promoted and prohibited in the colonial era, for it was viewed as both a sign of Christian conversion as well as an insidious subterfuge for performing pagan idolatry.

This chapter explores this tension as well as the underlying questions that undergird writings about dance in the colonial era: How is dancing a technique for social and religious conversion? What financial and governance structures does it require? Where and under what supervision does conversion take place? What are the physical expressions of social and religious transformation?

Consider one of the most demonstrable indicators that colonial authorities recognized that dancing could meaningfully contribute to the formation of a New Spain. On October 30, 1526, Maestros Pedro and Benito de Begel petitioned the *cabildo* (town council) of Mexico City for permission to build a dance school in order to "ennoble the City" (see app. J). The *cabildo* granted approval to build a school 50 feet long by 30 feet wide in the plaza, for which the petitioners were to pay 40 pesos in rent to cover the income that would be lost from the market space the school would replace. The council minutes say nothing else about the school, its students, or its curriculum, except for giving the names of its founding dancing masters. In his *True History*, Bernal Díaz includes a necrology of fallen conquistadors that confirms that these two dancing masters were conquistadors. Maestro Pedro was a harpist from Valencia. Benito de Begel played the drum and tambourine in Cortés's expeditions both in Europe and Mexico. Both men died "natural deaths." (Díaz also mentions a "teacher of dancing" named Ortiz, who "died at the hands of the Indians.")[8]

Thus, two conquistadors were the first dance mas-

FIG. 5.1 Eagle and jaguar warriors dancing before the Spaniards. *Códice de Tlatelolco*. Reproduced with permission of the National Institute of Anthropology and History (INAH), Mexico.

ters in New Spain. While the council-sanctioned dance school was likely intended to serve the children of Spanish colonists, Indians performed songs and dances as part of Church-sponsored feasts, processions, and *autos*, the plays based on biblical figures and Christian history. Many of the missionary dramas, which were performed by and for the natives as a Christian conversion tactic, coincided with Corpus Christi, the Christian festival that celebrates the mystery of the sacrament of communion. Established by a papal bull in 1264, by 1350 Corpus Christi was celebrated throughout Europe, typically with processions of the Eucharist and mystery plays.[9]

In New Spain, some of the best evidence of dance's role in these religious *autos* comes from Motolinía, who is most likely responsible for staging several of them in Tlaxcala. For instance, he refers to processions and performances connected to Corpus Christi Day and Saint John the Baptist's Day in 1538 and explains that the Indians danced to Christian hymns that missionaries had translated into Nahuatl.[10] He describes how nine *niños* danced before the Blessed Sacrament as well as a procession that weaved throughout the city, stopping first at the church door, where others performed joyous *danzas y bailes*.[11] After performing the *Magnificat* (a Christian hymn) and spending hours on their knees in prayer, sometime at two or three in the afternoon the natives gathered in the patio of the church to perform a dance "in their ancient manner" (*el baile á su modo antiguo*), most likely as a reward for their profession of Christian devotion.[12]

There is another group of references to dancing related to Corpus Christi festivals in Mexico City in the proceedings of the town council (*Actas de Cabildo de México*). For the most part, the records indicate how monies were to be disbursed to participants in the Corpus Christi festivals. Dorothy Tanck de Estrada reports that throughout the sixteenth century the cities of Toluca, Tehuacán, and Tejupan spent the greatest amount of their municipal funds for Corpus Christi festivals, next only to those associated with Holy Week and patron saint ceremonies.[13] These funds were often entrusted to a *mayordomo*, or a treasurer and manager of a *cofradía* (a "brotherhood" or "an organization of laymen dedicated to the financing of religious ceremonies and charitable works").[14]

The proceedings give a fascinating glimpse into Corpus Christi festivals that have gone otherwise undocumented. For example, in 1593 Señor Alonzo Dominguez arranged to pay 300 pesos for silk and iron necessary to the construction of *gigantes*, large puppets used during processions (*acta* #5435). On June 28, 1596, the council voted to pay Indian men to perform dances such as the *panadero* and *pelas*. It also agreed to pay *gitanas* (gypsy women) to perform with them (*acta* #5723). On March 5, 1598, the *cabildo* deputized Señores Geronimo Lopez and Guillen Brondat with "contracting the dances, giants, games, and what is usually done for the celebration of Corpus Christi" (*acta* #5878). This duty seems to have been formalized the following year, when on May 28, 1599, the council voted to appoint Señor Francisco Escudero as "the commissioner for the festivals of Corpus" (*acta* #5991). Apparently this position was created to remedy corruption in the relations between the *cabildo* and the *cofradías*, as is evident from the related order that "the *mayordomo* should be paid half now and half after the octave, and Señor Francisco Escudero, in case some of the funds are missing, should not pay for what is missing" (*acta* #5993). A month later, Escudero appeared before the council with a detailed accounting of his expenditures: "forty pesos for the dance of the *gitanas* [gypsy women], twenty-nine pesos for the *negros* [blacks] who carry the *gigantes*, forty pesos for the *pelas* dance [a dance with sticks], and forty pesos for the adornment of the *gigantes*, and for the *dança de villanos* [a peasant dance], thirty pesos."

One of the fascinating aspects of these town council minutes, apart from revealing the degree to which the council participated in the governance of the Corpus Christi festivals, is the reference to *las gitanas* and *los negros* who participated in the festival. Gypsy music and dance were integrated into Corpus Christi festivals in Spain during the seventeenth century, though it is unclear which dances and songs they performed or what significance was attached to the participation of a persecuted minority group in a Christian ceremony. The reference to *los negros* likely refers to *cofradías* of black slaves. Between 1519 and 1650, Spaniards trafficked over 120,000 African slaves to New Spain in order to replenish the native slave labor on ranches and mines, which had been depleted by the smallpox epidemic in 1520–1521.[15] Thus, this *acta* makes an early albeit oblique reference to the relatively undocumented role of Africans in colonial Mexican performance.

Jesuit missionary Andrés Pérez de Ribas (1576–1655) offers another glimpse. He incorporates a letter from Padre Andrés Tutino about the inauguration of a church in the northern city of San Gregorio, where he reports that Indians gathered "from a distance of a hundred miles for the inauguration ceremonies, which lasted eight days" and during which time "the visiting Indians performed colorful and attractive dances."[16] Spaniards contributed to the celebration by presenting a religious play and performing a joust on horseback. One of the striking aspects of this letter is its rare reference to the fact that Africans were integrated into the performance alongside Spaniards and Indians: "Negroes who had come from the south to work in the mines, now being members of the newly built church, also staged a play, presenting attractive dances in their fashion." While the letter suggests that church celebrations were a means of integrating Africans and Indians as "new members" into the social and religious fabric of the church, it also raises the possibility that these ceremonies were another opportunity for Spaniards to assert their religious and military dominance, especially since "during the festivities the Spaniards, at intervals, would deliver salvos from their arquebuses, using altogether ten *arrobas* [250 pounds] of powder in these demonstrations." These militarized displays might well have been demonstrations of Spanish strength in the face of ongoing slave uprisings.

The entries in the *Actas de Cabildo de México* suggest that the colonial administration in New Spain promoted religious and civic spectacles, even if only to exert financial and social control over them. However, other municipal bodies and religious juntas attempted to assert control over performances by prohibiting them, especially those aspects of performances that potentially allowed for the retention of native idolatry. In 1576 Sahagún expressed this anxiety explicitly by warning that Indians "remembered through *areítos* that secretly and at night they perform in honor of their idols."[17] For other clerics and administrative bodies, the unease about clandestine native revivalism focused on the Indian songs and dances, even those performed in the context of Church-sanctioned festivals, such as *moros y cristianos*, missionary plays, religious festivals, and cathedral inaugurations. Cervantes de Salazar expressed this anxiety thusly: "For certain it would be better to strip them of all the relics and traces of their paganism, because according to credible clergy, it has happened that they dance around a cross and hide their idols beneath it, making it seem that they address their songs to the cross [but] directing them to their idols in their heart."[18]

Juan de Zumárraga (1468–1548), the first bishop of Mexico and archbishop of New Spain, led an inquisition to root out Indian idolatry and sorcery, an effort that led to the trial and execution of Indians. In 1539, he headed an ecclesiastic junta that explicitly prohibited dancing in church patios for similar reasons. The junta "agreed and decreed that the *areítos* be omitted from the churches" based on the suspicion that by singing and dancing the Indians maintained a connection to the "time of their faithlessness." Only dances that "would assist them to become good Christians" were permitted, provided that "someone who understands and knows the language" could affirm that the songs to which they dance do not contain any heathen significance.[19]

Gerónimo de Mendieta relates a fascinating anecdote regarding Zumárraga's prohibition of dancing. In the wake of the archbishop's death, the junta temporarily lifted the ban against dancing—until a miracle occurred that persuaded the junta to restore the stay.

> The most important miracle refers to the fact that some years before his death he had prohibited some indecent dances and representations performed in connection with the general procession at the Feast of Corpus Christi. This in his fair judgment required a dignified and reverential performance. In order to ensure the observation of this reforming measure once and for all, he published in conjunction with a tract by Dionisio Cartujano a catechism expressing the view that processions should always be performed with dignity and reverential comportment. After his death and while the archiepiscopal seat was still vacant this servant of God appeared to some members of the chapter who had been responsible for the dances in the past. As they were getting ready on the day of the holy feast, it began to rain cats and dogs in the morning and this made it impossible to hold a street procession. Seeing this, the chapter realized that on the suggestion of this saintly man, heaven had intervened to prevent them from breaking Zumárraga's rule. They decided that all future performances and dances be re-

moved from the festivities and this rule was observed during the six years the see remained vacant.[20]

In 1555 a decree from the First Provincial Council of Mexico augmented the junta's prohibition when it "ordered and commanded that in their dances, *areitos* or *mitotes*, [Indians] do not use masks or emblems that give any suggestion of idolatry." It restricted dancing to public spaces (and specified that dances not be performed inside churches) and to the time between the morning's high mass and the vesper bells, at which time "they should leave the *mitote* to attend the services."[21]

On April 28, 1550, the *cabildo* of Tlaxcala passed an *acta* that prohibited Indians from dancing with feathers, especially those plucked from the crosses and litters used in Church ceremonies. In all likelihood, the prohibition was enacted not only to protect Church property but also to forbid dancing with said feathers, which the *cabildo* and Church leaders saw as an expression of native beliefs and practices under the guise of Christian ceremony. Moreover, the *cabildo* established a prohibitive fine for such an offense—"80 pesos of mine-gold"—which was to "be divided in to two parts: one part will belong to the treasury and exchequer of his majesty, and an equal amount will belong to the judge."[22]

The descriptions of, laws about, and prohibitions against dancing among Indians in the early colonial era express anxiety and ambivalence about its effects: was dancing an authentic expression of Christian devotion, or was it a way to hide in plain sight their worship of Nahua gods? Even missionaries who were best poised to answer this question offer only arbitrary explanations, vigilant defenses, or heightened assurances about the significance of Indians dancing in the context of Christian ceremony. What follows is an examination of three exceptional texts about dance in colonial New Spain that, when read against and alongside each other, give a historical perspective on the integration of dance into Christian worship during roughly the first century following the conquest. These sources also bring into dramatic relief the broader cultural and philosophical questions about the principles and practices of dance in relation to colonial governance and as a symbol of and technique for religious and political conversion.

The "God of Dance" in the Garden of Eden: Diego Durán and the *Cuicacalli*

Describing his participation in a Pentecost procession, Dominican missionary Diego Durán expressed deep ambivalence about the Indians' performance of Christian devotion. He sensed that the recently converted Indians, who carried flowers instead of the traditional candles, were actually paying tribute to the god Tezcatlipoca instead of Christ. He wrote: "I see these things, but I am silent, since I realize that everyone feigns ignorance. So I pick up my staff of flowers like the rest and walk along, thinking of our gross ignorance, for great evils may be concealed under these customs."[23] With this statement, Durán admits to yielding to what he perceived as profound disillusionment among missionaries who convinced themselves that the evangelization of the Indians had been a success.

Durán's momentary participation in "gross ignorance" was but one of his many responses to the Indian dances and rites he saw performed throughout colonial New Spain. In some instances he insists that the pagan ways of the past were but a distant memory: "The problem [of paganism] has been solved."[24] In others he claims that "the Christian religion and the heathen ways found a common ground."[25] In some, admittedly more rare, moments he concedes that conversion was a failure, owing to the fact that his "adversary [was] subtle and tricky."[26]

Durán's writings about dance in New Spain are exceptional as compared to those of his contemporary missionaries not only because he was as interested in the colonial present as he was in the pagan past, but also because, unlike his contemporaries, Durán was both a keen observer of the colonial world and a product of it. Durán was born in Seville and traveled with his parents to New Spain at the age of five or six.[27] He spent his youth in Texcoco and Mexico City, and, at the age of nineteen, became a novice of the Dominican order at the monastery of Santo Domingo in Mexico City. He was an eyewitness to the physical and social transformation of the Aztec empire into a Spanish colony. He attended school and church among the ruins of the former empire and entertained himself by venturing into the ancient barrios of the former Tenochtitlan.

Because he had learned Nahuatl, he was better prepared than most chroniclers to pursue answers to the questions that colonial New Spain presented him: about the customs and offerings in the market, about the skeleton-like trees that emerged from the lakes, about the bloodstained stones that lined the new cathedral, about the natives' obsession with bathhouses, and, most especially, about the esoteric songs and dances performed on the various feast days. Durán never experienced a "new" world or a "new" Spain. While other missionaries came to know the New World through their knowledge of the Spanish past, Durán came to know the Spanish past through the New World.

According to Tzvetan Todorov, Durán was "the most accomplished cultural hybrid of the sixteenth century," and his writings, "the summit of sixteenth-century Spanish scholarship with regard to the Indians."[28] These writings included his two ethnographic works, *The Book of the Gods and Rites* (ca. 1574–1576) and the *Ancient Calendar* (ca. 1579), as well as his *History of the Indies of New Spain* (ca. 1581), a transcription of an anonymous and now missing Nahuatl chronicle known today as *Crónica X*.[29]

Todorov argues that the shifting racial, religious, and class distinctions of colonial New Spain profoundly shaped the nature of Durán's ethnohistoriographic ideas, especially his borderline obsession with identifying continuities and collisions between Christian and indigenous ritual. Durán's writings focus on the connections between Aztec and Spanish rituals, which Todorov describes as a "syncretic" act in and of itself: "What seemed to Durán the greatest infamy—religious syncretism—characterized his own outlook."[30] Todorov argues that Durán's syncretic outlook was animated by his desire to understand his own cultural "hybridity" and his identity as a Spaniard raised in colonial New Spain. Todorov also provocatively but unconvincingly suggests that Durán himself came from a family of converted Jews, and that his attempt to theorize the relatedness between Christianity and Nahua cosmology reflected a similar process he had previously undergone in trying to reconcile his Jewish and Christian identities.

One of Durán's most deeply held yet widely rejected beliefs was that the Indians of New Spain were descendants of the Jews. Durán based this idea on the myriad resemblances he identified between the two religions. In the first chapter of the *History of the Indies of New Spain*, Durán suggests that Topiltzin, a leader of the Toltec, the ancestors of the Mexica, was an apostle sent to the New World by God. He made this claim in large part as a result of his study of Indian rituals: "Because of their nature we could almost affirm that they are Jews and Hebrew people, and I believe that I would not be committing a great error if I were to state this fact, considering their way of life, their ceremonies, their rites and superstitions, their omens and false dealings, so related to and characteristic of those Jews."[31]

Durán was committed to exposing the Indians' ability to conceal the expression of native beliefs through the performance of Christian rites, as well as the clergy's willingness to turn a blind eye toward it. His pursuit of knowledge of ancient ritual was stymied by the conquistadors and early missionaries, who destroyed many ancient codices, which Durán was certain had held the key to unlocking the mystery of Aztec ritual: "They left us without a light to guide—to the point that the Indians worship idols in our presence, and we understand nothing of what goes on in their dances, in their marketplaces, in their bathhouses, in the songs they chant (when they lament their ancient gods and lords), in their repasts and banquets; these things mean nothing to us."[32] Durán therefore pursued knowledge of their "tightly guarded secret" by other means.[33] He encouraged his fellow priests to ask the natives during confessions to reveal their dreams, which he believed harbored reminiscences of pagan times. He also reconstructed the ancient ritual calendar, Durán's Rosetta Stone, which enabled him to "translate" Aztec into Roman, and more specifically Dominican, time.[34] With his newly acquired knowledge of the Aztec calendar, he was better able to concretely identify the vestiges of the specific pagan songs, rites, and dances he intuitively sensed existed.

Durán was well aware that ancient rites and dances were performed throughout New Spain for decades following the conquest, even if only "by exception." He says as much in his discussion of a dance performed for the goddess Xochiquetzal ("Flower Feather"). The dance involved young boys decked out as birds and butterflies who climbed trees and "suck[ed] the dew of the flowers." Then men and women dressed as "gods" would appear and with blowguns shoot the birds and butterflies from the trees. A representative of Xochiquetzal would then gather other god representatives and seat them beside her. The ceremony clearly held religious significance, as is evident from its representation and display of gods. However, Durán curiously admires it, adding that it was "the most solemn dance in the land" as well as "the dance they most enjoyed."[35]

Durán dedicates a relatively lengthy passage to dancing in his treatment of the festival of Xocotl Huetzi, or "Feast of the Falling Fruit."[36] One of the ceremonies involved placing a bird made of dough at the top of a high pole, which young boys then scaled in a race to capture it. Durán makes a comparison between this dance and a game performed among Spanish sailors, a game with which he admits he himself was not familiar:

> Those who were brought up in Spain will have seen how this game was conducted. According to the story (since I must confess that I have not seen this done), it is that [in Spain sailors] place lengths of velvet rope on top of a smooth, greased mast of the ship. Those who are to run strip, stand in order, then assault the mast in a wild rush, those in advance tussling among themselves. (As Saint Paul says) all run, but only one manages to reach the top first and take the prize, being the lightest and most adroit.
>
> Well, try to imagine the same thing: these [Mexica] youths forming, stripping, placing themselves in order, and climbing the pole.[37]

One of the interesting features of this comparison is that Durán reveals that he was more familiar with the Aztec ritual than with the Spanish tradition. Seemingly to compensate for his own "ignorance," he makes an obscure comparison between the Aztec pole-climbing contest and a scene in the life of Saint Paul, wherein he allegedly avoided a shipwreck en route to Rome by way of masterfully manipulating the sails of his slave ship. Durán then further explains that following the competition, the young men were ritually purified and bathed as in "a Jewish rite."[38] If Durán's comparisons seem overwrought (likening the *xocotl* feast to Spanish sailors, a Christian saint, and a Jewish rite), it is because he sought to understand the world of the "other" through the lens of a "self" that he did not entirely know.

The same is true of his description of the *cuecuechcuicatl* (a "tickling dance" or "dance of the itch"), which Durán compares to the Spanish *sarabande*, "with all its wriggling and grimacing and immodest mimicry." To make this comparison, Durán relies on the impressions of Spanish missionaries, as he likely had never seen a *sarabande*. He advises missionaries against permitting Indians to dance the *cuecuechcuicatl* "because it is highly improper." Durán adds, "Men dressed as women appear there."[39]

Durán describes another dance associated with the Xocotl Huetzi. This description is based on his understanding of the ceremony as it was performed by the Tecpanecs in the Franciscan-dominated area of Coyoacan:

> The leader of the dance, who stood in front of the others, was dressed according to the native fashion. This god was disguised as a bird or a bat, its wings and crest made of large and splendid feathers. From his wrists and ankles hung gold bells; in both his hands he carried native rattles. He made much noise and clamor with these [rattles] and with his own mouth. He went twisting along completely out of order and rhythm with the other dancers. From time to time he spoke loudly, using terms which few—and perhaps none at all—understood. Thus this man went along merrily.
>
> Let our priests and laymen take note of what they may have seen often in the native dances. How common it is to see one or two natives precede the circling dancers without following the rhythm of the rest; yet [this man] is their guide. He dances as he pleases; he is attired in a different disguise. Once in a while he becomes merry and makes pleasant sounds which I have described.
>
> How ignorant we are of their ancient rites, while how well informed [the natives] are! They show off the god they are adoring right in front of us in the ancient manner. . . . It behooves our priests to remember my warning so as to recognize things that are evil.[40]

Durán includes an illustration of the above-mentioned dance leader so that missionaries could visually recognize the "warning" signs of his "evil" dance (fig. 5.2). It is important to note that Durán bases his discussion of these dances as they were performed by (or explained by) Tecpanecs of Coyoacan,

FIG. 5.2 Dance leader in Xocotl Huetzi. Diego Durán, *Book of the Gods and Rites*, fol. 277v. Courtesy of Biblioteca Nacional de España.

an indigenous community that was under the control of the Franciscan order. His insistence that the ancient beliefs endured in their dances was as much a criticism of the ineffectiveness of the Franciscan missionaries in converting natives as it was a statement about the dances themselves.

Almost every chronicler of New Spain wrote about the ubiquitous *juego de palo*, and Durán was no exception. However, unlike most chroniclers, who stop short of admiring the dance/game for its athleticism, Durán addresses some of the missionaries' concerns that the *juego* was a "diabolic art." He mollifies these concerns by asserting his long-standing experience with the game:

> Another performance with dance and song dealt with rogues. A simpleton appeared who pretended to understand all his master's words backward, turning around his words. With this dance came [a juggler who manipulated] a round log with his feet with such skill that the tricks and turns he performed with it caused astonishment, to such an extent that some [Spaniards] believed it to be done through diabolic arts. Considering it carefully, [I believe] it is no more than the sleight of hand played in Spain. Here we could call it "sleight of foot." I myself can be a witness. When I was a lad, I remember a school of this game in the San Pablo Ward, where there was an Indian who was most skillful in this art. There many young Indians from different provinces learned how to juggle the log with their feet. Therefore, I can affirm that this dance and its trickery was more trickery of the foot than art of the devil. In some places when the Indians heard that the people were shocked by it, [considering it diabolic], they let it fall into disuse and do not dare to perform it nor many other dances, gay and refined, with which they made merry and fêted their gods.[41]

Here Durán defends the dance based on his own intuition about its significance: "I myself can be a witness." One might even argue that through his defense of this dance, Durán sought to defend his own perception of himself as a subject of New Spain, or at least his childhood memory of being affected by the dance's alleged diabolic charms. In fact, Durán admits that the songs and dances he witnessed moved him emotionally: "These songs were so sad that just the rhythm and dance saddens one. I have seen these danced occasionally with religious chants, and they are so sad that I was filled with melancholy and woe."[42]

As much as the Indians' dances moved Durán to experience "melancholy and woe," they also inspired in him a great sense of awe and respect, especially those among the peoples of Tlahuic, a lush region south of Mexico City then also known as the Marquesado, presently the state of Morelos. Durán idealized the Marquesado, describing it as "one of the most beautiful lands in the world," and noting that "were it not for the great heat it would be another Garden of Eden."[43] He goes on to mention the "delightful springs, wide rivers full of fish, the freshest of woods, and orchards of many kinds of fruits, many of them native to Mexico and others to Spain." Durán had a special affinity for the region—as did many wealthy Spaniards, including Cortés, for whom the region was named and who maintained a residence there in the postconquest years. Durán expresses his great respect for the region through his writing about its local dances.

> Who will not wonder on gazing upon a dance in which forty or fifty men appear around the drum, on stilts six or twelve feet tall, moving and turning with their bodies as if they were on their own feet?
>
> Who will not consider it a skillful and mighty thing that three men walk about upon one another's shoulders, the lower one dancing with his arms outstretched and his hands filled with feathers or with flowers, and the one in the middle doing the same, and the third one doing the same—each without more support than his feet on the other's shoulder? It is true that this shows not only skill and dexterity but also an amazing strength in the feet.[44]

This "Garden of Eden" once had a "God of Dance," whom the Tlahuica worshiped at the *cuicacalli*—"House of Song"—the school where the children of Aztec nobility learned music and dance. Although Durán notes that natives of Texcoco and Tlacopan maintained their own *cuicacalli*, he emphasizes that the God of Dance was particular to the Tlahuica.[45] For Durán, the *cuicacalli*, above all other Aztec institutions—the marketplace, the bathhouses, the temples—was the ultimate expression of Aztec order, civility, and reason. In fact, Durán dedicated one of the final chapters of his *Book of the Gods and Rites* to "The God of Dance" and the *cuicacalli*.[46] In this chapter he makes his most impassioned defense of the native society, as exhibited by the customs of the *cuicacalli*. He upholds the school as a model of "harmony, good organization, and social order" to which some Spaniards should aspire, for he "confessed" that there was a "coarse lower class, rude, dirty, bestial people that exist in Spain who are as brutish as these Indians or more so."[47] He introduces the *cuicacalli* and the god of dance with the following rhetorical questions:

> Which nation on earth has sustained so many ordinances and laws for common welfare, so just, so well codified, as those the natives had in this land? Where were the sovereigns so feared, so well obeyed, together with their laws and commandments, as in this country? Where were great men, knights, and lords so respected, so revered? Where were their feats and deeds so richly rewarded as in this nation?[48]

Durán melds Christian thought with native Indian practices throughout the "God of Dance" chapter, especially when describing dance rituals and practices. In fact, if Durán thought of Tlahuic as Eden, he seems to describe the *cuicacalli* as its church. For Durán, the *cuicacalli* was the ideal subject for demonstrating Aztec honor, for it was a stage for instilling social discipline. Durán focuses on the obligations of inclusion as well as the threats of exclusion, noting that breaking the rules of the *cuicacalli* could lead to "excommunication" and that failure to perform the dances with physical and rhythmic accuracy could lead to severe punishment.[49] He also admired the protocols that governed the relations between men and women. (Elsewhere he expressed his dissatisfaction with the commingling of men and women in the bathhouses.) Dancing at the *cuicacalli* represented the ideal of gendered relations, which is represented in an image about which Durán writes (fig. 5.3).

The image conveys the sense of order, balance, and harmony Durán envisioned for New Spain. When he inquires whether holding hands in the dance led to "any misbehavior or instigation to evil," he learns that boys would promise girls from other wards their hand in marriage during dances.[50] Such arrangements were unconventional, for as Durán notes, most marriages were arranged by a *tecihuatlanque*, a "petitioner of women" or a "matchmaker." However, in exceptional cases, the *cuicacalli* would provide the space for boys and girls promised to each other to maintain physical and social contact until they were mature enough to marry, usually at the age of twenty-one. His focus on the positive social dimensions of the *cuicacalli* is unflinching, even in cases when it facilitated activity that diametrically opposed its primary disciplining function. Taking it one step further, Durán reports that during the day "in that same building and school" the *cuicacalli* was attended by warriors and prostitutes, with whom they would dance "in fine style."[51] Durán once again makes this observation without any criticism, apparently forgiving the warriors and prostitutes on the basis of their dancing virtuosity.

Durán's writing about the *cuicacalli* is actually a lament, for by the time he wrote about the school it had already been outlawed by Spanish authorities. If Durán seems to idealize the *cuicacalli*, it is because he understood it to have a valuable disciplinary function

FIG. 5.3 Dancing at the *cuicacalli*. Diego Durán, *Book of the Gods and Rites*, fol. 305r. Courtesy of Biblioteca Nacional de España.

in native society. Durán even attributes the prevalence of lawlessness and drunkenness among the young Indians to the disbanding of the *cuicacalli*:

> When they see the young people today, eighteen and twenty years old—living in perdition, utterly shameless, drunkards, thieves, murderers, bandits, disobedient, rude, cocky, gluttons, loaded with girls—they affirm that under the old law there was not the dissoluteness or insolence they observe in the unruly youth of today. No one used to dare drink pulque or become drunk unless he was an old man, for warmth and comfort of his old age (and this applied as much to the ruling class as to the rest of the people).... This law was kept with a terrible vigor and was also applied to fornicators and adulterers, as I have described. The things I mention are not at all divorced from my theme but well describe the refinement of these courtly and polished people. Not only did this refinement exist, but it was the law of the state of a people who are not barbarous, as some pretend.

Curiously, Durán gives few details about the so-called God of Dance mentioned in the chapter's title.

He does not even identify said god by name, which is particularly perplexing given that the *Book of the Gods and Rites* otherwise provides detailed information about the gods and myths associated with them: explanations of their names, descriptions of their physical representations, and, of course, the rituals performed in their honor, no matter how local the god's manifestation and sphere of influence. Below is the only mention Durán makes about the "God of Dance" in the chapter:

> Occasionally they pretended that the idol was angry and that he did not wish them to dance. To placate him, they composed new chants in his praise, glory, and honor, making sacrifices and offerings to him. This idol was made of stone, with his arms open like a man who dances. In his hands were holes in which feathers or flowers were placed. He was kept in a chamber in a courtyard where the usual dances were held. It is said that during some feasts he was brought into the courtyard and was set down next to the drum that is called the *teponaztli*.[52]

It is not clear exactly which god Durán is referring to in this passage. Several Mesoamerican deities are associated with dancing, especially Macuilxochitl ("Five Flower") in the form of Xochipilli ("Flower Prince"). In the *Florentine Codex* Sahagún describes Macuilxochitl/Xochipilli as the "god of the palace folk" or "the persons who served for the amusement or pastime of the great—hence first and foremost the players, dancers, and singers."[53] However, Durán refers to Macuilxochitl only as "the god of dice," without ever mentioning his association to dance.

A sculpture of Xochipilli in the collection of the National Museum of Anthropology in Mexico conforms remarkably to Durán's description of the "God of Dance" sculpture (fig. 5.4). In this sculpture, the Flower Prince is seated cross-legged, apparently in some state of ecstatic stupor from ingesting mind-altering mushrooms, representations of which cover the pedestal upon which he sits. As such, it is possible that Xochipilli is the unnamed god of dance to which Durán refers.

Moreover, Durán mentions Xochiquetzal in his "God of Dance" chapter and notes that she was "represented with her arms open like a woman who is dancing" (as was the figure in the sculpture he describes) and emphasizes that dances associated with her feast were the "most enjoyed" and the "most solemn." Although Durán refers to the "God of Dance" as "he," is it possible that Xochiquetzal was the god of dance among the Tlahuica (see fig. 5.5).

Also in the "God of Dance" chapter Durán mentions a dance of "Old Humpbacks, who wore masks representing old men. It was extremely gay, merry, and funny in the native fashion."[54] Could this have been a dance of the trickster Huehuecoyotl ("Very Old Coyote"), the god of dance and song, oratory, deceit, and sexuality? The *Codex Borbonicus* depicts Huehuecoyotl dancing to the beat of Xochipilli's drum, illustrating yet another deity duo's shared association to music and dance (fig. 5.6).

Within Durán's chapter there are references to at least three dancing "gods": Xochipilli, Xochiquetzal, and Huehuecoyotl. This leaves open the possibility that Durán misunderstood (or perhaps was misled by) his informants about the existence of a singular "God of Dance." Given Durán's deep admiration for the *cuicacalli*, it is conceivable that he refers only to a single "God of Dance" so as to portray the devotees of the "God of Dance" as a monotheistic cult primed for Christianity. After all, as Durán openly admits in the closing remarks of the chapter, he was perfectly willing to withhold certain incriminating "details" about the principles and practices of Aztec dance:

> Thus I shall end here my description of native dances, for I have noted the essential things within the subject of dancing. I could add a few trifling details of little importance if I felt they could be useful as an admonition. In that case I would set them down as a warning [to our priests], but the problem [of paganism] has been solved, praised be our Lord.[55]

Durán's own past was intimately tied to the dancers and dances about which he wrote. As such, his dance writings are riddled with arbitrary explanations, perfunctory admonishments, and ambiguous praise, yet collectively they confidently assert his belief that dancing held a "guarded secret" that had to be revealed in order for people to fully understand the transition between a pagan past and a Christian future, as well as his own relation to it.

Dancing in Good Harmony:
José de Acosta and Andrés Pérez de Ribas

Durán criticized Franciscan missionaries for failing to recognize the syncretic dimension of the dances and feasts they sponsored, yet his criticism also could have applied to Jesuit missionaries who arrived in New Spain in 1572, almost fifty years after the other orders.[56] The writings of José de Acosta and Andrés Pérez de Ribas give a unique perspective on the early years of the Jesuit mission in New Spain. These two missionaries built upon (and perhaps even drew di-

FIG. 5.4 Xochipilli, "The God of Dance." Museo Nacional de Antropología, Mexico City. Photograph © John Bigelow Taylor.

FIG. 5.5 Xochipilli and Xochiquetzal. *Codex Borgia*, pl. 58. Courtesy of Dover Publications.

rectly from) Durán's remarks that allowing dance was a necessary aspect of good government.

José de Acosta (ca. 1540–1600) wrote *Natural and Moral History of the Indies* (*Historia natural y moral de las Indias*), first printed in Seville in 1590.[57] The *Historia* was partially based on a manuscript by Juan de Tovar, which itself was based on a now missing manuscript called *Crónica X*, which also, as mentioned above, a source for Durán.[58] Acosta dedicates a chapter of his history to the dances and festivities of the Indians. Its opening paragraph echoes Durán's remarks about the relationship between dance and "good government": "Because it is an element of good government for a commonwealth to have its recreations and pastimes on appropriate occasions, it would be well to describe what the Indians—especially the Mexicans—were accustomed to doing in this regard. No group of men living in common has been discovered that does not have some method of entertainment and recreation, with games or dances and pleasant exercises."[59]

From his travels throughout Peru and New Spain in 1586–1587, Acosta saw Peruvian *taquis*, which he equates with *areítos* and *mitotes* (a Nahuatl word for "dance"), the *puella* (a dance with sticks), dances associated with various occupations (shepherds, farmers, fishermen, and hunters), and a game wherein men balance on each others' shoulders, which he calls *pelas* after a similar Portuguese tradition. He dismisses attempts among missionaries to "avoid such dances." In fact, Acosta suggested allowing Indians to perform their dances as a "form of recreation and rejoicing." Acosta's relatively lengthy description of the dances of New Spain was published in Theodor de Bry's *America* (book 9). The book includes an engraving depicting dance in New Spain: "Of All the Manners of Strange Dances Among the Indians (*De toda suerte de extrañas danzas de los Indios*)" (fig. 5.7).

Acosta emphasizes that "the method of recreation most enjoyed by the Mexicans is the solemn *mitote*, which is a dance that had so much prestige among them that sometimes the kings danced it." By *mitote*, Acosta refers to sacred dances, akin to what Motolinía called the *macehualiztli*. He describes a version of a *mitote* he saw performed in the church courtyard in the city of Tepoztlán, though he shares no distinguishing descriptions of the dance he saw, he echoes Durán's warning that dancing was "a good thing to occupy and entertain the Indians." He also relativizes: "Recreation that is public and harms no one has fewer disadvantages than others that the Indians might perform by themselves should these dances be taken away from them." Acosta supports his claim by referencing Pope Gregory I (ca. 540–604), who had advocated incorporating Anglo-Saxon pagan rituals into Christian festivities in order to advance the conversion process. He applies that papal teaching to the Indians of the New World by suggesting that missionaries "try to channel their festivals and rejoicings toward the honor of God and the saints whose feasts are being celebrated."

Acosta concludes the chapter about the dances of New Spain with a promise to dedicate an entire book to "the usages and customs of the Mexicans." He never fulfilled that promise. However, approximately a decade after Acosta completed his *Natural and Moral History*, another Jesuit missionary arrived in New Spain and would go on to fill the lacunae surrounding the role of the *mitote* in the spiritual conquest.

Andrés Pérez de Ribas (1575–1655) left for New Spain in 1602. Between 1604 and 1620 he served in

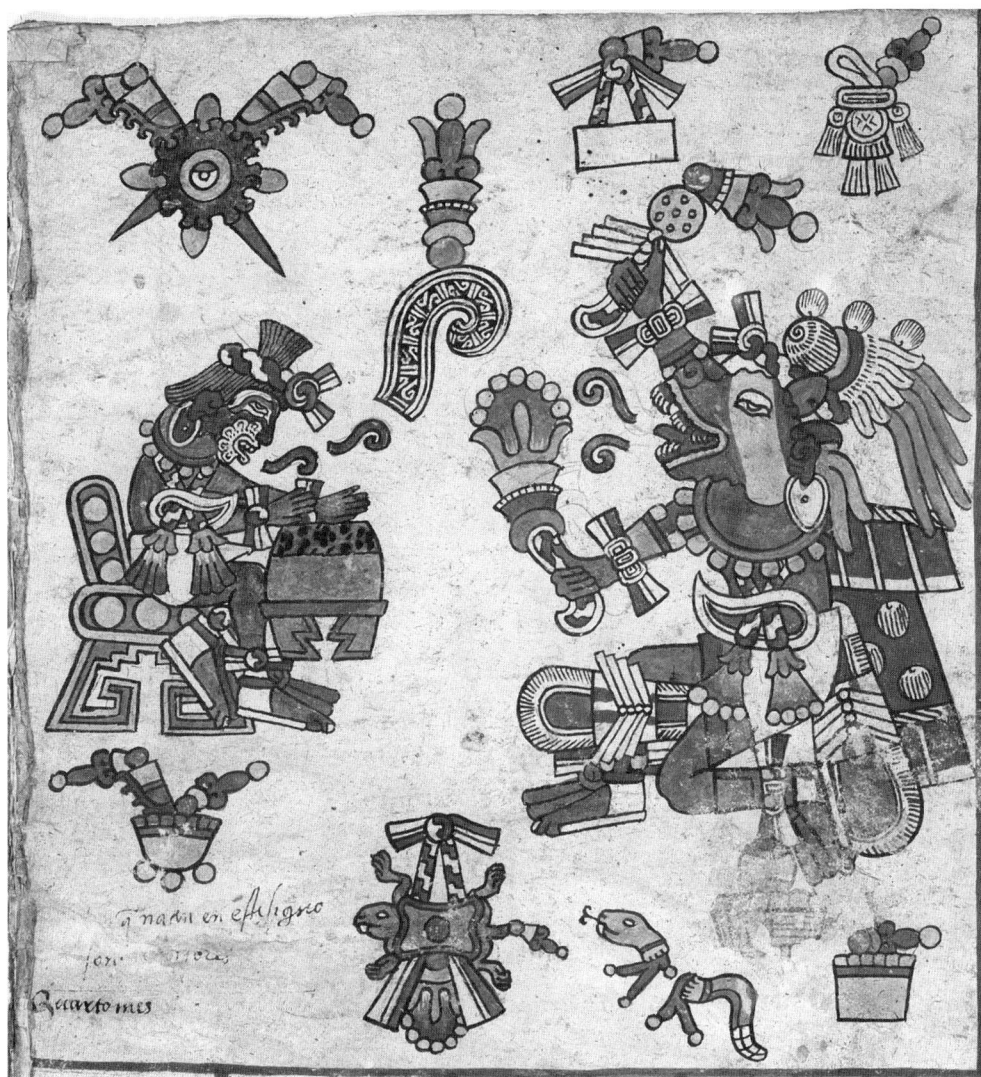

FIG. 5.6 Xochipilli drumming and Huehuecoyotl dancing and singing. *Codex Borbonicus*, fol. 4. Courtesy of ADEVA, Akademische Druck-u. Verlagsanstalt, Graz, Austria.

northern Mexico, especially in the region of Sinaloa, which he considered the most "barbarous and fierce" of the Indian territories. Due to failing health, he was called to Mexico City to convalesce, later taking on a role as rector of the Jesuit College at Tepotzotlán, a city situated northeast of Mexico City and the former center of the indigenous Otomí peoples. In 1638 Pérez de Ribas became *padre provincial* of the Jesuit order in New Spain. In 1645 he published *History of the Triumphs of Our Holy Faith amongst the Most Barbarous and Fierce Peoples of the New World* (*Historia de los triunfos de nuestra santa fe entre gentes las más bárbaras y fieras del Nuevo Orbe*), which chronicles the Jesuit mission's evangelical "triumphs" in New Spain.

Throughout the *History*, Pérez de Ribas takes every opportunity to praise the Jesuits for educating the Indian youth, especially the sons of Indian elites, who were trained in theology, music, and reading. Many of their Indian seminarians returned to their cities to become governors and, among other things, organize "unusual festivals" to win the attention of "poorer Indians" who had not yet integrated into the Church and who were particularly "restless" during

FIG. 5.7 "Of All the Manners of Strange Dances Among the Indians." Theodor de Bry, *America*, part 9 (1601). Courtesy of the John Carter Brown Library at Brown University.

the ceremonies of Holy Week. In fact, Pérez de Ribas dedicates a chapter to the life and work of Don Lorenzo, one of the Indian seminarians who was "an example for the Christian Indians of other nations to follow."[60] Born to a noble family in Mexico City, Lorenzo entered the seminary at Tepotzotlán where he had become a master teacher of Nahuatl. He was a model Indian, Pérez de Ribas explains, for he refused gifts, liquor, and chocolate, and made significant contributions to the missionary theatre. Don Lorenzo had his pupils "act out the principal biblical scenes, the children being richly adorned in what Don Lorenzo conceived to be the manner of dress of those ancient days. These pageants became so famous that Spaniards, as well as Indians, came from afar to enjoy them."[61]

The most detailed of Pérez de Ribas's descriptions of "unusual festivals" concerns the "Dance of the Emperor Montezuma," a *mitote* that he explains was "once performed for their pagan people" but had since been "dedicated to the King of Kings, Christ our Lord."[62] His account is based on a performance that took place in 1645 at the Cathedral of San Gregorio el Magno in Mexico City. Pérez de Ribas's "digression" into his description of this dance was meant to highlight San Gregorio as a "triumph" of Christian education. San Gregorio was a seminary where noble Indian youths were taught to convey Christian themes in their indigenous language as well as in dance and song. Each year at the commencement of the Lenten season, students performed the "Dance of the Emperor Montezuma," a dramatization of the *tlatoani*'s royal entrance and the subsequent prostrations of his court. The ceremony was so impressive that it attracted the attention of "important persons, lords, and archbishops who [had] come from Spain."

The dance took place in a plaza strewn with flowers and made to resemble Montezuma's palace. At one end of the plaza sat a small red and gilded stool that represented the emperor's throne; at the other was a drum, surrounded by a chorus of elders who sang and danced "a grave step without much movement." The dance began with the elders singing: "Go forth, Mexicans! Dance the Tocotín, for here we have the King of Glory." Pérez de Ribas explains that *tocotín* is a dance and a rhythm, so named for the vocables that are sung to the rhythm of the beating drum: *to-co-tin*. To the sound of the beating *teponaztli*, a group of fourteen dancers entered in two rows, "as in the Spanish *hacha*" (a "torch dance" from the Spanish court).[63] They wore elaborate dress that recalled "the ancient Mexican princes" as well as the "Roman emperors": richly embroidered mantles tied in a rosette knot over the right shoulder, a doublet, and matching trousers. They also wore pyramid-shaped diadems encrusted with gold and precious stones. In the left hand each carried a feathered wand, and in the right, a rattle called an *ayacaztli*. They moved in a manner that was "subdued and grave, executed in rhythm, not only with the feet but with the arms and hands."

Following the procession, a dancer portraying Montezuma entered the plaza with three young courtiers, two of whom swept the emperor's path and scattered flowers at his feet while the other carried a large fan of feathers over the emperor's head "in the manner of a canopy." The emperor then took to his throne as his court performed a *sarao* for him, waving their wands and rattles in unison so as to demonstrate their reverence, "as though they would like to place themselves beneath his feet." Following the spectacle of submission, the emperor then took center stage to dance with a rare combination of "modesty" and "majesty." As the emperor danced, the members of his court "remain[ed] stationary in their positions, bowing down to the ground," except for when he approached them, at which point they touched his feet with one of their feathered wands "as a sign of humility." Upon completing his dance, the emperor sat in his throne and watched a series of additional court dances, which Pérez de Ribas notes were all similar yet "pleasing and not tiresome."

Two eighteenth-century colonial histories include visual depictions of the "Dance of the Emperor Montezuma." The first is the *Crónica de Michoacán* (ca. 1788), which includes a map that illustrates a series of events connected to the 1521 arrival of conquistador Cristóbal de Olid in the city of Michoacán (fig. 5.8).[64] With a set of theatrical circumstances that are similar to those surrounding the arrival of the Spaniards in Tenochtitlan, the map shows King Caltzontzin watching a dance as he receives word of Olid's arrival. The image reads: "Here they are dancing for the King (*Aqui le estan bailando al Rey*)." Like Pérez de Ribas's description of the "Dance of the Emperor Montezuma," the scene in the *Crónica* depicts an enthroned emperor watching as mantle-clad dancers move in unison to the rhythm of the *teponaztli* drum (albeit far fewer than the fourteen Pérez de Ribas mentions).

The second depiction is in Antonio de Basarás y Garaygorta's unpublished *Origen, costumbres y estado presente de mexicanos y philipinos* (1763), which illustrates the moment in the "Dance of the Emperor Montezuma" when the emperor processes between two rows of dancers who point their feathered fans at his feet (fig. 5.9). Despite its eighteenth-century European dress and architecture, this image more accurately illustrates details in Pérez de Ribas's account. For instance, it represents the feathered shield used to protect the emperor from the sun. It also depicts European instruments, such as the harp, coronet, and bassoon, which Pérez de Ribas notes augmented the indigenous drum and singers—and which indicated to him that the music was "already Christian."

Neither of these images portrays the *mitote* as a distinctly Christian ceremony. Moreover, there is virtually nothing in Pérez de Ribas's account that explains how or why he perceived this dance as an act of Christian devotion, apart from his references to "Christian" music and the brief aside that the dancers made reverences to the Blessed Sacrament. What led Pérez de Ribas to believe that the dance was

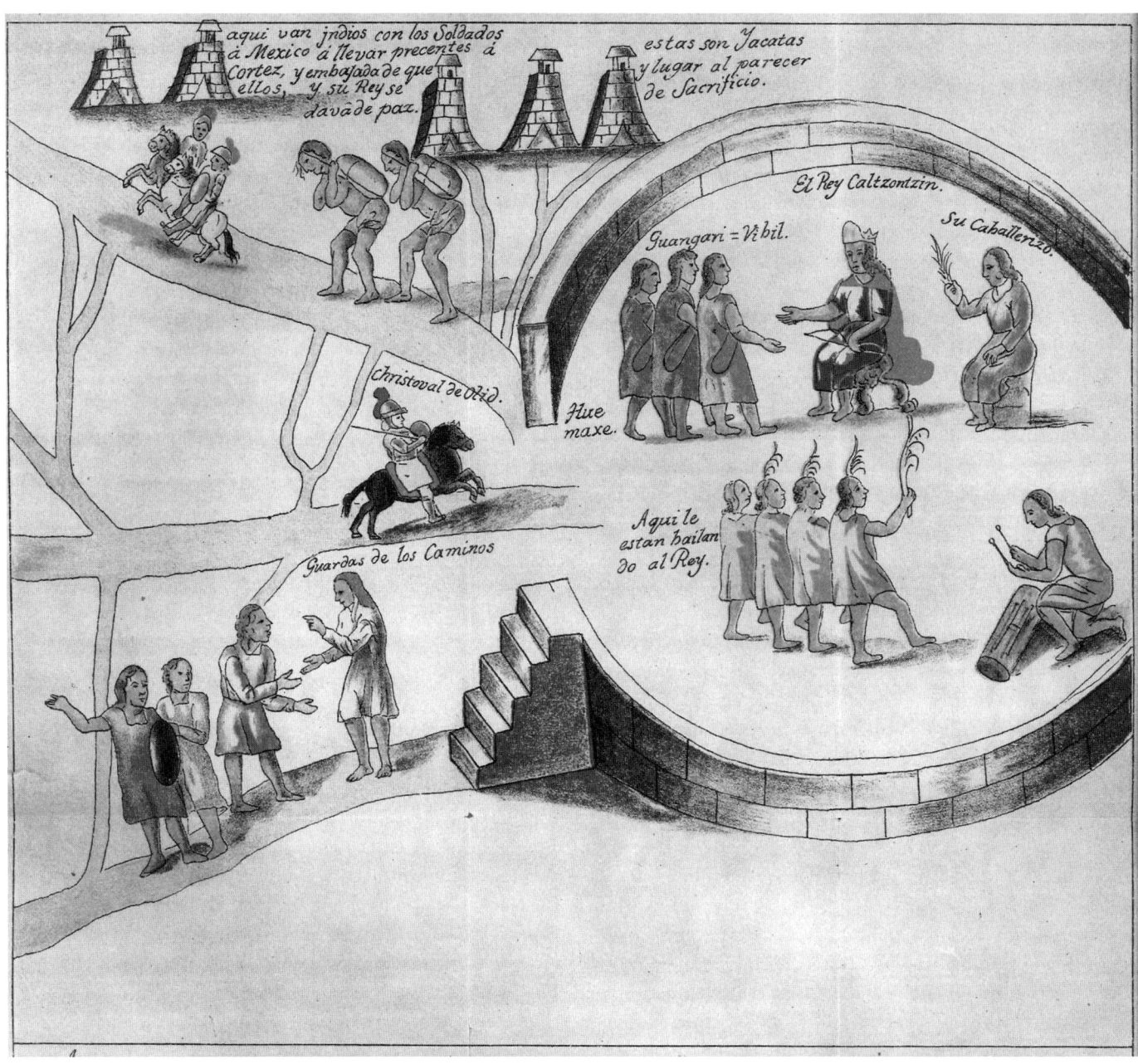

FIG. 5.8 Dance of the Emperor. *Crónica de Michoacán*, v. 18. Courtesy of the Archivo General de la Nación, Mexico.

"used in the service and recognition of the one who is King of Kings, our sacramental lord Jesus Christ"? What specifically about this dance led audiences of Spaniards to believe in the faithfulness of the Indians' conversion, especially when its dramaturgical elements seem to bear so little relation to Christian iconography, doctrine, or history? What allowed Montezuma to stand in for God?

One possible answer is that colonial and Church authorities permitted Indians to dance as a substitute for participating in the Christian sacrament of the Holy Eucharist. In sixteenth-century New Spain, only a select few of Spaniards participated in the sacrament of the Holy Eucharist. Recently converted Indians were routinely denied permission to partake since clerics were uncertain whether the Indians were able to understand the theological significance of transubstantiation. (However, note that the Mexica had their own eucharistic practices, wherein dough-shaped figures of the Aztec god Huitzilopochtli were ritually created and then eaten.) In colonial Christian celebrations, the Eucharist appeared "as an object to be looked at and adored, more than received."[65] While no missionary explicitly explains why Indians danced with, around, near, and for the Eucharist, it is plausible that dancing was a surrogate form of communion with the Body of Christ.

For example, in the course of describing the "Dance of the Emperor Montezuma," Pérez de Ribas qualifies the Indians' expressions of devotion with the following aside: "Today it has been changed, and this entire obeisance is made to the Blessed Sacrament on the altar."[66] He also "was moved to describe" a performance of the *danza de los voladores* that took place immediately following the "Dance of the Emperor Montezuma" and that similarly integrated the Blessed Sacrament. In a description similar to that of Oviedo, as discussed in chapter 1, he explains that young men erected a pole at the center of the plaza and climbed it until they reached a platform at its apex. They then attached themselves by cords to the pole before they leapt from its platform, tracing progressively wider cycles around the pole as they descended, all the while playing rattles and other instruments. Pérez de Ribas emphasizes that their flight coordinated with a procession of the Holy Sacrament in the plaza below, essentially dramatizing a choreographed communion between Aztec *voladores* and the procession of Christ's body.[67] Although he does not explicitly explain the dance in theological terms, he stresses that the ceremony engenders great religious significance: "And it cannot fail to be pleasing to faithful Catholics to see the ancient Mexican nobility vanquished at the feet of the redeemer, whom they did not know formerly and now adore and recognize with every demonstration of joy that they can put forth."

Pérez de Ribas's text suggests that dancing was both a substitute for the sacrament of the Holy Eucharist as well as a confirmation of the Indians' fidelity to Christianity. He sensed the sacramental quality of their dances not only in their choreographic design, but also in the kinesthetic qualities of their movements. For Pérez de Ribas, and presumably for the alleged flocks of Spanish administrators and clergy who came to see the *mitotes*, dancing had

FIG. 5.9 Dance of the Emperor Montezuma. Joaquín Antonio de Basarás y Garaygorta, *Origen, costumbres, y estado presente de mexicanos y philipinos* (1763), lam. 3, 118. Courtesy of the Hispanic Society of America, New York.

transformed the Indians' barbaric impulse into a noble reflex. That much is clear from the way his descriptions focus on the dancers' physical stability over mobility, their physical repression over expression, and their labor over pleasure. For example, he makes note of the elders, who make "a grave step without much movement," the emperor, who moves with "modesty," and the court dancers, who move in a manner that is both "subdued and grave," especially when they "remain stationary" while in deep prostration or perform gestures of "humility" and "obeisance."

The refined, ordered, and balanced quality of the Indians' dancing led Pérez de Ribas to the remarkable epiphany that the during the "pomp" of the ceremonies, "these children ... often resemble the sons of Spanish lords."[68] The uncanny experience of witnessing Indians convincingly perform idealized versions of Spanish selfhood is presumably what distinguished the "Dance of the Emperor Montezuma" from the "ordinary *mitotes*" performed by "commoners." However, although Pérez de Ribas recognized a motional resemblance between dancing Indians and Spanish lords, his writing continually reinscribes difference by way of marking the ways that the Indians' movements express the physical labor, discipline, and repression necessary to producing the colonial ideal. In that sense, Pérez de Ribas's description of the "Dance of the Emperor Montezuma" configures dancing as a sphere of colonial mimicry that produces "a reformed, recognizable Other as a subject of difference that is almost the same but not quite."[69]

Interestingly, for Pérez de Ribas, as well as for Durán, dancing was not only a form of colonial mimicry, wherein Indian colonial subjects imitated Christian gestures and steps, but also a type of "*primitive* mimicry," in which the Indians lampooned the rituals of their indigenous ancestors. For example, Durán once observed a festival wherein Indians performed their "heathen" rites, but only so that they could "laugh and mock them."[70] Pérez de Ribas similarly notes that the Indian seminarian Don Lorenzo "incorporated the *mitote* dances made famous by the great Emperor Montezuma, employing in them the dances of the Aztec peoples. In these dances, however, he took great care to express the abomination felt for the cruel sacrifices of so many thousands of people before the coming of the Padres."[71] If we accept Pérez de Ribas's claim that Don Lorenzo "took great care" to consciously choreograph *mitotes* so as to repudiate the rites of the Aztec ancestors, then we may conclude that dancing was a means by which the Indians simultaneously embodied the idealized codes of physical comportment associated with the Spanish lords *and* disembodied their pagan pasts.

Pérez de Ribas's description of the "Dance of the Emperor Montezuma" affirms the claims Acosta made about the relationship between dance and "good government" and fulfills the prophesy Durán had made just over a half-century earlier that the Indians would restore order, harmony, and balance through dancing.[72] In some way, the Seminary of San Gregorio el Magno was the culmination of both the Aztec *cuicacalli* and Maestros Pedro and Benito de Begel's dancing school, in that its seminarians transformed dances associated with Aztec sacrifice into sacramental acts of Christian devotion.

Conclusion: Miraculous Dancing

Trexler succinctly explains that "because of the power of Spanish soldiers and administrators, the missionaries were able to choreograph the 'Indian' culture they imagined and force the natives to perform that imagination."[73] In this chapter I examined diverse types of writing about dance in colonial New Spain—prohibitions against dancing, *actas* that governed dance festivals, and missionary interpretations of dance among converted Indians. These writings are saturated with colonial anxieties and aspirations about the role of dance in the spiritual conquest that suggest that forcing "the natives to perform" a Christian worldview was a far more ambiguous process than Trexler would have us believe.

Those anxieties and aspirations are vividly illustrated in one of the final folios of the *Codex Azcatítlan* (fig. 5.10). Like Pérez de Ribas's description of the *danza de los voladores*, this codex depicts *voladores* descending from the pole in tandem with the administering of a Christian sacramental rite, in this instance, a baptismal scene wherein a missionary douses a native youth in a baptismal font. To affirm the fidelity of the *danza* as an expression of Christian devotion, the *voladores* are shown as angels with

FIG. 5.10 Missionaries gazing at *voladores* and baptism. *Codex Azcatítlan*, fol. 27. Courtesy of Bibliothèque nationale de France.

wings attached to their backs.[74] The image also validates the baptismal rite by means of the legitimizing gaze of nine missionaries, whose disembodied heads form a figurative watchtower. However, by exposing the mechanisms of surveillance by which colonial performance was scaffolded, the *Codex Azcatítlan* begs questions similar to those explored in this chapter about the performative dimensions of perception: What exactly did the missionaries look for when watching Indian dances? How did they determine whether dances were expressions of Christian devotion or Nahua revitalism?

Durán, Acosta, and Pérez de Ribas similarly believed that the dancing Indian body exemplified order, discipline, and balance, and thus represented a preparedness for Christian conversion—although they arrived at this conclusion by different means. Durán relied on a combination of instinct and experience to determine whether dances were expressions of Christian belief. Acosta assumed that there were always slips of paganism, yet thought dancing was a preferred "evil" to other indigenous customs and traditions. He reasoned that even if dancing had not indoctrinated the Indians, it at least kept them under close scrutiny, as compulsory religious ceremonies diverted the Indians' attention away from the altars they maintained in their homes.[75] Pérez de Ribas interpreted the meaning of *mitotes* by how well the Indians' physicality resembled that of Spanish lords, as well as by the level of pleasure and interest the dances elicited from Spanish audiences.

Missionaries recognized that dance was a mysterious realm of expression and sought to control its potentially ambiguous meanings by producing narratives that linked dancing to experiences of miraculous conversion. For example, dancing Indians are at the center of three defining accounts concerning the literal and figurative foundation of Mexican Christianity. For some curious reason, all three of these events allegedly transpired in 1531, though they were not chronicled until decades later.

According to Motolinía, on Easter Day in 1531 (April 16) the Spaniards founded the city of Puebla de los Ángeles, one of the only major colonial cities that was not built from the remains of a preexisting indigenous city. To celebrate, Indians from neighboring villages entered the city while singing, drumming, and holding banners: "Others came with boys dancing and with many dances so that it seemed that they were driving away demons."[76]

Could these boys have been performing the "hand-waving dance" of the feast of Ochpaniztli, wherein the Mexica would perform purifying gestures with flowers in order to prepare the roads for Toci? Did this choreographed procession have anything to do with "Ilamateuchtli's Leap," the dance performed during the festival of Tititl by young boys dressed as the menacing spirits of the *cihuateteo* to drive their negative energies away?

According to another legend, on July 25, 1531, Don Nicolás de San Luis Montáñez, a *cacique* of Queretero, led Chichimeca warriors into battle against Christians at the Hill of San Gremal. The Chichimeca, the infamous "barbarians" of New Spain, were "screaming and dancing in their *mitotes* and *bailes*" during their prolonged battle with the Christians, when a Holy Cross miraculously appeared in the sky and reflected the image of Santiago—a sign that forced the Chichimeca to put down their arms and to dedicate themselves to Jesus Christ. The following day the Chichimeca erected a cross made of stones and danced around it for a whole week with their bows and arrows.[77]

Were they dancing the serpent's dance? Perhaps just as it was performed during the *veintena* Izcalli, when Montezuma led his lords around a temple four times in order to consecrate it? Or did they circle the cross in the manner that bathed slaves circled the temple to prepare to sacrifice themselves during the Mexica festival of Panquetzaliztli? There, on the site of San Gremal, did the Chichimeca prepare themselves for their sacrifice to Christianity? Or was theirs an act of resistance? Was this procession just a ruse so that the warriors could replenish and rededicate their energy, just as they once had by circling the *xocotl* pole dedicated to ancestral warriors during the feast of Xocotl Huetzi?

A third dancing miracle took place in 1531, this one connected to the defining narrative of Mexican identity. In that year, Our Lady of Guadalupe miraculously and repeatedly appeared to Juan Diego Cuauhtlatoatzin, then a recently converted Indian *macehual*, now the first indigenous saint. The Virgin Mother compelled Juan Diego to petition Bishop Zumárraga to erect a shrine in her honor in the very place she appeared to him, on Tepeyac Hill. The bishop refused Juan Diego's requests, until one day Juan Diego appeared before the bishop with a cloak full of flowers that he had collected at the insistence of the Virgin Mother. Per her instruction, Juan Diego unfurled his cloak before the bishop to reveal the flowers. When he did, they were shocked to find that the flowers had miraculously emblazoned an image of the Virgin Mother on his cloak. Finally convinced of her divine presence, the bishop ordered the construction of a shrine on Tepeyac Hill dedicated to the *Virgen de Guadalupe*, where the relic could be displayed for all to behold. According to the legend, several unconverted Indians were near the shrine when priests were transferring the *tilma* to its altar. These pagan Indians were so moved by the image's power as it crossed their path that they spontaneously converted to Christianity and danced in praise and honor of the image.[78]

Could this dance, if indeed it was performed as the legend stipulates, have related to the *toxcatl* leap, when during the Festival of Toxcatl young boys and girls danced in front of the amaranth dough image of Huitzilopochtli? Could the relic of the Virgin have carried the same transformative power as the limbs of women who died in childbirth, with which thieves would dance to entrance and manipulate unsuspecting victims?

Of course, we have no way of knowing what went through the minds and bodies of the Indians as they performed these alleged dances of conversion— nor did the missionaries. However, that did not deter these accounts of "miraculous" dancing from being used to substantiate broader narratives about the origins of Mexican Christianity. By portraying the conversion of Aztecs into Christians as an involuntary, spontaneous, and divinely inspired dance, chroniclers, missionaries, and Indians alike concealed the carefully choreographed acts of the spiritual conquest. The references to dancing in colonial chronicles, missionary ethnographies, municipal and Church records, and post-conquest codices discussed in this chapter give us an idea about the degree to which Indian bodies were orchestrated, controlled, and directed to perform these miraculous acts of belief.

Conclusion

Fernando de Alvarado Tezozómoc was born into an Aztec royal family fifteen years after the conquest of Mexico. His father was a descendant of the Mexica ruler Axayacatl; his mother was one of Montezuma's daughters. As the descendant of two ruling lineages, he had unique access to the Aztec codices as well as to oral histories about his royal ancestors, their history, and customs. He was also a student at the Colegio Imperial de Santa Cruz de Tlatelolco, a school for indigenous nobles that Franciscan missionaries established in 1536. This remarkable set of circumstances conspired to make him the first full-blooded Mexican to write a postconquest chronicle of the Aztec past, the *Crónica mexicana* (1598).

Tezozómoc weaves references to dance throughout his narration of epic events, offering rare glimpses into the role of dancing in the highest spheres of Mexica society. He dedicates an entire chapter to the description of a funerary ceremony that honored the unprecedented loss of Mexica warriors during their prolonged military conflict with the Chalca in the fifteenth century. The ceremony began with a procession led by the relatives of the deceased, who carried the bows, arrows, and feathered shields of the slain warriors, as children performed a very sad song and dance (*la música con canto y baile triste*): "The death that our fathers, brothers, and children received, what happened to them wasn't just. . . . We will remember you forever!" They proceeded to the "House of War," where for four days they performed more dances of mourning (*bailar llorando*). As they danced, their songs of collective anguish were transformed into chants of revenge: "Loving children, have strength, as much as you can. Glory will be revenge, and a lot of it!" Following the dance, they brought an anthropomorphic figure of Huitzilopochtli to his temple and burned it, along with the bodies of their beloved.[1]

Even if only a few choreographic details survived the more than one hundred years between the performance of this dance and Tezozómoc's memorialization of it, the *Crónica* conveys the sense that dancing was an intense form of social memory for the Aztec by depicting the affective responses to performance. In this instance, the *bailar llorando* was a way to collectively experience and share grief. It was also an act of resistance, not only against murderous enemies, but also against the dancers' own bodies, which defied the physical and emotional duress that came with dancing for four days.

Tezozómoc never explains how he came to know about this particular funeral, although it is near certain that one of his sources was the now-missing *Crónica X*. We know this because Diego Durán, who similarly relied on this source, also references this mourning ritual, though he barely mentions any details about its physicality or how it inspired violent ideations.[2] Tezozómoc must have had an additional source. Perhaps he consulted one of the pictorial codices before they were destroyed? Or maybe he learned of the ceremony directly from a relative, possibly even one who had participated in it? We may never know how Tezozómoc came to learn about this dance or why he chose to write about it at a critical turning point in his history of the Mexica, yet it highlights one of the central questions that runs throughout this book: When does choreography (the writing of dance) become historiography (the writing of history), and vice versa?

At the outset of researching this book, I wanted to identify written and visual representations of dance, dancers, and dancing in the chronicles of the New World. My primary interest was to trace a history of dance in the Americas and the role of embodied experience in the New World encounter. As I began to examine the broad and diverse representations of dance in colonial discourse, it became apparent that many allusions to dance are intimately tied to death. Dance seems always to be a sign of impending violence, a spectacle of sacrifice, a reenactment of history, or an interaction with ancestors. As with Tezozómoc's description of the *baile llorando*, nearly every chronicler draws upon the inherent power of the dancing body to represent otherwise unrepresentable embodiments of and responses to death. Indeed, the chroniclers powered their histories with the agency, presence, and corporeality of dancing Indians. We see this in the early accounts of discovery and settlement, with Europeans and Indians attempting to communicate across linguistic boundaries, often with violent consequences.

The first chroniclers marveled at the idea that dancing was a mode of connecting with ancestors and gods, as well as a technique for representing the past. Motolinía and his counterfeiters fabricated statistics about the number of dancers who participated in Aztec rituals, but those numbers were only body counts, perverse indices of the incalculable genocide eventuated by the conquest. The *Florentine Codex* reveals the ways that dancing made human sacrifice meaningful in the production, maintenance, and representation of Aztec identity and imperial power. In the accounts of the Massacre of the Festival of Toxcatl, both Mesoamerican and Christian chroniclers assert competing perspectives about the political, religious, and social significance of the conquest through their mythistorical depictions of dancing bodies. Even later generations of missionary ethnographers—most of whom upheld Aztec dancing as an expression of a supremely governed, disciplined, and noble culture—sought to transform Indian dances dedicated to sacrificed indigenous gods into acts devoted to a resurrected Christ.

In order to represent their evolving ideas about indigenous culture, the chroniclers had to discover and borrow terms for "dance." The early chroniclers "invented" the concept of *areíto* so as to reflect their own preoccupations with its historiographic function. Motolinía outright rejects *areíto*, instead preferring to write about the Nahuatl *macehualiztli* and *netotiliztli*, which he discursively baptized to reflect his own ideal view of the Mexica as penitent Christian commoners. Sahagún's extensive study yielded a range of terms specific to the principles and practices of Aztec dance. He reports terms such as the "serpent's dance," the "captive's dance," the "hand-waving dance," "dancing with the limbs, skins, and severed heads." Indeed, the *Florentine Codex* leaves a whole lexicon with which to understand Aztec rituals of purification and sacrifice. With succeeding generations of chroniclers came even more terms—*tocotín*, *mitote*, *moros y cristianos*—all of which reflect the early convergences o Spanish and Nahua cultures.

Tezozómoc inherited this polyglottal lexicon for "dancing" that had come to circulate within colonial discourse by the end of the sixteenth century. For the most part, he uses the Spanish terms *baile* and *danza*, but he also employs *areíto*, *macehualiztli*, *mitote*, and *tocotín*, sometimes in remarkable combinations. For example, when writing about the coronation ceremony of the *tlatoani* Tizoc, he says the nobles prepared themselves to perform an *areíto y baile de macehualiztli*.[3] Roughly translated, this phrase means "the (Taíno) song-dance and the (Spanish) dance of the (Aztec) sacred dance." This discursive act stretches the limits of language to represent the complex embodiments of time and space that dancing uniquely instantiates. In this compressed phrase, we can see an impulse that flows throughout colonial representations of dance: to choreograph racial, cultural, and religious difference into the historiography of a unified New World.

This impulse is evident in one of the earliest references to dance in the discourse of the New World, Christopher Columbus's account of "discovering" Indians in the West Indies, an encounter that led to a profound experience of alterity for Spaniards and Indians alike, and ultimately to violence. Over a hundred and fifty years later, Andrés Pérez de Ribas had a similar encounter with dancing, yet had a radically different experience. Instead of "otherness," he saw a reflection of himself and his fellow Spaniards in the providential movements of the Indians who performed the "Dance of the Emperor Montezuma." How is it that dancing could produce such radically different experiences of identity and identification?

In the years between Columbus's "discovery" and Andrés Pérez de Ribas's epiphany, conquistadors, missionaries, chroniclers, colonial administrators, and artists attempted to portray their perspectives of and from the New World through visual and written representations of indigenous dance. In so doing, some left behind discriminatory portrayals of Indians as barbarians. However, it is also true that some expressed the most passionate critiques of and sincere laments about the Spanish conquest. While this study has shown that these representations of dance are often ambivalent, ambiguous, fictionalized, and sometimes outright deceptive—and thus reveal little about the actual social history of the Aztec empire or its conquest—they are relevant as evidence that dancing was in many ways central to Europeans' experience of the New World, which they often memorialized as a dance between the self and the other.

APPENDIX A

Two Accounts of the *Areíto* of Anacaona

Bartolomé de las Casas, *Historia de las Indias*, Volume 2, Book 1, Chapter 114

Trans. Francis Sullivan in Las Casas, *Indian Freedom: The Cause of Bartolomé de las Casas, 1484–1566: A Reader*, 37–38.

When the Christians saw the army, Don Bartholomew signaled that he came to do them no harm, but to visit them, spend time among them, and he wanted to see King Behechio and his country. The Indians relaxed, as if they had gotten great pledges from the Christians, and it would be impossible for them to fail in their word. So messengers went flying off to King Behechio, or, if he was already there, he sent orders that his whole court and all of his people, plus his sister Anacaona, a remarkable and gracious woman, should go out and welcome the Christians, and that they should put on all the festivities usually done for their own rulers, the full panoply of their traditional celebrations. The Indians and the Christians went a further thirty leagues to reach the city of Xaragua because it is some sixty leagues from Santo Domingo. A whole host of people, including many chiefs and nobles, came out to meet them, a gathering of the entire region with King Behechio and Queen Anacaona, his sister, singing their songs, dancing their dances, which they call *areítos*, a happy, happy thing to see, especially when performed jointly by large numbers. Thirty women led the procession, the wives of King Behechio, they were stark naked except their lower bodies were covered with cotton skirts, white skirts beautifully woven which they call *naguas*, and which covered them from waist to thigh.

They carried green branches in their hands, and they sang and danced and leaped with grace in a womanly way, expressing great, great delight, excitement, and festival joy. The women danced up to Bartholomew Columbus, sank to the ground on their knees, and with great respect, presented him with the palm branches they carried. The rest of the people, a huge, huge number all danced in jubilation, and in that festive, celebratory fashion—almost beyond description—they led Bartholomew Columbus to the royal house, the Palace of King Behechio, where a huge feast was ready and waiting, of native foods, i.e., cassava bread, rodents—rabbit-like creatures of the island—roasted or stewed, and all sorts of fresh and salt water fish that run in that area.

. . . .

Next day, the Indians gathered in the town plaza to offer further and varied festivities so they brought Don Bartholomew and the Christians to watch. During the events, two troops of men, armed with bows and arrows, naked otherwise, suddenly appeared and started to skirmish in a war game, one against the other. At first it was like the wooden-sword fights in Spain, but little by little the men got heated up, then it was as if they were battling their worst enemies, so much so that wounded each other and severely, four were soon dead and many quite hurt. And this was done with all the exhilaration and zest and enthusiasm in the world, making no more of the wounded or dead than if someone had flicked them in the face. The bash would have kept up and many more died if King Behechio, at the request of Don Bartholomew and the Christians, had not ordered to halt it. . . .

Anacaona was a very remarkable woman, very prudent, very gracious and cultured in her speech, in crafts, in relationships, and very friendly toward the Christians. She was as well, Queen of Maguana, because she was the wife of King Caonabo.

Peter Martyr d'Anghera, *De orbe novo*, Vol. 1, "First Decade," Book 5

Trans. Francis Augustus MacNutt in *De orbe novo: The Eight Decades of Peter Martyr d'Anghera*, vol. 1, 119–120.

"We do not pretend," continued the Adelantado, "to exact tribute from anybody which cannot be easily paid, or of a kind not obtainable; but we know that this country produces an abundance of cotton, hemp, and other similar things, and we ask you to pay tribute of those products." The *cacique*'s face expressed joy on hearing these words, and with a satisfied air he agreed to give what he was asked, and in whatever quantities they desired; for he sent away his men, and after dispatching messengers in advance, he himself acted as guide for the Adelantado, conducting him to his residence, which, as we have already said, was situated about thirty leagues distant. The march led through the countries of subject *caciques*; and upon some of them a tribute of hemp was imposed, for this hemp is quite as good as our flax for weaving ships' sails; upon others, of bread, and upon others, of cotton, according to the products of each region.

. . . .

When the company approached, some thirty women, all wives of the *cacique*, marched out to meet them, dancing, singing, and shouting; they were naked, save for a loin-girdle, which, though it consisted but of a cotton belt, which dropped over their hips, satisfied these women devoid of any sense of shame. As for the young girls, they covered no part of their bodies, but wore their hair loose upon their shoulders and a narrow ribbon tied around the forehead. Their face, breast, and hands, and the entire body was quite naked, and of a somewhat brunette tint. All were beautiful, so that one might think he beheld those splendid naiads or nymphs of the fountains, so much celebrated by the ancients. Holding branches of palms in their hands, they danced to an accompaniment of songs, and bending the knee, they offered them to the Adelantado. Entering the chieftain's house, the Spaniards refreshed themselves at a banquet prepared with all the magnificence of native usage. When night came, each, according to his rank, was escorted by servants of the *cacique* to houses where those hanging beds I have already described were assigned to them, and there they rested.

Next day they were conducted to a building which served as a theatre, where they witnessed dances and listened to songs, after which two numerous troops of armed men suddenly appeared upon a large open space, the king having thought to please and interest the Spaniards by having them exercised, just as in Spain Trojan games (that is to say, tourneys) are celebrated. The two armies advanced and engaged in as animated a combat as though they were fighting to defend their property, their homes, their children or their lives. With such vigor did they contest, in the presence of their chieftain, that within the short space of an hour four soldiers were killed and a number were wounded; and it was only at the instance of the Spaniards that the *cacique* gave the signal for them to lay down their arms and cease fighting.

APPENDIX B

Areítos and *Bailes cantando* of the Indies

Gonzalo Fernández de Oviedo y Valdés,
Historia general y natural de las Indias, Part 1,
Book 5, Chapter 1

Trans. Paul Scolieri with Liam Moore from *Historia general y natural de las Indias*, ed. Juan Pérez de Tudela Bueso, 112–116.[1]

"Which treats the images of the devil the Indians had, and of their idolatries, and of the areítos *and* bailes cantando, *and their form of preserving the memory of past events which they wish recalled by their descendants and their people."*

By every means at my disposal, from the time I came to these Indias, I have tried with much earnestness to learn, both on these islands and on the Tierra Firme, how the Indians recall the matters of their origins and ancestors, and whether they have books, or by what signs and symbols they keep from forgetting the past. And on this island, as far as I have been able to find out, their songs, which they call *areítos*, are their only books or memorials to pass from person to person, from parents to their children, from present to future generations, as will be explained here.

. . . .

Let us pass on to the *areítos*, or songs, which were the second thing promised in the title to this chapter. These people had a good and gracious way of remembering the past and ancient things; and this was in their songs and dances, which they call *areíto*, which is the same thing that we today call *bailar cantando* ["a sung dance"]. Livy says that the Etruscans were the first dancers to come to Rome and that they organized their voices and their movements go together. This was done to forget the work and pestilence and death the year Camillus died; and this I say must be like the *areítos* or *cantares en corro* ["song circles"] of the Indians. The *areíto* was performed thus. When they wished to have pleasure, celebrating some notable feast among them, or lacking that, as a simple pastime, a great many Indians of both sexes would come together, sometimes only the men, at others the women alone. In the general festivals, such as celebration of a victory or defeat of their enemies, or the marriage of the *cacique* or chief of their province, or for other causes which brought pleasure to everyone, men and women were mixed together. And to increase their joy and pleasure they would join hands sometimes, and other times link arms, or form a line or a circle, and one of them (whether man or woman) would take the office of leader, and he would take certain steps backward and forward, as if in a very orderly step of the *contrapás*. And at the same time, everyone goes about in the same way he acted and spoke, singing in that high or low key which the leader set for them, the rhythm of the steps measured and coordinated with the verses or words they sing. And as he sings, the whole crowd responds with the same steps and words and order; and while they answer him, the leader is silent, although he does not cease dancing the *contrapás*. When the response is finished, that is, the repetition or saying the same that the leader has said, the leader proceeds immediately, without delay, to another verse and words that the chorus repeats in turn. In that way, without stopping, they go on for three or four hours or more, until the master or leader of the dance finishes his history, and at times it lasts from one day to another.

Sometimes they add to the chant a drum that is made from a log of wood. It is hollow, concave, and as thick as a man, which is more or less how they like to make it. It sounds like the muted drums that the *negros* make, but they put no skin on it, but rather there are some holes and slits that go through to the hollow part, and therefore they have an unpleasant sound. And thusly, with or without that terrible instrument, in their song (as I have said) they relate their memories and past history, and in these songs they relate how the past *caciques* died, and how many there were and what they were like, and other things that they do not wish to be forgotten. Sometimes they change the *guías o maestro de la danza* ["leaders or master of the dance"] and continue the same story with a change in tune or step, the new one continues the same story, or if the first has ended, they tell another story with the same or another tune.

This manner of dance is somewhat similar to the songs and dances of farmers in some parts of Spain when in the summer men and women entertain themselves with tambourines. And in Flanders I have seen the same manner of singing, with men and women dancing in circles, responding to what the leader sings first, as they say.

At the time that the Comendador Mayor Don Frey Nicolás de Ovando governed this island, Anacaona, the wife of the *cacique* or chief Caonabo, who was a great lady, held an *areíto* before him. More than three hundred maids participated in the dance, all of them her servants and unmarried women, because she did not wish that either a man or a married woman, or one who had known a man, should enter into that dance or *areíto*.

So, going back to our subject, this manner of singing in this island and the others (as well as on a good part of the Tierra Firme, is *una efigie de historia* ["an effigy of history"] or a remembering of things past, wars as well as times of peace, because with the continuation of such songs great deeds and events of the past are not forgotten. And these songs remain in their memory, in the place of books, through this recalling; and in this form they revive the genealogies of their *caciques* and kings or lords that they have had, and the works that they have done, and the good or bad periods that have occurred or that have befallen them; and whatever else they want to impart to both the young and the old so that they are well known and firmly carved in memory. And to this end they continue these *areítos*, in order not to forget these things, especially the famous victories in battle.

Concerning the *areítos* of the Tierra Firme, other things will be said further on, because the ones of this island, which I saw in 1515, did not seem to me as notable as those that I saw earlier on the mainland and that I have seen since then in that region. Let it not seem to the reader that this is savagery, for in Spain and Italy they do the same; and in many other Christian countries, and even infidel ones, I think it must be thus. What else are the *romances* and the songs based on true events, but part and memory of past history? At least among those who cannot read, it is because of the songs that they know that King Don Alfonso was in the noble city of Seville and he was inspired to besiege Algeciras. That is in a romance, and indeed it really happened that way: King Don Alfonso XI left Seville and took Algeciras on the 28th of March, 1344. Thus there are, in this year of 1548, 204 years that song or *areíto* covers.

. . .

During these songs or *contrapases* or *bailes*, other Indian men and women walk about giving drink to those who dance. Not a single one stops to drink. Instead they keep moving their feet as they swallow what they are given. And what they drink are certain concoctions that they use amongst themselves, and when the festival is over, the greater part of the men and women are intoxicated and unconscious, and lie on the ground for many hours. And so when one of them falls down inebriated, they remove him from *la danza* and the rest carry on; so it is drunkenness that brings the *areíto* to conclusion. This is the case when the *areíto* is solemn and done for weddings or funerals or for a battle, or a significant victory and celebration; because they often perform other *areítos* without drunkenness. Some do it on account of this vice and others because they want to learn this kind of music, but all know this manner of telling stories, and sometimes other similar songs and dances are created by people who are held among the Indians as discriminating and with great talent in this art.

APPENDIX C

Areítos of Nicaragua and Its Vicinity

Gonzalo Fernández de Oviedo y Valdés, *Historia general y natural de las Indias*, Part 3, Book 4, Chapter 11

From Fernández de Oviedo y Valdés, *Historia general y natural de las Indias*, trans. Alice Gillespie, 96–110.[1]

"Which treats the areítos *and other details of the province of Nicaragua and its vicinity; and likewise of various rites and ceremonies of the people thereof, in addition to and beyond those which this history has already related."*

It was the custom of the ancients (in the autumn), when the fruits of the earth had been harvested, to assemble in the temples, and make festivals and sacrifices, thus affording pleasure to themselves and doing honor to their gods (Aristotle, Eth. Chap. VIII). Since such a custom prevailed of old among the people so advanced, it is not strange that the Indians should have adopted it. And I speak of the Plaza of the Cacique Viejo, so called because he was in truth very aged. I myself knew him and spoke with him. His real name was Agateyte, and his plaza and domain was Tecoatega. He was one of the greatest chiefs in the province of Nicaragua, and had actually six thousand Bowman, and more than twenty thousand vassals, including men and women, small and great. And I went thither one day, to see an *areíto*, which they call there *mitote*, and singing in chorus, as it is a custom of the Indians to do; and it was at the close of the harvesting of the fruit of the *cacao*, which is the nut used amongst these people as money, and of which they make the beverage which they consider so excellent; and the ceremony was as follows. About sixty persons, all men, some of whom were disguised as women, danced a *contrapás*; they were all painted, and wore much gorgeous plumage, and sandals, and motley doublets of variegated patterns and colors; and they were naked, for the sandals and doublets of which I speak were painted; but in a matter so true to life that anyone would have taken them to be as well attired as any pagan German or Teutonic soldier. And this paint was of cotton lint (first spun) resembling the waste left by the scissors of the shearers, and was by as many colors as could be found, all very brilliant. Some wore masks like those faces of birds and they danced around the plaza, two by two, each three or four paces apart; and in the middle of the plaza, was erected a tall stake more than eighty palms high, on the upper end of which was seated up brightly painted idol, which they call the God of *cacaguat*, or *cacao*; and there were four poles suspended so as to form a frame around the upper part of the stake, and a rope of hemp (or of *agaye*) as thick as one's two fingers was wound around the latter. [*Voladores*], two boys of seven or eight years of age, were fastened to both ends of this cord, one of them holding in one hand a bow and in the other a bundle of arrows, and the second carrying a brilliant fan of feathers and a mirror. At a certain time during the dance, these boys would let themselves drop from the frame, and hang in the air, revolving around the pole as the rope unwound, flying farther out at every revolution, and counterbalancing each other; and during the descent of these boys, the sixty dancers continued their measure in a very orderly manner, to the music furnished by those who were singing and speaking upon certain tambours and kettle-drums; for there were ten or twelve persons engaged in singing and playing, very poorly, and the dancers did not converse, but observed the most complete silence.

This festival of singing and dancing lasted more than half an hour. At the end of this time, the boys began to descend, and were as long in reaching the ground as one would take to repeat the *Credo* five or six times. As the rope unwound, the boys moved through the air with considerable swiftness, moving their arms and legs so that they appeared to be flying. As the rope is of a certain length, when it is all unwound they suddenly come to a stop at a palm's length above the ground. When they find themselves approaching the ground, they contract their limbs, and extend them at the same moment, so that they remain standing about thirty paces from the pole which stands upright, one on one side and one on the other; and on the instant, the dance and the singers and musicians cease with a loud shout, and with this the festival is over (see fig. 1.2).

The pole is left standing for eight or ten days, at the end of which one hundred or more Indians disassemble and remove it, taking down the *cemi* or idol, from its top and bearing it to its place of worship and the temple of its sacrifices, where it remains until the same feast comes around again in the following year. The spectacle is undoubtedly a pleasing one; but what pleased me most was the style of adornment or dress described, and the many wonderful feather crests they wore, and the manner in which they were divided into groups of two or four, each of these groups being painted in a special manner, all well matched. The dancers were all handsome men, and would have been so considered in Spain, France, Italy, and Germany, or any other part of the world.

I witnessed another kind of *areíto* in the same plaza of Tecoatega, which took place after the death of said Cacique Viejo, who was succeeded by his son, a pleasing youth. It took place on a Sunday, the sixteenth day of May—Pentecost Day—and was as follows: before the chief's *buhio* was a *barbacoa*, beneath which were about twenty Indians, painted *bixa* and *xagua* [red and black], and wearing many gorgeous feathers, who stood singing to the accompaniment of three or four kettle-drums; and in the plaza, about twenty paces in front of the shed where these musicians stood, were ten or twelve young warriors, masked and much painted also in red and black, with their feathers and stripes and fans and cotton lint, dancing a kind of *contrapás*. About ten paces to the right of them were four well-built men painted in the same manner, their faces dyed red as blood. [Upon their heads were ornaments with bunches of feathers, as they wear them when they got to war.] Three of these four stood still and motionless, while the fourth danced and walked, in the manner of a *contrapás*, not going more than a pace or two one side or the other from Tecoatega, the *cacique* of the district, who threw rods at the dancer from three or four paces away, often striking him on both sides—flanks, belly, arms, and legs—or wherever he aims, but never the head. And as the *cacique* launched the sticks at him, the dancer would try to avoid them, twisting his body from side to side, or stooping, or turning his back, so that they often failed to strike him; but more often they hit smart blows, which raised large welts. [As he retired,] another of the four would take his place, undergoing some ten or twelve shots, or whatever number the *cacique* willed. And another of the four stood his turn until about thirty rods had been broken on them. These rods are lighter than chains, like reeds, and about as thick as the smallest finger of one's hand, and the thickest end being covered with a *cipote*, or head of wax, so that though the blows were not dangerous. It was a brutal game, those men being naked. And he who received the stripes made no complaint, nor did he alter his expression, or feel of the wounds, or lament any blow; but immediately prepared to receive another, with unchanging countenance and expression; and, also, the *cacique* threw the same rod three or four times, until it broke, or else missed, and fell beyond its mark.

In this manner, he expended some thirty of the aforesaid rods on the four Indians; and if there was a large crowd of Indian men, large and small, and women, watching the said festival when the rod throwing was over, the *cacique* sent for *cacao*, and with his own hands gave to each of the four up to five hundred grains and nuts of the said *cacao*. This done, they, with the dancers, and musicians, and singers, departed, with a great clamor, and followed by a large crowd went on to other plazas and other *caciques* and lords, to repeat the performance and undergo a similar number of shots; this being undertaken by four more youths, of those who were sounds and not battered; and for the purpose they themselves took with them two Indians each bearing armfuls of the rods.

After they had departed, I asked the *cacique* the reason for this ceremony and whether its purpose was to celebrate one of their feast days, and what mysterious significance it had; and he replied that it was not a festival [*fiesta*] but that these Indians were from other plazas and were youths who went about for their own pleasure, as on a New Year's expedition to obtain gifts of *cacao* from the various lords and *caciques* who had it, and who gave it to them as he had done; but before doing so the custom was to break twenty or thirty rods upon them as has been described, by which it appeared that they proved themselves to be youths of good courage and strong and capable warriors, able to endure wounds. And, verily, the said *cacique* cast the rods with great force, for he was young and strong, which created welts the size of one's finger or greater.

. . . .

Other *areítos* and songs, together with dancing and the *contrapás*, are customary with the Indians, and are of frequent occurrence, as I have stated in other parts of this history, and many of these take place during the burial ceremonies of the principal chiefs; and they take the place of history, as a method of recalling things of the past, and the events are added to as time goes on. And there are others [to conceal treason],[2] as was the case after the slaying of Don Cristóbal de Sotomayor, on the Island of [Saint John], which I narrated in book 16, chapter 5.

They have other more common *areítos* to celebrate their debauches of drunkenness [*beoderas*], during which wine is as plentiful as are songs, and they end by becoming drunken wine-skins, and falling in a stupor upon the ground. Many of them who become thus intoxicated lie where they fall, until the effect of the wine wears off, or till daybreak; those of their companions who see them succumb feel it to be enviable, rather than disgraceful. It is not so much to dance as to drink that they come together. But I shall speak here of another of these [drunken feasts],[3] during which I, and a priest, and four or five other Spaniards who were present wished ourselves far from there, because on seeing seventy or eighty Indians and their chief all drunk, and knowing them to be a people of such bestiality and idolatry and so full of vices. I believe that in truth, they take no joy in the Christians, for, from their former condition of masters, the latter have reduced them to slavery, and have restrained them in their rites, and ceremonies and vices. How can one feel sure of their friendly disposition? In addition to this we were far from any Christian aid or rescue, and in the house of one of the most important chiefs of that province and by land and by sea as well they had the equipment to carry out whatever they should undertake; all these considerations justified us in feeling fear at what we saw. It was true that one of the *caciques* who most valued the friendship of the Spaniards is this one who is called Nicoya, and he has been baptized and given the name of Don Alonso and as an Indian he is called Nambi, and when we would ask him for Indians for whatever reason we might happen to need them, he would reply: "I have no Indians, but only Christians, and if you want Christians, I will give them to you."

"Then give us Christians to perform this of which we have need," and he would immediately give us as many Indians as we asked, and they did whatever we bade them.

But hear what this *cacique* and his people did, after their baptism, which was as follows:

One Saturday, on the twenty-ninth day of August, 1528, in the plaza of Nicoya, under the *cacique* of that province, Don Alonso, known by another name as "Nambi," which in his Chorotega language means "dog," two hours before nightfall, about eighty or one hundred Indians began to sing and dance in an *areíto*, in one part of the plaza; they must have been of the vulgar and plebian people because in another part of the same plaza the *cacique*, with much enjoyment and festivity, seated himself on a *duho*, or small bench, and his chief officials and about seventy or eighty other Indians on similar *duhos*. A girl began to bring them drinks in small gourds, like bowls or cups. This was *chichi*, very strong and rather acid wine which they make of maize; and which in its color resembles chicken broth into which the yokes of one or two eggs have been broken. And as soon as they had begun to drink, the *cacique* himself brought forward a handful of rolls of tobacco, each as long as the distance from the end of one's forefinger, and consisting of a certain leaf, rolled up and tied with two or three thin cords of *agave* fiber.

. . . .

The drinking continued, Indians of both sexes coming and going with that beverage, and bringing in gourds or large cups of the *cacao*, cooked as they are accustomed to drink it (but of this they took only three or four mouthfuls, and it went from hand to hand, now to one, now to another, and they took puffs of smoke at intervals; some of them drumming, with their hands, and others singing). Thus occupied, they remained till after midnight, until most of them fell senseless on the ground, drunk; and as drunkenness has different effects upon different men, some would appear to sleep motionless, while others ran around weeping and howling, and stumbling foolishly. When they reached this state, their wives and friends or children came and took them back to their houses to sleep, which they did till noon of the following day or some even till the next night, and more or less according to the extent that they had drunk and participated in the drunken revelry [*beodera*]. He among those people who does not follow this custom of theirs is [held in little regard] among them and considered unfit to be a warrior.

While they wept and shrieked, it was a fearful thing to see their mad acts; and during the time that they were becoming further inebriated, it was more so; for the more the dubious occurrences of the affair were concealed from us, the greater the danger we thought ourselves to be in. Their women behave in the same manner, but apart, and only those of highest rank. At one time we thought that the *areíto* and debauch would end badly for the six or seven Spaniards who were present, so we remained on our guard and with weapons in hand; for, though there were not enough of us for a successful defense against so many, we determined at least to sell our lives very dearly, and to try to slay the *cacique*, and as many of his chiefs as possible, without whom the lower people are of little account, and very disorderly and cowardly without their captains.

When the debauch was over, I asked the *cacique* why they held such drunken feasts [*borracheras*] since he himself was a Christian and claimed that his chiefs and many of these people were likewise. A man in such a condition, having lost his reason, is no more than any beast, or a low and vile animal; and saying that he well knew that man's best attribute is his power of reason and judgment, and that he who has the greatest degree of it has an advantage over his fellows, and is deservedly honored and esteemed by them, while according as he is more foolish, mad or ignorant, he is nearer the lower animals; that he himself knew well that among his vassals were chiefs of higher station, and more closely related to himself then Don Diego (who was one of his favorite chiefs), but he had told me that he preferred the latter to all others because of his greater wisdom and bravery, for he was the more esteemed on account of his good sense. Therefore why did they lose their reason, and intoxicate themselves, and remain senseless like beasts?

. . . .

He replied that as to these drunken revelries, he was aware that they were evil, but that such was the custom, and such has been the custom of his ancestors and if he did not continue it, his people would dislike him and look upon him as poor-spirited and mean and would depart from the land.

. . . .

To all of this I replied as seemed best to me, trying to make him understand his error, and that all these were great sins, and worthy of an infidel, rather than a Christian; he agreed with what I said, saying that my counsel was good and that he would gradually mend his ways. But, in the end, he had a name like his deeds, and his deeds were as his name, Nambi, which as I have said means "dog."

Among others, they have an *areíto* or rite [*rito*], which is as follows: three times a year, on stated days which are now regarded as principal feast days, the *cacique* of Nicoya, his chiefs, and most of his people, men as well as women, painted and adorned with feathers, according to their usual custom, dance an *areíto* similar to a *contrapás*, the women holding each other by the arms and hands, and the men surrounding them, linked in similar fashion, with an interval of four or five paces between the two circles, for in the space between them others go in and out, giving drink to the dancers who do not cease moving their feet, nor drinking of that wine of the theirs; and the men gesticulate with their bodies and heads and the women imitate them. On that day, the women wear *gutaras* [new shoes]; and after this dance—which takes place around the sacrificial mounds before the principal temple in the plaza—has lasted four hours or more they seize a man or woman (whom they have previously selected for a sacrifice) and ascending to the top of the sacrificial mound, they cut open the victim's breast, and remove the heart. The first blood is offered in sacrifice to the Sun. Then they decapitate that body and several others upon a stone slab which is placed on the summit of the said mound, and the blood of the rest they offer to their particular idols and gods, whose images they anoint with it. The intercessors or priests—or to put it better, their hellish ministers and executioners—afterward smear it on their own faces and lips; and they extend the dead bodies, which roll down the mound and are picked up at the base thereof, and afterwards eaten, as a holy and very precious viand. As soon as this accursed sacrifice is accomplished, all the women give a loud shriek and flee towards the mountains and woods and sierras, singly or in couples, in spite of the efforts of their husbands and kinsmen, who bring them back, some with entreaties, others with promises and gifts and in some cases, where severer methods are necessary, they are beaten and kept bound until the frenzy has passed, and she who is captured furthest away is greatly admired and receives most praise.

. . . .

Since I have fully described their *areítos*, let us process to the other matters that I proposed to say in this chapter. Other kinds of *areítos* have been mentioned in other parts of this history, because, as these people differ in their languages and customs, so do they vary in their songs, and dances, and many other things.

APPENDIX D

Bailes and Songs of the Indies

Bartolomé de las Casas, *Apologética historia sumaria*, Volume 2, Book 3, Chapter 243

Trans. Paul Scolieri with Liam Moore.

"Continuing the material from the previous chapter, especially concerning bailes *and songs"*

All the people of these provinces that we have been describing have many kinds of *bailes* and songs. These customs are widespread throughout the Indies, in the same way that they existed in the ancient nations of both Jews and Gentiles, just as we have explained at length above. Every time the lord of a province or a village married off a son or daughter, or buried someone close to him, or wanted to plant some crops or make a sacrifice, he ordered the principal men of his land to come together at a great festival. They sat around a large plaza, or in the widest part of his house, holding drums and flutes and the other instruments that they use. After them, many men and women would arrive, each one adorned with their best jewelry, and if they were dressed at all, they (at least the women) wore the best they had. They put strings of bells made of gold or bone on their wrists and their ankles. If they were all nude, they painted their bodies and faces red, and if they could get feathers, they wore them over the body paint, and so what our justice prescribes as a penalty for witches or pimps, for them is their finery. Everyone sang or responded following the music played on the instruments, just like our people often do in Spain.

What they said in their songs was a recounting of the deeds and riches and lordships and peace and government of their past, the life they had before the Christians arrived, as well as the arrival of the latter and how they violently entered their land, how they took their women and children after stealing from them all the gold and goods they inherited from their parents and achieved through their own work. Other songs tell of the speed and violence and ferocity of the horses; others about the fierceness and cruelty of the dogs, who in an instant could rip them into pieces; and others about the fierce valor and resolution of the Christians, since so few of them vanquished, pursued, and killed so many multitudes of people. Finally, whatever story that is for them sad and bitter is embodied in the songs that represent their miseries and calamities. In some places, after those people have sung, armed men come in screaming as if they had broken in during a battle and they take away the women that seem to them the best in the circle. They go out with them for some time, without the husbands who are present interfering, even if they are the men's own lords, in order not to break such a praiseworthy tradition—so that even in their jokes, weapons are unfortunately used with some audacity. This gives the image of the very unpleasant bacchanals that the Romans and other peoples celebrated, and that some may still do even today, as we mentioned in the above chapter, though in these parts they do not seem to me by far as unpleasant and dishonest as those, and this should be very clear from what I said above.

When they had become tired from dancing and singing and recalling and crying over their misfortunes, they sat to eat on the ground, where they had waiting their poor meals. Although they intended to make the food splendid, all that the Indians could put together was miserable compared to our excessive and riotous banquets. They prepared hens, or venison, or rabbits, or fish from the sea or from the rivers, depending on which was closest to them. They boiled or roasted the meat without making them exquisite and superfluous delicacies as we do. And although the meal lasted two or three hours, they did not take a single sip of drink, but rather only when they were full did they serve the drink, which was wine made from corn and was powerfully intoxicating. This was brought in a golden cup (for those who had one) and also in certain gourds, much more beautiful and useful than ours, that those of this island of Hispaniola called *hibueras* and those of New Spain call *xícaras*. They drank until they could drink no more, or until they had finished the wine they had brought with them and the vessels were empty. They say that they drank to each other's health, like our Flemish do, and even our Spaniards, who easily adopt foreign customs, and are never ashamed to do so, because when we criticize the defects of these peoples, we are spitting in the wind.

In those drinking parties or revels, after they become very intoxicated, they discussed and decided matters of justice or warfare, or other serious matters that they had to attend to—if what the Spaniard I mentioned above named Tobilla wrote about the people of these regions is true. And because this upset him a great deal, we must remember that the Germans and other nations that I named in a chapter above do the same thing after becoming very full of wine.

In the entire land and in its provinces that we discuss in this chapter and the preceding one, or at least in its greater part, the aforementioned gentleman (and no other) said that the people living there had none of the three defects of which others have been accused, namely, eating human flesh, sacrificing men, and the sin of sodomy. Tobilla only says that certain Spaniards found in a certain province three men dressed in women's clothes, who were judged only because of that to have been corrupted by that sin, and without further proof they then let loose the dogs they had on those men, who were then torn apart and eaten alive, as if they were their judges. But it is possible that those men had not committed that sin, that perhaps for those people the costume of women was used by the men who wore them not so that they would be women and make their defect public, but rather because they had to do the tasks and duties of women, as is done in other nations, just as we have noted in a chapter above. And we can be sure that if there were more news of more people of this land being blemished with that vice and those defects, the Spaniards would not have been quiet about it, nor would Tobilla have failed to write about it.

APPENDIX E

Bailes of Mexico

Toribio de Benavente "Motolinía," *Memoriales*, Chapter 91

Trans. Scott Metcalfe.[1]

"Of the manner of dances these natives had; of the great dexterity and conformity that all maintained in dance and song; and many other things of this kind; so that this chapter and those that follow are no less noted than those previous."

One of the principal things that there were everywhere in this land were the songs and dances, not only to celebrate the festivals of their demons which they honored as gods, with which they thought they were making a great service, but also for simple rejoicing and delight. And for this reason they gave two names for *baile*, as is explained below, for it was something that was made much of in each *pueblo*. Each lord in his house he had a chapel of singers, composers of dances and songs, and they sought those of good talent for composing songs in the type of meter or verses that they had. And good *contrabajos* were much valued, for the lords in their houses had them sing frequently in a quiet voice.

Ordinarily, they sang and danced during the major *fiestas* that occurred every twenty days, and on other minor festivals. The most important *bailes* took place in the plazas, at other times in the house of the greatest lord, in the patio, for all the lords had grand patios; they also danced in the houses of the other lords and nobles.

When there had been some victory in war or when they elevated a lord, or when marriage to a noblewoman took place, or some other notable event, the masters composed a new song, in addition to those generally appropriate for the festivals of the demons, or those celebrating the historic feats or departed lords.

The singers rehearsed that which they had to sing several days before the festival. In the large towns there were many composers and if there were new songs and dances, they gathered together so that there would be no flaw on the day of the festival. On the day they were to dance, in the morning they put a large straw mat in the middle of the plaza where they were to position the drums, and they dressed themselves and gathered in the house of the lord, and from there came out singing and dancing. Sometimes they started the dances in the morning and other times at the hour of high mass. At nightfall they returned singing to the palace, and there the singing and dancing ended at dark or when the night was well advanced or at midnight.

There were two drums: one tall and round, wider than a man, five palms in height, made of good wood, hollow inside, well-wrought and painted on the outside. Across the mouth they bound deerskin, tanned and tightly stretched. From the edge to the middle it sounds a perfect fifth, and they play it according to the notes and melodies, which rise and fall, accompanying the singers and tuning the drum to them. The other drum is of a kind that is difficult to explain without a picture; it serves as a *contrabaxo*, and both make a fine sound and can be heard from afar. When the *dançantes* [dancers] are in position they get ready to play the drums: two singers, the two best, act as *sochantres* [subcantors], in order to start the songs. The large drum with the skin is played with the hands and this one is called *huehuetl* and the other, like drums in Spain, with sticks, although of a different design, and they call it the *teponaztli*. The lord, with other nobles and elders, goes dancing before the drums; they spread out three or four braces[2] wide around the boards [drums], and with them a multitude, widening and filling the circle. In the large towns, those dancing here in the middle [used to] number more than a thousand, and sometimes more than two thousand. Besides these, around the radius goes a procession of two lines of dancers, young men, great dancers. In front are two men chosen from among the great dancers, who lead the dance without holding hands. In these two lines [rings], in certain turns and curtsies they sometimes face and partner a person in front, and in other dances the person behind. It is no small number of people who dance in these two lines, often reaching as many as about a thousand, and other times more, depending on the town and the festival. [In the past,] before the wars, when they would freely celebrate their *fiestas*, in the large towns, three or four thousand or more would gather to dance; since the conquest, half as many, until the number was steadily diminishing and shrinking.

When they are ready to begin the dancing, three or four Indians sound some very lively whistles, then they begin to play the drums in a low tone, gradually increasing the sound. And when *la gente bailadora* [the dancing people] hear the drums begin, they all listen to the song and begin the dance. By their tune they know the song and the dance, and then they begin it. The first songs are pitched low, as if in the soft hexachord, and slow. The first song is particular to the festival, and those same two leaders always begin the song; and then the entire ring [choir] proceeds to sing and dance together. And that whole multitude coordinates their feet as well as the most skilled dancers from Spain. And what is more remarkable is that their entire bodies, the head as well as arms and hands, are so synchronized, measured, and ordered that they do not differ from one another or come apart for even a half measure; but that which one does with his right foot or with the left, all of them do the same, and at the same time and on the same beat; when one lowers his left arm and raises his right, all do likewise and at the same moment, so that the drums and the song and the dancers all keep their beat exactly together. They all synchronize precisely, so that not one differs an iota from another, which astonishes good dancers from Spain when they see it, and they greatly esteem the dances of these natives and the great coordination and feeling they have put into them.

Those furthest away, in the outside ring, we might say they adopt a *compasillo*, that is, in the time of one measure to make two; they dance more rigorously and put more effort into the dance. And these in the outer ring all match each other. Those in the middle of the circle follow their regular *tactus* [*compás entero*], and the movements of their feet and bodies are graver. Some of them [certainly they] raise and lower their arms with much grace. Each verse or couplet is repeated three or four times, and they go on moving and singing in good intonation, so that neither the singing nor the drums nor the dance comes apart from the rest. When one song is finished—and, granted, that the first ones seem much longer because they go more slowly, they take nothing like an hour—when one is finished the pitch that the drum sounds is changed. All stop singing [the drum barely changes its pitch, when all leave off singing], and after several measures of pause in the song, but not the dance, the leaders begin another song, somewhat higher and in a faster tempo. Thus the pitch and sounds of the songs rise continually, as if a bass were to change by degrees into a high voice, and a dance into a *contrapás*.

Some youths and children join the dancing, sons of nobles, seven or eight years of age (and some of four or five), who sing and dance along with their fathers. Since the boys sing in an unbroken voice (or treble), they add much grace to the song. Occasionally trumpets are played, and some small flutes, not very well in tune, and others whistle on little bones, which make a loud sound. Others wear costumes and disguise their voices, imitating people of other nations, altering their speech. These I speak of are like jesters; they whirl and leap about, pulling a thousand faces and telling a thousand jokes and witticisms, which make those who see and hear them laugh;

some go about like old women, and others like fools. At times they bring them drinks, and some leave to rest and to eat, and when these return, others leave and thus all rest without the dance stopping. Sometimes they wear clusters of roses and other flowers or bouquets to carry in their hands and garlands on their heads, besides the costumes they wear for dancing, of rich mantles and plumage, and others carry in their hands, instead of bouquets, small and beautiful feathers. In these dances, many emblems and tokens are worn by those who have been valiant warriors.

From the hour of vespers until nightfall, the songs and dances become ever more lively and higher in pitch, and the sound is ever more attractive; [so] it seems they are singing some melody of the hymns that carry a cheerful tune, and the drums too play always higher. And since there is a large crowd [dancing], it can be heard from a great distance, especially when the wind carries the voice, and even more so at night [when all is quiet], when they used many large torches. Certainly it was something to see.

Spaniards call these dances *areítos*, which is a term from the islands, but up to now I have never known anyone who could account for or explain, in writing or in speech, the words of that island language. They do not write down what it means, nor do they know if it is a noun or a verb, if it is singular or plural, if it is an active verb or a passive verb. Like unskilled negroes [*los negros bocales*] who are beginning to speak our language and say "If understand do, if know your mercy, Sir." The words used in the language of the islands are just like this, and so this word *areíto* is *impersonal* (without gender) and may mean "to dance" or "everybody in the ring dances." When I passed through the islands, I saw very rustic dancing and singing, not at all like that of New Spain, where, as is described here, they dance with great delicacy and refinement.

APPENDIX F

Macehualiztli and *Netotiliztli*

Toribio de Benavente "Motolinía," *Memoriales*, Chapter 92

Trans. Scott Metcalfe.

"How the dance of these people has two names, which dances they offered to their demons, and of the dances and songs performed upon the victories which God granted to the fathers of the Old Testament."

In this language of Anáhuac the dance [*dança o bayle*] has two names: one is *macehualiztli* and the other *netotiliztli*. This latter properly means "dance of rejoicing," with which the Indians delight and take pleasure in their festivities, as well as the lords and princes in their houses and at their weddings. And when they dance thus they say *netotilo*, "they dance," [*baylan o dançan*], *netotiliztli*, "a dance" [*bayle o dança*].

The second and principal name of the dance [*dança*] is *macehualiztli*, which properly means "merit"; *macehualon* means "to merit." They regarded this dance as a meritorious work, much as we say one "earns merit" through works of charity or of penitence, or by other virtuous deeds done for a good end. From this verb *macehualo* derives the compound *tlamacehualo*, for "to do penance or confession." And those most solemn dances were performed during their general festivals, and also particularly those of their gods, and they performed them in the plazas. With these not only did they call and honor and praise their gods with songs of the mouth, but also with the heart and gestures of the body. In order to do this well they had and made use of many signifying gestures [*memorativas*]; thus by the movements of their heads, arms, and feet, and with their entire bodies, they labored to call upon and serve the gods. For this reason, the laborious care devoted to raising their hearts and feelings to their demons and to serving them with all the humors of the body, and that work of persevering all day and a large part of the night, they called *macehualiztli*, "penance and merit." And because they did this at the principal festivals, and in songs more than in any other thing they praised and extolled their demons, they called this *macehualizti*, "confession of merit."

These Indians of Anáhuac in their books and manner of writing recorded the defeats and victories which they had had over their enemies. And their songs remembered these things and they celebrated them with dances, saying prayers and confessing to their demons, through whom they believed that they had won victories against their enemies. And for these commemorations, at their festivals they performed these acts, works and songs, *macehualiztli*, that is, "merit," for they held that they were highly acceptable to their gods and worthy of merit. And by *macehualo* they meant that all those in the circle earned merit and praised the gods through song and dance. From this verb *macehualo* for "to work or to earn merit, or work of merit" comes *macehuali*, which means "laborer," or in the plural *macehualtin*, "laborers." The Spaniards say *los macehuales*, that is, "the common laboring folk."

APPENDIX G

Aztec Myth of the Origin of Music and Dance

Gerónimo de Mendieta, *Historia eclesiástica indiana*, Book 2, Chapter 3

Trans. John Bierhorst in *Ballads of the Lords of New Spain*, 210.

"Of how Tezcatlipoca appeared to a man who was his devotee and sent him to the House of the Sun."

It is said that the men who were devotees of these dead gods, who had left them their mantles as memorials, went about with the mantles wrapped around their shoulders, sadly and pensively, looking to see if they could find their gods or if they would appear to them. It is said that the devotee of Tezcatlipoca, who was the principal idol of Mexico, persevering in his devotion, reached the seacoast, where he did appear to him, in three shapes, or forms, and called to him and said, "Come here, you! Since you are such a friend of mine, I want you to go to the House of the Sun and bring back singers and instruments so you can make festivities for me, and for this purpose you must call out to the whale, the mermaid, and the turtle, so they can form a bridge that you can walk across." And so, as the bridge was made, and the Sun heard him giving out with a song he happened to be singing, the Sun warned the people around him and his servants not to answer the song, because whoever answered would have to go with him. And so it occurred that some of them, finding the song mellifluous, did answer him, and he took them away, together with the [skin] drum they call *huehuetl* and [the log drum known as] the *teponatztli*; and this, they say, was the beginning of the festivities and dances that they make for their gods: and the songs they sing in those *areítos* [sacred dances] they consider to be prayers, performing them in concert with a particular melody [*tono*] and choreography [*meneos*], with much concentration and gravity, without any disagreement in the voices or in the dance steps. And they preserve this same synchronization nowadays. But it is much to be advised that they not be allowed to perform the ancient songs, because all of these are filled with memories of idolatry, or be allowed to perform them with diabolical or suspicious insignias, which represent the same. And it should be noted, with regard to what has been said above, that the gods killed each other by [opening] the breast, and from this, so they say, came the custom that was later practiced, of killing people as sacrifices, opening the breast with a flint knife, and taking out the heart as an offering to their gods.

APPENDIX H

Charges Drawn by the *Audencia* of Mexico against Pedro de Alvarado (1529)

Translated in John E. Kelly, *Pedro de Alvarado, Conquistador*, app. B, 239–240.

Item 5

And the charge is made against the said Pedro de Alvarado that at the time that the said Hernán Cortés left this city to proceed against Pánfilo de Narváez, he left the said Pedro de Alvarado to guard this city and in his power, Montezuma, the Lord thereof, together with all of the gold and treasure which up to that time had been accumulated which was a great quantity and at the time of departure, Montezuma asked permission of Cortés to hold certain feasts and dances which his people were accustomed to celebrate at such time of the year and the said Cortés gave the requested permission, and the time having come for the said feasts and dances, the said Montezuma ordered them held and there being one day in the house of the said Montezuma a great number of Indians dancing and celebrating their feast the said Pedro de Alvarado, together with the Spaniards under his command, entered into the fort where the said Montezuma was prisoner together with many Lords and principal chiefs and their servants, and entering into the patio where all were dancing, without any cause or reason whatsoever, fell upon the Indians and killed all of the Lords captive with Montezuma and four hundred principal chiefs who were present and a great number of Indians who were dancing to the number of three thousand for which reason the tribes rose in arms because their fellows had been killed without reason and because of this war, more than two hundred Spaniards died at the hands of the Indians, many horses were lost and more than four hundred thousand Indians were killed in the said war. Much gold was lost, much of which belonged to His Majesty and to the soldiers. All of which is a charge against Pedro de Alvarado because he killed Indians who were dancing in a state of peace by license of the said Cortés.

APPENDIX I

Pedro de Alvarado's Response to Charges Brought by the *Audencia* of Mexico

Trans. Paul Scolieri with Liam Moore from *Proceso de residencia contra Pedro de Alvarado*, 66–68.

Item 5, Regarding the Massacre at the Festival of Toxcatl (June 4, 1529)

Moreover, to answer the fifth charge against me, which says that at the same time that Don Hernando Cortés left the City to go against Pánfilo de Narváez, he left me in charge of the City and of Montezuma and of the gold and the rest of what had been in that City; and that the aforesaid Montezuma asked and received permission from the aforesaid Don Hernando Cortés to have dances and *areítos*. And that after he left the City, they had their dances and festivals, and along with the armed Spaniards, I attacked the aforesaid Indians that were performing their *areítos*, and I killed many of them as well as those that were with Montezuma. And that this was the reason that this City was lost and many Spaniards were killed and the gold that had been collected was lost. . . . I say that I am not required to answer the aforesaid charge and accusation, nor do I need to explain that at the time that we entered this City with the aforesaid Don Hernando Cortés, the crowd of Indians that were in it had agreed to rise up against us and kill us. That was public and well known among our friends and the inhabitants of Tlaxcala, and as they saw that Don Hernando Cortés had gone to where Narváez was, and since in the *areítos* and dances they gather together a large number of people, in order to justify their wicked plan they asked for the aforesaid permission for the aforesaid gathering; since it is very usual among them that when they want to perform sacrifices or some harm or evil, they have the aforesaid festivals. And since they saw that I had few men, and seeing that the aforesaid Montezuma was prisoner in that city where we were, they took away our food and when we sent for it, they did not want to give it to us, and they beat our Indian servants with rods, and they caught one of our Indians when she was doing the washing and drowned her, and they said and announced that the same should be done to the Spaniards. That following morning at dawn, there were a number of stakes stuck into the ground of the courtyard of the Huitzilopochtli and there was a taller one at the main temple. When I went to the aforesaid courtyard, I asked them why they had stuck those stakes there and they said to me publicly and in the presence of the people who had come with me that they were to put all of the Spaniards on and to kill them, and that the tall one was for me. Seeing their evil plan, I went to the courtyard where the Huitzilopochtli was, all canopied in precious fabrics, and many Indians were sacrificing before it, taking out the hearts of other Indians and giving them to him through his mouth or his body. Having seen what was happening above, I took one of the Indians that were to be sacrificed so that they wouldn't kill him and asked him for information. He told me that they had agreed to take the Huitzilopochtli to the main temple and take out from there Our Lady, and that there were many warriors in the City that had come together to kill me. Having learned and seen the above mentioned, I went to Montezuma and I told him what was happening and what I knew, and that he should interfere. He answered me that he couldn't interfere, and so to find out more about the truth I went to another Indian from Tezcuco named Don Hernando and I asked him what the Indians had planned to do. He told me it was true that they wanted to kill me and the Spaniards that were with me, and that they were going to pull down Our Lady from where she was and put up Huitzilopochtli, their idol. He also said there were many people in the fortress and its courtyard with clubs and other weapons with which to strike the guards watching over Montezuma, and the aforesaid Montezuma had another gilded club under his bed. Apart from what I already mentioned, there were many other people surrounding the fortress outside with a number of ladders to climb so they could kill the Spaniards. That all of this happened this way was public and well known. Since I was surrounded, the aforesaid Montezuma sent a message to me saying I should go see them put Huitzilopochtli up in the temple and knock down Our Lady. I told him that he must not do that and that I would not consent to it, since it had been consecrated and Mass had been said there and that it was not right that they put Huitzilopochtli there. Since the Indians about had wicked plans and wished to attack me, I left the fortress, leaving the number of men I thought necessary to guard it, and went to the courtyard where the Huitzilopochtli was. There I saw a large number of people who had come to raise him up and defend him, and I saw many people who began to fight with us, and many Indians came out from the chambers fighting against us, and in the fight they seriously wounded me and killed one of my Spaniards and wounded the rest. We were in a great deal of danger for our lives and if we hadn't done what we did, they would have killed all of us, and we would have lost the territory, and when the aforesaid Don Hernando Cortés came, they wouldn't have let him into the City, which would have been a disservice to Your Majesty. So in this way I held and defended this City more than forty days until the aforesaid Don Hernando Cortés came, and once he arrived I handed over the aforesaid fortress and Montezuma and everything else he left under my guard, without a single thing being lost, by which it is apparent that while I had that commission I did everything appropriate for a good captain and one at the service of Your Majesty. Doing otherwise, we would not have held the territory the way we did, and the witness who claims the matter of the accusation must have done so to ingratiate himself, as he has done in other affairs, for at the time when the above-mentioned occurred, he did not say what he is saying now, if what was done was not good, he did not say so at the time.

APPENDIX J

Founding of the First Dance School in New Spain

Trans. Paul Scolieri with Liam Moore from *Actas de Cabildo de la Ciudad de México*, vol. 1, 109–110.

Acta #132

[In the margin:] Site for the dance school.

On Monday the 30th of the aforementioned month of October in the year 1526.

On this day being in session the town council and government according to the practice and custom of the very noble attorney Señor Marcos de Aguilar, chief justice of New Spain, [the presence] should be noted of the aforesaid Señor attorney and Juan García Xaramillo, mayor in the aforementioned City, and García Holguín and Luys de la Torre and Andres de Barrios and Cristóbal de Salamanca and Juan de Salzedo, councilmen of the aforementioned City.

Maestros Pedro and Benito de Begel presented a petition to the aforementioned Gentlemen through which they asked that they would grant the favor of giving them a site where they can build a dance school where the market is at present, for the betterment of the City.

And having examined it, the aforesaid Gentlemen gave them a license to build a house fifty feet long and thirty wide to be held as long as they wish, as long as every year they give to the City the forty pesos of income of those who had lived in the aforesaid shop which they leave without impediment to the City each time they are ordered with all that has been built.

And they ordered that they be given the title to it in the proper form. And they ordered that the abovementioned present the City with the aforesaid amount of the aforesaid gold pesos.

NOTES

ABBREVIATIONS

FC — Bernardino de Sahagún, *Florentine Codex: General History of the Things of New Spain*. 13 vols. (1st ed. and 2nd ed. rev.). Translated from the Aztec into English with notes and illustrations by Arthur J. O. Anderson and Charles E. Dibble. Monographs of the School of American Research (Santa Fe, NM: School of American Research; Salt Lake City: University of Utah, 1950–1982).

Handbook — Manuel Aguilar-Moreno, *Handbook to Life in the Aztec World* (New York: Facts on File, 2006).

HMAI — Robert Wauchope, ed., *Handbook of Middle American Indians* (Austin: University of Texas Press, 1964–1976).

OEMC — Davíd Carrasco, ed., *The Oxford Encyclopedia of Mesoamerican Cultures* (Oxford: Oxford University Press, 2001).

INTRODUCTION

1. Certeau, *Writing of History*, 3.
2. Agustín Millares Carlo's Spanish translation of Martyr's original Latin text refers to the "slave" as a "servant" (*criado*) as well as a "young man" (*joven* or *muchacho*), *Décadas del Nuevo Mundo* (vol. 2), 537–549. The following quotes are drawn from Martyr, *De orbe novo* (vol. 2, "Fifth Decade," ch. 10), 202–204.
3. Certeau, *Writing of History*, 3.
4. Carrasco, *City of Sacrifice*, 190.
5. Clendinnen, *Aztecs*, 90.
6. My argument draws its critical momentum from deconstruction, a critical theory associated with Jacques Derrida, who developed a critique of the "metaphysics of presence"—Western philosophy's privileging of presence in the formation of claims to reality, truth, identity, and representation. By destabilizing the hierarchy between binaries such as presence and absence (and the related binaries of self–other, male–female, speech–writing, life–death), Derrida challenged the logocentrism of Western philosophical thought. Derrida proposed instead that all language has a trace, or a differential "force," that undergirds claims to meaning-making. For Derrida, the idea of the trace complicates the temporal and spatial fixation so central to ontological and epistemological claims to subject formation and representation. Derrida's "grammatology" ("the science of writing") has significantly influenced all disciplines, and has particularly generative implications within the field of dance studies. Derrida's "science" approaches writing as a performance that constructs meaning through a strategic "play" of presences and absences. Whereas dance is often considered as writing's "other"—it defies the permanence of writing, and its ephemerality resists the materiality of the page—for Derrida, writing is like dance, leaving "traces" of the movement of meaning. Throughout this book, I explore how the relationship between dancing and death dramatizes the interaction between absence and presence that formed the basis of colonial writings about the Indian as a subject.
7. Martyr, *De orbe novo* (vol. 2, "Fifth Decade," ch. 10), 191.
8. Clark, *History, Theory, Text*, 120.
9. Hulme, *Colonial Encounters*, 2.
10. Foucault, *Archaeology*, 49.
11. Nebrija, *Gramática de la lengua castellana*, 13.
12. Delgado Gómez, *Spanish Historical Writing*, 42.
13. *Handbook*, 384.
14. The other two missionaries were Johannes Dekkers and John der Auwera Tecto. Later Ghent moved to Tenochtitlan, the former center of the Aztec empire, where he trained students at a school called San José de Belén de los Naturales. He emphasized singing and performing folk dramas to teach and convert the natives.

15. In Burkhart, *Holy Wednesday*, 80.
16. Sparti in Guglielmo, *On the Practice or Art of Dancing*, 57.
17. Sparti in Guglielmo, *On the Practice or Art of Dancing*, 57.
18. Robert Stevenson, "Spagna," in *Medieval Iberia*, ed. Gerli, 760.
19. Kamen, *Philip of Spain*, 6.
20. Among these dancers, the king favored Catherina "La Comare," who from 1417 to 1424 performed Moorish dances in what may have been an early instance of Oriental dancing (Maricarmen Gómez Muntané, "Dance," in *Medieval Iberia*, ed. Gerli, 275). The Aragonese court of Pedro IV (1319–1387) featured two French-inspired female troubadours (*trobadors de dances*), Jacme Fluvia of Mallorca and Pere de Rius.
21. Coleman, *Creating Christian Granada*, 123.
22. Weiditz, *Authentic Everyday Dress of the Renaissance*, 43: "In this manner the Moriscos dance with each other, snapping with fingers at the same time"; and "This is the Morisco dance music; they make noises also like calves."
23. Brooks, *Dances of the Processions of Seville*, 206.
24. Ivanova, *The Dance in Spain*, 46.
25. See Clark, *Dance of Death*, 1–2. Gómez Muntané points out that the *Llibre vermell de Montserrat* ("Red book of Montserrat"), a collection of late medieval musical compositions for dance dating from approximately A.D. 1400, includes extant "dance of death" musical compositions, which minimally suggests that there was not only a literary and artistic tradition but also the basis of a performance tradition, at least in the late fourteenth century in the region of Montserrat, from where the collection of songs hails ("Dance," in *Medieval Iberia*, ed. Gerli, 275–276).
26. Werner L. Gundersheimer in Holbein, *Dance of Death*, xiii.
27. Whyte, *The Dance of Death in Spain and Catalonia*, vii–viii.
28. "Dance of Death," in *Encyclopedia of Death and the Human Experience*, ed. Bryant and Peck, 254.
29. Brooks, *Dances of the Processions of Seville*, 36.
30. Olive, *Diccionario de sinónimos de la lengua castellana*.
31. See Lepecki, *Exhausting Dance*, 25–27. The term *chorégraphie* was coined by Feuillet in his 1798 treatise on dancing, *La chorégraphie; ou, L'Art de décrire la danse par caractères, figures et signes démonstratifs*.
32. Arbeau, *Orchesography*, 15.
33. Susan Leigh Foster characterizes Arbeau's writing as an "inventory" (*Choreographing Empathy*, 29).
34. Arbeau, *Orchesography*, 12.
35. Arbeau, *Orchesography*, 13.
36. Arbeau, *Orchesography*, 12.
37. Taylor, "Scenes of Cognition," 356.
38. Nevile, *The Eloquent Body*, 2.
39. This information is based on the work of Cline, who compiled and analyzed reports from the House of Trade in Seville regarding Cortés's first return visit to Spain in 1528 ("Hernando Cortés and the Aztec Indians in Spain").
40. The term "Anáhuac" was originally used to describe the "Aztec" peoples by Jesuit chronicler Francisco Javier Clavigero in his *Storia antica del Messico* (1780–1781).
41. Clendinnen, "Cost of Courage in Aztec Society," 68.
42. Eduardo Matos Moctezuma gives the figure of 250,000 ("Tenochtitlan," *OEMC* 3:198–200); Aguilar-Moreno says 200,000 (*Handbook*, 227); and Coe estimates 11 million (*Mexico*, 227).
43. *Handbook*, 74.
44. *Codex Ramírez*, 83. Also in Brundage, *Jade Steps*, 107.
45. See table 3 in "Major Deities of the Late Pre-Hispanic Central Mexican Nahua-Speaking Communities," *HMAI* 10:395–446.
46. Hugo G. Nutini, "Witchcraft, Sorcery, and Magic," *OEMC* 3:332–334.
47. The Aztec called this energy *tonalli*.
48. *Handbook*, 208.
49. See Köhler, "On the Significance of the Aztec Day Sign 'Olin.'"
50. *Handbook*, 208.
51. Sahagún, *FC* (bk. 4, ch. 2), 6.
52. Durán, *Book of the Gods and Rites*, 402–403.
53. Boone, *Cycles of Time*, 36.
54. Durán, *Book of the Gods and Rites*, 187.
55. *Handbook*, 208. Martí was a proponent of the idea that the symbol represented the joining of the four quarters of the Aztec universe (*Canto, danza y música precortesianos*, esp. 259).
56. Las Casas, *Short Account*, 50–51.
57. Boone, "Migration Histories as Ritual Performance," 145.
58. Thomas makes a convincing case for this date (*Conquest of Mexico*, 387).
59. Tezozómoc, *Crónica mexicana* (ch. 18), 278–281.

CHAPTER 1

1. In Irving, *Life and Voyages* (vol. 1), 211–212. There are various versions of this encounter that are believed to have derived from Columbus's now-missing journal. Las Casas includes a thirdhand account in Bartolomé de las Casas, *Historia de las Indias* (vol. 1, ch. 58), 392–395. For more on Columbus's journal, see Reid, *Myths and Realities*, 117–120.
2. Columbus, *Select Letters* ("Third Voyage"), 116.
3. Columbus, *Select Letters* ("Third Voyage"), 123.

4. See Ellingson, *Myth*, for a thorough study of the origins and development of this term.

5. Vespucci, *Letters* ("First Voyage"), 6.

6. Vespucci, *Letters* ("First Voyage"), 10. Following this report, Vespucci describes his march inland, where he encountered other Indians who were dancing savagely: "Here we were received with so many barbarous ceremonies that the pen will not suffice to write them down. There were songs, dances, tears, mingled with rejoicings and plenty of food. We remained here for the night. Here they offered their wives to us, and we were unable to defend ourselves from them" (15).

7. White, *Tropics of Discourse*, 153.

8. Vespucci, *Letters* ("First Voyage"), 15; and see n. 6.

9. Scillacio, *De insulis meridiani*, 75, 77.

10. Scillacio, *De insulis meridiani*, 79.

11. Scillacio, *De insulis meridiani*, 89.

12. Greenblatt, "Resonance and Wonder," 20.

13. Greenblatt, *Marvelous Possessions*, 135.

14. Throughout the chronicles the term appears in various permutations (*arreyto, areito, areíto*).

15. Ortiz, "La música y los areítos de los indios de Cuba," 127 (my translation).

16. Thompson, "'Cronistas de Indias' Revisited," 191.

17. Certeau, *Writing of History*, 86.

18. Taylor, *The Archive and the Repertoire*, 28–31.

19. Las Casas (see app. A); Martyr, *De orbe novo* (vol. 1, "Third Decade," bk. 9), 387.

20. Ortiz, *La africanía de la música*, 58, as translated and quoted in Kuss, *Music in Latin America*, 1:133. For more on these debates, see Moore, *Nationalizing Blackness*, esp. 261, n. 21; Thompson, "'Cronistas de Indias' Revisited"; and Stevenson, *Music in Aztec and Inca Territory*.

21. Las Casas, *Short Account*, 22.

22. Las Casas, *Short Account*, 27–28.

23. Oviedo, *Conquest and Settlement*, 23–26. It is hard to resist speculating that the legend of Sotomayor and Guanina inspired Arthur Brooke's poem "The Tragical History of Romeus and Juliet," the precursor to Shakespeare's *Romeo and Juliet*, given its underlying territorial dispute, "star cross'd lovers," a "masquerade," and the discovery of bodies lost through miscommunication and suicide.

24. See Thompson, "'Cronistas de Indias' Revisited" for its relation to music history and Brokaw, "Ambivalence, Mimicry, and Stereotype" in relation to discourse.

25. Arrom in Pané, *An Account of the Antiquities*, xi.

26. Pané, *An Account of the Antiquities*, 20.

27. Pané, *An Account of the Antiquities*, 20.

28. Martyr, *De orbe novo* (vol. 1, "Third Decade," bk. 7), 361.

29. Martyr, *De orbe novo* (vol. 1, "First Decade," bk. 7), 146.

30. Martyr, *De orbe novo* (vol. 1, "Third Decade," bk. 7), 361–362.

31. Gómara, *Historia general de las Indias* (vol. 1, ch. 33), 52–53.

32. According to Sebastián de Covarrubias Orozco's 1611 dictionary *Tesoro de la lengua castellana o española*, a *zambra* is a Moorish dance performed to the sound of bagpipes and flutes. The *zambra* was named for the *zimr*, a folk oboe used to accompany a festival of the same name and danced with a small brass cymbal ("North Africa" in *International Encyclopedia of Dance*, ed. Cohen, vol. 4, 664).

33. Gómara, *Historia general de las Indias* (vol. 1, ch. 29), 48.

34. Myers, *Fernández de Oviedo's Chronicle of America*, 1.

35. Oviedo, *Historia general y natural de las Indias* (bk. 17, ch. 4), 389.

36. Oviedo, *Historia*, trans. Gillespie (bk. 4, ch. 11), 112.

37. Oviedo, *Sumario de la natural historia de las Indias* (1526) (ch. 10) in Vedia, ed., *Historiadores primitivos de Indias*, 484. See also app. B for a passage about the dance leader. For Stoudemire's complete English translation of the *Sumario* passage, see Oviedo, *Natural History of the West Indies*, 38–39: "Then they sing of these matters in their songs which are called *areítos*. The *areíto* is something that may be described as follows: when the Indians want to amuse themselves and sing, a great company of men and women get together and catch hands, alternately men and women. The leader, who is called *tequina*, man or woman, takes a few steps forward and then back, something like a contradance, and they go around in this fashion, and he sings in a low or medium voice anything that he cares to, making the measure of his voice keep time with the steps. And what he speaks is repeated by the multitude that takes part in the contradance or *areíto*, in the same steps and order, but in a louder voice. This goes on for three or four hours or longer, or from one day to another. At the same time there are other people who walk behind those who were dancing, giving them wine which they call *chichi*, which will be described further on. They drink so much that often they get so drunk that they appear to lose all senses. In these drunken orgies they tell how the *caciques* died, as was mentioned above, and they also sing of other things that may strike their fancy. And often they order their treason against those they love.

Sometimes the *tequinas*, or leaders who direct the dance, are changed, and the new guide of the dance changes the tune and the contradance and the words. This type of song-dance is very similar to the form of the songs used among the farmers and villagers when in summer men and women for the pleasure join in the *panadero* [a clog dance]. In Flanders I have seen this form of song-dance also."

38. Livy, *History of Rome*, 55.

39. See Lada-Richards, *Silent Eloquence*, esp. 177, n. 14.

40. Brokaw, "Ambivalence, Mimicry, and Stereotype," 144.

41. Sahagún, *FC*, "Al lector" section of the "Arte divinitoria," in García Icazbalceta, *Bibliografía*, 321–322. The claim was repeated by historian Juan de Torquemada. See Bierhorst, *Cantares mexicanos*, 528, n. 27.

42. Myers, *Chronicle of America*, 69.

43. O'Gorman, *The Invention of America*, 140.

44. Brokaw, "Ambivalence, Mimicry, and Stereotype," 149.

45. Bhabha, *Location of Culture*, 86. Also in Brokaw, "Ambivalence, Mimicry, and Stereotype," 149.

46. His description of this particular ceremony is unique for at least two reasons. First, Oviedo makes no claim to having witnessed it, whereas with his other descriptions he is certain to situate himself as a "witness," sometimes even memorializing the date on which he had seen the ceremony. Second, the passage is uncharacteristically devoid of judgment. Oviedo expresses neither pleasure nor terror, which leads me to suspect that Oviedo did not directly observe this ceremony, but learned about it through an elder. In all likelihood, such sacrifices would have been banned after the Spanish arrival in the region of Nicoya in 1522.

47. Las Casas, *In Defense of the Indians*, 348.

48. *Historia de las Indias* (vol. 3, bk. 2, ch. 60), 307.

49. Las Casas, *Apologética historia sumaria* (bk. 3, ch. 204), 349–350.

50. See Hanke, *All Mankind Is One*, 41–44. Hanke points out that Oviedo's position concerning the Christians' ability to convert the Indians evolved over time.

51. Las Casas, *Apologética historia sumaria* (bk. 3, ch. 193), 290.

52. Las Casas, *Obras escogidas* (vol. 1), 200.

53. Las Casas, *In Defense of the Indians*, 348.

54. Las Casas, *Obras escogidas* (vol. 3), 88–89; translation by Sanderlin in *Bartolomé de las Casas*, 124. Interestingly, Las Casas bases this claim on reports concerning the Indians who boarded Columbus's ship and exhibited "fondness" for dancing.

55. Las Casas, *Apologética historia sumaria* (vol. 1, bk. 2, ch. 34), 181.

56. Las Casas, *Witness*, 109. Also *Apologética historia sumaria* (ch. 28 and 37).

57. *Bartolomé de las Casas*, 124. Also, *Obras escogidas* (vol. 3), 124–125.

58. Las Casas, *Short Account*, 50–51.

59. Translated and discussed in Mignolo, "When Speaking Was Not Good Enough," 313.

CHAPTER 2

1. This account is relayed by Friar Gerónimo de Mendieta, *Historia eclesiástica indiana* (bk. 3, ch. 12), 211: "Ese será mi nombre para toda la vida."

2. Bauer, "Millennium's Darker Side," 41.

3. Baudot, *Utopia and History in Mexico*, 131.

4. Baudot, *Utopia and History in Mexico*, 399. For debates concerning the dates of *Historia*, see Foster in Motolinía (*History of the Indians of New Spain*, 18) and Baudot (*Utopia and History in Mexico*, 376).

5. Bauer, "Millennium's Darker Side," 35.

6. Mendieta, "Carta del P. Fr. Gerónimo de Mendieta," in García Icazbalceta, ed., *Nueva colección de documentos* (vol. 1), 6. Also in Baudot, *Utopia and History in Mexico*, 86.

7. In Baudot, *Utopia and History in Mexico*, 277.

8. Motolinía, *History of the Indians of New Spain* (bk. 1, ch. 14), 96.

9. Motolinía, *History of the Indians of New Spain* (bk. 3, ch. 12), 238.

10. Motolinía, *History of the Indians of New Spain* (bk. 3, ch. 12), 238.

11. Baudot, *Utopia and History in Mexico*, 279.

12. Bk. 1, ch. 15.

13. Dyer explains that *boçal* referred to a recently arrived slave (*Memoriales*, 541, n. 4). Perceval defines *boçal* as a "muffler, a muzzle, one that sayeth and trieth to speak a toong, yet cannot" (*A Dictionarie in Spanish and English*, 46).

14. Motolinía memorializes the tension between him and Las Casas (and between Franciscans and Dominicans more generally) in a 1555 letter to Charles V (*Carta al Emperador*). Church officials also used the term, such as in the Ecclesiastical Junta of 1539, which prohibited the performance of *areítos*. As such, it is also possible Motolinía's remarks were aimed at Church authorities more broadly.

15. Metcalfe, *Motolinía on Music*, esp. 44–45.

16. The terms appear as *maceua* and *maceualiztli* (fol. 50r and v).

17. Sahagún, *Historia general* (vol. 1, bk. 1, ch. 16), ed. López Austin and García Quintana, 95. Sahagún's native informants, whose original Nahua testimony is presented in the *Florentine Codex*, rarely use *macehualiztli* to signify "dance." Interestingly, in the few instances that linguistic forms based on *macehua* appear in the text, they are often, although not exclusively, associated with the Aztec emperor (*tlatoani*).

18. Lockhart, *Nahuas after the Conquest*, 503, n. 2.

19. *Introduction to Classical Nahuatl*, 450. Several descriptions of dance in Sahagún's *Florentine Codex* distinguish between dances that do and do not have hand gestures, giving credence to the possibility that *macehualiztli* might refer to a particular type of nongestural dance.

20. Motolinía, *History of the Indians of New Spain* (bk. 1, ch. 8), 72.

21. Baudot, *Utopia and History in Mexico*, 378.

22. Baudot, *Utopia and History in Mexico*, 378.

23. Cervantes de Salazar, *Crónica de la Nueva España* (1914) (bk. 1, ch. 20), 39; Mendieta, *Historia eclesiástica indiana* (bk. 2, ch. 31), 140–143; Muñoz Camargo, *Historia de Tlaxcala* (fol. 142v), 194; Gómara, *Cortés* (ch. 70), 147–148.

24. Baudot explains that "loose folios" of Motolinía's drafts circulated between New Spain and Europe, which explains why Gómara had access to them prior to 1552 (*Utopia and History in Mexico*, 367). Gómara's account also relied on his interviews with Andrés de Tapia, who fought alongside Cortés in the conquest of Mexico and later returned to Spain with the marqués in 1528.

25. Cortés, "Second Letter," *Letters from Mexico*, 111.

26. Cortés, "Second Letter," *Letters from Mexico*, 111–112.

27. Gómara uses this information again to describe the dancing that took place at the Massacre at the Festival of Toxcatl. See chapter 4.

28. Motolinía, *History of the Indians of New Spain*, 239.

29. *HMAI* 13:70.

30. Cervantes de Salazar, *Crónica* (bk. 4, ch. 7). See chapter 5 of this book for the other chapter about dance in Cervantes's *Crónica*, "About the dances or *areítos* of the Indians (*De los bailes ó areítos de los indios*)" (bk. 1, ch. 20). Based on an unknown source, this chapter is interesting because it uses the Nahuatl term *ximitote* (a variant of *mitote*) to signify "dance."

31. See Nieto Jiménez, *Nuevo tesoro lexicográfico del español*. The term *sarao* first appears in 1591 as "a hall to daunce in" (Perceval, *Bibliotheca hispanica*). In 1601 Francisco del Rosal defined it as follows: "In Latin it is the *corro*, dance, or ordered procession, if it's not *hebreo*, which they call *ceder*" (*Origen y etimología de todos los vocablos originales*). In 1611 Covarrubias similarly asserted that a *sarao* is a regal event, based on the premise that *sarao* is a Hebrew word for *señor* (*Tesoro de la lengua castellana o española*).

32. Cervantes de Salazar, *Crónica de la Nueva España* (bk. 4, ch. 102), 462–463.

33. For more on the history of the *matachine*, see Harris, *Aztecs, Moors, and Christians*, esp. 227–232.

34. Fabian, *Time and the Other*, 31.

35. Fabian, *Time and the Other*, 143.

36. Fabian, *Time and the Other*, xi.

37. Motolinía (app. E); Gómara, *Cortés* (ch. 70), 147–148; Cervantes de Salazar, *Crónica de la Nueva España* (bk. 4, ch. 7), 287 and (bk. 1, ch. 20), 38–39; Benzoni, *History of the New World* (bk. 2), 151; Hernández, *Antigüedades* (bk. 2, ch. 6), 94–96. Benzoni and Hernández seemingly drew upon parts of Motolinía's *Memoriales*, but their accounts are sufficiently distinct so as not to be considered "counterfeits."

38. Motolinía (app. E); Mendieta, *Historia* (bk. 2, ch. 31), 140–143; Muñoz Camargo, *Historia de Tlaxcala* (fol. 142v), 194.

39. Hernández, *Antigüedades* (bk. 2, ch. 6), 94–96. The surviving version of Hernández's chapter on the *netotiliztli* is written in Latin, making it more difficult to compare to Motolinía's in terms of diction and syntax. In a chapter about the Aztec market (bk. 1, ch. 27), Hernández points out that the Aztec "have species of edible birds, whose feathers are used for clothing, and whose wings are used by bird hunters, and all for dancing and dances known as *netoteliztli*" (*Mexican Treasury*, 76).

40. Some of these song and dance names are mentioned by Franciscan friar Bernardino de Sahagún, who in 1570 had just completed his *Historia general de las cosas de Nueva España*. However, Hernández includes information that is not found within Sahagún's work. For a detailed comparison between Hernández and Sahagún with respect to their treatment of songs and dances, see Hernández, *Antigüedades*, 277–282.

41. A notable exception is Oviedo's attempt to question a *cacique* about the significance of one of the *areítos* he had seen.

CHAPTER 3

1. Book 5 addresses "The Omens," and Book 11, "Earthly Things."

2. *Historia general*, ed. López Austin (vol. 1), 8: "Que trata del calendario, fiestas, y cerimonias, sacrificios, y solenidades que estos naturales désta Nueva España Hacían a Honra de sus Dioses."

3. Klor de Alva, "Sahagún and the Birth of Modern Ethnography: Representing, Confessing, and Inscribing the Native Other," in *Work of Bernardino de Sahagún*, ed. Klor de Alva et al., 47.

4. Sahagún identified his "trilinguals" as Antonio Valeriano of Azcapotzalco, Alonso Vegerano and Pedro de San Buenaventura of Quauhtitlan, and Martín Jacobita of Tlatelolco. *FC* (intro.), 55.

5. Mexican historian Francisco del Paso y Troncoso gave the *Primeros memoriales* its title.

6. Luis Nicolau D'Olwer and Howard F. Cline, "Bernardino de Sahagún, 1499–1590," in *HMAI* 13:196.

7. H. B. Nicholson, "Bernardino de Sahagún," in *OEMC* 3:105–113.

8. According to Edmonson, between 1575 and 1580 Sahagún worked on a later version that is known as the *Tolosa Manuscript* (*Sixteenth-Century Mexico*, 9).

9. *FC* (intro.), 45.

10. Translator Fanny R. Bandelier claims that "we can now recognize [Sahagún] as the first true ethnologist" as well as "the first great historian" (in Sahagún, *A History of Ancient Mexico*, ix). Klor de Alva, Nicholson, and Quiñones Keber subsequently subtitled their edited volume about Sahagún "Pioneer Ethnographer of Sixteenth-Century Aztec Mexico." In that volume, Klor de Alva examines Sahagún in relation to "the birth of modern ethnography." And it is Miguel León-Portilla's biography of Sahagún that enthusiastically claims the missionary as the "First Anthropologist."

11. Browne, *Sahagún and the Transition to Modernity*, 9–13.

12. Klor de Alva, "Sahagún and the Birth of Modern Ethnography," 33.

13. Sahagún, *A History of Ancient Mexico*, 21. Todorov argues that Sahagún was not an ethnologist but instead a "comparatist" who "puts certain *objects*, all of which are external to him, on the same level, and he himself remains the sole *subject*" and "does not put the Other on the same level as oneself." An ethnologist, by comparison, "contributes to the reciprocal illumination of one culture by another" (*Conquest of America*, 240–241).

14. López Austin in Edmonson, *Sixteenth-Century Mexico*, 125.

15. López Austin in Edmonson, *Sixteenth-Century Mexico*, 126.

16. *A History of Ancient Mexico* (bk. 2), 75.

17. See chapter 1 above for a complete discussion of the term *areíto* and its influence on missionary writings about dance.

18. López Austin, "Cosmovision," in *OEMC* 1:268–274.

19. *FC* (bk. 7, ch. 6), 7.

20. *Handbook*, 291.

21. See *Handbook*, 292.

22. Boone, *Cycles of Time*, 17.

23. Broda, "Festivals and Festival Cycles," in *OEMC* 1:406–409.

24. *FC* (bk. 2, ch. 26), 93 and *FC* (bk. 2, ch. 15), 27.

25. *FC* (bk. 2, ch. 20), 46.

26. *Handbook*, 291. These periods were called "Iquiza-Tonatiuh" (6 a.m. to 12 noon); "Nepantla-Tonatiuh" (12 noon to 6 p.m.); "Onaqui-Tonatiuh" (6 p.m. to 12 midnight), and "Yohualnepantla" (12 midnight to 6 a.m.).

27. *FC* (bk. 2, ch. 26), 93.

28. *FC* (bk. 2, ch. 28), 110.

29. *FC* (bk. 2, ch. 37), 165.

30. *FC* (bk. 2, ch. 30), 118. During the month of Teotleco, the serpent dance began "at midday" (*FC* [bk. 2, ch. 31], 130). And during Toxcatl, "night fell as there was dancing. Thus the feast day ended when the day came to an end" (*FC* [bk. 2, ch. 6], 76).

31. *FC* (bk. 2, ch. 27), 101.

32. See López Austin, *Human Body and Ideology*, vol. 1, esp. 203–229.

33. Carrasco, *City of Sacrifice*, 57–58.

34. *Handbook*, 229.

35. *Handbook*, 228.

36. Durán, *Book of the Gods and Rites*, 189.

37. Carrasco, "Myth, Cosmic Terror, and the Templo Mayor," 127.

38. The first New Fire Ceremony was performed in 1195 CE and seven times thereafter. The last New Fire Ceremony was recorded in November 1507, under the reign of Montezuma. The next would have occurred in 1559.

39. *Handbook*, 298.

40. Broda, "Festivals and Festival Cycles," in *OEMC* 1:406–409. Brundage, *Jade Steps*, 3–39.

41. This description is based on the work of H. B. Nicholson, who wrote some of the most exhaustive studies of Mesoamerican religion. See Nicholson, "Religion in Pre-Hispanic Central Mexico," in *HMAI* 13:395–446.

42. Brundage, *Jade Steps*, 92.

43. *Handbook*, 99.

44. *FC* (bk. 3, ch. 5), 56–57.

45. *FC* (bk. 8, ch. 17), 51 and 55.

46. *FC* (bk. 8, ch. 17), 57.

47. *FC* (bk. 8, ch. 14), 43–45. See chapter 5 for a full discussion of the *cuicacalli*.

48. *FC* (bk. 8, ch. 9), 27.

49. *FC* (bk. 9, ch. 20), 91.

50. *FC* (bk. 8, ch. 9), 28.

51. *FC* (bk. 8, ch. 10), 29.

52. See *Códice Carolino*, 38, n. 24. Also López Austin, *Human Body and Ideology*, 308.

53. *FC* (bk. 4, ch. 7), 26.

54. *FC* (bk. 2, ch. 27), 101.

55. *FC* (bk. 8, ch. 17), 56.

56. *FC* (bk. 4, ch. 7), 25.

57. *FC* (bk. 8, ch. 17), 56.

58. *FC* (bk. 1, ch. 13), 30.

59. *FC* (bk. 1, ch. 13), 30 and (bk. 2, ch. 37), 164.

60. *FC* (bk. 2, ch. 37), 164. The tunic was called a *xicolli*, or a "sleeveless jacket."

61. *FC* (bk. 2, ch. 37), 164.

62. *FC* (bk. 2, ch. 28), 110.

63. For example, in the festival of Huey Tecuilhuitl, celebrants danced around an image of the corn goddess Xilonen. During Panquetzaliztli they danced around the image of Huitzilopochtli. During Izcalli, following the ritual sacrifice of four women, Montezuma offered incense to the god as others danced the serpent dance.

64. *FC* (bk. 2, ch. 24), 75.

65. *FC* (bk. 2, ch. 28), 110.

66. *FC* (bk. 2, ch. 29), 116.

67. *FC* (bk. 2, ch. 34), 142–143.

68. *FC* (bk. 2), 177. The serpent was not the only animal imitated in Aztec dance. During the ceremony of the twelfth month, Teotl Eco ("The Arrival of the Gods") there was a mass sacrifice by fire. As the victims were cast into the fire, two dancers, one arrayed as a squirrel, the other as a bat, went along dancing, whistling, and rattling.

69. *FC* (bk. 10, ch. 29), 173.

70. *FC* (bk. 10, ch. 29), 184.

71. *FC* (bk. 10, ch. 29), 183: "The gourd rattle rests in their hands; also they dance with it. And the men always carry their gourd rattles."

72. León-Portilla in Gossen, *South and Meso-American Native Spirituality*, 43.

73. For a complete discussion of Aztec notions of sacrifice in the work of Sahagún, see Köhler, "'Debt-Payment' to the Gods."

74. Brundage, *Jade Steps*, 57.

75. Carrasco, *City of Sacrifice*, 190.

76. Booth likened this underlying structure to the narrative of "incarnation," "sacrifice," and "epiphany" of Jesus Christ ("Dramatic Aspects of Aztec Rituals," 423).

77. Díaz del Castillo, *Discovery and Conquest of Mexico* (ch. 64), 214.

78. *FC* (bk. 9, ch. 10), 46.

79. *FC* (bk. 9, ch. 10), 46.

80. *FC* (bk. 2, ch. 1), 2. The short introductory descriptions of the *Florentine Codex* reference this dance, but there is no mention made of it in the long version of the *veintena* description therein, nor in the *Primeros memoriales*.

81. *FC* (bk. 2, ch. 20), 44.

82. In Durán, *Book of the Gods and Rites*, 178, n. 9.

83. *FC* (bk. 9, ch. 8), 38–39.

84. In *Primeros memoriales* (56) Sahagún specifies that the rite took place on Feb. 26.

85. Carrasco, *City of Sacrifice*, 162.

86. *Historia general* (vol. 1, bk. 2, ch. 21), ed. López Austin and García Quintana, 180.

87. *FC* (bk. 2, ch. 20), 46.

88. *FC* (bk. 2, ch. 20), 46.

89. *FC* (bk. 2, ch. 20), 46.

90. *Primeros memoriales* (fol. 250r), 57.

91. *FC* (bk. 2, ch. 21), 47–48.

92. *FC* (bk. 2, ch. 21), 48.

93. *FC* (bk. 2, ch. 21), 51; italics added.

94. *FC* (bk. 2, ch. 37), 163.

95. Clendinnen, *Aztecs*, 95.

96. *FC* (bk. 2, ch. 21), 52–53; italics added.

97. *FC* (bk. 2, ch. 21), 54.

98. *FC* (bk. 2, ch. 21), 54.

99. *Primeros memoriales* (fol. 250r), 57.

100. Durán, *Book of the Gods and Rites*, 83.

101. *FC* (bk. 2, ch. 21), 55.

102. *FC* (bk. 2, ch. 21), 55.

103. Durán, *History of the Indies*, 273.

104. Durán, *History of the Indies* (ch. 36), 276.

105. *FC* (bk. 2, ch. 21), 55.

106. *FC* (bk. 2, ch. 21), 55–56.

107. Carrasco, *City of Sacrifice*, 210.

108. Sahagún says June 26 in *Primeros memoriales* (fol. 251r), 60.

109. *FC* (bk. 2, ch. 27), 98.

110. López Austin translates "Cihuacoatl" as "serpent uterus" over the more common "serpent woman" to emphasize the goddess's relation to childbirth (see Shelton, "The Aztec *Cihuateteo*," 12).

111. *FC* (bk. 2, ch. 27), 101.

112. *FC* (bk. 2, ch. 27), 101.

113. *FC* (bk. 2, ch. 27), 102.

114. *FC* (bk. 2, ch. 27), 103.

115. *FC* (bk. 2, ch. 27), 104.

116. *FC* (bk. 2, ch. 27), 105.

117. *FC* (bk. 2, ch. 33), 139–140. *Primeros memoriales* (fol. 252r), 64, stipulates that during this offering there was "dancing of only the men; god-keepers sang to them."

118. *FC* (bk. 2, ch. 33), 139–140.

119. *FC* (bk. 2, ch. 26), 92.

120. *FC* (bk. 2, ch. 26), 93.

121. *FC* (bk. 2, ch. 26), 94.

122. *FC* (bk. 6, ch. 30), 167.

123. Shelton, "The Aztec *Cihuateteo*," 5.

124. Clenninnen, *Aztecs*, 179.

125. *FC* (bk. 4, ch. 33), 107.

126. *FC* (bk. 6, ch. 29), 161. The *Florentine Codex* refers to women who died during childbirth as *mociuaquetzque* and likens them to the *cihuateteo*.

127. The thief is also called a *macpalitoti*.

128. *FC* (bk. 10, ch. 11), 39: the *temacpalitoti* was a "guardian [of secret rituals]; a master of the spoken word, song. [He is] one who robs by casting a spell, who puts people to sleep; [he is] a thief. He dances with a dead woman's forearm; he robs by casting a spell, causing people to faint, to swoon."

129. *FC* (bk. 6, ch. 29), 162.

130. In describing the name "Tititl," Durán references a dance in which "men and women joined hands, danced," since, he explains, "Indians placed or imagined in the heavens two children pulling at each other, very much as we picture the sign Gemini in certain stars." This "stretching" may also refer to the stretching of the food supply during the rainy season (*Book of the Gods and Rites*, "Aztec Calendar," 463).

131. *FC* (bk. 2, ch. 36), 156.

132. Sahagún, *Historia General* (vol. 1, bk. 2, ch. 36), ed. López Austin and García Quintana, 257.

133. *Primeros memoriales* (fol. 253r), 66.

134. FC (bk. 2, ch. 36), 156. *Primeros memoriales* mentions that the priest dances in the flayed skin of the Ilamatecuhtli *ixiptla* as well as with her severed head.

135. FC (bk. 2, ch. 36), 156.

136. FC (bk. 2, ch. 30), 118.

137. FC (bk. 2, ch. 30), 118.

138. *Primeros memoriales* (fol. 251v), 62.

139. *A History of Ancient Mexico* (bk. 2), 113.

140. *Primeros memoriales* (fol. 251v), 62.

141. FC (bk. 2, ch. 30), 119.

142. FC (bk. 2, ch. 30), 121.

143. FC (bk. 2, ch. 30), 121.

144. FC (bk. 2, ch. 30), 123.

145. FC (bk. 2, ch. 30), 123–124.

146. Frazer, *Golden Bough* (1998), 26.

147. Frazer, *Golden Bough* (1911), pt. 3, 77.

148. Frazer, *Golden Bough* (1998), 27.

149. Frazer, *Golden Bough* (1998), 27.

150. Frazer, *Golden Bough* (1925), pt. 3, 11.

151. Girard, *Violence and the Sacred*, 32.

152. Girard, *Violence and the Sacred*, 5.

153. Girard, *Violence and the Sacred*, 7.

154. FC (bk. 2, ch. 21), 55.

155. Girard, *Violence and the Sacred*, 6.

156. Girard, *Violence and the Sacred*, 6.

CHAPTER 4

1. From the *Codex Chimalpahin* (vol. 2), 81.

2. The following descriptions of the Toxcatl dances are from Sahagún, FC (bk. 2, ch. 24), 71–77.

3. Thomas makes this estimate about the number of soldiers left behind with Pedro de Alvarado (*Conquest of Mexico*, 383).

4. On Saint John's Day, in Díaz del Castillo, *Discovery and Conquest of Mexico*, 296.

5. Gómara, *Historia general de las Indias* (vol. 1, p. 7): "La mayor cosa después de la creación del mundo, sacando la encarnación y muerte del que lo crió, es el descubrimiento de Indias, y así las llaman Nuevo Mundo." Translated and quoted in Restall, *Seven Myths*, 2.

6. White, *Tropics of Discourse*, 84.

7. Greenblatt, *Marvelous Possessions*, 7.

8. Clendinnen, "'Fierce and Unnatural Cruelty,'" 19.

9. Fogelson, "The Ethnohistory of Events and Nonevents," 143.

10. His expeditions took place between 1521 and 1524 (Kelly, *Pedro de Alvarado*, 173).

11. Pagden in Las Casas, *Short Account*, xxxi.

12. Pagden in Cortés, *Letters from Mexico*, xl.

13. Gibson, *Aztecs under Spanish Rule*, 58.

14. According to witness deposition of Juan Álvarez given on July 6, 1521, in Santiago de Cuba. Cortés, *Documentos cortesianos, I (1518–1528)*, 207–209.

15. "Respuesta del Conquistador," *Relación de méritos y servicios*, 105–113.

16. Thomas explains that in around 1527 Cortés accused Vázquez de Tapia of owing Cortés money, which ultimately landed Vázquez de Tapia in prison in Seville (*Who's Who of the Conquistadors*, 138).

17. The "Second Letter" is dated Oct. 30, 1520, and was published on Nov. 8, 1522. In 1527 the Crown suspended by royal decree further printings. See Pagden's introductory essay in Cortés, *Hernán Cortés: Letters from Mexico*, lviii.

18. *Historia general y natural de las Indias* (bk. 3, ch. 54) in Myers, *Fernández de Oviedo's Chronicle of America*, 166–174. The interview was published as a transcript, so as to give the semblance of objectivity to the exchange. Kathleen Ann Myers explains that Oviedo's use of direct discourse in his *History* "dramatizes the historical material" so as to provide authority to the text. Oviedo wrote decades after Cortés penned his second letter and was preoccupied with writing a history that could substantiate Cortés's claims. Interestingly, Cano's response to Oviedo's question about the legitimacy of his marriage involves a story about dance. Cano describes a custom whereby a bride and groom's marriage was recognized only after the couple had spent three consecutive days in a chamber to consummate the union. While the couple remained in sexual confinement, members of both families danced a *mitote*, a type of Aztec dance.

19. In Myers, *Chronicle of America*, 170.

20. In Myers, *Chronicle of America*, 170.

21. In Myers, *Chronicle of America*, 172.

22. In Myers, *Chronicle of America*, 170.

23. In Myers, *Chronicle of America*, 170.

24. In Myers, *Chronicle of America*, 170.

25. In Myers, *Chronicle of America*, 170.

26. Andrés de Tapia left his own account, but it does not cover the Festival of Toxcatl massacre. See Díaz et al., eds., *Conquista de Tenochtitlan* and Fuentes, ed., *The Conquistadors*.

27. Gómara, *Cortés: The Life of the Conqueror by His Secretary* (ch. 105), 207.

28. See chapter 2 for a complete discussion of Motolinía's writings about *netotiliztli* and *macehualiztli* and Gómara's appropriation of them.

29. Gómara, *Cortés: The Life of the Conqueror*, 208.

30. Leonard, *Books of the Brave*, 13.

31. Leonard mentions *Quatro libros de Amadís de Gaula*

(1508); the Castilian version of the *Tirant lo Blanch* (1511); and *Historia del caballero de Dios que avrá por nombre Cifar* (1512).

32. See J. H. Elliott's introductory essay in *Cortés: Letters from Mexico*, xvi.

33. Díaz del Castillo, *Discovery and Conquest of Mexico*, 190.

34. Díaz sent the manuscript to Spain in 1575, but it wasn't published until 1632.

35. Díaz, *The Discovery and Conquest*, 210.

36. Díaz, *The Discovery and Conquest*, 214. In this quote, I retain Díaz's use of the term *matachine*, which Maudslay translates as "Merry-Andrews."

37. Díaz, *The Discovery and Conquest of Mexico*, 294.

38. Díaz, *The Discovery and Conquest of Mexico*, 297.

39. Asked about this exchange in his interrogation, Vázquez de Tapia says he neither heard nor saw this exchange happen.

40. Anonymous Conqueror in Fuentes, ed., *The Conquistadors*, 169. This anonymous chronicle was first published in Italy in 1556. See "Anonymous Conqueror" in *HMAI* 13:65.

41. *The Discovery and Conquest of Mexico*, 436.

42. Díaz, *The Discovery and Conquest of Mexico*, 436–437.

43. Spanish nationalist Julián Juderías coined the term "black legend" in *La leyenda negra* (1914) and held that such negative indictments of Spain and Spaniards were based on "omission," "exaggeration," and "misinformation" about the Spanish expansion in the Americas and its conquest.

44. See "Introduction" of Greer, Mignolo, and Quilligan, eds., *Rereading the Black Legend*, esp. 5–9.

45. In 1542, with support from Las Casas, the New Laws were enacted, which prohibited colonists from enslaving Indians in hereditary *encomiendas*, yet still forced Indians to pay tribute to the Spanish through labor.

46. Dates are according to Henry Raup Wagner (in Las Casas, *Defense of the Indians*, xx) and Pagden, who says the *Apologetic History* was written "sometime after 1551" ("Ius et factum," 89).

47. *History of the Indies* was written between 1527 and 1559, according to Pagden, "Ius et factum," 89.

48. Las Casas's *A Brief Account* is dedicated to Prince Philip, the heir to the Spanish throne, and addressed to King Charles V, his father.

49. Las Casas reports on the infamous Spanish massacre of natives at Cholula, a southern city under the control of the Mexica, that had occurred a month prior to the Spanish arrival in Tenochtitlan. At Cholula, Las Casas explains, the Spaniards "stage[d] a bloody massacre of the most public possible kind in order to terrorize those meek and gentle people" (*Short Account*, 45).

50. Las Casas, *Short Account*, 50.

51. Las Casas, *Short Account*, 50. Saint James was the patron saint of the Spanish army.

52. Las Casas, *Short Account*, 51. Also discussed in the introduction.

53. Incidentally, Las Casas's cautionary tale proved true, for throughout Mexico, even until today, dances such as the *moros y cristianos*, which reenact the conquest of Mexico, are performed. See chapter 5 for origins of *moros y cristianos* in New Spain.

54. As noted by Hans Magnus Enzensberger in Las Casas, *The Devastation of the Indies*, 9.

55. The text was originally published as *Narratio regionum Indicarum per Hispanos quosdam deuastatarum verissima*.

56. Alexander, ed., in de Bry, *Discovering the New World*, 7.

57. The engravings are attributed to Iodocus a Winghe, one of de Bry's engravers.

58. Conley, "De Bry's Las Casas," 113.

59. Conley, "De Bry's Las Casas," 108.

60. Benzoni, *History of the New World* (bk. 2), 137.

61. Binski, *Medieval Death*, 157.

62. Binski, *Medieval Death*, 156.

63. Binski, *Medieval Death*, 157–158.

64. One of the earliest known examples of a dance of death mural dates from 1424 and appeared at the Cimetière des Innocents in Paris.

65. Gundersheimer, "Introduction," in Holbein, *Dance of Death*, ix–xiv. Holbein made the woodcuts in Basel between 1523 and 1526.

66. Whyte, *Dance of Death in Spain and Catalonia*, vii–viii.

67. Whyte, *Dance of Death in Spain and Catalonia*, 22.

68. Whyte, *Dance of Death in Spain and Catalonia*, 42.

69. Jáuregui in Carvajal, *Conquest on Trial*, 2, n. 1.

70. Jáuregui in Carvajal, *Conquest on Trial*, 22–24.

71. See the introduction for more about the Indians who traveled with Cortés on his return to Spain.

72. Carvajal, *Conquest on Trial*, 99.

73. Carvajal, *Conquest on Trial*, 101.

74. Jáuregui in Carvajal, *Conquest on Trial*, 49.

75. See chapter 5 for more on Durán's writings.

76. Durán, *The History of the Indies of New Spain*, 530–531.

77. Aguilar's *relación* is in the Real Biblioteca de San Lorenzo de El Escorial. Aguilar discusses the Mexica revolt, but does not mention that Alvarado instigated the attack. See *La Conquista de Tenochtitlan*, ed. Díez.

78. Durán, *Book of the Gods and Rites* (ch. 2), 78.

79. Durán, *Book of the Gods and Rites* (ch. 2), 77.

80. Aguillar in Fuentes, ed., *The Conquistadors*, 150.
81. Durán, *Book of the Gods and Rites*, 76.
82. Durán, *History of the Indies*, 536.
83. Durán, *History of the Indies*, 536.
84. Durán, *History of the Indies*, 537.
85. Durán, *History of the Indies*, 538.
86. Durán, *History of the Indies*, 537–538.
87. Muñoz Camargo, *Historia de Tlaxcala* (fol. 187r), 243. Keen says that Muñoz Camargo based his history on Sahagún's informants and Gómara's history, as well as his own informants (*Aztec Image*, 127).
88. Prescott, *History of the Conquest*, 595–596.
89. Muñoz Camargo, *Historia de Tlaxcala* (fol. 202v), 221.
90. Muñoz Camargo, *Historia de Tlaxcala* (fol. 202r), 221.
91. Restall, *Seven Myths*, 112–114.
92. Clendinnen, "Fierce," 16.
93. Tedlock, *Popol Vuh*, 64. Also in Boone (*Stories in Red and Black*, 15) and Restall (*Seven Myths*, xvii).
94. The manuscript is held in the Bibliothèque nationale de France in Paris. See León-Portilla, ed., *Broken Spears*, 128.
95. In *Broken Spears*, ed. León-Portilla, 129–131.
96. In *Broken Spears*, ed. León-Portilla, 129–131. For the Nahuatl account and its Spanish translation, see *Códice Aubin*, 82. *Macanas* are wooden clubs with obsidian blades.
97. The *Códice Aubin* is a pictorial manuscript with an accompanying Nahuatl text and was written in Mexico in the late 1550s by members of the San Juan district of Mexico City. The codex is also known as the *Códice de 1576* for the date given on the document—September 26, 1576—although Dana Leibsohn says its creation began "sometime after 1560s" (see Leibsohn, "Codex Aubin," in *OEMC* 1:60–61).
98. In *Broken Spears*, ed. León-Portilla, 80.
99. In *Broken Spears*, ed. León-Portilla, 81.
100. See chapter 3 for a complete discussion of Sahagún and the *Florentine Codex*.
101. Although Sahagún sought to objectively present the indigenous voices, his text bears the trace of his mediation. In fact, in a 1585 version of the *Historia general*, Sahagún revises his previous version of the massacre to justify Alvarado's attack, emphasizing the impending threat of native violence against the Spaniards. See Heyden's introduction to Durán's *History* (xxxiii) and Cline in Sahagún's *Conquest of New Spain: 1585 Revision* (7–9). Cline explains that Sahagún places a greater emphasis on the role of Cortés in the 1585 revision by justifying Alvarado's massacre as a means to forestall Aztec uprising and later attributed the decision to Cortés.

102. *FC* (bk. 12, ch. 19), 51.
103. *FC* (bk. 12, ch. 20), 53–54.
104. Florine Asselbergs, "Tlaxcala, Lienzo de," in *OMEC* 3:233–234.
105. *FC*, 1st ed. (bk. 3, ch. 1), 3.
106. *FC*, 1st ed. (bk. 3, ch. 1), 4; italics added.
107. See Carrasco, *City of Sacrifice*, esp. 62.
108. *FC*, 1st ed. (bk. 7, ch. 2), 5.
109. *FC*, 1st ed. (bk. 7, ch. 2), 5–6.
110. *FC* (bk. 3, ch. 7), 23.
111. *FC* (bk. 3, ch. 7), 24.
112. *FC* (bk. 3, ch. 7), 24.
113. *FC* (bk. 3, ch. 7), 23.
114. Todorov, *Morals of History*, 20.
115. For more on the evolving visual depictions of the Templo Mayor and its ceremonial patio, see Boone, "Templo Mayor Research, 1521–1978."
116. "Tipus sacrificiorum quæ in templis demonum Indi in maniter faciebant." The biblical passage inscribed at the bottom of the image is a commentary on the scene: "They sacrificed unto devils, not to God; to gods whom they knew not" (Deuteronomy 32:17, 1769 King James version).
117. The image is likely a copy of an engraving by J. Clark that appeared in the 1723 edition of Antonio de Solís's *The History of the Conquest of Mexico by the Spaniards* (1684), following p. 72.
118. *FC* (bk. 12, ch. 21), 57.

CHAPTER 5

1. Díaz del Castillo, *True History*, ed. García (vol. 4, bk. 14, ch. 174), 6.
2. In his studies on festivals of conquest, Max Harris presents several compelling ideas about how indigenous cultures enacted resistance against the official narratives of Christian triumph over native defeat.
3. Díaz del Castillo, *True History of the Conquest of Mexico* (ch. 4), trans. Keatinge, 437.
4. Cabeza de Vaca, *Relación*, 116.
5. The pictorial part of the codex covers the years 1554–1562 and dates from 1565. Robert H. Barlow claims that the scene depicted the foundation of the Metropolitan Cathedral in Mexico City in 1562 (*Obras de Robert H. Barlow*, vol. 2:325–358). Perla Valle Pérez has since made a convincing argument that the image depicts a ceremony held in 1557 to commemorate King Philip's oath in 1556 ("La sección VIII del *Códice de Tlatelolco*," 33–47).
6. Trexler, "We Think, They Act," 194.
7. I am referring to the work of theater scholars such as Fernando Horcasitas, María Sten, Louise Burkhart, Barry D. Sell, and Othón Arroniz; music scholars such as

Robert M. Stevenson, Gary Tomlinson, and Lourdes Turrent; and performance scholars such as Diana Taylor, Max Harris, and Linda A. Curcio-Nagy, who have provocatively and productively written about performance in ways that transcend the individual disciplines of "dance," "theater," and "music."

8. Díaz del Castillo, *The Conquest of New Spain* (vol. 5, bk. 17, ch. 205), 242–250.

9. Rubin, *Corpus Christi*, 1991.

10. Motolinía, *History* (bk. 1, ch. 13), 92.

11. Motolinía, *Historia* (bk. 1, ch. 15), 61.

12. In Mendieta, *Historia eclesiástica indiana* (bk. 4, ch. 19), 429–434.

13. Tanck de Estrada, *Pueblos de indios y educación*, 308.

14. Tanck de Estrada, *Pueblos de indios y educación*, 308. See also Tanck de Estrada, "Cofradía," in OEMC 1:227–230.

15. Davidson, "Negro Slave Control and Resistance," 236, based on Aguirre Beltrán's foundational study *La población negra de México, 1519–1810* (Mexico, 1946).

16. The letter is in Pérez de Ribas, *My Life*, 171.

17. "Relación etnográfica de Bernardino de Sahagún sobre la degeneración de la disciplina y de las costumbres indígenas causadas por la destrucción de sus 'Idolatrías'" in Suess, *La conquista espiritual*, 111. Also translated in Rostas, *Carrying the Word*, 173.

18. *Crónica de la Nueva España* (bk. 1, ch. 20), 38–39. "Cierto sería mejor desnudarlos del todo de las reliquias y rastros de su gentilidad, porque ha contescido, según dicen religiosos de mucho crédito, estar haciendo el baile alrededor de una cruz y tener debaxo della soterrados los ídolos y parescer que sus cantares los enderesçaban a la cruz, dirigiéndolos con el corazón a los ídolos."

19. "Capítulos de la Junta Eclesiástica de 1539" (number 7, art. 7), in García Icazbalceta, *Juan de Zumárraga*, 156–157.

20. Mendieta, *Historia eclesiástica indiana* (bk. 5, pt. 1, ch. 9), ed. García Icazbalceta.

21. Catholic Church, *Concilios provinciales, primero y segundo*, 146–147. This decree was repeated by the Third Council in 1585. See Llaguno, *La personalidad jurídica del indio*, 286.

22. Lockhart et al., *Tlaxcalan Actas* (fol. 58: calendar item 90), 70–71.

23. Durán, *Book of the Gods and Rites* (ch. 4), 103.

24. Durán, *Book of Gods and Rites* (ch. 21), 300.

25. Durán, *Book of Gods and Rites* (ch. 16), 247.

26. Durán, *Book of Gods and Rites* (ch. 16), 240.

27. According to Todorov (*Conquest of America*, 202).

28. Todorov, *Conquest of America*, 210 and 212.

29. *Historia de las Indias de Nueva España e islas de la Tierra firme* is also known as the *Codex Durán*. Doris Heyden and Fernando Horcasitas edited and translated the text into English and offer the following pithy description of the original manuscript: "The *Codex Durán*, the original manuscript, forms one corpus of 344 sheets of European paper, written in a clear script on both sides of each sheet and numbered only on the right-hand folio. Each sheet is made up of two columns averaging thirty-six lines each. The Spanish spelling would have been considered atrocious even in its time, and virtually no effort was made to lighten the reader's task by means of punctuation. The work is illustrated with 127 colored drawings, 70 in the *History*, 36 in the *Book of Gods and Rites*, and 21 in the *Ancient Calendar*" (*Book of Gods and Rites*, xviii). The manuscript is maintained by the National Library of Madrid, where it was discovered by José Fernando Ramírez in the nineteenth century. The Ramírez copy is preserved in the Historical Archives of the Library of the National Museum of Anthropology, Mexico. Heyden says that Durán wrote the *Historia* between 1574 and 1576 (*History of the Indies*, xxviii).

30. Todorov, *Conquest of America*, 208.

31. Durán, *The Aztecs: The History of the Indies of New Spain* (ch. 1), 3.

32. Durán, *Book of Gods and Rites* (intro.), 55.

33. Durán, *Book of Gods and Rites* (intro.), 55.

34. Sixteenth-century Dominican religious calendars included additional measurements for time appended to the basic Roman calendar. One of their additions included assigning each Sunday a letter. (For example, the first Sunday of the year would be referred to by the letter "a," and so forth.)

35. Durán, *Book of Gods and Rites* (ch. 21), 297.

36. Durán admits that he did "not know the Spanish word" for "Xocotl," but assumed it referred to the bird at the center of one of its rites.

37. Durán, *Book of the Gods and Rites*, 208.

38. Durán, *Book of the Gods and Rites*, 209.

39. Durán, *Book of Gods and Rites* (ch. 21), 295.

40. Durán, *Book of Gods and Rites* (ch. 12), 207.

41. Durán, *Book of Gods and Rites* (ch. 21), 297.

42. Durán, *Book of Gods and Rites* (ch. 21), 300.

43. Durán, "The God of Dance," *History of the Indians* (ch. 2), 15.

44. Durán, *Book of Gods and Rites*, 312–313. Durán's description of dances bleeds over into his chapter 23, which takes up the subject of the Mesoamerican ballgame.

45. In Tenochtitlan, the *cuicacalli* was situated just beyond the southwest corner of the ceremonial precinct, right along the eastern edge of where today stands Mexico City's *zócalo*, which also borders the National Cathedral and the National Palace (see map 2).

46. *Book of the Gods and Rites* (ch. 21), 287–300: "Which treats of the God of Dance and the schools of the dance which existed in the temples of Mexico in the service of the gods." Also in *Historia de las Indias* (vol. 1, ch. 21), 187–196: "De la relación del Dios de los bailes y de las escuelas de danza que había en México en los templos para servicio de los dioses."

47. Durán, *Book of the Gods and Rites* (ch. 21), 287.

48. Durán, *Book of the Gods and Rites* (ch. 21), 288.

49. Durán, *Book of the Gods and Rites* (ch. 21), 294.

50. Durán, *Book of the Gods and Rites* (ch. 21), 287.

51. Durán, *Book of the Gods and Rites* (ch. 21), 298.

52. Durán, *Book of the Gods and Rites* (ch. 21), 290.

53. Seler writes about this passage from the *Florentine Codex* (bk. 1, ch. 14) in *Codex Vaticanus*, 161.

54. Durán, *Book of the Gods and Rites* (ch. 21), 297.

55. Durán, *Book of the Gods and Rites* (ch. 21), 300.

56. Between 1767 and 1816, the Jesuits were exiled from New Spain.

57. *Handbook*, 81.

58. Heyden in Durán, *History of the Indians*, xxix.

59. "Of the Indians' Dances and Festivities," *Natural and Moral History of the Indies* (bk. 6, ch. 28), 374–375.

60. Pérez de Ribas, *My Life* (bk. 3, ch. 8), 247.

61. Pérez de Ribas, *My Life* (bk. 3, ch. 8), 248.

62. The following passages concerning the "Dance of the Emperor Montezuma" are from Bierhorst's translation in *Cantares mexicanos*, 88–90. Original in *Historia de los triunfos* (vol. 3, bk. 12, ch. 11), 324–327.

63. In *Discursos sobre el arte dançado* (Seville: Juan Gómez de Blas, 1642), Juan de Esquivel Navarro classified the *hacha* as a court dance (fol. 38). See Stevenson, *Music in Aztec and Inca Territory*, 165, n. 30.

64. *Crónica de Michoacán* was written by Franciscan intellectual Pablo de Beaumont based on various early colonial sources. The images that accompany the book are of an even later edition.

65. Lara, *Christian Texts for Aztecs*, 125.

66. Perez de Ribas in Bierhorst, *Cantares mexicanos*, 88–90.

67. There are several references within colonial discourse to Indians dancing before the Blessed Sacrament, including Motolinía's reference to *niños* who danced before the Blessed Sacrament during a Corpus Christi feast (in *Historia de los Indios* [vol. 1, ch. 150]).

68. Pérez de Ribas in Bierhorst (*Cantares mexicanos*, 88–90). Robertson's translation of this passage differs significantly: "That which has been described is now often imitated by sons of the principal Spanish families living in Mexico" (in *My Life* [bk. 3, ch. 7], 245–246). However translated, the passage reveals that Pérez de Ribas saw a meaningful relationship between the Spanish lords and the indigenous nobles in terms of physical comportment.

69. Bhabha, *Location of Culture*, 86.

70. Durán, "Ancient Calendar: Sixth Month," in *Book of the Gods and Rites*, 433.

71. Pérez de Ribas, *My Life* (bk. 3, ch. 8), 248.

72. John Bierhorst has developed a very different and controversial interpretation of Pérez de Ribas's description of the "Dance of the Emperor Montezuma." He argues that there is an "undeniable resemblance" between the *mitote* and the *cantares mexicanos* ("Songs of the Mexica"), a collection of ninety-one native "poem-songs" from the mid-sixteenth century. According to Bierhorst, who translated the *cantares*, most of the poem-songs were composed after the conquest and may be evidence of a "Mexican revitalization movement" similar to the Native American ghost dance ritual, wherein warriors performed ecstatic dances and songs dedicated to deceased warriors, calling their spirits down through ritual song and dance in order to support their ongoing resistance against colonizing forces. Bierhorst explains: "In response to the music, ghost warriors from paradise, led by ancestor kings, supposedly came 'scattering,' 'raining,' 'flying,' or 'whirling' to earth in the form of flowers or birds, reminiscent of the well-known *volador*, or 'flyer' dance, still being performed in various parts of Mexico and Guatemala" (*Cantares mexicanos*, 4). While there are undeniable references to preconquest Nahua ritual in the "Dance of the Emperor," it does not seem likely that musicians and dancers who performed the dance, and who enjoyed the sponsorship and protection of the local churches and *cabildos*—and thus held a relatively privileged position within colonial New Spain—would have participated in a revitalist movement.

73. Trexler, "We Think, They Act," 190.

74. Lara has made the association between the wings and Christian angels (*Christian Texts for Aztecs*, 84).

75. In Trexler, "We Think, They Act," 194.

76. Motolinía, *Memoriales* (ch. 57), 363–368.

77. *Crónica de Michoacán* (vol. 3, ch. 8), 102–110. This account is based on the testimony of Don Nicolás de San Luis Montáñez himself; it was incorporated into *Crónica de Michoacán*, most likely written in 1744, according to Warman, *La danza de moros y cristianos*. Susanna Rostas recounts this story as one of the mythical origins of contemporary *concheros*, the societies (*mesas* or *cofradías*) that integrate pre-Hispanic sacred rites in service of Christian devotion. They perform elaborate vigils, prayers, purifications, ceremonial songs, sacred pilgrimages, and dances such as *la danza de los concheros* ("Concheros of Mexico," 168 and 252, n. 8).

78. See Warman, *La danza de moros y cristianos*, 86. Also in Gonzáles, *Danza tu palabra*, 124–125.

CONCLUSION

1. *Crónica* (ch. 25), 300–302.
2. Durán, *History* (ch. 18), 149–168.
3. Tezozómoc, *Crónica* (ch. 59), 450.

APPENDIX B

1. For alternate translations of this appendix, see Daymond Turner in Oviedo, *The Conquest and Settlement of the Island of Boriquen or Puerto Rico*, 66–75, and select passages in Brokaw.

APPENDIX C

1. For an alternate English translation, see Squier, *Observations on the Archaeology and Ethnology of Nicaragua* (New York: Bartlett and Welford, 1845), 145–153.

2. Oviedo writes: "que ordenan sobre haçer alguna trayçion." Squier translates this as "to conceal treason," which reflects the meaning of the passage more accurately than Gillespie's translation: "appointed to commemorate some treacherous act."

3. Here and in other places in the text, Gillespie translates *beoderas* and *borracheras* as "orgies."

APPENDIX E

1. For an alternate translation of passages from this chapter, see Stevenson, *Music in Aztec and Inca Territory*, 97–100.
2. A brace is about six feet.

BIBLIOGRAPHY

Aa, Pieter van der. *Naaukeurige versameling der gedenkwaardigste zee en land-reysen na Oost en West-Indiën . . . : Beginnende met het jaar 1246. En eyndignede op dese tijd.* Leyden: P. vander Aa, 1707.

Acosta, José de. *Natural and Moral History of the Indies.* Ed. Jane E. Mangan; trans. Frances López-Morillas. Durham, NC: Duke University Press, 2002.

Adorno, Rolena. "The Discursive Encounter of Spain and America: The Authority of Eyewitness Testimony in the Writing of History." *William and Mary Quarterly* 49.2 (1944): 251–268.

Aguilar, Francisco de. *Historia de la Nueva España.* Mexico: Ediciones Botas, 1938.

———. *Relación breve de la conquista de la Nueva España.* Ed. Jorge Gurriá Lacroix. 8th ed. Mexico: Universidad Nacional Autónoma de México, Instituto de Investigaciones Históricas, 1980.

Aguilar-Moreno, Manuel. *Handbook to Life in the Aztec World.* New York: Facts on File, 2006.

Aguirre Beltrán, Gonzalo. *La población negra de México, 1519–1810.* Mexico: Ediciones Fuente Cultural, 1946.

Alvarado, Pedro de. *Cartas de relación y otros documentos: Pedro de Alvarado, Diego García Palacio, Antonio de Ciudad-Real.* 2, ed. San Salvador, El Salvador: Dirección de Publicaciones e Impresos, Consejo Nacional para la Cultura y el Arte (CONCULTURA), 2000.

———. *Proceso de residencia contra Pedro de Alvarado, ilustrado con estampas sacadas de los antiguos códices mexicanos, y Notas y noticias biográficas, críticas y arqueológicas por d. José Fernando Ramírez. Lo publica paleografiado del ms. original el Lic. Ignacio L. Rayon.* Mexico: Impreso por Valdes y Redondas, 1847.

Anales de Tlatelolco, unos anales históricos de la nación mexicana y Códice de Tlatelolco. Mexico: Antigua Librería Robredo, de J. Porrúa, 1948.

Andrews, J. Richard. *Introduction to Classical Nahuatl.* Austin: University of Texas Press, 1975.

Arbeau, Thoinot. *Orchesography.* New York: Dover, 1967.

Argyriadis, Kali. *Raíces en movimiento: Prácticas religiosas tradicionales en contextos translocales.* Mexico: CEMCA, IRD, CIESAS, ITESO, 2008.

Arrom, José Juan. "Fray Ramón Pané, Discoverer of the Taíno." In *Amerindian Images and the Legacy of Columbus,* ed. René Jara and Nicholas Spadaccini, 266–290. Minneapolis: University of Minnesota Press, 1992.

Arróniz, Othón. *Teatro de evangelización en Nueva España.* Mexico: Universidad Nacional Autónoma de México, 1979.

Baird, Ellen T. *The Drawings of Sahagún's* Primeros memoriales: *Structure and Style.* Norman: University of Oklahoma Press, 1993.

Barlow, R. H. *Obras de Robert H. Barlow.* Ed. Jesús Monjarás-Ruiz, Elena Limón, and Maricruz Paillés. Mexico: INAH, 1987.

———. "Some Remarks on the Term 'Aztec Empire.'" *The Americas* 1.3 (1945): 345–349.

Basarás y Garaygorta, Joaquín Antonio de. *Origen, costumbres y estado presente de mexicanos y filipinos* [1763]. Mexico City: Landucci, 2006.

Baudot, Georges. *Utopia and History in Mexico: The First Chroniclers of Mexican Civilization (1520–1569).* Trans. Bernard R. Ortiz de Montellano and Thelma Ortiz de Montellano. Niwot: University Press of Colorado, 1995.

Bauer, Ralph. "Millennium's Darker Side: The Missionary Utopias of Franciscan New Spain and Puritan New England." In *Finding Colonial Americas: Essays Honoring J. A. Leo Lemay,* ed. Carla Mulford and David S. Shields, 33–49. Newark: University of Delaware Press, 2001.

Benzoni, Girolamo. *History of the New World.* London: Hakluyt Society, 1857.

Berdan, Frances, and Patricia Rieff Anawalt, eds. *The Essential Codex Mendoza*. Berkeley: University of California Press, 1997.

Bhabha, Homi K. *The Location of Culture*. London: Routledge, 1994.

Bierhorst, John. *Ballads of the Lords of New Spain: The Codex Romances de los Señores de la Nueva España*. Austin: University of Texas Press, 2009.

———. *Cantares Mexicanos: Songs of the Aztecs*. Stanford: Stanford University Press, 1985.

Binski, Paul. *Medieval Death: Ritual and Representation*. Ithaca: Cornell University Press, 1996.

Boone, Elizabeth Hill. *Cycles of Time and Meaning in the Mexican Books of Fate*. Austin: University of Texas Press, 2007.

———. "Migration Histories as Ritual Performance." In *To Change Place: Aztec Ceremonial Landscapes*, ed. Davíd Carrasco, 121–151. Niwot: University Press of Colorado, 1991.

———. *Stories in Red and Black: Pictorial Histories of the Aztecs and Mixtecs*. Austin: University of Texas Press, 2000.

———. "Templo Mayor Research, 1521–1978." In *The Aztec Templo Mayor: A Symposium at Dumbarton Oaks, 8th and 9th October 1983*, ed. Elizabeth Hill Boone, 5–70. Washington, D.C.: Dumbarton Oaks Research Library and Collection, 1987.

Booth, Willard. "Dramatic Aspects of Aztec Rituals." *Educational Theatre Journal* 18.4 (1966): 421–428.

Brading, D. A. *Prophecy and Myth in Mexican History*. Cambridge: Centre of Latin American Studies, University of Cambridge, 1984.

Broda, Johanna, Davíd Carrasco, and Eduardo Matos Moctezuma. *The Great Temple of Tenochtitlan: Center and Periphery in the Aztec World*. Berkeley: University of California Press, 1988.

Brokaw, Galen. "Ambivalence, Mimicry, and Stereotype in Fernández de Oviedo's *Historia general y natural de las Indias*: Colonial Discourse and the Caribbean Areíto." *CR: The New Centennial Review* 5.3 (2005): 143–165.

Brooks, Lynn Matluck. *The Dances of the Processions of Seville in Spain's Golden Age*. Kassel: Ed. Reichenberger, 1988.

Browne, Walden. *Sahagún and the Transition to Modernity*. Norman: University of Oklahoma Press, 2000.

Brundage, Burr Cartwright. *The Jade Steps: A Ritual Life of the Aztecs*. Salt Lake City: University of Utah Press, 1985.

Bry, Theodor de. *América (1590–1634)*. Madrid: Ediciones Siruela, 1992.

———. *Discovering the New World*. Ed. Michael Alexander. New York: Harper and Row, 1976.

Bryant, Clifton D., and Dennis L. Peck, eds. *Encyclopedia of Death and the Human Experience*. Los Angeles: SAGE, 2009.

Burkhart, Louise M. *Holy Wednesday: A Nahua Drama from Early Colonial Mexico*. Philadelphia: University of Pennsylvania Press, 1996.

Cano, David Sanchez. "Dances for the Royal Festivities in Madrid in the Sixteenth and Seventeenth Centuries." *Dance Research: The Journal of the Society for Dance Research* 23.2 (2005): 123–152.

Carrasco, Davíd. *City of Sacrifice: The Aztec Empire and the Role of Violence in Civilization*. Boston: Beacon Press, 1999.

———. "Myth, Cosmic Terror, and the Templo Mayor." In *The Great Temple of Tenochtitlan: Center and Periphery in the Aztec World*, ed. Johanna Broda, Davíd Carrasco, and Eduardo Matos Moctezuma, 124–162. Berkeley: University of California Press, 1988.

———, ed. *The Oxford Encyclopedia of Mesoamerican Cultures*. Oxford, UK; New York: Oxford University Press, 2001.

Carvajal, Micael de. *The Conquest on Trial: Carvajal's Complaint of the Indians in the Court of Death*. Ed. Carlos A. Jáuregui; trans. Carlos A. Jáuregui and Mark Smith-Soto. University Park: Pennsylvania State University Press, 2008.

Catholic Church. Province of Mexico City (Mexico). Concilio Provincial (1st 1555; 2nd 1565). *Concilios provinciales, primero y segundo, celebrados en la muy noble y muy leal ciudad de México, presidiendo el illmo. y rmo. señor D. Fr. Alonzo de Montúfar en los años de 1555 y 1565 dalos a luz el illmo. Sr. D. Francisco Antonio Lorenzana, arzobispo de esta santa metropolitana iglesia*. Mexico: Imprenta de el Superior Gobierno, de Joseph Antonio de Hogal, 1769.

Certeau, Michel de. *Heterologies: Discourse on the Other*. Minneapolis: University of Minnesota Press, 1986.

———. *The Writing of History*. Trans. Tom Conley. New York: Columbia University Press, 1988.

Cervantes de Salazar, Francisco. *Crónica de la Nueva España*. Madrid: Hispanic Society of America, 1914.

———. *Crónica de la Nueva España*. Ed. Manuel Magallón. Madrid: Atlas, 1971.

Clark, Elizabeth A. *History, Theory, Text: Historians and the Linguistic Turn*. Cambridge, MA: Harvard University Press, 2004.

Clark, James Midgley. *Dance of Death in the Middle Ages and the Renaissance*. Glasgow: Jackson, 1950.

Clendinnen, Inga. *Aztecs: An Interpretation*. Cambridge: Cambridge University Press, 1991.

———. "Cost of Courage in Aztec Society." *Past and Present* 107 (May 1985): 44–89.

———. "'Fierce and Unnatural Cruelty': Cortés and the Conquest of Mexico." In *New World Encounters*, ed. Stephen Greenblatt, 12–47. Berkeley: University of California Press, 1993.

———. "Ways to the Sacred: Reconstructing 'Religion' in Sixteenth-Century Mexico." *History and Anthropology* 5 (1990): 105–141.

Cline, Howard F. "Hernando Cortés and the Aztec Indians in Spain." *Quarterly Journal of the Library of Congress* 26 (1969): 70–90.

Codex Azcatítlan. Paris: Bibliothèque nationale de France, Société des Américanistes, 1995.

Codex Borgia: A Full-Color Restoration of the Ancient Mexican Manuscript. Ed. Gisele Díaz and Alan Rodgers. New York: Dover, 1993.

Codex Chimalpahin: Society and Politics in Mexico Tenochtitlan, Tlatelolco, Texcoco, Culhuacan, and Other Nahua Altepetl in Central Mexico, by Domingo Francisco de San Antón Muñón Chimalpahin Quauhtlehuanitzin. Ed. and trans. Arthur J. O. Anderson and Susan Schroeder. Norman: University of Oklahoma Press, 1997.

Codex Ramírez. Mexico City: Editorial Leyenda, 1944.

Codex Vaticanus no. 3773 (Codex Vaticanus B): An Old Mexican Pictorial Manuscript in the Vatican Library. Ed. Eduard Seler. Berlin: T. and A. Constable, 1902–1903.

Códice Aubin. Historia de la nación mexicana: Reproducción a todo color del Códice de 1576. Ed. and trans. Charles E. Dibble. Madrid: J. Porrúa Turanzas, 1963.

Códice Carolino. Ángel Ma. Garibay K., "Códice Carolino: Manuscito anónimo del siglo XVI." *Estudios de Cultura Náhuatl* 7–8 (1967–1969): 11–58.

Códice de Tlatelolco. Facsimile, with an introduction by Perla Valle. 2 vols. Mexico: Instituto Nacional de Antropología e Historia; Puebla: Benemérita Universidad Autónoma de Puebla, 1994.

Coe, Michael D. *Mexico: From the Olmecs to the Aztecs*. New York: Thames and Hudson, 2008.

Coleman, David. *Creating Christian Granada: Society and Religious Culture in an Old-World Frontier City, 1492–1600*. Ithaca: Cornell University Press, 2003.

Columbus, Christopher. *Select Letters of Christopher Columbus, with Other Original Documents, Relating to His Four Voyages to the New World*. Trans. and ed. Richard Henry Major. London: Hakluyt Society, 1847.

Conley, Tom. "De Bry's Las Casas." In *Amerindian Images and the Legacy of Columbus*, ed. René Jara and Nicholas Spadaccini, 103–131. Minneapolis: University of Minnesota Press, 1992.

Cortés, Hernán. *Documentos cortesianos*. Ed. José Luis Martínez. Mexico: Fondo de Cultura Económica, 1990.

———. *Hernán Cortés: Letters from Mexico*. Trans. and ed. Anthony Pagden. New Haven: Yale University Press, 1986.

Covarrubias Orozco, Sebastián de. *Tesoro de la lengua castellana o española* [1611]. Ed. Felipe C. R. Maldonado. Madrid: Editorial Castalia, 1994.

Crónica de Michoacán, por fr. Pablo [de la Purísima Concepción] Beaumont. Mexico: Talleres Gráficos de la Nación, 1932.

Curcio-Nagy, Linda A. *The Great Festivals of Colonial Mexico City: Performing Power and Identity*. Albuquerque: University of New Mexico Press, 2004.

Davidson, David M. "Negro Slave Control and Resistance in Colonial Mexico, 1519–1650." *Hispanic American Historical Review* 46.3 (1966): 235–253.

Delgado Gómez, Angel. *Spanish Historical Writing about the New World, 1493–1700*. Providence, RI: John Carter Brown Library, 1994.

Díaz, J., et al., eds. *La conquista de Tenochtitlan*. Ed. Germán Vázquez. Historia 16. Madrid, 1988.

Díaz del Castillo, Bernal. *The Conquest of New Spain*. Nendeln: Kraus, 1967.

———. *The Discovery and Conquest of Mexico, 1517–1521*. Ed. Genaro García. Trans. A. P. Maudslay. New York: Farrar, Strauss, and Cudahy, 1956.

———. *Historia verdadera de la conquista de la Nueva España*. Mexico: Porrúa, 1955.

———. *The History of the Conquest of New Spain*. Ed. Davíd Carrasco. Albuquerque: University of New Mexico Press, 2008.

———. *The True History of the Conquest of Mexico* [1800]. Trans. Maurice Keatinge. Reprt. Salem, MA: Cushing and Appleton, 1803.

———. *The True History of the Conquest of New Spain* [1916]. Ed. Genaro García. Cambridge: Cambridge University Press, 2010.

Durán, Diego. *The Aztecs: The History of the Indies of New Spain*. Trans. and ed. Doris Heyden and Fernando Horcasitas. New York: Orion Press, 1964.

———. *Book of the Gods and Rites and the Ancient Calendar*. Trans. and ed. Fernando Horcasitas and Doris Heyden. Norman: University of Oklahoma Press, 1971.

———. *Historia de las Indias de Nueva España e islas de la Tierra Firme*. Ed. Angel Ma. Garibay K. Biblioteca Porrúa. Mexico: Porrúa, 1967.

———. *The History of the Indies of New Spain*. Trans. and ed. Doris Heyden. Norman: University of Oklahoma Press, 1994.

Earle, Rebecca. *The Return of the Native Indians and Myth-Making in Spanish America, 1810–1930*. Durham: Duke University Press, 2007.

Edmonson Munro S., ed. *Sixteenth-Century Mexico: The*

Work of Sahagún. Albuquerque: University of New Mexico Press, 1974.

Ellingson, Terry Jay. *The Myth of the Noble Savage*. Berkeley: University of California Press, 2001.

Esses, Maurice. *Dance and Instrumental Diferencias in Spain during the Seventeenth and Early Eighteenth Centuries*. Stuyvesant, NY: Pendragon Press, 1994.

Fabian, Johannes. *Time and the Other: How Anthropology Makes Its Object*. New York: Columbia University Press, 1983.

Feuillet, Raoul-Auger. *Chorégraphie; ou, L'Art de décrire la danse par caractères, figures et signes démonstratifs*. Paris: Feuillet and Brunet, 1700.

Flinchpaugh, Steven. "Economic Aspects of the Viceregal Entrance in Mexico City." *The Americas* 52.3 (1996): 345–365.

Fogelson, Raymond D. "The Ethnohistory of Events and Nonevents." *Ethnohistory* 36.2 (spring 1989): 133–147.

Foster, Susan Leigh. *Choreographing Empathy: Kinesthesia in Performance*. London: Routledge, 2011.

Foucault, Michel. *The Archaeology of Knowledge and the Discourse on Language*. Trans. A. M. Sheridan Smith. New York: Pantheon, 1972.

Frazer, James George, Sir. *The Golden Bough: A Study in Magic and Religion*. 3rd ed. London: Macmillan and Co., [1911–1915] 1925.

———. *The Golden Bough: A Study in Magic and Religion*. Ed. Robert Fraser. Oxford: Oxford University Press, 1998.

Fuentes, Patricia de, ed. *The Conquistadors: First-Person Accounts of the Conquest of Mexico*. Norman: University of Oklahoma Press, 1993.

García Icazbalceta, Joaquín. *Bibliografía mexicana del siglo XVI*. Mexico: Librería de Andrade y Morales, Sucesores, 1886.

———. *Juan de Zumárraga, primer obispo y arzobispo de México*. Mexico: Porrúa, 1947.

———, ed. *Nueva colección de documentos para la historia de México*. 5 vols. Mexico: Librería de Andrade y Morales, Sucesores, 1886–1892.

Gaudio, Michael. *Engraving the Savage: The New World and Techniques of Civilization*. Minneapolis: University of Minnesota Press, 2008.

Gerli, E. Michael, ed. *Medieval Iberia: An Encyclopedia*. New York: Routledge, 2003.

Gibson, Charles, ed. *Aztecs under Spanish Rule: A History of the Indians of the Valley of Mexico, 1519–1810*. Stanford: Stanford University Press, 1964.

———. *The Black Legend: Anti-Spanish Attitudes in the Old World and the New*. New York: Knopf, 1971.

Gillmor, Frances. *The King Danced in the Marketplace*. Tucson: University of Arizona Press, 1964.

Girard, René. *Violence and the Sacred* [1977]. London: Continuum, 2005.

Gómara, Francisco López de. *Cortés: The Life of the Conqueror by His Secretary* [1552]. Trans. and ed. Lesley Byrd Simpson. Berkeley: University of California Press, 1965.

———. *La conquista de México*. Ed. José Luis de Rojas. Crónicas de América 36. Madrid: Historia 16, 1987.

———. *Historia de la conquista de México*. Introducción y notas por d. Joaquín Ramírez Cabañas. México, D.F., Editorial Pedro Robredo, 1943.

———. *Historia general de las Indias y vida de Hernán Cortés*. Ed. Jorge Gurría Lacroix. Caracas, Venezuela: Biblioteca Ayacucho, 1979.

González Torres, Yólotl. *Danza tu palabra: La danza de los Concheros*. Mexico: Plaza y Valdés, 2005.

Gossen, Gary H., and Miguel León-Portilla. *South and Meso-American Native Spirituality: From the Cult of the Feathered Serpent to the Theology of Liberation*. New York: Crossroad, 1993.

Graulich, Michel. *Ritos aztecas: Las fiestas de las veintenas*. Mexico: Instituto Nacional Indigenista, 1999.

Greenblatt, Stephen, ed. *Marvelous Possessions: The Wonder of the New World*. Chicago: University of Chicago Press, 1991.

———. *New World Encounters*. Berkeley: University of California Press, 1993.

———. "Resonance and Wonder." *Bulletin of the American Academy of Arts and Sciences* 43.4 (Jan. 1990): 11–34.

Greer, Margaret R., Walter D. Mignolo, and Maureen Quilligan, eds. *Rereading the Black Legend: The Discourses of Religious and Racial Difference in the Renaissance Empires*. Chicago: University of Chicago Press, 2007.

Guglielmo, Ebreo da Pesaro. *De pratica seu arte tripudii (On the Practice or Art of Dancing)*. Ed. Barbara Sparti. Oxford: Clarendon Press, 1993.

Hanke, Lewis. *All Mankind Is One: A Study of the Disputation between Bartolomé de las Casas and Juan Ginés de Sepúlveda in 1550 on the Intellectual and Religious Capacity of the American Indians*. DeKalb: Northern Illinois University Press, 1974.

Harris, Max. *Aztecs, Moors, and Christians: Festivals of Reconquest in Mexico and Spain*. Austin: University of Texas Press, 2000.

———. *The Dialogical Theatre: Dramatizations of the Conquest of Mexico and the Question of the Other*. New York: St. Martin's Press, 1993.

Hernández, Francisco. *Antigüedades de la Nueva España*. Trans. Joaquín García Pimentel. Mexico: Editorial P. Robredo, 1945 (1946 colophon).

———. *The Mexican Treasury: The Writings of Dr. Francisco Hernández*. Ed. Simon Varey and trans. Rafael

Chabrán, Cynthia L. Chamberlin, and Simon Varey. Stanford: Stanford University Press, 2000.

Herrera y Tordesillas, Antonio de. *The General History of the Vast Continent and Islands of America, Commonly Call'd, the West-Indies, from the First Discovery Thereof: With the Best Accounts the People Could Give of Their Antiquities. Collect'd from the Original Relations Sent to the Kings of Spain*. 2nd ed. London: Wood and Woodward, 1740.

———. *Historia general de los hechos de los castellanos en las islas y tierrafirme del mar Océano*. Ed. Antonio Ballesteros-Beretta. Madrid: [Tipografía de Archivos], 1934–1957.

Holbein, Hans. *The Dance of Death by Hans Holbein the Younger* [1538]. New York: Dover, 1971.

———, and Sabas Martín. *La danza de la muerte: Códice de El Escorial*. Madrid: Miraguano, 2001.

Hulme, Peter. *Colonial Encounters: Europe and the Native Caribbean, 1492–1797*. London: Methuen, 1986.

Hvidtfeldt, Arild. *Teotl and ixiptlatli: Some Central Conceptions in Ancient Mexican Religion*. Copenhagen: Munksgaard, 1958.

International Encyclopedia of Dance. Ed. Selma Jeanne Cohen et al. New York: Oxford University Press, 2004.

Irving, Washington. *The Life and Voyages of Christopher Columbus*. London: Cassell and Company, Ltd., 1885.

Ivanova, Anna. *The Dance in Spain*. New York: Praeger, 1970.

Ixtlilxóchitl, Fernando de Alva. *Ally of Cortés: Account 13, of the Coming of the Spaniards and the Beginning of the Evangelical Law*. Trans. Douglass K. Ballentine. El Paso: Texas Western Press, 1969.

Jara, René, and Nicholas Spadaccini, eds. *Amerindian Images and the Legacy of Columbus*. Minneapolis: University of Minnesota Press, 1992.

Juderías, Julián. *La leyenda negra y la verdad histórica*. Madrid: Tip. de la "Rev. de Arch., Bibl. y Museos," 1914.

Kamen, Henry. *Philip of Spain*. New Haven: Yale University Press, 1997.

Keen, Benjamin. *The Aztec Image in Western Thought*. New Brunswick: Rutgers University Press, 1971.

Keller, Kate Van Winkle. *Dance and Its Music in America, 1528–1789*. Hillsdale, NY: Pendragon Press, 2007.

Kelly, John Eoghan. *Pedro de Alvarado, Conquistador*. Princeton: Princeton University Press, 1932.

Klor de Alva, J. Jorge, H. B. Nicholson, and Eloise Quiñones Keber, eds. *The Work of Bernardino de Sahagún: Pioneer Ethnographer of Sixteenth-Century Aztec Mexico*. Albany: Institute for Mesoamerican Studies, State University of New York, Albany, 1988.

Köhler, Ulrich. "'Debt-Payment' to the Gods among the Aztec: The Misrendering of a Spanish Expression and Its Effects." *Estudios de Cultura Nahuatl* (2001): 125–133.

———. "On the Significance of the Aztec Day Sign 'Olin.'" In *Proceedings of the Symposium "Space and Time in the Cosmovision of Mesoamerica,"* ed. Franz Tichy, 111–128. Munich: Wilhelm Fink, 1982.

Krippner-Martínez, James. *Rereading the Conquest: Power, Politics, and the History of Early Colonial Michoacán, Mexico, 1521–1565*. University Park: Pennsylvania State University Press, 2001.

Kuss, Malena, ed. *Music in Latin America and the Caribbean: An Encyclopedic History*. Austin: University of Texas Press, 2004.

Lada-Richards, Ismene. *Silent Eloquence: Lucian and Pantomime Dancing*. London: Duckworth, 2007.

Lara, Jaime. *Christian Texts for Aztecs: Art and Liturgy in Colonial Mexico*. Notre Dame: University of Notre Dame Press, 2008.

———. *City, Temple, Stage: Eschatological Architecture and Liturgical Theatrics*. Notre Dame: University of Notre Dame Press, 2004.

Las Casas, Bartolomé de. *Apologética historia sumaria*. 2 vols. Ed. Edmundo O'Gorman. Mexico: UNAM, 1967.

———. *Bartolomé de las Casas: A Selection of His Writings*. Trans. and ed. George Sanderlin. New York: Knopf, 1971.

———. *In Defense of the Indians. The defense of the Most Reverend Lord, Don Fray Bartolomé de las Casas, of the order of preachers, late bishop of Chiapa, against the persecutors and slanderers of the peoples of the New World discovered across the seas*. Trans. and ed. Stafford Poole. DeKalb: Northern Illinois University Press, 1974.

———. *The Devastation of the Indies: A Brief Account*. Trans. Herma Briffault. New York: Seabury Press, 1974.

———. *Historia de las Indias*. 5 vols. Madrid: M. Ginesta, 1875–1876.

———. *Indian Freedom: The Cause of Bartolomé de las Casas, 1484–1566: A Reader*. Trans. Francis Sullivan. Kansas City, MO: Sheed and Ward (an imprint of Rowman & Littlefield Publishers, Inc., in Lanham, MD), 1995.

———. *Obras escogidas de Fray Bartolomé de las Casas*. Ed. Juan Pérez de Tudela y Bueso. Madrid: Ediciones Atlas, 1957–1958.

———. *A Short Account of the Destruction of the Indies*. Ed. and trans. Nigel Griffin. London: Penguin, 1992.

———. *Witness: Writings of Bartolomé de las Casas*. Ed. and trans. George Sanderlin. Maryknoll, NY: Orbis, 1992.

Leonard, Irving Albert. *Books of the Brave: Being an Account of Books and of Men in the Spanish Conquest and Settlement of the Sixteenth-Century New World*. Berkeley: University of California Press, 1992.

León-Portilla, Miguel. *Bernardino de Sahagún, First An-

thropologist. Norman: University of Oklahoma Press, 2002.

———, ed. *The Broken Spears: The Aztec Account of the Conquest of Mexico*. Boston: Beacon Press, 1992.

Lepecki, André. *Exhausting Dance: Performance and the Politics of Movement*. New York: Routledge, 2006.

Levenson, Jay A., ed. *Circa 1492: Art in the Age of Exploration*. Washington, DC: National Gallery of Art, 1991.

Livy. *The History of Rome*. Vol. 2. Trans. Rev. Canon Roberts. London: J. M. Dent & Sons, 1905.

Llaguno, José A. *La personalidad jurídica del indio y el III concilio provincial mexicano (1585), ensayo histórico-jurídico de los documentos originales*. Mexico: Porrúa, 1963.

Lockhart, James. *The Nahuas after the Conquest: A Social and Cultural History of the Indians of Central Mexico, Sixteenth through Eighteenth Centuries*. Stanford: Stanford University Press, 1992.

———. *The Tlaxcalan Actas: A Compendium of the Records of the Cabildo of Tlaxcala, 1545–1627*. Ed. Frances Berdan, Arthur J. O. Anderson, and Tlaxcala de Xicohténcatl (Mexico). Salt Lake City: University of Utah Press, 1986.

———. *We People Here: Nahuatl Accounts of the Conquest of Mexico*. Los Angeles: University of California Press, 1993.

López Austin, Alfredo. *The Human Body and Ideology: Concepts of the Ancient Nahuas*. 2 vols. Trans. Thelma Ortiz de Montellano and Bernard Ortiz de Montellano. Salt Lake City: University of Utah Press, 1988.

———. "The Research Method of Fray Bernardino de Sahagún: The Questionnaires." In *Sixteenth-Century Mexico: The Work of Sahagún*, ed. Munro S. Edmonson, 111–149. Albuquerque: University of New Mexico Press, 1974.

Martí, Samuel. *Canto, danza y música precortesianos*. Mexico: Fondo de Cultura Económica, 1961.

———, and Gertrude Prokosch Kurath. *Dances of Anáhuac: The Choreography and Music of Precortesian Dances*. Chicago: Aldine, 1964.

Martyr d'Anghera, Peter. [Anglería, Pedro Mártir de.] *Décadas del Nuevo Mundo*. 2 vols. Ed. Edmundo O'Gorman. Trans. Agustín Millares Carlo. Mexico: Porrúa, 1964–1965.

———. [Anghiera, Pietro Martire d'.] *De orbe novo: The Eight Decades of Peter Martyr d'Anghera*. 2 vols. Trans. and ed. Francis Augustus MacNutt. New York: G. P. Putnam's Sons, 1912.

———. *The Discovery of the New World in the Writings of Peter Martyr of Anghiera*. Ed. Ernesto Lunardi, Elisa Magioncalda, Rosanna Mazzacane. Trans. Felix Azzola. Rome: Istituto Poligrafico e Zecca dello Stato, 1992.

Mendieta, Gerónimo de. *Historia eclesiástica indiana: A Franciscan's View of the Spanish Conquest of Mexico*. Trans. Felix Jay. Lewiston, NY: Edwin Mellen Press, 1997.

———. *Historia eclesiástica indiana: Obra escrita a fines del siglo XVI*. Ed. Joaquín García Icazbalceta. Mexico: Porrúa, 1980.

Metcalfe, Scott. *Motolinía on Music: An Anthology, Translation, and Study of Writings about Music in the Works of Fray Toribio de Benavente, called Motolinía (ca. 1490–1569)*. MA thesis, Harvard University, 2005.

[Mexico City. Cabildo.] *Actas de cabildo de la Ciudad de México*. Ed. del "Municipio libre." Mexico: I. Bejarano, 1889–.

Mignolo, Walter D. "When Speaking Was Not Good Enough: Illiterates, Barbarians, Savages, and Cannibals." In *Amerindian Images and the Legacy of Columbus*, ed. René Jara and Nicholas Spadaccini, 312–345. Minneapolis: University of Minnesota Press, 1992.

Molina, Alonso de. *Vocabulario en lengua castellana y mexicana* [1555]. Mexico: Porrúa, 1992.

Moore, Robin. *Nationalizing Blackness: Afrocubanismo and Artistic Revolution in Havana, 1920–1940*. Pittsburgh: University of Pittsburgh Press, 1997.

Motolinía, Toribio. *Carta al Emperador: Refutación a Las Casas sobre la colonización española*. Mexico: Editorial Jus, 1949.

———. *Historia de los indios de la Nueva España*. Ed. Edmundo O'Gorman. 2nd ed. Mexico: Porrúa, 1973.

———. *History of the Indians of New Spain*. Trans. and ed. Elizabeth Andros Foster. Berkeley: Cortés Society, 1950.

———. *Memoriales: Libro de oro (MS JGI 31)*. Ed. Nancy Joe Dyer. Mexico: El Colegio de México, Centro de Estudios Lingüísticos y Literarios, 1996.

Muñoz Camargo, Diego. *Historia de Tlaxcala [Relaciones geográficas de Tlaxcala]*. Ed. René Acuña. 2nd ed. San Luis Potosí: El Colegio de San Luis, 1999.

———. *Relaciones geográficas de Tlaxcala*. 2nd ed. San Luis Potosí: El Colegio de San Luis; Gobierno del Estado de Tlaxcala, [1984], 1999.

Myers, Kathleen Ann. *Fernández de Oviedo's Chronicle of America*. Austin: University of Texas Press, 2007.

Nájera-Ramírez, Olga, Norma Elia Cantú, and Brenda M. Romero, eds. *Dancing across Borders: Danzas y bailes mexicanos*. Urbana: University of Illinois Press, 2009.

Nebrija, Antonio de. *Diccionario latino–español (Salamanca 1492)*. Barcelona: Puvill, 1979.

———. *Gramática de la lengua castellana*. Ed. Antonio Quilis. Madrid: Ediciones de Cultura Hispánica, 1992.

Nevile, Jennifer. *The Eloquent Body: Dance and Humanist Culture in Fifteenth-Century Italy*. Bloomington: Indiana University Press, 2004.

Nicolau d'Olwer, Lluís. *Fray Bernardino de Sahagún, 1499–1590*. Salt Lake City: University of Utah Press, 1987.

Nieto Jiménez, Lidio, and Manuel Alvar Ezquerra. *Nuevo tesoro lexicográfico del español (s. XIV–1726)*. Madrid: Arco, 2007.

Núñez Cabeza de Vaca, Alvar. *The Account: Alvar Núñez Cabeza de Vaca's* Relación. Trans. Martin A. Favata and José B. Fernández. Houston: Arte Público Press, 1993.

O'Gorman, Edmundo. *Guía de las Actas de Cabildo de la Ciudad de México, siglo XVI*. Mexico: Departamento del Distrito Federal; Fondo de Cultura Económica, 1970.

———. *The Invention of America: An Inquiry into the Historical Nature of the New World and the Meaning of Its History*. Bloomington: Indiana University Press, 1961.

Olive, Pedro María de. *Diccionario de sinónimos de la lengua castellana*. 2nd ed. Paris: Impr. de Madame Lacombe, I. Boix, 1852.

Olivier, Guilhem. *Mockeries and Metamorphoses of an Aztec God Tezcatlipoca, "Lord of the Smoking Mirror."* Trans. Michel Besson. Boulder: University Press of Colorado, 2003.

Ortiz, Fernando. *La africanía de la música folklórica de Cuba*. Havana: Letras Cubanas, 2001.

———. "La música y los areítos de los indios de Cuba." *Revista de Arqueología y Etnología* 6.7 (1948): 115–189.

Oviedo y Valdés, Gonzalo Fernández de. *The Conquest and Settlement of the Island of Boriquen, or Puerto Rico*. Trans. and ed. Daymond Turner. Avon, CT: Limited Editions Club, 1975.

———. *Historia general y natural de las Indias*. Ed. José Amador de los Ríos. Madrid: La Real academia de la historia, 1855.

———. *Historia general y natural de las Indias*. Ed. Juan Pérez de Tudela y Bueso. Madrid: Atlas, 1959.

———. *Historia general y natural de las Indias: Part 1 (1535)*. Research at King's College, London: Early Modern Spain. http://www.ems.kcl.ac.uk/index.html.

———. *Historia general y natural de las Indias: Part 3, Book IV*. Trans. Alice Gillespie. Tozzer Library, Harvard University, 1919.

———. *Natural History of the West Indies*. Trans. and ed. Sterling A. Stoudemire. Chapel Hill: University of North Carolina Press, 1959.

———. *Sumario de la natural historia de las Indias*. Ed. José Miranda. Mexico: Fondo de Cultura Económica, 1950.

Pagden, Anthony. "Ius et factum: Text and Experience in the Writings of Bartolomé de las Casas." In *New World Encounters*, ed. Stephen Greenblatt, 85–100. Berkeley: University of California Press, 1993.

Pané, Ramón. *An Account of the Antiquities of the Indians: Chronicles of the New World Encounter*. Ed. José Juan Arrom. Trans. Susan C. Griswold. Durham: Duke University Press, 1999.

Pedelty, Mark. *Musical Ritual in Mexico City: From the Aztec to NAFTA*. Austin: University of Texas Press, 2004.

Perceval, Richard. *Bibliotheca hispanica*. London, 1591.

———. *A Dictionarie in Spanish and English*. London: Edm. Bollifant, 1599.

Pérez, Perla Valle. "La sección VIII del Códice de Tlatelolco: Una nueva propuesta de lectura." In *De tlacuilos y escribanos: Estudios sobre documentos indígenas coloniales del centro de México*, ed. Xavier Noguez and Stephanie Gail Wood, 33–47. Zamora, MI: El Colegio de Michoacán, 1998.

Pérez de Ribas, Andrés. *Historia de los triunfos de nuestra santa fe entre gentes las más bárbaras y fieras del Nuevo Orbe*. Mexico: Editorial Layac, 1944.

———. *History of the Triumphs of Our Holy Faith amongst the Most Barbarous and Fierce Peoples of the New World*. Trans. Daniel T. Reff. Tucson: University of Arizona Press, 1999.

———. *My Life among the Savage Nations of New Spain*. Trans. Thomas A. Robertson. Los Angeles: Ward Ritchie Press, 1968.

Polo, Marco. *Il milione*. Florence: Successori le Monnier, [1916].

Pomar, Juan Bautista. *Relaciones de la Nueva España*. Ed. Germán Vázquez. Madrid: Historia 16, 1991.

Prescott, William Hickling. *History of the Conquest of Mexico* [1843]. New York: Modern Library, 1998.

Quiñones Keber, Eloise. *Codex Telleriano-Remensis: Ritual, Divination, and History in a Pictorial Aztec Manuscript*. Austin: University of Texas Press, 1995.

———, ed. *Representing Aztec Ritual: Performance, Text, and Image in the Work of Sahagún*. Boulder: University Press of Colorado, 2002.

Reid, Basil A. *Myths and Realities of Caribbean History*. Tuscaloosa: University of Alabama Press, 2009.

Restall, Matthew. *Seven Myths of the Spanish Conquest*. Oxford: Oxford University Press, 2003.

Ricard, Robert. *The Spiritual Conquest of Mexico: An Essay on the Apostolate and the Evangelizing Methods of the Mendicant Orders in New Spain, 1523–1572*. Berkeley: University of California Press, 1966.

Rosal, Francisco del. *Origen y etimología de todos los vocablos originales de la lengua castellana* (1601). Biblioteca Nacional de España, MS 6929-T.127. Madrid.

Rostas, Susanna. *Carrying the Word: The Conchero Dance in Mexico City*. Boulder: University Press of Colorado, 2009.

———. "The Concheros of Mexico: A Search for Ethnic Identity." *Dance Research: The Journal of the Society for Dance Research* 9.2 (1991): 3–17.

Rubin, Miri. *Corpus Christi: The Eucharist in Late Medieval Culture.* Cambridge: Cambridge University Press, 1991.

Sahagún, Bernardino de. *Conquest of New Spain: 1585 Revision.* Ed. S. L. Cline. Trans. Howard F. Cline. Salt Lake City: University of Utah Press, 1989.

———. *Florentine Codex: General History of the Things of New Spain.* 13 v. (1st ed. and 2nd ed. rev.) Trans. Arthur J. O. Anderson and Charles E. Dibble. Monographs of the School of American Research. Santa Fe, NM: School of American Research; Salt Lake City: University of Utah Press, 1950–1982.

———. *Historia general de las cosas de Nueva España.* Ed. Angel María Garibay K. Mexico: Porrúa, 1956.

———. *Historia general de las cosas de Nueva España.* Ed. Alfredo López Austin and Josefina García Quintana. 3rd ed. Mexico: Consejo Nacional para la Cultura y las Artes, 2002.

———. [*Historia general de las cosas de Nueva España*] *Historia universal de las cosas de Nueva España: Codice Laurenziano Mediceo Palatino, 218, 219, 220.* 3 vols. Italy: Giunti, 1996.

———. *A History of Ancient Mexico.* Trans. Fanny R. Bandelier. Nashville: Fisk University Press, 1932.

———. *Primeros memoriales.* Trans. Thelma D. Sullivan. Ed. H. B. Nicholson. Norman: University of Oklahoma Press, 1997.

Scanlan, Thomas. *Colonial Writing and the New World, 1583–1671: Allegories of Desire.* Cambridge: Cambridge University Press, 1999.

Schwartz, Stuart B. *Victors and Vanquished: Spanish and Nahua Views of the Conquest of Mexico.* Boston: St. Martin's Press, 2000.

Scillacio, Niccolò. *De insulis meridiani atque Indici maris nuper inventis.* Trans. John Mulligan. Ed. James Lenox. New York, 1860.

Scolieri, Paul A. "Choreographing Empires: Aztec Performance and Colonial Discourse." PhD diss., New York University, 2003.

Seed, Patricia. "Colonial and Postcolonial Discourse." *Latin American Research Review* 26.3 (1991): 181–200.

Sell, Barry D., and Louise M. Burkhart. *Nahuatl Theater.* Norman: University of Oklahoma Press, 2004.

Shelton, Anthony Alan. "The Aztec *Cihuateteo*: An Image of the Apocalyptic Woman." *Ancient America: Contributions to New World Archaeology,* ed. Nicholas J. Saunders, 1–17. Oxford: Oxbow, 1992.

Solís, Antonio de. *The History of the Conquest of Mexico by the Spaniards.* Trans. Thomas Townsend. London: Printed for T. Woodward, J. Hooke, and J. Peele, 1724.

Spence, Lewis. *The Gods of Mexico.* London: T. F. Unwin, 1923.

Squier, E. G., ed. "Observations on the Archaeology and Ethnology of Nicaragua." *Transactions of the American Ethnological Society,* vol. 3, part 1. New York: George P. Putnam, 1853.

Sten, María. *Ponte a bailar, tú que reinas: Antropología de la danza prehispánica.* Mexico City: Editorial Joaquín Mortiz, 1990.

Stevenson, Robert Murrell. *Music in Aztec and Inca Territory.* Berkeley: University of California Press, 1976.

Stone, Martha. *At the Sign of Midnight: The Concheros Dance Cult of Mexico.* Tucson: University of Arizona Press, 1975.

Suess, Paulo, ed. *La conquista espiritual de la América espanōla: 200 Documentos–Siglos XVI.* Quito: Abya-Yala, 2002.

Tanck Estrada, Dorothy. *Pueblos de indios y educación en el México colonial, 1750–1821.* Mexico: El Colegio de México, Centro de Estudios Históricos, 1999.

Tarducci, Francesco, and Henry F. Brownson. *The Life of Christopher Columbus.* Detroit: H. F. Brownson, 1890.

Taylor, Diana. *The Archive and the Repertoire: Performing Cultural Memory in the Americas.* Durham: Duke University Press, 2003.

———. "Scenes of Cognition: Performance and Conquest." *Theatre Journal* 56.3 (2004): 353–372.

Tedlock, Dennis. *Popol Vuh: The Definitive Edition of the Mayan Book of the Dawn of Life and the Glories of Gods and Kings.* New York: Simon and Schuster, 1996.

Tezozómoc, Fernando Alvarado. *Crónica mexicana.* Ed. José M. Vigil. Mexico: Imprenta y litog. de I. Paz, 1878.

Thomas, Hugh. *The Conquest of Mexico.* London: Hutchinson, 1993.

———. *Who's Who of the Conquistadors.* London: Cassell, 2000.

Thompson, Donald. "The 'Cronistas de Indias' Revisited: Historical Reports, Archeological Evidence, and Literary and Artistic Traces of Indigenous Music and Dance in the Greater Antilles at the Time of the 'Conquista.'" *Latin American Music Review* 14.2 (1993): 181–201.

Todorov, Tzvetan. *The Conquest of America: The Question of the Other.* New York: Harper and Row, 1982.

———. *Morals of History.* Trans. Alyson Waters. Minneapolis: University of Minnesota Press, 1995.

Toriz Proenza, Martha. *La fiesta prehispánica: Un espectáculo teatral. Comparación de las descripciones de cuatro fiestas hechas por Sahagún y Durán.* Mexico: Instituto Nacional de Bellas Artes, 1993.

Torquemada, Juan de. *Monarquía Indiana*. 3 vols. Mexico: Porrúa, 1975.

Townsend, Richard. *The Aztecs*. New York: Thames and Hudson, 2000.

Trexler, Richard C. "We Think, They Act: Clerical Readings of Missionary Theatre in Sixteenth-Century New Spain." In *Understanding Popular Culture: Europe from the Middle Ages to the Nineteenth Century*, ed. Steven L. Kaplan, 189–228. Berlin: Mouton, 1984.

Turner, Daymond. *Gonzalo Fernández de Oviedo y Valdés: An Annotated Bibliography*. Chapel Hill: University of North Carolina Press, 1967.

Turrent, Lourdes. *La conquista musical de México*. Mexico: Fondo de Cultura Económica, 1993.

van Groesen, Michiel. *The Representations of the Overseas World in the de Bry Collection of Voyages (1590–1634)*. Vol. 2. Leiden: Brill, 2008.

Vázquez de Tapia, Bernardino. *Relación de méritos y servicios del conquistador Bernardino Vázquez de Tapia . . .* Mexico: Antigua Librería Robredo, 1953.

Vedia, Enrique de, ed. *Historiadores primitivos de Indias*. Madrid: M. Rivadeneyra, 1852–1853.

Vespucci, Amerigo. *The Letters of Amerigo Vespucci and Other Documents Illustrative of His Career*. Trans. Clements R. Markham. London: Hakluyt Society, 1894.

Warman, Arturo. *La danza de moros y cristianos*. Mexico: Secretaría de Educación Pública, 1972.

Wauchope, Robert, ed. *Handbook of Middle American Indians*. Austin: University of Texas Press, 1964–1976.

Weiditz, Christoph. *Authentic Everyday Dress of the Renaissance: All 154 plates from the* Trachtenbuch. New York: Dover, 1994.

White, Hayden V. *Tropics of Discourse: Essays in Cultural Criticism*. Baltimore: Johns Hopkins University Press, 1985.

Whyte, Florence. *The Dance of Death in Spain and Catalonia*. New York: Arno Press, 1977.

Ybarra, Patricia A. *Performing Conquest: Five Centuries of Theater, History, and Identity in Tlaxcala, Mexico*. Ann Arbor: University of Michigan Press, 2009.

INDEX

Note: Italic page numbers refer to figures and maps.

Acosta, José de, 22, 139–140, 146, 147
Africans (*negros*), 130, 131, 156. See also *negros bocales*
Aguilar, Francisco de, 110–111, 181n77
Aguilar, Gerónimo de, 92
alcohol and drugs: *chichi*, 36, 159, 175n37; drinking parties (*beoderas* or *borracheras*), 36, 38, 40, 64, 72, 156, 159–160, 163, 166, 175n37, 185n3 (app. C); drunkenness, 137, 156, 159–160; hallucinogenic mushrooms, 72, 138; in human sacrifice rituals, 72; inebriated tricksters, 2; *peyote*, 70; prohibition of, 64, 137; pulque, 64, 137; *teooctli* ("divine wine"), 72
Alfonso V (king of Aragon), 7
Alhambra Decree, 5
Alvarado, Pedro de: and Cortés, 98, 99, 100; interrogation of Toxcatl festival dancers, 96, 97, 102; and Massacre at the Festival of Toxcatl, 19, 92, 93, 94–97, 98–99, 100, 101, 102, 103–104, 105, 111–114, 115, 123, 169, 170–171, 181n77, 182n101; Tlaxcalans as allies of, 95, 112, 113, 118
Álvarez, Francisco, 96
Álvarez, Juan, 96–97, 98, 99, 102
Anacaona (Taína *cacica*), 28–29, 30, 156. See also "*Areíto* de Anacaona"
Anáhuac, 167, 174n40
ancient Greece: and Ariadne's Dance, 86, 87; dances of, 11, 31, 40, 86; and Las Casas, 42
ancient Rome: dances of, 11, 31, 34–35, 37, 40, 42, 155, 162; Durán on, 112, 134; and elaborate dress, 143; *gesticulatores*, 52, 53; and killing performances, 70
Anderson, J. O., 71
Andrews, J. Richard, 48
animals, and Aztec ritual dances: bats, 179n68; headdresses and masks of, 50, 51, 52; in myth of Aztec ritual origins, 61; squirrels, 179n68. See also eagle and jaguar warriors; serpents, and Aztec ritual dances
Annals of Tlatelolco, 114
Anonymous Conqueror, 101, 181n40
Arawak, 20
Arbeau, Thoinot, 12–13, 174n33
"*Areíto* de Anacaona," 28–29, 153–154. See also Anacaona (Taína *cacica*)
areítos (song-dances): Acosta on, 140; Alvarado on, 95, 96, 97; *bacanales* compared to, 40; Cano de Saavreda on, 99; definitions of, 20–21, 151; and distinction between sacred and secular performance, 38, 42, 43, 47; divinatory properties of, 20, 33, 42, 43; as expression of knowledge, 35, 42; Gómara on, 33, 49; Las Casas on, 30, 31, 39–42, 43, 45–46, 103, 104, 153–154; literary staging of, 29–30; and *macehualiztli*, 48, 53; Martyr d'Anghera on, 31, 32–33, 34, 35, 42, 154; as method for memorializing history, 20–21, 31–33, 35, 37–38, 41, 42, 43, 46, 104; Motolinía on, 45–46, 47, 49, 151, 166; Oviedo y Valdés on, 31, 33–39, 37, 40, 41, 42, 43, 46, 48, 155–161, 175n37; Pané on, 31, 33, 34, 35, 42, 43; prohibition of, 131, 132; as resistance, 37, 42; Sahagún's use of term, 12, 48, 60, 61, 73, 131, 151; as term for dance, 11, 20, 28, 34; and Tezozómoc, 151; of Toxcatl festival, 96; violence resulting from, 36, 39, 95
Ariadne's Dance, 86, 87
Aristotle, 40, 41, 102
Arronix, Othón, 182n7
Atamalqualiztli festival, 68, 69
Atlcaualo festival, 72, 87
audencia (judicial court): Alvarado's response to, 95, 170–171; charges against Alvarado, 94–95, 96, 97, 169; establishment of, 5, 44; and Massacre at the Festival of Toxcatl, 94–95, 97
Augustine, Saint, 40
Axacayatl (*tlatoani*), 76, 92, 95–98, 103, 114, 150
Aztec ceremonies: and Aztec calendars, 22, 59; and captives, 72–77, 95, 97; in *Florentine Codex*, 59–63; role of dance in, 57; role of social stratification in, 64–68, 70; *veintenas*, 17, 62, 67, 72–77, 85–86, 88, 95. See also specific festivals
Aztec codices, 6, 14, 17, 20, 133
Aztec deities: and auto-sacrifice, 61; and Aztec calendars, 17–18; categories of, 17; and cults, 64; and ritual debt payment, 61, 70, 72; role of dance in relation to, 56, 61; and women, 77–78. See also *ixiptlas* (human representations of Aztec deities)

197

Aztec empire: and anthropomorphic supernaturalism, 18; and Aztec as term, 14–15; enemies of, 17, 19, 91, 92, 112, 113; ethnography of, 14–20; fall of, 118, 127; map of surrounding region, 16; map of Tenochtitlan, 15; and Massacre at the Festival of Toxcatl, 113–115, 117–122; military in, 17, 19; population of, 15, 174n42; priesthood in, 17; religious and political structure of, 16–17; role of dance in, 23; social stratification of, 14, 16, 18, 59–60, 61, 64–68, 70; and Tenochtitlan, 6, 14, 15–16, 15, 18; Tezozómoc's postconquest history of, 22–23; transformation to Spanish colony, 1, 101

Aztec ritual dances: as acts of transference, 88; and agricultural fertility, 3, 80; Arbeau on, 13; captives' dance, 62, 72–77, 80, 85, 151; and choreography, 46, 57, 61, 62, 63, 72–76, 77, 80, 81, 83, 85, 87, 88, 90–91, 96, 145; chroniclers of New World on, 1, 3–4; and colonial discourse, 5; *cuecuechcuicatl*, 134; and *cuicacalli*, 136, 137; dancers' raiments, masks, and props, 57, 65–68, 66, 73, 76, 80, 82, 83, 98; "dancing with the limbs, skins, and severed heads," 151; descriptions in *Florentine Codex*, 6, 67–68, 70, 72, 86; diplomatic pageants, 85; and divination, 56; as embodying history, 20; ethnography of, 14; and fire, 62, 63–64, 90; as form of social memory, 3, 19–20, 150; "hand-waving dance," 83–84, 88, 148, 151; human sacrifice reenacted in, 2–3, 22, 57, 61, 70–72, 83–85, 88, 89, 151, 180n134; Ilamatecuhtli's Leap, 83, 148; and *ixiptlas*, 71, 72, 77–78, 80, 81, 82–83; "Kiss of Huitzilopochtli," 91; location of, 57, 63–64, 85; and magic, 86–87; and market, 71, 84; meaning of, 86, 87, 89, 97, 100, 112, 122; and Montezuma, 65, 66, 67, 75, 76, 90, 95, 100, 148, 178n63; Motolinía on, 21–22, 40, 45, 46–49, 140, 151, 164–166, 167, 184n58; and music, 11, 56, 57, 60–61, 65, 67, 80, 101, 106, 114, 117; performances for Spanish court, 9, 10–11, 12, 14; "popcorn dance," 91; and punishment, 67, 78, 79, 91; realities of, 2; as representational practice, 18; and resistance dances, 72, 75, 80–81, 83, 85, 150; and riddles, 56; role in colonization, 23, 126, 128, 146, 151; and sacred ceremonies, 45; serpent dances, 67–68, 85, 91, 148, 151, 178n63, 179n68; severed heads dance, 73, 76, 83, 180n134; social context of, 22, 56; and social hierarchy, 57, 64–68, 70, 77, 81, 85, 88; "Sowing of the Rattles" dance, 74–75; and Templo Mayor, 19, 120–121, 124, 125, 126; time of, 57, 61–63, 85; "Toxcatl Leap," 91; types of, 18; and women, 62, 70, 71, 75, 77–78, 80–85, 90. *See also* representations of indigenous dances; *and specific festivals*

Aztec rituals: astronomical rites, 56; and Aztec codices, 133; as bridges between celestial and terrestrial realms, 61, 64, 70; and Fifth Sun, 61; in *Florentine Codex*, 59, 60; as forms of military, sacred, and political theatre, 18; and human sacrifice, 18, 22, 56, 57, 61, 64, 70, 88; and *ixiptlas*, 70–72; and *nextlaoailli* (debt payment), 61; "Placing upon Straw," 75; rules of ritual engagement in, 59; "She Tramples on Her Marketplace," 84; and social stratification, 59–60; "They fight with grass," 84

Bachiller y Morales, Antonio, 28
bailar cantando (sung dance), 28, 34, 35, 38, 155–156
bailar llorando (dances of mourning), 150–151
baile, as term for dance, 11, 12, 20, 60, 130
Bandelier, Fanny R., 178n10
Barlow, Robert H., 15, 182n5
Basarás y Garaygorta, Antonio de, "Dance of the Emperor Montezuma," 143, 145
bathhouses, 133, 136
Baudot, Georges, 44, 177n24
Begel, Benito and Pedro de, 128, 146, 172
Behechio (*cacique*), 28, 29
Benzoni, Girolamo, 54, 105, 177n37
Bhabha, Homi, 38, 184n70
Bible: passages on dance, 11, 46, 47, 53; sacrifice in story of Isaac, 89
Biblioteca Medicea Laurenziana, Florence, 58
Bierhorst, John, 184n63, 184n73
Binski, Paul, 108

"Black Legends," 93, 94, 102–113, 181n43
Black Plague, 10
Boone, Elizabeth Hill, 20
Booth, Willard, 179n76
Broda, Johanna, 62, 64
Brokaw, Galen, 35, 38
Brondat, Guillen, 130
Brooke, Arthur, 175n23
Brooks, Lynn Matluck, 8, 12
Browne, Walden, 59
Brundage, Burr Cartwright, 64, 71
Burkhart, Louise, 182n7

Cabeza de Vaca, Álvar Núñez, 127
calendars: Aztec, 6, 17–18, 22, 42, 56, 59, 61–64, 81, 90, 133; Dominican, 133, 183n35; Julian, 59
calmecac (Aztec school for priests), 17, 59–60, 64
cannibalism: and human sacrifice, 70, 71, 75, 101; Las Casas on, 40–41
Cano de Saavedra, Juan, 34, 98–99, 102, 180n18
cantares mexicanos ("Songs of the Mexica"), 184n73
captives: and Aztec ceremonies, 72–77, 95, 97; captives' dance, 62, 72–77, 80, 85, 151; and human sacrifice, 3, 64, 71, 72, 73, 74–77, 80, 81, 85, 95, 97, 101
Carlo, Agustín Millares, 173n2
Carrasco, Davíd, 63, 71, 73, 77
Carvajal, Michael de, 109–110, 112
Casa de Contratación, 5
Cathedral of San Gregorio el Magno, Mexico City, 142–143, 146
Catholic Church: appropriation of pagan funerary rituals, 10; dance as symbol of power relations within, 9, 14, 22; and dance of death imagery, 9, 108; in New Spain, 6; and syncretic nature of dancing, 22. *See also* Franciscan missionaries; Spanish missionaries
Certeau, Michel de, 2, 4, 13, 28
Cervantes de Salazar, Francisco, 49, 50–51, 52, 54, 131, 177n30
Charles V (Holy Roman emperor): and chroniclers of New Spain, 98; and Cortés, 2, 127; and debates of Valladolid, 41, 102; and Franciscan missionaries, 6; Indians' performance for, 2, 9, 10–11, 12, 14, 23; and Las Casas, 104, 181n48; and Moorish

dances, 7–8; and Oviedo y Valdés, 33; peace treaty with France, 127–128
Chichimeca, 70, 148
Chilcotin Indians, 86, 87
children, and human sacrifice, 3, 18, 72
chivalric *romances*, 94, 99–100, 115
Cholula, Spanish massacre of, 181n49
choreography: and *areítos*, 32, 34, 38, 40, 42; and Aztec ritual dances, 46, 57, 61, 62, 63, 72–76, 77, 80, 81, 83, 85, 87, 88, 90–91, 96, 145; choreographed reenactments, 125–126; choreographed retribution for Massacre at the Festival of Toxcatl, 101; of dance of death imagery, 109, 112; and fall of Aztec empire, 118; and historiography, 20, 150, 151; of history, 94; and lexicon of terms for dance, 12, 14, 174n31; and Motolinía, 50, 51; and music, 22; and practices of falling, 118–122; of resistance, 14; of Spanish conquest, 104; of Spanish warfare, 97; of violence, 88, 107; as writing of dance, 13, 20
Christian conversion: and *areítos*, 39; and clandestine native revivalism, 132; Durán on, 132; and Franciscan missionaries, 45; and Hatuey, 30; Las Casas on, 40, 42; methods and merits of, 2; miraculous conversion and dancing, 148–149; and Motolinía, 45, 47; Oviedo y Valdés on, 40, 176n50; and papal bull on number of baptisms, 45; and resistance, 148; role of dancing in, 128, 132, 146, 147, 148, 151; role of missionary theatre in, 129; and sacrament of the Holy Eucharist, 144–145, 184n68
Christian evangelization: and Aztec tradition of public spectacle, 6; dance and theatre used in, 9, 20; and *Florentine Codex*, 58; and Jesuit missionaries, 141; music in, 128; performance as method of, 45; success of, 132
chroniclers of New World: and *areítos*, 28, 31–32, 34; and chivalric *romances*, 99–100; and colonial discourse, 5; documentation of indigenous dances, 1, 2–3, 4, 7, 13–14, 15, 128; erasure of indigenous distinctions, 14; and eyewitness accounts, 31, 33; and lexicon of terms for dance, 11, 12; and Massacre at the Festival of Toxcatl, 98, 122; and *moros y cristianos*, 127;

preoccupation with indigenous performance, 31; proto-ethnographical writings of, 54; and representations of indigenous dances, 49–54, 151; and secondhand reports, 32, 33, 46, 49–54
Cicero, 13
Cihuacoatl ("Serpent Uterus"), 78, 179n110
cihuateteo (women who died in childbirth), 20, 21, 81–82, 83, 87, 148, 179n126
Clark, J., 182n117
Claudius, 13
Clavigero, Francisco Javier, 174n40
Clendinnen, Inga, 15, 70, 75, 93, 114
Cline, Howard F., 174n39, 182n101
Codex Azcatítlan, 118, 120–121, 146, 147
Codex Borbonicus, 138, 141
Codex Borgia, 20, 21, 140
Codex Durán, 183n30
Codex Ramírez, 17
Codex Telleriano-Remensis, 19
Códice Aubin, 114–115, 116, 182n97
Códice Carolino, 66
Códice de Tlatelolco, 128, 129, 182n5
cofradías, 130
Colegio Imperial de Santa Cruz de Tlatelolco, 58, 150
Coleman, David, 7–8
colonial discourse: and *areítos*, 31; and colonial relationship, 5; complex issues of, 4–5; copying of Motolinía's dance writings in, 22; documentation of indigenous dance in, 1, 2, 4–7, 55, 152; and *encomienda* system, 5, 96; and historiography of Spanish conquest, 93; and history of dance, 13; and lexicon of terms for dance, 11; and Massacre at the Festival of Toxcatl, 95; and perspectives of "Indian," 6–7; tension between dance and death in, 4
colonial mimicry, 38, 146
colonization: and *areítos*, 35; and dance of death imagery, 110, 122; eyewitness role in, 132; Las Casas on, 39, 40, 42; and *moros y cristianos*, 127; and performances, 128, 147, 147; role of Aztec ritual dances in, 23, 126, 128, 146, 151; Sepúlveda on, 42; and Spanish assertion of dominance, 22, 131. *See also* New Spain
Columbus, Bartholomew, 29

Columbus, Christopher: accounts of indigenous dances, 20, 24–25, 27, 30, 31, 42, 152, 174n1, 176n54; letter on indigenous dances, 1; perceptions of Indians as mythical "wild man," 25; and Spanish global empire, 5
Coma, Guglielmo, 27
concheros, 184n78
Conley, Tom, 104–105
contagious magic, 86, 87
contrapás, 34, 38, 46, 155–156, 157, 158, 159
Corpus Christi festivals, 9, 22, 129–130, 131, 184n68
Cortés, Hernán: Cline on, 174n39; death of, 33; Gómara's biography of, 49–50, 99; and Indians' performances in Spain, 2, 9, 14; and Marquesado, 135; and Massacre at the Festival of Toxcatl, 93–94, 95, 97–98, 99, 102, 111–112, 182n101; and Montezuma, 50, 92, 95, 98, 104, 105, 111, 112, 113, 115; and Nahuatl, 92; and Narváez, 92, 95, 96, 98, 99, 100, 111, 169, 170; Oviedo y Valdés on, 98, 180n18; *relaciones* of, 97–98, 99, 180n17, 180n18; and Spanish conquest, 19, 92–93, 97–98; and Vázquez de Tapia, 97, 180n16; and Velázquez de Cuéllar, 96
Costa Rica, 35
Council of the Indies, 5, 32, 40, 58, 96, 102
Covarrubias, Sebastián de, 12, 175n32, 177n31
Coyolxauhqui Stone, 119, 122
Crónica de Michoacán, 143, 144, 184n78
Crónica mexicana (Tezozómoc), 150
Crónica X, 133, 140, 150
Cuauhtémoc (*tlatoani*), 93
Cuauhtlatoatzin, Juan Diego, 148
cuecuechcuicatl ("tickling dance"), 134
cuicacalli ("House of Song"), 14, 15, 64, 65, 78, 84, 136–138, 137, 146, 183n46
Cuitlahuac (*tlatoani*), 93
Curcio-Nagy, Linda A., 183n87

dance and dancing: as allegory of power relations, 9, 11, 14; as court entertainment, 7; cultural differences in meaning of, 25, 70; as form of historiography, 7, 11, 13, 20, 55; and Iberian folk dances, 8–9; lexicon of terms for, 11–13, 174n31; perceptions

dance and dancing (*continued*)
of "primitive dance" and magic, 86–87; as political resistance, 20, 31, 132; and space of the alien, 27; as tribute, 23. *See also* alcohol and drugs; Aztec ritual dances; dance of death imagery; dancing masters; representations of indigenous dances; *and specific dances*

dance of death imagery, 9–11, 14, 75, 85, 87, 94, 108–110, 112, 115, 122, 174n25, 181n64. *See also* death scenarios

dancing masters: and Guarionex (cacique) 32; *guías*, 34; "masters of youth" as, 64, 90, 91; Motolinía on, 48; Oviedo y Valdés on, 155–156. *See also* Arbeau, Thoinot; Begel, Benito and Pedro de; *tequinas*

danza, as term for dance, 11, 12, 20, 60, 130

danza de los voladores, 145, 146–147, 147

Danza general de la Muerte (poem), 109

death scenarios: and *areítos*, 30; dancing associated with funerary rituals, 10, 25, 26–27, 30, 150; and representations of indigenous dances, 3–4, 25, 27, 150, 151. *See also* dance of death imagery; human sacrifice

de Bry, Theodor de: *America*, 26–27, 26, 105, 107, 140, 142; and dance of death imagery, 108–109, 110; "First encounter between Cortés and Montezuma," 104, 105; "The Massacre at the Festival of Toxcatl," 105–107, 107, 110, 112; "Montezuma watches as conquistadors attack his court dancers," 104, 106; "Of All the Manners of Strange Dances Among the Indians," 140, 142; "Vespucci in Paria," 26–27, 26

Dekkers, Johannes, 173n14

Derrida, Jacques, 173n6

Díaz del Castillo, Bernal, 71, 100–102, 127, 128, 181n34

Dibble, Charles E., 71

discovery of New World: invention of New World compared to, 38; leading to violence, 152; and Martyr d'Anghera, 23, 32; and representations of indigenous dances, 20, 25–27, 35, 42–43, 151. *See also* Columbus, Christopher

disease: and *areítos*, 35; Las Casas on, 41; smallpox epidemics, 92–93, 130

Dominguez, Alonzo, 103

Durán, Diego: and colonization, 132; on *cuicacalli*, 136–137, 137, 184n47; and Dominican calendar, 133, 183n35; ethnography of, 133; on human sacrifice, 72, 75, 76; on Indians dancing in Christian contexts, 22, 132–138, 135, 140, 146, 147; on *juego de palo*, 135–136, 183n45; on Massacre at the Festival of Toxcatl, 94, 110–112; "The Massacre at the Festival of Toxcatl," 110, 111; on mourning dances, 150–151; on *ollin*, 18; on religious syncretism, 133, 139; on Tititl festival, 179n130; on Xocotl Huetzi festival, 134–135, 183n37

Dutch empire, 102

Dyer, Joe, 176n13

eagle and jaguar warriors, 17, 75, 128, 129

Ebreo da Pesaro, Guglielmo, 7

Edmonson, Munro S., 177n8

Eighty Years' War, 102

encomienda system, 5, 6, 39, 96, 102, 181n45

epistemology, 11, 31, 59, 173n6

Escudero, Francisco, 130

ethnography: of Aztec empire, 14–20; confession-generated ethnographic process, 57; and Franciscan missionaries, 6, 44; and manipulation of time, 54; and representations of indigenous dances, 7, 20; and Sahagún's methodology, 58–59, 178n10, 178n13; of Spanish missionaries, 6, 20, 44–45, 49, 57, 114, 128, 133, 149, 151

Etruscan dances, 34–35, 37, 155

European humanism, 7, 13–14

eyewitness role: in chroniclers' accounts of New World, 31, 33; in colonization, 132; in historiography, 2, 4, 93, 103; and Massacre at the Festival of Toxcatl, 95, 96–97, 98, 101–102, 103, 114, 115; in representations of indigenous dances, 4, 22; in Spanish official histories, 96

Fabian, Johannes, 54

Ferdinand (king of Spain), 7, 9, 14

Feuillet, Raoul-Auger, 174n31

fiestas: for Cortés, 127; Las Casas on, 103; Motolinía on, 46, 54, 164–166; Oviedo y Valdés on, 36, 38, 157–161. *See also* Aztec ceremonies

Fifth Sun, 19, 61, 119

First Provincial Council of Mexico, 132

Flemish missionaries, 6

Florentine Codex (Sahagún): as authoritative source on Aztec culture, 6, 22, 56, 57, 151; and Aztec calendars, 61–64; Aztec dancers and musicians, 65, 65; and captives and dance, 72–77; and cycle of violence, 77, 87–88, 117, 118; on day sign "Four Movement," 18; and human sacrifice and dance, 70–72, 83–85, 88, 89, 151, 180n134; instruments and equipment for dance, 66; and *ixiptlas*, 71; limitations of, 59–60; and location of dances, 63–64, 65, 85; and *macehualiztli*, 48, 176n17, 176n19; on Macuilxochitl, 138; and Massacre at the Festival of Toxcatl, 115–117, 117, 118, 121, 125, 182n101; and meanings of dances, 86, 89; mediated process of informant interviews, 57, 59–60; and myth of Coyolxauhqui's fall, 118–119, 122; and myth of creation of sun and moon, 119; and myth of destruction of Tula, 119; and myth of Nanauatzin's fall, 119, 121; and Nahuatl, 58, 60, 115; and patterns of silence, 57, 89; prohibitions against documentation of indigenous belief systems, 86; as proselytizing tool, 6; purpose of, 58–59; role of dancing in, 56–57, 60–72; and sacrifices of representation, 57–58, 59, 85–86, 87; sacrificial quality of, 57, 87–88, 89; and Sahagún's assistants, 58, 59, 85, 86, 89, 115, 177n4, 182n101; Sahagún's preface to, 59, 60; Sahagún's writing of, 58, 60, 86, 89, 182n101; social hierarchy in dances, 64–68, 70, 77, 81; and Spanish conquest, 113, 117; and time of dances, 61–63, 85; *tlatoani*'s dance array, 65, 66–67, 66; and women and dancing, 77–79, 80–85

Fluvia, Jacme, 7, 174n20

Fogelson, Raymond D., 94

footprints, representing physical movement, 20

Foster, Susan Leigh, 174n33

Foucault, Michel, 5

Franciscan missionaries: and Christian conversion, 45; Durán on, 135, 139;

and education, 150; and ethnography, 6, 44; and Tecpanecs, 134–135
Francis I (king of France), 127–128
Francis of Assisi, Saint, 44
Frazer, James, 18, 86–87, 88, 89
Fuenleal, Sebastián Ramírez de, 44
Fuller, J., "The Great Temple of Mexico" in *The American Traveler*, 123, 125

games: Durán on, 134, 135–136, 183n45; *juego de cañas*, 29, 30; *juego de palo*, 9, 10–11, 135–136, 183n45
Gante, Pedro de, 42
gesticulatores, 52, 53
Ghent, Pedro of, 6, 173n14
Girard, René, 87–89
Gómara, Francisco López de, 33, 49–52, 54, 93, 94, 99, 177n24, 177n27, 182n87
Gómez Muntané, Maricarmen, 174n25
Gonzales, Juan, 30
Greenblatt, Stephen, 27, 93
Gregory I (pope), 140
Guacanagari (*cacique*), 24
Guanina (native princess), 30, 175n23
Guarionex (*cacique*), 32
Guatemala, 44, 95
Gundersheimer, Werner L., 9

hacha (Spanish court dance), 143, 184n64
Hanke, Lewis, 176n50
Harris, Max, 182n2, 183n7
Hatuey (*cacique*), 29–30, 43
Hernández, Francisco, 54, 55, 177n37, 177n39, 177n40
Herrera y Tordesillas, Antonio de, 51
Heyden, Doris, 183n30
Hispaniola: and Anacaona, 28–29; and *areítos*, 33, 35, 39, 46, 49, 53; dance among natives of, 20, 27; Spanish missionaries on, 31
historiography: *areítos* as form of, 42–43; and choreography, 20, 150, 151; dance as form of, 7, 11, 13, 20, 55; eyewitness role in, 2, 4, 93, 103; historical representation as literary staging, 28; Martyr d'Anghera on, 4; principles of, 2; of Spanish conquest, 93, 152
Holbein, Hans, the Younger (*Dance of Death*), 10, 108, *108*
Horcasitas, Fernando, 182n7, 183n30
Huehuecoyotl ("Very Old Coyote"), 138, 141

Huey Tecuilhuitl festival, 67, 77–78, 78, *79*, 80, 178n63
Huitzilopochtli ("Hummingbird of the South"): birth of, 118–119; and eucharistic practices, 145; as patron deity of Mexica, 15, 17, 67, 90, 119; temple of, 23, 64, 73, 85, 90, 97, 150; and Toxcatl festival, 90–91, 96, 97, 101, 111, 114, 148
human sacrifice: Aztec ritual dances reenacting, 2–3, 22, 57, 61, 70–72, 83–85, 88, 89, 151, 180n134; and Aztec rituals, 18, 22, 56, 57, 61, 64, 70, 88; and captives, 3, 64, 71, 72, 73, 74–77, 80, 81, 85, 95, 97, 101; flayed skins of victims, 71, 72–77, 83, 84, 85, 87, 101, 180n134; and *ixiptlas*, 18, 57–58, 70–72, 73, 75, 83, 85–86, 89, 91, 97, 101; Las Casas on, 39, 40–41; Oviedo y Valdés on, 38, 39, 40, 43, 176n46; physical and mental condition of victims, 72; sanguinary rites, 70, 74, 75, 91, 101; and *teomiqui*, 61; violence of, 70, 87, 88, 95; and women, 72, 77, 78, 80–84
Humboldt, Alexander von, 15

Ilamatecuhtli ("Old Lady"), 82–83, 88, 148
imitative magic, 18
Indian identity, 4, 39, 53
Indians: dancing in Christian contexts, 22, 129–140, 142–148, 152, 184n73; as descendants of Jews, 133, 134; Las Casas's defense of, 39, 41, 42, 102–103; perceptions of as mythical "wild man," 25; performances in Spain, 2, 9, 14; performing songs and dances for religious dramas, 129–130; prohibition of dancing among, 131–132, 146. See also Aztec empire; Mexica people
indigenismo, 93
indigenous cultures, distinctions in, 14, 34, 39, 70
Isabella (queen of Spain), 5, 7, 9, 12
Itzcoatl ("Obsidian Serpent"), 23
Itzcohuatzin (*cacique* of Tlatelolco), 114
Ivanova, Anna, 9
ixiptlas (human representations of Aztec deities): children as, 72, 87; and human sacrifice, 18, 57–58, 70–72, 73, 75, 83, 85–86, 87, 91, 97, 101; as representations of gods, 18, 57, 70–71, 88; women as, 72, 77–78, 80, 81, 82–83
Izcalli festival, 62, 67, 75, 148, 178n63

Jáuregui, Carlos, 109
Jesuit missionaries, 139–146, 184n57
Jews: converted Jews, 9, 133; expulsion from kingdom of Spain, 5; Indians as descendants of, 133, 134
Juderrías, Julián, 181n43
juego de cañas, 29, 30
juego de palo (indigenous log-rolling game), 9, 10–11, 135–136, 183n45

Keen, Benjamin, 182n87
Klor de Alva, J. Jorge, 59, 178n10

Lara, Jaime, 184n75
Las Casas, Bartolomé de: on Anacaona, 29; on *areítos*, 30, 31, 39–42, 43, 45–46, 103, 104, 153–154; on *bailes*, 162–163; and Charle V, 104, 181n48; on Cholula massacre, 181n49; on Columbus's encounters with indigenous dancing, 174n1; and dance of death imagery, 108–109, 110; defense of Indians, 39, 41, 42, 102–103; and *encomienda* system, 39, 102, 181n45; on Hatuey, 29–30, 43; on human sacrifice, 39, 40–41; on Indian nature, 41, 176n54; on indigenous dances, 20; on *juego de cañas*, 29; on Massacre at the Festival of Toxcatl, 19, 41, 94, 102, 103–104, 108–109, 112
Leibsohn, Dana, 182n97
Leonard, Irving A., 99
León-Portilla, Miguel, 70, 178n10
leylas (Moorish wedding dances), 7–8
Lienzo de Tlaxcala, 118
Livy, 34–35, 37, 40, 155
Lopez, Geronimo, 130
López Austin, Alfredo, 59, 179n110
Lorenzo (Indian seminarian), 142, 146

macanas, 114, 182n96
macehual, 148
macehualiztli (sacred dance): and *Florentine Codex*, 48, 176n17, 176n19; and Gómara, 52, 99; and Massacre at the Festival of Toxcatl, 51–52, 99; and Molina, 47–48; and Motolinía, 47–48, 51, 52, 53, 54, 99, 140, 151, 167; as term for dance, 11, 13; and Tezozómoc, 151; and van der Aa, 51, 52–53, *53*

Macuilxochitl ("Five Flower"), 138
magic, and perceptions of "primitive dance," 18, 86–87, 88, 89
Maiobanex (*cacique*), 32
Malintzin (La Malinche), 19, 92, 115
Marquesado, 135
Martí, Samuel, 174n55
Martín I of Aragón, 7
Martyr d'Anghera, Peter: on *areítos*, 31, 32–33, 34, 35, 42, 154; and European dancing, 7; and humanist curriculum, 7, 32; official Spanish history of discovery of New World, 23, 32; representations of indigenous dances, 2–4, 9, 14, 20, 23, 173n2
Massacre at the Festival of Toxcatl: and Alvarado, 19, 92, 93, 94–97, 98, 98–99, 99, 100, 101, 102, 103–104, 105, 111–114, 115, 121, 169, 170–171, 181n77, 182n101; and Aztec ritual dance imagery, 115, 117, 121; and chroniclers of New World, 98, 122; and conspiracy theories, 111–112; contradictory accounts of, 94, 95, 98, 100; and Cortés, 97–98, 115; de Bry's engraving of, 105–107, 107; Díaz de Castillo on, 100–102; Durán on, 94, 110–112; European accounts of, 19, 22, 122; eyewitness account of, 95, 96–97, 98, 101–102, 103, 114, 115; and *Florentine Codex*, 115–117, 117, 118, 121, 125, 182n101; and Gómara, 52, 99, 177n27, 182n87; historical consequence of, 22; indigenous accounts of, 19, 22, 93, 94, 113–115, 117–122; Las Casas on, 19, 41, 94, 102, 103–104, 108–109, 112; location of, 93, 99; and *macehualiztli*, 51–52, 99; and meaning of dancing, 19, 92, 97, 98–99; Mexica retaliation for, 92; narratives of, 94, 95–96, 110, 113–114; and practices of falling, 94, 118–122; representations of, 93, 114, 151, 169; and Spanish conquest, 19, 22, 91, 94, 100–101, 102, 151; Spanish conquistador accounts of, 94–102, 110, 112, 115, 122; Spanish missionary accounts of, 22, 93, 102–113, 121; and Templo Mayor, 52, 91, 93, 94, 114–115, 117–118, 118, 120–121; time of, 93, 99
matachines, 52, 54, 100, 181n36
Maya language, 92
mayhabao (percussion instrument), 31
Mendieta, Géronimo de: "Dance of the Indians" at the Templo Mayor in *Historia eclesiástica indiana*, 123, 124, 182n116; and Motolinía, 45, 49, 54; on origins of Aztec ritual, 60, 168; on prohibition of dancing, 131–132
Mendoza, Antonio de, 3, 6, 127
Mendoza, Diego de, 58
Mesoamerica, 14, 15
Metcalfe, Scott, 47
Mexica people: and Aztec as term, 15; eucharistic practices of, 145; legendary accounts of, 67, 90; and smallpox epidemic, 92–93; social order of, 68; and Spanish conquest, 91, 92–93. *See also* Aztec empire; Massacre at the Festival of Toxcatl
Mexico, and historiography of Spanish conquest, 93
Mexico City: and Corpus Christi festivals, 130; dance school in, 128–129, 172
military theatre, 18, 128
mimesis: and Motolinía, 21, 47; and ritual sacrifice, 88
miracles, 131–132
mitotes (dances): Acosta on, 140; "Dance of the Emperor Montezuma," 142–146, 144, 145, 152, 184n63, 184n73; Las Casas on, 103; Pérez de Ribas on, 140, 142–148; prohibition of, 132; as term for dance, 11, 13, 33–34, 54, 151, 177n30; and Tezozómoc, 151. *See also ximitote*
Mixcoatl ("Cloud Serpent"), 17, 80
Molina, Alonso de, 47–48
Montezuma: and Aztec ritual dances, 65, 66, 67, 75, 76, 90, 95, 100, 148, 178n63; and Cortés, 50, 92, 95, 98, 104, 105, 111, 112, 113, 115; "Dance of the Emperor Montezuma," 142–146, 144, 145, 152, 184n63, 184n73; and day sign "Four Movement," 18; de Bry's engravings of, 104, 105, 106, 107; and Gómara, 51; imprisonment at palace of Axacayatl, 95–98, 103, 114; Oviedo y Valdés on, 98; and severed heads dance, 73; and Spanish conquest, 19, 92
Montúfar, Alonso de, 128
Moore, John Hamilton, "The Rejoicings of the Mexicans, at the Beginning of the Age" in *A New and Complete Collection of Voyages and Travels*, 123, 126
Moors: *areítos* compared to *zambras*, 31, 33, 42, 46; and choreographies of resistance, 14; and dance as court entertainment, 7–8, 9, 174n20; Morisco dances, 8, 8, 174n22
Morales, Andreas, 32
moros y cristianos: and clandestine native revivalism, 131; and colonization, 127; and dance of death imagery, 10; as reenactment of military battles, 8–9, 14; and Spanish conquest, 9, 20, 181n53; as term for dance, 151
Moses, 13
Motolinía, Toribio de Benavente: on Aztec ritual dances, 21–22, 40, 45, 46–49, 140, 151, 164–166, 167, 184n58; and Cervantes de Salazar, 49, 50–51, 54; and Christian utopia in New World, 47; and ethnography, 6, 44–45; on founding of Puebla de los Ángeles, 148; and Gómara, 50, 51, 54, 99, 177n24, 180n28; and Las Casas, 39, 40, 45–46; and mimesis, 21, 47; Motolinía name as reverse baptism, 44, 48; and *netotiliztli*, 47, 49, 50, 51, 52, 53, 54, 99, 151, 167, 177n39; and Oviedo y Valdés, 46, 59; and religious dramas, 130
Muñoz Camargo, Diego, 49, 54, 113, 182n87
music: and Aztec ritual dances, 11, 56, 57, 60–61, 65, 67, 80, 101, 106, 114, 117; and choreography, 22; in Christian evangelization, 128; and dance of death imagery, 9, 174n25; Gypsy music and dance, 130; instruments and equipment for dances, 65, 66, 70, 179n71
Myers, Kathleen Ann, 180n18

Nahua: cosmology of, 133; as term, 15
Nahuatl: Christian hymns translated into, 130; dramas of, 128; Durán's knowledge of, 133; and *Florentine Codex*, 58, 60, 115; and Malintzin, 92; and Motolinía, 47–48; Nahua as speakers of, 15; Ribera's knowledge of, 2, 4; Sahagún's knowledge of, 58, 60; and Spanish conquest accounts, 114; terms for dance, 11–12, 22, 33; Tezozómoc's use of for Aztec empire chronicle, 23, 150
Nambi (*cacique*), 36
Narváez, Pánfilo de, 92, 95–96, 98–100, 111, 169–170

National Cathedral of Mexico, 52
Native American ghost dance ritual, 184n73
Navarro, Juan de Esquivel, 184n64
Nebrija, Antonio de, 5, 12
negros bocales, 45, 176n13
nemontemi (five extra days), 17, 62
Nero (Roman emperor), 112
netotiliztli (social dance): and Cervantes de Salazar, 51; Hernández on, 55, 177n39; and Herrera y Tordesillas, 51; and Motolinía, 47, 49, 50, 51, 52, 53, 54, 99, 151, 167, 177n39; as term for dance, 11, 13; and van der Aa, 51, 52
Nevile, Jennifer, 13–14
New Fire Ceremony, 63–64, 178n38
New Laws (1542), 5, 181n45
New Spain: African slaves in, 130; colonial administration in, 131; Cortés as governor of, 127; Motolinía on, 44, 46–47; role of dancing in, 20, 22, 128, 132; social hierarchy of, 133; territory of, 6; viceroyalty of, 5–6. *See also* colonization
New World. *See* chroniclers of New World; discovery of New World
Nicaragua, 35, 40, 44, 157–161
Nicholson, H. B., 17, 178n10, 178n41
"noble savage" theme, 25, 26
Noche Triste ("Sad Night"), 92, 113

Ochpaniztli festival, 62, 67, 82, 83–85, 84, 88, 148
O'Gorman, Edmundo, 38
Olid, Cristóbal de, 143
Olive, Pedro M. de, 12
ollin (day sign), 18–19, 19, 174n55
Olmos, André de, 6, 44, 49
orchesography, 12–13
Ortiz, Fernando, 28
Otomí peoples, 141
Our Lady of Guadalupe, 148–149
Ovando, Nicolás de, 28, 29
Oviedo y Valdés, Gonzalo Fernández de: on *areítos*, 31, 33–39, 37, 40, 41, 42, 43, 46, 48, 155–161, 175n37; on *cacique* ceremony, 36, 38, 177n41; and Cano de Saavedra interview, 98–99, 180n18; on Christian conversion, 40, 176n50; eyewitness account of, 33; on human sacrifice, 38, 39, 40, 43, 176n46; on indigenous dances, 20; Las Casas on, 39; and Massacre at the Festival of Toxcatl, 98; and Motolinía, 46, 49; on *voladores*, 35–36, 37, 145, 157–158

paganism: Acosta on, 147; and *areítos*, 42; and choreographies of resistance, 14; colonial prohibition of, 131, 132; dance as sign of, 11, 57, 128, 131–132; dancing as disembodying pagan past, 22, 30, 48, 57, 146; Durán on, 132, 133, 138; and *Florentine Codex*, 6, 57; and funerary rituals, 10; Gregory I on, 140; Las Casas on, 30; Martyr d'Anghera on, 3; and Motolinía, 48
Pagden, Anthony, 103, 181n46
Pané, Ramón, 31, 33, 34, 35, 42, 43
Panquetzaliztli festival, 62, 68, 148, 178n63
Paso y Troncoso, Francisco del, 177n5
patronato real, 6
Paul, Saint, 44, 134
Pedro IV (king of Aragon), 7, 174n20
Pérez, Fernand, 39
Pérez, Perla Valle, 182n5
Pérez de Ribas, Andrés: on Indians dancing in Christian contexts, 22, 130–131, 142–148, 152, 184n73; as Jesuit missionary, 140–142; on physical comportment of Indians, 146, 147–148, 184n69
performances: *areítos*, 28, 34–35, 36, 38, 39, 40, 41, 42; of Aztec ritual dances for Spanish court, 9, 10–11, 12, 14; and captives' dance, 74; and Christian conversion, 146; and colonization, 128, 147, 147; distinction between sacred and secular performance, 38, 42, 43, 47; as embodied meaning, 39; human sacrifice as killing performances, 70; indigenous performance as model for writing history, 28, 31; and military theatre, 128; and Motolinía, 45, 47; of religious dramas, 6, 9, 20, 45, 129–130; and symbolic geography of Aztec rituals, 63; writings about, 31–32
Peruvian *taquis*, 140
Philip II (king of Spain), 7, 42, 102, 127, 181n48, 182n5
politics: political theatre, 18; role of dancing in, 20, 31, 132; structure of Aztec empire, 16–17
Polo, Marco, 24
Ponce de León, Juan, 30
Prescott, William H., 15, 113, 114

Primeros Memoriales (Sahagún): and Atamalcualiztli festival, 68, 69; on Aztec ritual dances, 58, 59, 73, 179n117, 180n134; and Ochpaniztl festival, 84; and Tlacaxipehualiztli festival, 74, 74, 76
Protestantism, 94, 102, 107
Protestant Reformation, 102
puella (dance with sticks), 140
punishment, and Aztec ritual dances, 67, 78, 79, 91

Quecholli festival, 80, 82
Quetzalcoatl ("Feathered Serpent God"), 67, 113
Quiñones Keber, Eloise, 178n10

Ramírez, José Fernando, 183n30
religious dramas (*autos*), performance of, 6, 9, 20, 45, 129–130
religious syncretism, 22, 133, 139
representations of indigenous dances: and colonial discourse, 1, 2, 4–7, 55, 152; and counterfeit histories, 49–54; and dance of death imagery, 10–11; and death scenarios, 3–4, 25, 27, 150, 151; and discovery of New World, 20, 25–27, 35, 42–43, 151; and embodied experience, 151; and Hernández, 54, 55, 177n37, 177n39, 177n40; lack of social reality in, 5, 7, 55, 152; Martyr d'Anghera's paradigms of, 2–4, 9, 14, 20, 23, 173n2; and mute bodies, 2, 3, 4; and numbers of dancers, 54; perspectives shaping, 1–2, 27; and spatial displacement, 53, 54. *See also Florentine Codex* (Sahagún)
Restall, Matthew, 113–114
revivalism, 131–132, 133, 134
Ribera, Juan de, 2, 4
Rius, Pere de, 7, 174n20
romances (ballads), 33, 35, 38, 156
Rostas, Susanna, 184n78

Sahagún, Bernardino de: on *areítos*, 12, 48, 60, 61, 73, 131, 151; and ethnographical methods, 58–59, 178n10, 178n13; interviews with native informants, 6, 22, 55, 56–60, 89, 115, 182n101; and lexicon of terms for dance, 11–12, 60; and Nahuatl, 58, 60; on song and dance names, 74, 151, 177n40; on *voladores*, 36; writings on Aztec world, 56, 58, 177n8, 182n87.

INDEX 203

Sahagún, Bernardino de *(continued)*
See also *Florentine Codex* (Sahagún); *Primeros Memoriales* (Sahagún)
saltare, as term for dance, 11
San Buenaventura, Pedro de, 177n4
San Francisco de Mexico, 85
San José de Belén de los Naturales, 173n14
San Luis Montáñez, Nicolás de, 148, 184n78
Santo Domingo monastery, Mexico City, 132
sarabande, 134
saraos, 51, 54, 143, 177n31
Scillacio, Niccolò, 27, 30
Sell, Barry D., 182n7
Sepúlveda, Juan Ginés de, 42, 102, 103
Sequer, Rodrigo de, 58
serpents, and Aztec ritual dances, 67–68, 85, 91, 148, 151, 178n63, 179n68
slaves and slavery: African slaves in New Spain, 130; and *areítos*, 35, 45; and Aztec ritual dances, 3, 68, 70, 71–72, 80, 82; and Aztec rituals, 18, 57; and human sacrifice, 18, 71; as *ixiptlas*, 71, 82, 83, 84, 88; Las Casas on, 39, 40, 41, 42, 102; Oviedo y Valdés on, 36; Sepúlveda on, 42, 102
social hierarchy: and Aztec ritual dances, 57, 64–68, 70, 77, 81, 85, 88; and dance of death imagery, 9–10, 108, 109; of New Spain, 133
social memory, Aztec ritual dances as form of, 3, 19–20, 150
Socrates, 13
Soderini, Pietro, 25
Solís, Antonio de, 182n117
Sotomayor, Cristóbal de, 30, 36, 159, 175n23
Spanish conquest: Aztec chronicle of, 1; and Aztec's Fifth Sun, 19; and chivalric *romances*, 100, 115; conquistador accounts of Massacre at the Festival of Toxcatl, 94–102, 110, 112, 115, 121; conquistadors as dance masters, 128–129; constellation of myths of, 113–114; and dance of death imagery, 110; dances dramatizing, 20, 22; dances of conquest, 125–126; and debates at Valladolid, 102; documentation of indigenous dances, 1, 3, 20, 54; and enemies of Aztec empire, 17, 19, 91, 92, 112, 113; events leading to, 92–93; and *Florentine Codex*, 113, 117; historiography of, 93, 152; indigenous accounts of, 114; indigenous resistance against official narratives of, 182n2; Las Casas on, 40, 41, 103, 104; Martyr d'Anghera on, 4; and Massacre at the Festival of Toxcatl, 19, 22, 52, 91, 94, 100–101, 102, 151; and *moros y cristianos*, 9, 20, 181n53; narratives of, 3, 4, 93; role of Aztec ritual dances in, 23, 56; theatricality of, 97
Spanish imperialism: expansion of, 5; Protestant critiques of, 94, 102; violence of, 102
Spanish Inquisition, 9, 58
Spanish missionaries: and ambiguous meanings of dance, 148; and *areítos*, 43; and Aztec rituals, 59; documentation of dances, 1, 3, 27; and documentation of human sacrifice, 70; ethnographies of, 6, 20, 44–45, 49, 57, 114, 128, 133, 149, 151; function of, 6; on Indians lacking written language, 42; Jesuits, 139–146, 184n57; and Massacre at the Festival of Toxcatl, 22, 93, 102–113, 115, 121; and *moros y cristianos*, 9; and Nahuatl, 48; role of missionary theatre, 6, 9, 22, 45, 126, 128, 129–130, 131; and surveillance mechanisms, 147, 147. *See also specific missionaries*
Sparti, Barbara, 7
Sten, María, 182
Stevenson, Robert M., 183n7
sympathetic magic, 86
synesthesia, and Aztec ritual dances, 73

Taíno: and *areítos*, 33, 38, 60; and lexicon of terms for dance, 11, 12
Tanck de Estrada, Dorothy, 130
Tapia, Andrés de, 99, 177n24, 180n26
taqui, as term for dance, 11
Taylor, Diana, 13, 28, 183n7
Tecpanecs, 134–135
Tecto, John der Auwera, 173n14
Tecuilhuitontli festival, 62, 81, 82
Tedlock, Dennis, 114
telpochcalli ("Youth House"), 16, 17, 64, 78
temacpalitoti (thief), 81–82, 82, 85, 87, 179n128
Temple of Tecanman, 75
Templo Mayor: and Aztec ritual dances, 19, 121–122, 124, 125, 126; and Aztec rituals, 16, 63; and Coyolxauhqui Stone, 119; and Massacre at the Festival of Toxcatl, 52, 91, 93, 94, 114–115, 117–118, 118, 120–121; and New Fire Ceremony, 64; visual depictions of, 182n115
Tenochtitlan: and Aztec empire, 6, 14, 15–16, 15, 18; and Aztec ritual dances, 76; ball court of, 63; ceremonial precinct of, 22, 57, 61, 63, 64, 183n46; colonial representations of, 122; and Cortés, 19, 92; dances consecrating, 63; fall of, 20, 121; images of preconquest past, 121, 124, 125, 126; *imago mundi* of, 63; and Massacre at the Festival of Toxcatl, 19, 91, 92, 100, 112, 121; Olmos's study of, 44; and Spanish conquest, 91, 100–101
teohuatzin ("Keeper of the God"), 64
teomiqui, 61
Teotleco festival, 178n30, 179n68
Tepeyac Hill, 148
Tepoztlán, 140, 142
tequinas (dance masters), 34, 48, 175n37
Texcoco, 15, 44, 45, 127
Tezcatlipoca ("Smoking Mirror God"), 17, 60–61, 71, 168
Tezozómoc, Fernando de Alvarado: on *bailar llorando*, 150–151; and lexicon of terms for dance, 12, 151; lineage of, 148; on post-conquest history of Aztec empire, 22–23, 150
Thomas, Hugh, 180n3, 180n16
Thompson, Donald, 28
Tititl festival, 82–83, 85, 88, 148, 179n130
Tizoc (*tlatoani*), 151
Tlacaxipeualiztli festival, 67, 72–77, 73, 74, 87, 88, 179n84
Tlacopan, 15
Tlahuica, 135–136, 138
Tlaloc (rain god), 17, 68, 72, 87
tlamacehua (penance through sacrifice), 70
Tlatelolco, 14, 15, 15, 59, 66, 114
tlatoani (ruler), and Aztec ritual dance, 65, 66–67, 66
Tlaxcala: Cortés's pillaging of, 92; Motolinía's religious dramas in, 130; Olmos's study of, 44; prohibition of dancing in, 132
Tlaxcalans: as Alvarado allies, 95, 112, 113, 118; as Mexica enemy, 17, 19, 92; Motolinía on, 50

Tlaxochimaco festival, 62
Tobilla, Diego de la, 40–41
Toci ("Mother of the Gods"), 83, 84–85, 148
tocotín, 143, 151
Todorov, Tvetzan, 113, 121, 133, 178n13
Tolteca, 70, 119–121, 133
Tomlinson, Gary, 183n7
tonalli, 62
Toral, Francisco de, 58
Torquemada, Juan de, 176n41
torture, 39. *See also* human sacrifice; violence
Totonaque, 70
Tovar, Juan de, 140
Toxcatl festival: Alvarado's interrogation of dancers, 96, 97, 102; and Aztec ritual dances, 90, 96, 99, 101, 148, 178n30; and Cortés, 95, 115; and Huitzilopochtli, 90–91, 96, 97, 101, 111, 114, 148. *See also* Massacre at the Festival of Toxcatl
Treaty of Granada (1491), 5
trecenas, 62, 63
Trexler, Richard C., 128, 146
Trinidad, 24–25
Triple Alliance, 15
Turrent, Lourdes, 183n7
Tutino, Andrés, 130–131

Valadés, Diego, 123
Valeriano, Antonio, 177n4
Valladolid, debates of (1550–1551), 41–42, 102
Valley of Mexico, 15
van der Aa, Pieter: *Macehualiztli* in *Naakeurige versameling*, 51, 52–53, 53; *Netotiliztli* in *Naakeurige versameling*, 51, 52

Vázquez de Tapia, Bernardino, 97, 98, 99, 102, 180n16, 181n39
Vegerano, Alonso, 177n4
veintenas (twenties) ceremonies, 17, 62, 67, 72–77, 85–86, 88, 95
Velázquez de Cuéllar, Diego, 92, 96
Venezuela, 25, 33, 39
Vespucci, Amerigo: accounts of indigenous dances, 20, 25–27, 175n6; and Bry's *America* engraving, 26–27, 26; and "wild man" construct, 25–26, 30
violence: and Black Legend, 110; choreography of, 88, 107; dance as sign of, 151; discovery of New World leading to, 152; and *Florentine Codex*, 77, 87–88, 117, 118; of human sacrifice, 70, 87, 88, 95; material reality of, 125; representations of traumatic witnessing of violence, 104–105, 106, 107, 107, 110, 121; resulting from *areítos*, 36, 39, 95; of Spanish conquest, 121; of Spanish imperialism, 102; in *veintenas* ceremonies, 88, 95
Virgin Mother, 148–149
voladores (flyers): *danza de los voladores*, 145, 146–147, 147; Oviedo y Valdés on, 35–36, 37, 145, 157–158
Vulcan (god), 13

Wagner, Henry Raup, 181n46
Warman, Arturo, 127
Weiditz, Christoph: "Aztec acrobat in Spain," 9, 10–11; "Morisco dance," 8, 8, 174n22
Welford, J. Mack, 10
White, Hayden, 93
"wild man" construct: Columbus's use of, 25; Vespucci's use of, 25–27, 30

women: and Aztec ritual dances, 62, 70, 71, 75, 77–78, 80–85, 90; and childbirth associations, 78, 81–82, 82, 83, 84, 85, 87, 179n110, 179n126; and *cuicacalli*, 136; gypsy women, 130; and human sacrifice, 3, 18, 72, 77, 78, 80–84; as *ixiptlas*, 72, 77–78, 80, 81, 82–83; and maize imagery, 77, 78, 80; and Massacre at the Festival of Toxcatl, 106–107; and Montezuma's ritual dancing, 66; and *netotiliztli*, 51; and New Fire Ceremony, 63; "pleasure girls," 77, 78, 80, 84, 85; role in Aztec rituals, 59, 77, 80; and thief dancing with forearm, 81–82, 82, 85, 87
wonder, discourse of, 27

Xilonen (goddess of green maize ear), 77, 80
ximitote, 177n30
Xipe Totec ("Flayed Lord"), 73, 76
Xiuhtecutli ("The Fire God"), 67
Xochipilli ("Flower Prince"), 17, 138, 139, 140, 141
Xochiquetzal ("Flower Feather"), 133–134, 138, 140
Xochitlolinqui (*tlatoani* of Cuitlahuac), 23
Xocotl Huetzi festival, 68, 134–135, 135, 148, 183n37

zambras (Morisco dances), 8, 8, 33, 50, 53, 174n22, 175n32
Zumárraga, Juan de, 44, 131–132, 148